HAWKER SIDDELEY TRIDENT

A PIONEER IN AVIATION TECHNOLOGY

Graham M Simons

AIR WORLD

First published in Great Britain in 2026 by
Air World
An imprint of
Pen & Sword Books Ltd
Yorkshire – Philadelphia

ISBN 978 1 03619 332 4

A CIP catalogue record for this book is available from the British Library.

Typeset in 11pt Times by GMS Enterprises
Printed and bound in India by Replika Press Pvt. Ltd.

The Publisher's authorised representative in the EU for product safety is Authorised Rep Compliance Ltd., Ground Floor, 71 Lower Baggot Street, Dublin D02 P593, Ireland.
www.arccompliance.com

For a complete list of Pen & Sword titles please contact
PEN & SWORD BOOKS LIMITED
47 Church Street, Barnsley, South Yorkshire, S70 2AS, England
E-mail: enquiries@pen-and-sword.co.uk
Website: www.pen-and-sword.co.uk
or
PEN AND SWORD BOOKS
1950 Lawrence Road, Havertown, PA 19083, USA
E-mail: uspen-and-sword@casematepublishers.com
Website: www.penandswordbooks.com

Contents

Acknowledgements

A book of this nature would not have been possible without the help of many people and organisations.

For many years Darryl Cott, the Staff Photographer at BAe Hatfield and Stuart Howe of the De Havilland Aircraft Museum at Salisbury Hall were the very greatest of help and assistance - the former making freely available to me the tremendous archive from the 'DH Days' that were then in his care. I also wish to record my thanks to Gary Bishop of BAe Product Support for allowing me access to the techical details and specifications of so many aircraft.

It goes without saying that my deepest possible thanks go to the late Group Captain John Cunningham CBE, DSO and Two Bars, DFC and Bar, De Havilland test pilot and an all-round gentleman!

Thanks are also offered to the usual 'guilty parties' for their endless, unfailing support over the years: John Stride, David Lee, John Hamlin, Vince Hemmings, Brian Cocks, Mick Oakey, Ian Frimston, Warrant Officer Paddy Porter BEM and many others too numerous to mention, but not forgotten! Finally, thanks also go to everyone at my publishers, Pen & Sword!

I am indebted to many people and organisations for providing photographs for this story, but in some cases it has not been possible to identify the original photographer and so credits are given in the appropriate places to the immediate supplier. If any of the pictures have not been correctly credited, please accept my apologies.

Introduction

Not long after the maiden flight of the prototype Trident on 9 January 1962, British European Airways chairman Sholto Douglas, 1st Baron Douglas of Kirtleside, wrote in the carrier's staff magazine: *'BEA's hopes lie with the Trident in the same way as ten years ago our future lay with the equally revolutionary Viscount. It is the last word in jet transport and especially designed for our work.'*

The second part of that last sentence encapsulates the controversy that has exercised aviation historians and observers ever since. The Trident was closely tailored to BEA's requirements, and it is often claimed — without unanimous agreement — that the corporation's directive to reduce the aircraft's capacity during its development process limited its wider market appeal. However, the fairness of this criticism remains debated.

The British European Airways Corporation was a significant force in Europe by the late 1950s with its world-beating Vickers Viscount turboprops leading the way. The arrival of turboprops and jets quickened both airline and airliner progress. This in turn required frequent planning and frequent changes to forecasts. Starting in 1956, BEA worked with the Ministry of Supply, the Treasury, and top manufacturers to evaluate the many turbo-prop and pure-jet options. They evaluated, proposed, counter-proposed, refined and reviewed their requirements with care. Eventually, they chose De Havilland (not Bristol or Vickers) for the airframe and Rolls-Royce (not Bristol) for the engines.

In a policy document of 15 May 1956, BEA's chairman said jet airliners were *...economically unjustifiable,* but by just over a year later in July 1957 pure jets were back in play, its planning committee conceding they would be needed to remain competitive, especially on longer routes. Responding to a proposal for an aircraft to suit both BEA and BOAC, BEA outlined its requirements for a jet with two or more engines capable of flying 1,500 miles fully loaded, accommodating no fewer than fifty-five and no more than one hundred and ten passengers, with its operating costs to be no higher than ten per cent above those of the Vickers Vanguard. On 31 July, a revised paper stated, *'Ideal size is seventy passengers with a payload of 19,000 pounds, required for service in 1967'*. BEA concluded a month later that it needed a *'small number of jets'* for major routes. In other words, someone kept moving the goalposts.

With hindsight, both the airlines and aircraft manufacturers appeared to be influenced by political considerations, and the airlines presented themselves as having clear strategies, although evidence suggests a massive underlying uncertainty regarding their requirements.

BEA's insistence on a design specifically tightly tailored to them severely limited any broader market success. Additionally, De Havilland's decision to share its proposal with Boeing may have almost certainly affected its competitive position.

Eventually, something was salvaged from the debacle, and what finally emerged was a five - if you count the Auxilliary Power Unit - engined airliner capable of carrying up to one hundred and eighty passengers on short-haul routes, but by then if was far too late. This is the story.

Before proceeding on to the main narrative, a number of technical things need explaining. Firstly, it has proved impossible to put the photographs in any semblance of chronological order. Please accept my apologies on this, but they are where they are!

As usual, I have had to face the decision about the use of poorer-quality images: I have always taken the view that a rarely seen, but poor-quality, image is worth more than a good-quality, but often-seen, picture. So it is here, and I have included poorer pictures for scarcity value and the information they contain.

Secondly, the Trident was designed and built in the era of Great Britain using Imperial measurements. Therefore, I will be using feet and inches, pounds, and gallons throughout. This is mainly because I detest the appearance of conversions: twelve inches is one foot; converted to metric, it is 304.80 millimetres or 30.48

centimeters. It gets even more ridiculous when you convert gallons to litres! For those who need a formula, multiply 1 inch by 25.4 to get the metric equivalent!

I'm proud to say I started my aviation career as a 'spotter' at Heathrow, Gatwick, and Luton in the late 1960s. At Heathrow Terminal Two and the Queen's Building roof area, we saw many types of Tridents and I made lifetime friends with many spotters watching them - for me they both became a background of sight and sound at the airport. Of course, I quickly began taking and collecting photographs. Being asked to do a book on the Trident definitely took me back to my youth! *Back Every Afternoon* was our nickname for British European Airways (don't ask about BOAC!) and their press office often sent us large packs of photographs on request. The aircraft manufacturers did the same, and of course we could and did collect all sorts gizzit-plunder at the Farnborough or Paris Air Shows!

Standing on top of the Queens Building, binos around the neck, long-lens camera slung over the shoulder with a talking pocket in the coat on one side and a reggie-notebook in the other. To complete the ensemble, an authentic college scarf adds a touch of 'cool' - danger, spotter and future author at work!

Whilst mentioning photographs, it may seem strange to see something that was applied to the reverse of many of the photographs used in this book, a simple publication clearance stamp, as shown below. A similar declaration came in the attached letters from BEA and the other airlines.

Unfortunately, in recent years, this has become especially important to demonstrate, given the proliferation of websites that seem to think it is perfectly acceptable to take any image, apply their own watermark, and then demand exorbitant 'fees' from authors.

Well, guys, I have news for you. This book was compiled with images scanned from prints obtained long before the internet, and you opportunists were around, and to prove it, here is the rubber stamp stating that *'Photograph Courtesy of British Aerospace Hatfield. This photograph may be published without payment of any fee'*, and is just a representative example of the many hundreds so marked I have in my collection and have used. It was applied by Darryl Cotts, enabling so many rarely seen images to appear here in print. We discussed and eventually decided that, even though Hatfield is no more, I would credit as requested.

Chapter One

In the Beginning

The cancellation of two United Kingdom aviation projects did more than anything else to blight the prospects of British airliner sales and development in the late fifties and the sixties. It was not the disappointment of the Avro Tudor, the abandonment of the Bristol Brabazon and the SARO Princess, or the calamities that befell the De Havilland Comet 1, which ultimately left air transport sales largely in American hands. The cause lay in the decision to stop building the Vickers V.l000 long-range jet and to scale down the original De Havilland Trident 1 airliner. In one case, it was the Government's and an airline's bad judgment; in the other, the manufacturer's and an airline's.

The pioneering development of commercial jet transport by Great Britain, particularly the De Havilland Aircraft Company, has been extensively chronicled. As detailed in my work *'Comet - the World's First Jet Airliner'* (Pen & Sword Aviation 2013), the company propelled the world into a new era of jet transportation with the first flight of the Comet I prototype from Hatfield on 27 July 1949, development of which started as early as 1944. This four-engined jet aircraft was the world's first purpose-built jet airliner to take to the skies, a truly momentous event in the history of aviation.

The earliest origins of the Trident may be traced back to 1944, when De Havilland conducted preliminary studies on how the newly arrived

From No.118, August 1960 edition of De Havilland *Gazette* tin-house magazine: The new look: an impression of the De Havilland Trident short-haul airliner, which is now taking shape at Hatfield and will commence flight trials late in 1961. Essentially a second-generation jet, it is pictured against an airport building such as may be typical of the future. The 121 is expected to have a career life running well into the 1970s. De Havilland is the first manufacturer to cut metal on a second and entirely new jet-airliner design. *[Photograph Courtesy of British Aerospace Hatfield.]*

turbojet engine could be exploited for civil use. The company's first thought was that the high consumption of early centrifugal engines would limit their practical use to short- and medium-haul flights. They envisaged a three-engined airliner with tail booms and engines buried in the rear of a short fuselage, somewhat on the lines of a scaled-up Vampire, capable of carrying twenty passengers over stages up to seven hundred and fifty miles and operating from 3500-4000 foot runways.

The availability of longer runways built mainly for military operations, and the desire to exploit the jet's speed over longer stages, led De Havilland away from this idea onto the Comet series of aircraft.

The wheel turned full circle again by 1956, however, when British European Airways (BEA) first showed interest in adopting the jet for their European network. Much had happened in the intervening years, the most significant fact being the striking improvement in the efficiency of the engines available or projected. The table below displays a comparison of the important properties of the Rolls-Royce Spey I engines, as fitted to the Trident, and the D. H. Ghost 50's, fitted to the first Comets - the developments for the engines were the basis for the 1944 studies.

It will be seen from the table that the thrust-to-weight ratio doubled, and the thrust/unit frontal area was multiplied by four. The cruising-specific consumption had been reduced by nearly forty per cent, while the specific consumption at typical holding conditions has been almost halved, this latter improvement being of particular value to short-haul aircraft.

In 1951, the Comet 1 with four Ghost turbojets was well on the way to entering service as the world's first pure jet commercial transport, while the Viscount was in production at Weybridge as the first turboprop commercial airliner. At Filton, Bristol, the prototype of the long-range turboprop aircraft, the Britannia, was being built. All three machines were based on the original Brabazon Committee specifications from the Second World War. It appeared that Britain was on the way to capturing a massive slice of the world market for short-, medium-, and long-haul aircraft.

When the Comet was first delivered to the British Overseas Airways Corporation (BOAC) in 1951-52, it was positioned as a medium-range aircraft for use on what was then termed 'The Empire Routes' - airline services from the United Kingdom to India and Australia via the Far East, and across Europe and then down to Africa. The concept was designed to serve the remnants of the British Empire and what was fast becoming the British Commonwealth under the auspices and reign of Queen Elizabeth II. This design, with a maximum gross weight matching the Trident and a range of 1,500 miles, was a testament to the innovative approach of the De Havilland Aircraft Company. Despite its cruising speed being lower than the Trident's and its payload being about half that of the Trident's, it was a clear indicator of the progress made in jet aircraft design over the decade.

Engine Development 1951 - 1962

	DH Ghost 50	R.R.Spey 1
Static Thrust @ take-off rpm S.L. ISA	5000 lbs	10,400 lbs
Thrust @ take-off rpm @ 100 kts S.L. ISA = 15 deg	4430 lbs	8700 lbs
Thrust @ Max Cruise prm @ 30,000 ft; M=0.85 ISA	1900 lbs	3290 lbs
Corresponding Specific Consumption	1.22 lbs/lb/hr	0.766 lbs/lb/hr
Specific Consumption @ 200 kts @ 5,000 ft with thrust @ 25% of Max Static S.L. value:	1.36 lbs/lb/hr	0.766 lbs/lb/hr
Weight of engine and essential accessories: (no silencer, no reverser)	2230 lbs	2200 lbs
Approx Frontal area of bare engine:	15.3 sq ft.	6.7 sq ft.

Interestingly, some of De Havilland's pre-Comet studies for a jet airliner envisaged a design based on the Vampire fighter airframe powered by three jet engines, all buried in the rear fuselage, the centre one below the tail. The aircraft was, however, expected to accommodate only six passengers, but it did offer the longer London-New York range.

A Painful, and Convoluted Gestation.
Around the same time, the Royal Air Force started putting through its key programme to re-equip Bomber Command with high-altitude four-jet aircraft. The first of these, the Vickers Valiant, flew on 18 May 1951. Powered by four Rolls-Royce Avon engines buried in the wings, the Valiant had a compound sweep wing, a speed of over 560 mph at 30,000 feet, a service ceiling of 54,000 feet and a range, with under-wing fuel tanks, of 4,500 miles. With this impressive performance, it was not unnatural that Vickers and the Ministry of Supply should consider a transport development of this type as a long-range successor to the Comet.

The Ministry of Supply requested Vickers to submit designs for such a transport derivative. BOAC, which also needed a much bigger aircraft than the Comet, took part in the studies from an early stage. Vickers realised that it was not just a simple matter of putting a pair of Valiant wings on a transport fuselage. An entirely new structure was required with a huge pressurised hull and higher-powered engines than those on the Valiant. The entire design was under George Edwards' control.

Sir George Robert Freeman Edwards OM CBE FREng FRS DL started work as a design draughtsman in 1935 at Vickers. He was promoted in 1940 to the Experimental Department Manager and in 1945 he became the Chief Designer of the Vickers-Armstrongs team that produced the Viking airliner, Valetta military transport, Varsity trainer, Viscount airliners and Valiant strategic bomber. He later became Managing Director of the company, during which time the Vanguard, VC.10 and (post-merger) BAC TSR-2 strike bomber were developed. He was knighted in 1957 and President of the Royal Aeronautical Society in 1957–58. When Vickers merged into the newly created British Aircraft Corporation, he became executive director. During this period, he initiated the BAC One-Eleven, initially a Hunting Aircraft design. BAC was also a partner on international Concorde projects, for which he led the British team. He was involved in the Anglo-French SEPECAT Jaguar and the Panavia Tornado.

To make a jet transport economical compared to piston- and turboprop-engined types, a new engine would be required with more power and better specific fuel consumption than the Avon. Rolls-Royce had the answer in the Conway engine, which featured a duct around the high-pressure compressor and the combustion chambers, feeding cold air into the hot gas stream of the turbine.

Christened the 'by-pass' engine by Rolls, the Conway showed better fuel consumption because of the greater mass of slower-moving air at the back, which meant better propulsive efficiency. Rolls-Royce ran its bypass engine in 1950, and the following year, it was developing the Conway for a thrust rating of 13,000 pounds. The Conway was accordingly adopted as the basic power plant for the V. 1000.

Sir George Robert Freeman Edwards OM CBE FREng FRS DL (*b.* 9 July 1908, *d.* 2 March 2003). Sir George is seen here in the Chair of the Royal Aeronautical Society.

Vickers was delighted that it seemed possible to develop a military transport for the RAF and a commercial airliner for BOAC concurrently. This meant not only better backing for the project, but improved facilities for test-flying and development.

From the outset, Edwards saw the V.1000 as a stepping stone to the civil version, designated the VC.7, which could operate not only on BOAC's 'Empire' routes but could also fly the North Atlantic. It was for this reason that the standard fuselage diameter was established

The prototype V.1000 during construction at Wisley. The aircraft was around eighty per cent complete when the Government of the day cancelled the project. *[Vickers]*

to give six-abreast seating, and the wing made slightly over-generous to allow for maximum fuel.

Work on the definitive V.1000 started in October 1952 to meet Ministry of Supply Specification C. 123D, the actual order for a prototype and a structural test specimen being placed in January 1953. It was not until June 1954 that the Secretary of State for Air, William Phillip Sidney, 1st Viscount De L'Isle, known as Lord De L'Isle and Dudley, announced the production order for the V.l000 for the RAF. Numbers were not revealed at the time, but the quantity later became publicly known as six.

The development of the V.1000 was an order of magnitude greater than any transport previously procured by the RAF. Neither the Ministry of Supply nor the manufacturers were seemed to be aware that in building a massive jet from scratch, the whole concept was far more complex than the Comet and, of course, much larger. Inevitably, under such stringent specifications, the gestation period of V.l000 began to elongate. Wind tunnel tests were protracted due to the need for high-speed and short-field performance, while the structure and systems took the Vickers team into entirely new fields.

The design finally selected for the V.l000 was larger than the RAF initially required, so that both the V.l000 and the VC.7 would be virtually the same basic airframe. Much of the design from the Valiant crossed over to the internal wing-mounted engines, but the structure underwent radical changes. Although the faults in the Comet structure were not yet known, Vickers took great pains to ensure the integrity of the pressure cabin and the engine bay, using fail-safe techniques.

Prototype construction of the V.1000 was laid down at Wisley, the Vickers test airfield, and flight trials were to be conducted from there. Apart from delays, all seemed to be going well until the summer of 1955, when it became clear that all-up weight of the V.l000 would be of the order of 248,000 pounds, a considerable, but not disastrous, increase over the original 230,000 pounds. Clearly, the Conway engine needed uprating. By now, politics had come into play, and the RAF were having second thoughts about the V.1000 concept, with the Air Staff under fire from the Treasury over expenditure. As one of the most expensive items in the inventory, the V. 1000 came top of the list for cancellation, a fact that coincided with Air Staff dictum that a jet transport had no requirement to operate at the same speeds and heights as the V-bombers.

In addition, there was considerable pressure from the Government for the RAF to back the turboprop Bristol Britannia, the prototype having first flown in August 1952. The Britannia had been ordered by BOAC in July 1949, and there was a very heavy investment in the type by the MoS and BOAC, both of which were worried about the length of time it was taking to get the aircraft into service. Bristol also dangled a carrot in the shape of a long-term second-generation 500 mph Britannia with a thin wing and a new high-powered turboprop, the Bristol B.E. 25 Orion, which promised exceptionally low fuel consumption; BOAC had already announced an order for sixty Orions.

William Sidney, 6th Baron de L'Isle and Dudley (1909–1991).

The final nail in the V.1000 coffin was the urgent need to get production work into Short Brothers and Harland in Belfast. Shorts had been hard hit by the cancellation of the Swift and the abandonment of the Comet 2, for which types they were tooled to build in quantity. It was agreed in Whitehall that if the RAF was to place a substantial order for Britannias to be produced at Shorts, then it might save the day.

The RAF took the line of least resistance and cancelled its contract for the V.1000. Reginald Maudling, the Minister of Supply, still had faith in the project and hoped that it could be kept going as the VC.7 for BOAC, but Sir Miles Thomas, Chairman of BOAC, would have none of it. His airline had suffered severely as a result of the Comet crashes, having invested £5 million in the Comet 1 and lost its orders for the Comet 2s and 3s. Because of Britannia's delays, BOAC obtained Whitehall approval to purchase ten Douglas DC-7Cs, on the condition that they would be resold upon delivery of long-range Britannias. Despite opposition from the Treasury, a full-scale rescue operation had been mounted following the Comet 1 investigation, and BOAC were fully committed to the new Comet 4.

Reginald Maudling (7 March 1917 – 14 February 1979)

Maudling was a British politician who served as Chancellor of the Exchequer from 1962 to 1964 and as Home Secretary from 1970 to 1972. Following the 1951 election, Churchill made him a junior Minister at the Ministry of Civil Aviation. However, his experience in preparing economic policy led to his speaking on behalf of the Treasury on the 1952 budget and, later that year, to an appointment as Economic Secretary to the Treasury. With his mentor Rab Butler as Chancellor of the Exchequer, Maudling worked to reduce taxes and controls in order to move from post-war austerity to affluence. When Anthony Eden took over as prime minister in 1955, Maudling was promoted to head a department as Minister of Supply.

Behind the scenes, a tremendous sales and public relations battle was being waged between pure jet and turboprop. In the United States, the Boeing 707 and Douglas DC-8 were on their way, while every effort was made by the turboprop faction, led by Bristol, to suggest that large pure jets would be totally uneconomic.

In 1953, after the British European Airways Corporation (BEA) had put the world's first turboprop airliner - the Viscount -

into service, the airline began to study requirements for its successor. Even though major manufacturers in the United States and France were actively pursuing pure jet designs, BEA decided to stick to turboprops on economic grounds. A speed of 370 knots and seating for 100 passengers were requested, and in May 1953, the Rolls-Royce RB.109 Tyne engine was chosen as the powerplant. It was not until two years later, after continuous study and design work, that the design crystallised as the 901. More modifications and compromises remained to be worked out before a contract for twenty Vickers type 951 Vanguard aircraft was finally placed on 20 July 1956. It was more than a year after the first flight of the new Sud Caravelle airliner with twin rear-mounted Avons, which was to pioneer the jet in the short-haul field just as the Viscount had with turboprops.

BEA was beginning to realise it would face stiff competition from the new jets.

As far as can be ascertained, Vickers undertook a number of studies from November 1956 for an aircraft that became known as the Vanjet, with

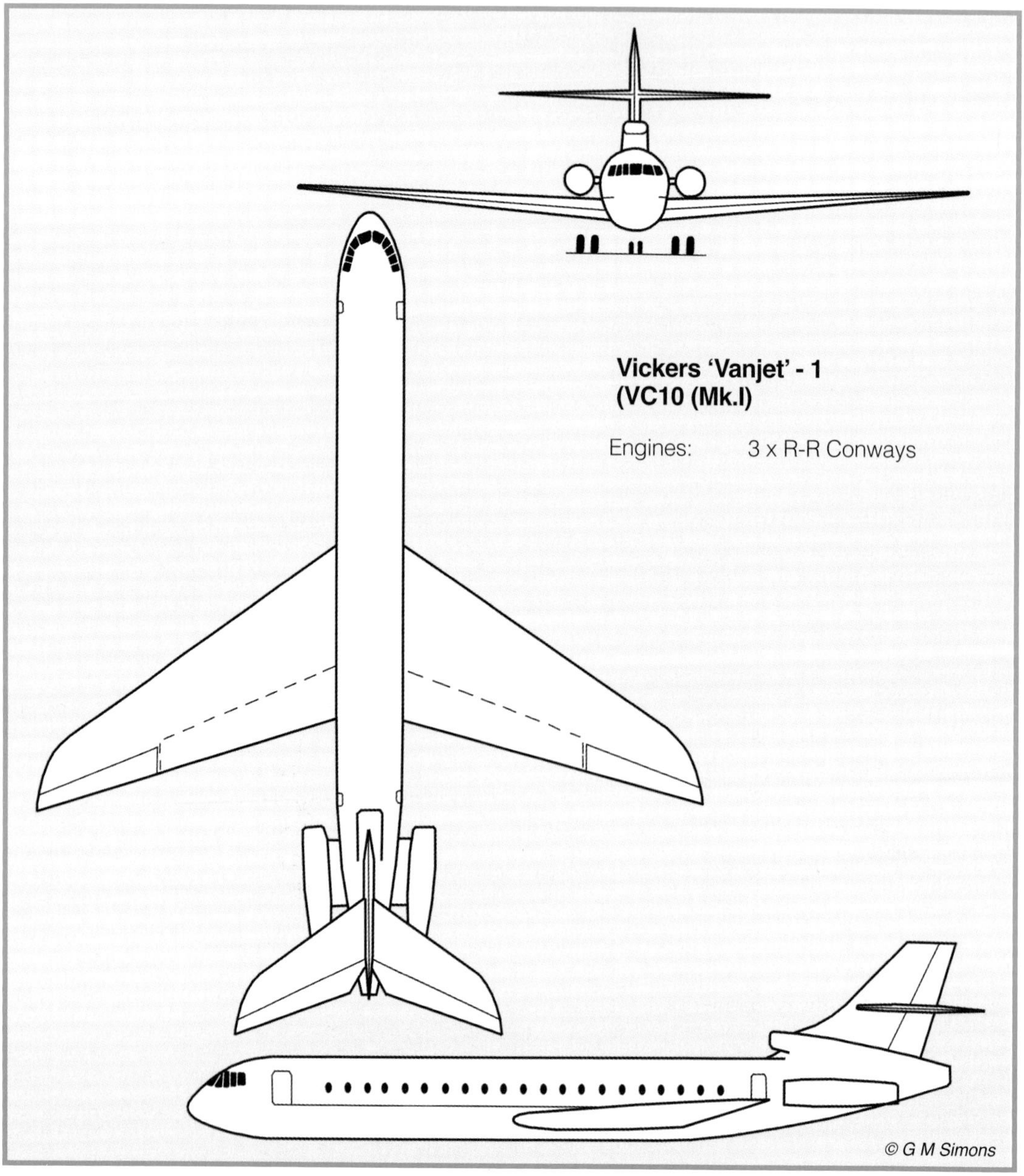

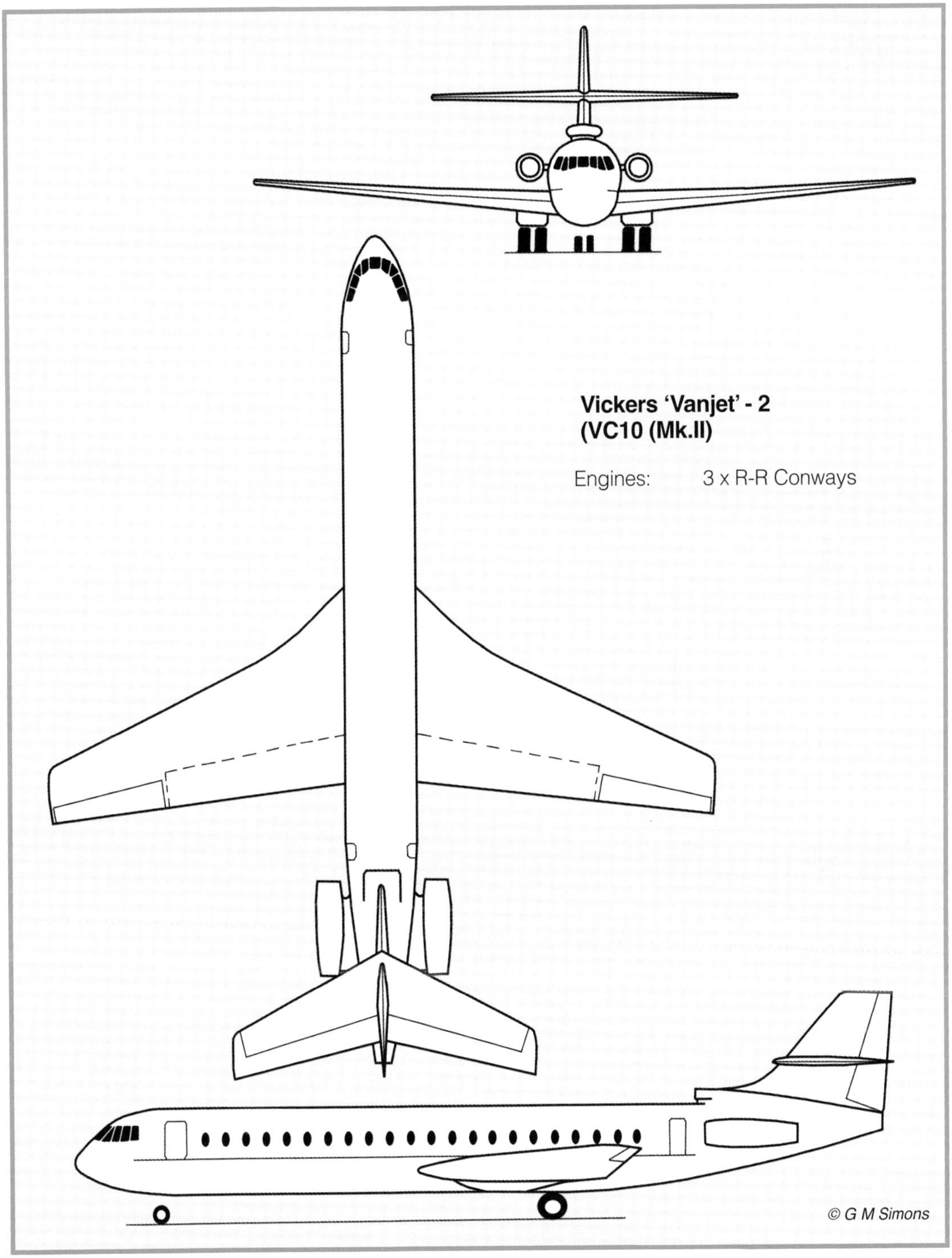

three Avon or Conway engines at the rear. Their idea was to take a Vanguard fuselage, put on a new swept wing and create a machine with medium range that could carry up to one hundred passengers with an all-up weight of 650,0000 pounds.

Concerned at the sudden interest in a jet rather than a turbine-powered regional airliner, Vickers undertook studies of a trijet version of the Vanguard, dubbed the 'Vanjet'. The aircraft featured a new swept wing, and three Rolls-Royce Avons mounted on the rear fuselage, two in pods

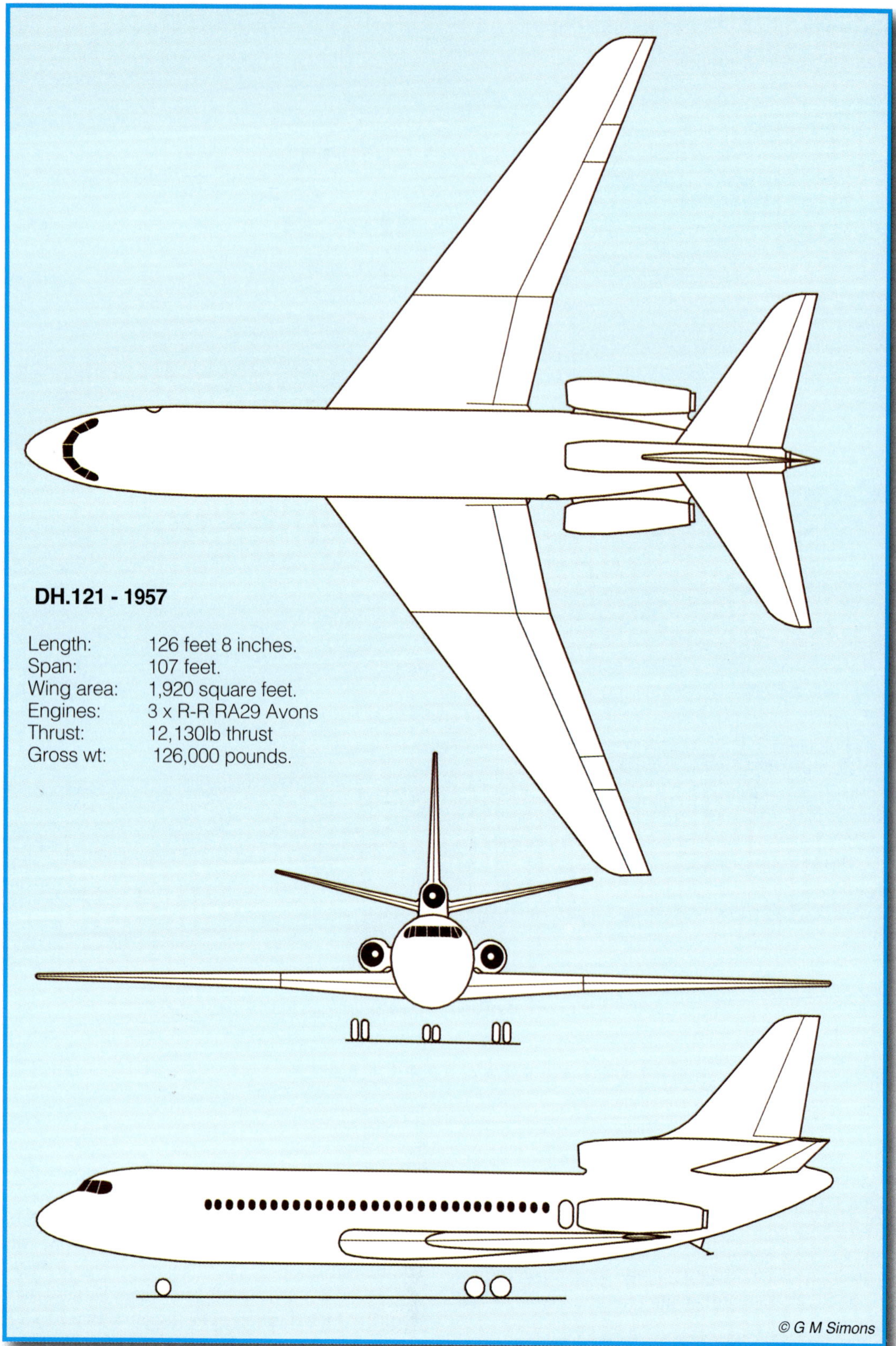
DH.121 - 1957
Length: 126 feet 8 inches.
Span: 107 feet.
Wing area: 1,920 square feet.
Engines: 3 x R-R RA29 Avons
Thrust: 12,130lb thrust
Gross wt: 126,000 pounds.
© G M Simons

on either side and the third buried in the tail. The cruciform tailplane layout was borrowed from the Caravelle. In addition, Vickers used a novel installation for its central engine, with its air intake located on the top of the fuselage feeding the engine through an 'S'-shaped intake duct. The structure was similar to the Martin XB-51 light bomber of 1949 and the proposed trijet Caravelle.

The Vanjet was effectively Vickers' insurance against the loss of the BEA and Trans-Canada Airlines launch orders for the Vanguard, in the event of the two airlines rethinking their selection of the turboprop. In the end the orders remained, and so the Vanjet failed to materialise. However, the Van-jet's design was to be influential in other manufacturers' proposals for the BEA requirement.

When it became clear that BEA were going to stick with the Vanguard, the Vanjet concept faded away and Vickers increased the size and power of the design, and it emerged in a very different guise as the VC.10 for BOAC.

When the RAF decided to scrap the V.1000, Sir Miles Thomas had done nothing so foolish as to back his interest with an order. His first reaction was to call for an up-to-the-minute VC.7 specification and a statement of price, delivery dates etc. For the VC.7, Vickers was offering one hundred to one hundred and fifty seats, a maximum take-off weight of 247,000 pounds, cruising speed of 440 knots and a London to New York range with 21,600 pound payload. A developed version with two 5,000-pound fuel slipper tanks was also offered at an all-up weight of 266,500 pounds.

BOAC was not the only operator interested. Gordon McGregor, President of Trans-Canada Airlines, had shown enthusiasm for the VC.7. When he heard that the project was about to be thrown overboard, he flew to Britain and saw Maudling and the Permanent Secretary to the MoS. He said he wanted the VC.7 and that Vickers should be allowed to go on with it. Sir Miles Thomas was adamant - he was not going to buy the VC.7. The weight increases had penalised the aircraft's performance so much that it would not be suitable for the North Atlantic as a non-stopper. All that was required was extra thrust from the Conway engine, but BOAC could not see this being made available. In reality, this was a smokescreen to cover the Corporation against having to support another British aircraft in addition to the Comet 4 and the Britannia.

By early November the newspapers were full of rumours regarding changed RAF transport policy and imminent demise of the V.1000. On 11 November, a press conference was called at the Ministry of Supply, where a wide-ranging review of aircraft procurement was given which included the cancellation of V.1000. Referring to the conference and the V.1000, *Interavia Air Letter* for 15 November 1955 stated: *'The MoS spokesman then dealt with the Vickers 1000. According to the official report, it has been decided, as a result of a review of equipment plans for Transport Command, to cancel the orders for the development and production of the V. 1000. It has taken longer than was hoped to overcome some of the problems of meeting the specification that was laid down for the V. 1000, and the urgency of the need to re-equip Transport Command therefore led to the decision to take the long-range Britannia, which has been developing well and which can be made available earlier. It is not intended to develop a civil version of the V.1000 since BOAC have no requirement for it as they consider that the aircraft which they already have on order will fully meet their needs until well into the 1960s. The Britannias now to be ordered for Transport Command will be built by Short Brothers & Harland Ltd. at Belfast. These aircraft, known as the 251 LR, will later be followed by further orders*

Ronald Eric Bishop CBE FRAeS (*b.* 27 February 1903, *d.* 11 June 1989), commonly referred to as R E Bishop, was a British engineer who was the chief designer for De Havillands from 1936.

to cover replacement of the present Handley Page Hastings fleet. However, Vickers feel that the Ministry has not done justice to the V.1000 in either their decision or their statement, and Managing Director George Edwards states that "it is a decision we shall regret for many years". The Rolls-Royce Conway engine is to be continued, as it is showing great promise. It will be used in one of the V-bombers, probably the Handley Page Victor.'

William Sholto Douglas, 1st Baron Douglas of Kirtleside, GCB, MC, DFC (*b.* 23 December 1893, *d.* 29 October 1969), seen during his early days of chairmanship of BEA, with a number of company Vickers Vikings behind,

Much later, Sir George Edwards was to remark, *'The V.1000 cancellation was the biggest blunder of all.'* In *Flight* for 13 July, 1961, Mr. Geoffrey Rippon, Parliamentary Secretary to the Ministry of Aviation, was reported as saying that the V.1000 was a 'terrible tragedy.' Supply Minister, Reginald Maudling, called in the leading air correspondents for a private session after the official announcement in November 1955. He expressed great regret at the demise of V.1000, but explained that with the Treasury wielding the economy axe and both potential customers unwilling to order, he had no alternative.

Nearly £4 million had been spent by the taxpayer on V.1000 prototype at Wisley and was eighty per cent complete with the first flight scheduled for mid-1956. The civil version, the VC.7, could have been in non-stop Atlantic service in 1959/60, while Transport Command would have got its V.1000s in 1959, to which year it had to wait for its Britannias. In addition, the VC.7 would have been the world's first by-pass or fan-engined aircraft on the long haul routes. On the Atlantic, the long-range Boeing entered service in August 1959 and the rival intercontinental DC-8 two years later. From 1958 to 1959, jet services on the North Atlantic were one stop with short-range Boeings and the Comet 4.

Despite the initial setback of the original Comet's untimely withdrawal from airline operations in April 1954, the world's aircraft manufacturers were spurred into action to develop their own jet transports. The four-engined Avro Canada Jetliner, which took flight just two weeks after the first Comet, was envisioned from the start for short to medium range intercity routes. It was on track to become the world's first 'regional jet airliner'. However, Avro was forced to shelve the design by the Canadian Government in favor of military jet development, a testament to the intense competition in the industry.

At the time of the V.1000's cancellation, BOAC was performing an extraordinary double act, on the one hand, insisting that the turboprop

De Havilland personalties!
From left to right: Richard Milroy Clarkson OBE FCGI FRAeS (*b.*14 July 1904 *d.*7 October 1996), Charles Clement Walker CBE FRAeS (*b.* 25 August 1877, *d.* 30 September 1968) C W Long, Charles Timothy Wilkins OBE, FRAeS (1913-1979).

was the only economic answer for long range, and on the other hand, extolling the virtues of a British paper project rival to V.1000, the DH.118. At the beginning of November 1956, the Ministry of Transport and Civil Aviation and BOAC announced that the Corporation and De Havilland were urgently discussing the DH.118. This was a development of an earlier design, the Comet 5, which had four pod-mounted Conways and was to cruise at around 550 mph. BOAC claimed that the DH.118 *'...will be sufficiently flexible to meet our requirements on our worldwide routes including the North Atlantic.'* The DH.118, however, was on the drawing board while the V.1000 prototype was nearing completion.

Despite all this ballyhoo, less than one year later, on 24 October 1956, Harold (later Lord) Watkinson, the Minister of Transport and Civil Aviation, announced that the Government had approved the purchase by BOAC of fifteen Boeing 707-436s. The total cost was £44 million. Even more ironic was that these airliners were powered by four Rolls-Royce Conway 508 engines, each rated at 17,500 pounds thrust. Apparently, the Conway could deliver the power for the 707 though not for the VC.7. The V.1000/VC.7 affair marked the point at which British airliner development really began to go wrong, and there has never been a full recovery. The bean counters and the Sir Humphrey Applebys of the Civil

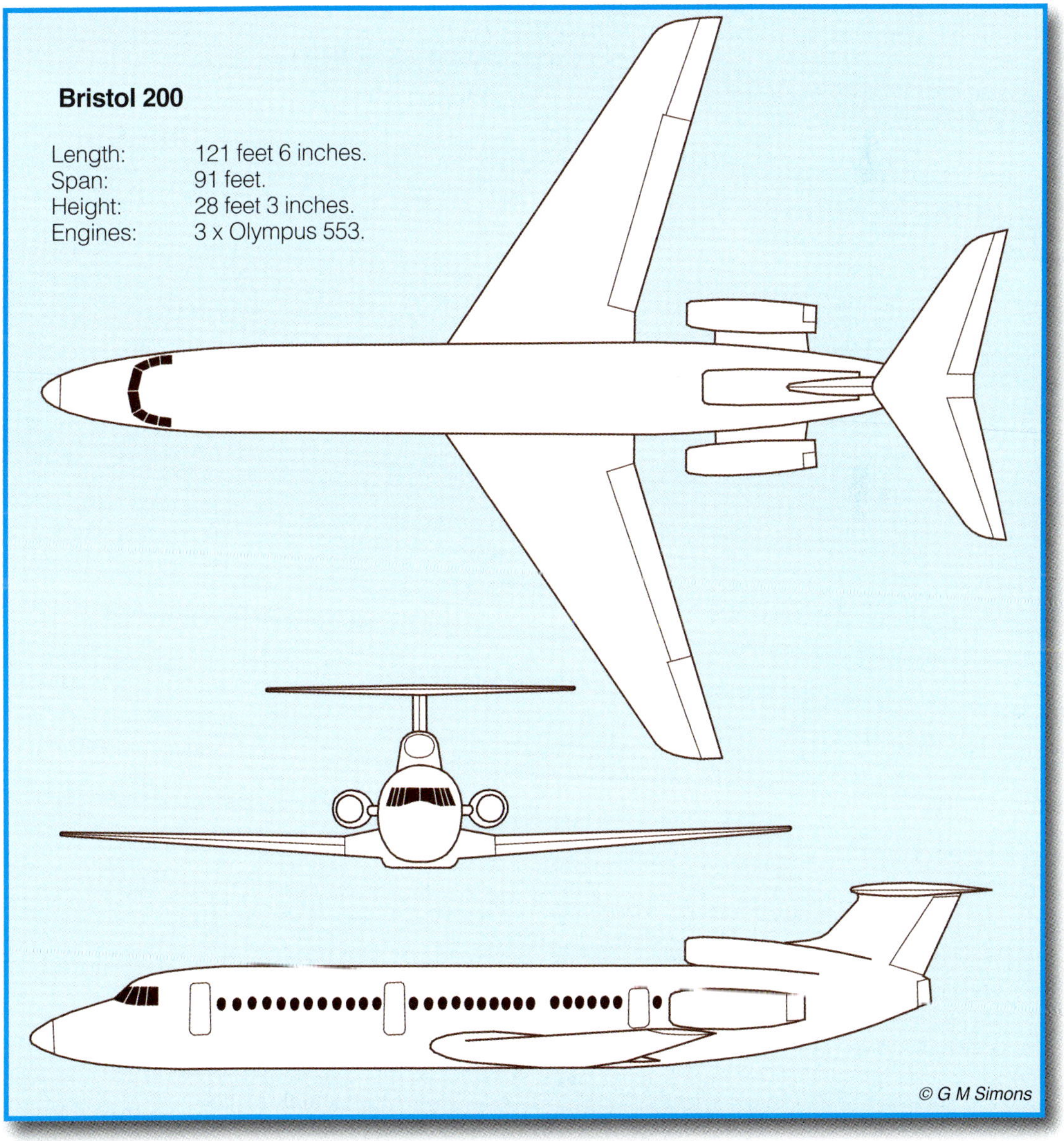

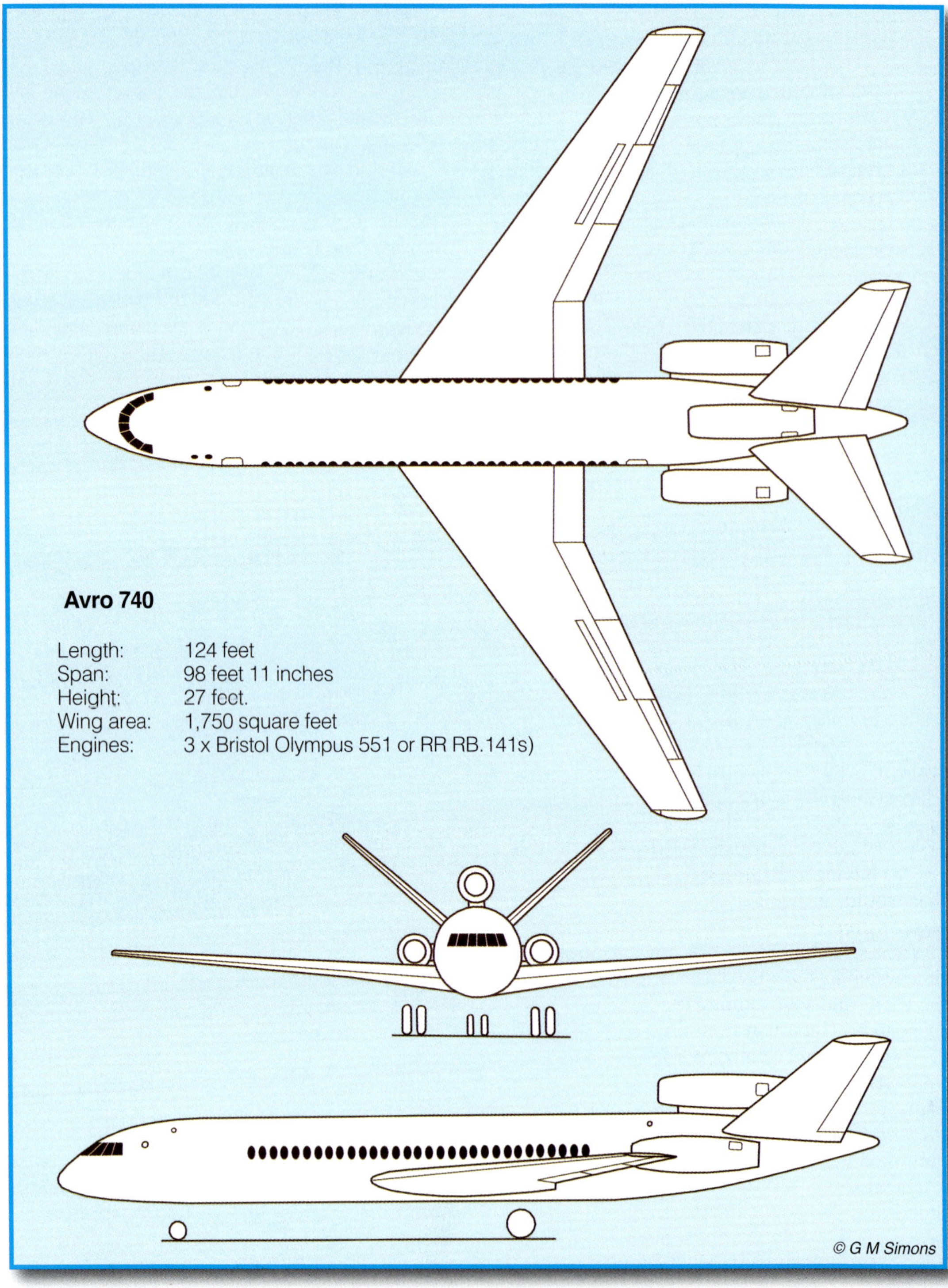

Service had taken over, and now the lunatics were running the asylum!

If there had been any understanding of the air transport business in the Government at the time, then the RAF would have been asked to continue with V. 1000 and BOAC pressed to take the VC.7. A highly competitive aircraft would therefore have been available which would have sold well in the world market and would certainly have broken even or better. More important still, Britain would have had continuity of experience in the long-haul jet field which would have allowed sustained competition with the American giants Boeing and Douglas. The overall solution to the civil problems of 1955 would have been for BEA to buy the Rolls-Royce Tyne-engined Britannia which was on offer, and for the order to be placed on Short Bros and Harland at Belfast - thereby overcoming the unemployment situation there. The Britannia programme would thus have been greatly expanded and export prospects improved. Transport Command would have got its long-range jets, which it eventually had to buy in the shape of the VC. 10, and BOAC would have been able to operate the North Atlantic and the 'Empire' routes with the British-made VC.7 and its derivatives. Or would they?

When I wrote *The British Overseas Airways Corporation - A History* (Air World, 2019), I discovered that one man was tasked with providing the BOAC Board with information on future aircraft projects. This was Alan Campbell Orde CBE, AFC, FRAeS, He was BOAC's Operations Development Director. Further research revealed that he was tasked with having to juggle firstly with his own bias for buying the latest and best American or Canadian airliners, to ensure BOAC could compete with and still make a profit against the likely international airline scene in the 1950s; secondly to convince his own Chairman this was the right course to follow; and thirdly to try to prevent his Chairman being prevailed upon by British Government sources to opt for buying British designed and built aircraft that would, in his words, *'be years behind the latest American designs in comfort and performance.'* Campbell Orde spent a considerable time watching the emerging new jet airliners from the USA, and sent running commentaries on the scene to his Chairman from time to time.

I came across Cambell Orde years later when I assisted Fiona Somerville with her book on the man *'Alan Campbell Orde Pioneer Aviator, Test Pilot and Airline Chief'* a long time before it was published by Fonthill Books.

In regard to the VC-7, Sir Miles Thomas, Basil Smallpeice, Whitney Straight, and Campbell Orde inspected the progress in September 1955 and decided in the following December not to maintain any further interest in the VC-7 project but to order Boeing 707s, which were much further advanced, the prototype having already flown. BOAC's competitors were now ordering them, also the Douglas DC-8, which was some way behind Seattle production. They regarded the VC-7 as being uncompetitive, and it was much too late.

Publicly, there appeared to be no planning of any sort. The V. 1000/ VC.7 project died, and BOAC, through the efforts of Alan Campbell-Orde became wedded to Boeing, and BEA insisted on having its own big turboprop, the Vickers Vanguard, which sold to only two operators and cost Vickers a small fortune in the process.

Boeing developed the 707 jet via the intermediate KC-135 tanker design for the US Air Force from the earlier 'one off' Model 367 Dash Eighty, whilst McDonnell Douglas followed its long line of piston 'DCs' with the four-jet DC-8. By the second half of the 1950s De Havilland had overcome the Comet's teething problems and the type was about to re-enter service with BOAC in an enlarged, re-engined, longer range form, known as the Comet 4. The Comet and the 707 inaugurated transatlantic jet services - again with the revitalised Comet taking the lead - during the autumn of 1958 with BOAC and Pan American respectively.

Yorkshireman Sir Roy Dobson (*b.*1891, *d.*1968) who rose from being an apprentice tool fitter to a major figure in the development of AV Roe and later Hawker Siddeley. He joined the company in 1914 and graduated from being an apprentice to a role in the drawing office where he also learned to fly and for a time was a designer and test pilot.

With the market apparently now saturated with four-engined long range jetliners, Convair developed a smaller high speed subsonic jet airliner, the 880, which offered less capacity than the Boeing and Douglas products but was capable of cruising at over 600mph, making it the fastest jet transport of its day and considerably faster than its rivals. Unfortunately for Convair, the speed gimmick did not really catch on.

During 1957 De Havilland began finalising plans for a shorter range, higher capacity version of the Comet 4, which eventually received a launch order from BEA in the form of the Comet 4B in August 1957.

In the meantime, the French manufacturer Sud Aviation had developed the world's first true short-range jet airliner in the form of the twin-engined SE.210 Caravelle. The aircraft had been launched into production in 1953, and the prototype made its first flight from Toulouse on 27 May 1955. Although initially proposed as a trijet with its centre engine buried in the tail, the aircraft evolved as a twin-engined design powered (initially) by two 10,000 pound thrust Rolls-Royce Avon turbojets. The launch customer Air France placed orders for twelve in February 1956 to operate on its European regional routes, and the aircraft entered revenue service with the airline in April 1959. Scandinavian Airlines System (SAS) became the first export customer for the type when it ordered six plus nineteen options in June 1957.

Once the Caravelle entered service, BEA rapidly recognised the passenger appeal of pure-jet airliners, with its market research finding that many travellers actively requested the French aircraft. Seeing the immediate and significant loss of share on its most important routes, the corporation ordered De Havilland DH106 Comet 4Bs as a stopgap but identified a need for twelve entirely new short-haul jets by 1964 and twenty-four by 1966.

As the pressure of design work on the Comet eased in 1956, the next major project to engage the inventive energies of the De Havillands came under active contemplation. For many months, the advisability of undertaking a larger jet airliner to meet the Atlantic and general needs of BOAC from the middle 1960s and into the 1970s was weighed. The company's special experience in the field of medium-size jet transport also claimed consideration, and finally it was agreed that in this direction lay the best opportunity for a useful contribution to the future of civil aviation, not only for British operations but also for world markets.

The full resources of the aerodynamics department were applied to this study as they had been ten years earlier to the theoretical evolution of a formula for the first jet airliner. Richard M Clarkson, turning increasingly towards research into future possibilities and working with Ronald E Bishop, devoting more time to forward thinking in the complementary design department, assessed the relative merits of all the new developments in airframe form and structure and consulted the most advanced thinking in the Engine Company and elsewhere on power-plant efficiency.

Despite the rapid development of jet transports in both the short and long-range markets, British European Airways (BEA) believed that propeller turbine power (turboprop) was the more viable option for shorter routes. This was due to the lower fuel consumption and quieter operation of turboprops, which made them more suitable for the shorter distances and frequent take-offs and landings typical of European regional routes. Having successfully introduced the fifty-seat turboprop Vickers Viscount into regular service in April 1953, BEA issued a detailed specification for a larger turboprop-powered successor, which led to the development of the Vickers Vanguard.

The introduction of the pure-jet Caravelle prompted BEA to reassess its strategy. With the prospect of Air France introducing a jet that would compete on its routes before its turboprop Vanguards were due to come online, BEA was faced with the possibility of its new Vanguards becoming obsolete before they even started operating on its European network.

In July 1956, the same month that BEA finalized its contract for the Vanguard and just four months after Air France placed its Caravelle order, BEA issued a detailed requirement for a new jet airliner. The airline was in need of a 100-seat 600 mph-plus jet airliner that could carry a payload of up to 19,000 pounds. This meant it should be capable of carrying seventy first-class passengers out of six thousand foot runways over 1,000-mile sectors. The aircraft should offer the best seat-mile costs over ranges from 500 - 1,000 nautical miles and be available to enter service by 1964. Importantly, BEA's requirement stated that its new jet should be faster than the Caravelle. BEA also expressed a preference for more than two engines, with a preference for rear-mounting.

Despite the requirement for a faster jet than the Caravelle, at the end of 1956, BEA Chairman, Sholto Douglas, 1st Baron Douglas of Kirtleside, stated that the core of the airline's fleet would

Artwork from *'The Gazette':* A Comet 4 and Trident - around 1959.
[Photograph Courtesy of British Aerospace Hatfield]

continue to be with the British turboprop. However, he conceded that the company could need to acquire a few jets to counter the competition. Less than nine months later, the Chairman stated, *'we were at one time hoping to go on indefinitely with turboprops,'* and now seemed resigned to the fact that it was going to have to follow its fellow European airlines into acquiring jets. This transition was evident in the introduction of the Vickers Vanguard, a key part of BEA's strategy to compete in the evolving aviation market.

William Sholto Douglas, 1st Baron Douglas of Kirtleside, GCB, MC, DFC had been a senior commander in the Royal Air Force. After serving as a pilot, then a flight commander and finally as a squadron commander during the First World War, he served as a flying instructor during the inter-war years before becoming Director of Staff Duties and then Assistant Chief of the Air Staff at the Air Ministry.

During the Second World War, Douglas clashed with other senior commanders over strategy in the Battle of Britain. Douglas supported Air Chief Marshal Trafford Leigh-Mallory, who argued for a 'Big Wing' strategy, i.e. using massed fighters to defend the United Kingdom against enemy bombers promulgated by legless Battle of Britain pilot, Douglas Bader.

After the Battle of Britain, Douglas became Air Officer Commanding-in-Chief of Fighter Command in which role he was responsible for rebuilding the command's strength after the attrition of the Battle of Britain, but also for bringing it on the offensive to wrest the initiative in the air from the German Luftwaffe.

Douglas went on to be Air Officer Commanding-in-Chief of RAF Middle East Command. He became commander of the British Zone of Occupation in Germany after the war. From 1949 to 1964, he served as chairman of British European Airways.

Privately, a paper by BEA's chairman on 4 October 1956 conceded any jet design should have export potential, so givng a nod to the hopes of the manufacturers.

A line in a draft report evaluating the options for BEA, prepared by the Royal Aircraft Establishment around the same time, emphasised that while the evaluation was against the airline's requirements, *'if the final choice is to be a commercial success, it should also appeal to other operators, who may require a longer range than BEA'*. The line had been manually altered from *'should also appeal'* to *'must* [underlined twice] *also appeal'*.

De Havilland proposals that eventually led to its submission of the Model 121 to BEA could be traced back to late 1956. Following the BEA requirement of July 1956 and a need by BOAC for a new long-range jet, De Havilland conceived the DH.118 in the autumn of 1956, although this proposal was aimed primarily at the BOAC requirement. The DH.118 was a development of the proposed Comet 5, itself a derivative of the Comet 4, with four pod-mounted Rolls-Royce Conway turbofans capable of cruising at around 550mph. At the end of 1956, BOAC was believed to be in negotiation with De Havilland to purchase up to fifteen DH.118s.

By the end of the year, the De Havilland proposal had developed into the DH.119 powered by four Rolls-Royce RA.29 Avons and aimed more closely to BEA's requirement. The engine installation on the '119 was behind the rear wing spars with air intakes below the wings, and this layout was carried over to its successor, the DH.120, which aimed at satisfying both corporations' requirements. The '120 was proposed with either the four Rolls-Royce RA.29 Avons of the DH.119 or RB.140s that were, in reality, scaled down Conways.

However, the DH.119 and DH.120 designs satisfied neither BOAC nor BEA, the former already favouring Vickers' scaled up Vanjet, the VC-10, whilst the DH.120 was too big for the latter. De Havilland, therefore, decided to aim directly at BEA's requirement and conceived the Model 121 in May 1957.

Initially, the 121 (De Havilland's 121st design) was proposed as a 79-seat 126,000 pound gross weight aircraft powered by either three or four 'bypass jets' in the 8 - 12,000 pounds thrust class. De Havilland, however, favoured the trijet design, which featured three 12,130-pound thrust RA29 Avons with the Caravelle/Vanjet-inspired tail layout, albeit with the tailplane positioned below the central engine. Both designs envisaged fully powered flying controls. The choice of a trijet design and the specific engine configurations were significant as they influenced the aircraft's performance and operational costs.

A Choice of Configuration

The desire to offer the fastest practicable subsonic cruising speed dictated a wing sweep of thirty-five degrees, and the most critical decisions determining the layout were connected to the location and number of power units. These two factors were closely related, since there was only one practical location for the centre engine if three were chosen. However, most considerations in choosing the number of engines can be treated independently of their location.

Number of Engines: The total thrust required for an aircraft with a specified payload may be dictated by either the cruising speed or the take-off and airworthiness climb requirements. The thrust required for a given cruising speed is broadly independent of the number of power units. In contrast, the total thrust required for a given take-off or climb compliance is strongly influenced by the number of units and the required range.

Engine thrust-to-weight ratio does not vary much with engine size, but the ratio of thrust to cost does vary widely. The general trend is clearly a fall in engine price per pound of thrust as engine

More artwork from *'The Gazette'*: a Trident in BEA colours, probably 1958.
[Photograph Courtesy of British Aerospace Hatfield]

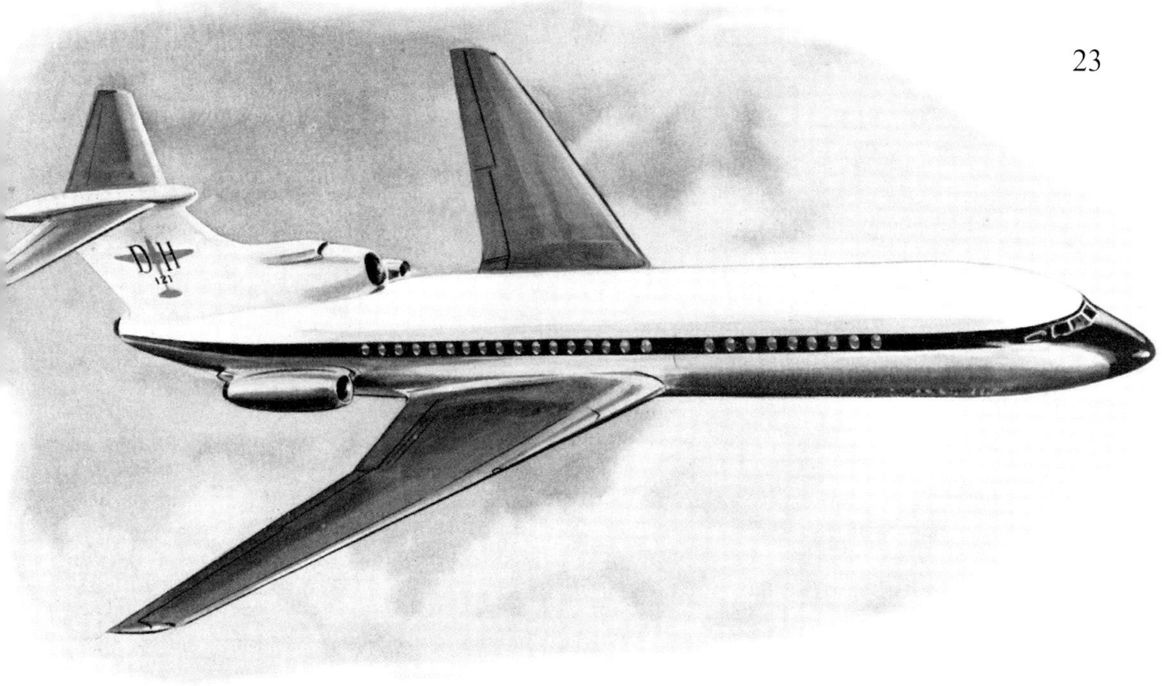

This time its artwork from a Hawker Siddeley brochure. This, and a few other artworks show the DH logo on the tail with '121' overlaid. There also appears to be an additional intake of some kind above engine No.2.
[Photograph Courtesy of British Aerospace Hatfield]

size increases. To take an example in 1962 values: A total thrust of 30,000 pounds would cost $432,000 if supplied by two engines; $523,000, by three units; or $606,000 by four units.

The twin-engined aircraft provides the most economical solution at the shortest ranges, but there is then a broad band of stage lengths over which the three-engined aeroplane is pre-eminent. Nowhere within the ranges considered does the four-engined case appear attractive. Variations in the basic specification will, to some extent, shift the crossover points between the various engine numbers, and in particular, the case for the twin is improved if the speed requirement is relaxed. However, speed is the primary commodity that air transport has to offer, and experience has often shown it to be decisive in a competitive situation. For operation at around 600 mph, therefore, there is no doubt that the three-engined formula is the most attractive for short and medium stage operations.

This argument sets out what might be called the theoretical case for the three engined airliner, but consideration must also be given to more practical aspects. In almost every case such aspects were found to reinforce the choice of three engines, and no instances of serious conflict arose. The more significant of these considerations are:

1. The three-engined machine has a better en route performance after failure of one engine, and the consequences of a second engine failure or the subsequent failure of an engine-driven power source are not catastrophic as compared to a twin failure. It is therefore more suitable for operation on stages over water or other inhospitable territory and can be expected to provide a higher schedule reliability in any area of operation. In the event of a landing away from base with one engine inoperative, the three-engined machine may be ferried back to base for the engine change, thus leading to economies in the provision of spare engines on a widespread route network as compared with those for a twin.
2. The three engines provide three independent power sources for all systems and hence a high standard of reliability and safety, suitable for the use of power controls and for the eventual application of all-weather automatic landing.
3. The three-engined layout can provide good separation of engines as compared to four engines at the rear, and there are no serious problems in ensuring complete independence of engines from a safety viewpoint.
4. The centre engine can be positioned behind and below all the main structural members; it is not a buried engine.

Location of Engines: To judge from design trends in use at the time, engine location was a less controversial issue than that of the number of engines. The principal factors that led to the choice of the rear position in the case of the Trident were as follows:

1. Experience with the Comet has shown the great safety advantage of minimising the yawing moment arising from engine failure. This is preserved with rear engines.
2. It permits an uninterrupted wing, both aerodynamically and structurally.
3. It gives the least possible cabin noise, and it exposes the minimum of the airframe to noise damage from the engine exhausts.
4. The engine intakes are at a good height from the ground, and the side intakes are protected by the flaps from water and debris thrown up by the wheels.
5. The engine installation does not dictate the wing dihedral.
6. The engines are well away from the fuel tanks, and very little primary structure is exposed to danger in the event of an engine break-up.
7. The relatively expensive engines are well protected in the event of a 'wheels-up' landing or minor taxiing mishap.
8. There is a penalty on wing weight as compared with that for pods because of the lack of relief weight, and there is a weight penalty in adapting the rear fuselage structure and fitting a high tail. These penalties together amount to around 1,500 pounds. However, the increased flap effectiveness due to the clean wing is more than able to carry this extra weight and therefore there is no net penalty in wing area, thrust, or operating cost.
9. There is a tendency for an abnormally large c.g. travel; in the case of the Trident this has been handled with a moving tailplane fitted with a geared slotted flap, giving a wide trim range at low speeds and a powerful control at high Mach numbers.

Having decided in favour of three engines mounted at the rear, considerable further work went into the more detailed engine location problem. The side engine's fore-and-aft position was determined by a self-imposed requirement that the plane of the turbines lie behind the pressure dome.

This is a very desirable safety feature, since although engines can be armored to contain a detached turbine blade, it is impractical to design for containment of a failed turbine disc. The position of the centre engine is very much tied up with that of the tailplane, and in the early stages of design a low tail was considered with the centre engine mounted above it. This was eliminated for fairly obvious reasons, and the present layout has proved to be the most practicable because it meets as it does the following considerations:

1. Engine mounted as far forward as possible, to minimise c.g. range and trim problems.
2. Tailplane arm to c.g. as great as possible.
3. Tailplane clear of wing downwash to minimise pitch-up tendency.
4. Tailplane clear of reverse thrust efflux field.
5. Easy changing and servicing of center engine.

Aerodynamic Features

Wing Design for High Speed - To be fully competitive in speed as well as operating with the best attainable economy, a considerable effort was invested during the early stages of design in getting the most favourable drag rise characteristics from the thirty-five degree swept wing. This, of course, meant maintaining the sweep of the isobars on the wing surface right up to the fuselage side, an aim that body waisting, wing planform changes, wing section changes, or some combination of all three could achieve. De Havilland's attention was mainly focused on wing-section changes, as it was estimated that these would involve lower weight and drag penalties than drastic wing-planform changes. Body waisting was regarded as a matter to be considered only as a last resort.

The proposed aircraft had an overall length of 110 feet 4 inches, and a wingspan of 111 feet. Wheel track was 19 feet 4 inches and the wheelbase 45 feet 7 inches. A conventional undercarriage layout was adopted, with a twin nosewheel unit and four-wheel bogey main units.

The centre engine was positioned atop the rear fuselage, fed by a straight-through air intake. The four-engined proposal featured four 8,550 pounds thrust Rolls-Royce RB.140 engines mounted in paired pods on the rear fuselage (as with the VC-10). A further proposed trijet derivative featured the proposed Rolls-Royce RB.141 engine rated at 11,660 pounds thrust each. The aircraft was expected to have a cruising speed of 605 mph at 24,000 feet and a maximum range of 1,140 miles. It was interesting that in the proposal put to BEA, De Havilland stated that it considered the aircraft might be the last subsonic short-range jet to be designed in Great Britain.

As initially proposed, the '121 featured two ventral airstairs (something never fitted on the production aircraft), one situated centrally in the rear fuselage; however, the other installation was far more novel. Positioned in the forward fuselage just behind the flightdeck, the airstair would be lowered from the nose gear bay through which passengers would enter and exit.

The number of engines for the new short-haul jet was a subject of intense technical debate. The BEA requirement for 'more than two engines' effectively ruled out a twin. The major airlines in the United States had also stated that they were not interested in anything less than three engines for those sort of ranges. This technical debate was a crucial part of the decision-making process, engaging all stakeholders in the project.

The preference, and later the decision, to opt for 'less than four engines' was a significant development in the 1950s aviation industry. This choice was primarily driven by the need to reduce direct operating costs (DOCS). Studies carried out by Rolls-Royce, and De Havilland showed that a four-engined aircraft would have between thee and five per cent higher DOCS. Similarly, a twinjet design capable of 600 mph would require a higher aspect ratio wing and would have been significantly overpowered in the cruise, as its total available thrust would have to cope with engine-out take-off requirements.

By July 1957, the DH.121 proposal had been re-thought and featured a gross weight of 107,000 lb with three 10,400 lb thrust Rolls-Royce RB-140-141 bypass engines, later called Medways, selected for the powerplant. As the DH.121's design was refined, a T-tail arrangement was adopted with the tailplane being moved to the top of the fin. At the same time, the Vanjet's buried central engine and 'S-shaped intake duct layout was incorporated.

During 1957 two other manufacturers submitted designs to BEA to meet its future short haul jet needs. Bristol proposed its Model 200, which in its final form was similar in layout to the 121 with three (initially four) engines mounted on the rear fuselage, the central one fed by an 'S' duct.

Manchester's A.V. Roe & Co (known simply as Avro) had in fact been the first company publicly to reveal its proposals for a short range jet for BEA. In the July 1957 edition of *Avro News,* the company's Managing Director Sir Roy Dobson referred to its proposal as a 'determined attempt to enter the civil airliner markets'. He also stated that the company could not afford to 'underestimate the opposition' and emphasised the fact that Avro would be 'risking many millions of our own money in this venture, so it had better be successful...'

Avro presented the Model 740, a design that stemmed from earlier work by Armstrong Whitworth. Powered by three Olympus 5515 engines, the design set itself apart from the De

After the size shuffle, BEA was finally ready to sign a contract with De Havilland for its new short haul jet. This occurred on 12 August 1959 and a signing ceremony at BEA's HQ at Keyline House.

Here Sir Aubrey Burke, Managing Director of Airco (left) is seen shaking hands with Anthony Milward, Chief Executive of BEA, after signing the £28 million contract for 24 DH121s plus 12 options.

From *'The Gazette'*: is what is almost certainly a mock-up of the Trident cabin at Hatfield.
[Photograph Courtesy of British Aerospace Hatfield]

Havilland and Bristol offerings with its innovative three-engined layout. The central engine was mounted in a pod on top of the fuselage between two V-fin tailplanes, while the other two engines were in pods on the rear fuselage, similar to the DH.121 and Bristol 200. Notably, Avro's proposal was unique in that it offered to finance the development of its project (estimated at £17 - £20 million) through export orders, a strategic move that piqued the interest of industry observers.

In August 1957, BEA satisfied its immediate jet requirement by announcing that it would order six De Havilland Comet 4Bs, a short range, higher capacity development of the intercontinental Comet 4, for delivery from the end of 1959. However, this was an interim measure and it would appear that at the same time BEA selected the DH.121 over the Bristol 200 and Avro 740 for its longer term requirements.

Up to this point, the Bristol 200 was believed to have been BEA's favoured design. However, as far back as July 1957, De Havilland had promoted the DH.121 as a supplement as well as an eventual replacement for BEA's anticipated fleet of Comet 4Bs. It would seem that BEA's interim requirement for jets, satisfied by the Comets, swayed its preference away from the Bristol offering towards the De Havilland 121. At this time, BEA wanted to start taking delivery of its all-new jets before the end of 1962.

Until BEA approached the Treasury for the necessary financial support to launch its jet airliner project, it was widely assumed that the government would be prepared to support the project financially. Of the three offerings, only Avro's proposal was planned to be financed privately. Therefore, it came as a shock when Harold Watkinson, Minister of Transport, announced on 9 December 1957 at the BIATA (British Independent Air Transport Association) annual dinner that the new trijet would have to be financed privately, a surprising turn of events that caught many off guard.

It was during 1957 that the then Conservative government began to encourage its policy of combining the many British aircraft manufacturers into larger, less numerous groupings. This was achieved by using its control of the state airlines to push through its belief that collaboration was the answer to future projects. As the government was to provide BEA with the finances for its new fleet in the form of a loan, the order would have to be subject to its approval.

As neither Bristol nor De Havilland could finance their projects individually, the turn of the year saw some frantic rejigging as various new proposals were put to the Minister. De Havilland proposed a consortium to BEA to build the '121, which it would lead (building the fuselage) and would include Hunting, Fairey and its rival Bristol who would be responsible for building the wings. Bristol, not keen on playing second fiddle to De Havilland, announced on 27 December 1957 that it was joining forces with Hawker Siddeley to produce the '200, with the shareholding split 35:65 per cent respectively. This strategic alliance between Bristol and Hawker Siddeley brought a sense of optimism to the industry, as it effectively eliminated the Avro offering, given that the company was a division of the Hawker Siddeley Group (and had been since the group was formed in 1935).

The formation of the Bristol-Hawker Siddeley consortium in 1958, with a combined asset value exceeding £200 million, was a significant event in the aviation industry. The consortium was chaired by Sir Frank Spriggs, the Managing Director of Hawker Siddeley Group, and included other influential figures such as Avro Managing Director Sir Roy Dobson, Sir Reginald Verdon Smith, Chairman and joint MD of Bristol, and Short Brothers/Bristol Chairman, Rear-Admiral Sir Matthew Slattery.

In a statement issued in January 1958 the consortium stated that *'the new company operating with the full support of the parent companies, will employ the strongest resources of the two parent companies in engineering, manufacture and sales, so as to develop and produce the aircraft as rapidly as possible, and on a scale to enable it to be offered in world markets at dates, times and prices which will be internationally competitive. To this end the new company will hold the contract, will have a direct relationship with BEA and other customers on all aspects of the project, and will be responsible for specification, airworthiness, planning and progressing, sales, engineering and promotion.'*

It was planned to divide design and production to enable the civil aviation experience of Bristol and the high subsonic speed experience of Hawker Siddeley to be deployed to the best advantage.

There had been suggestions that BEA's previous selection of the De Havilland design over the Bristol 200 was unlikely to have been on technical preference as it was purported that there was little to choose between them at this early stage. BEA's favouring of the De Havilland 121 was more likely to do with the commercial continuity that the company could offer in jet airliner design, having already built and delivered the Comet. This would explain the emphasis made in the Bristol-Hawker Siddeley statement over the consortium members' experience in their relevant fields of aviation.

The creation of the Bristol 200 consortium was to put governmental pressure on BEA to change direction away from the '121 as it awaited final government approval for its purchase of twenty-four DH.121s. The Corporation's board met on the afternoon of Friday 3 January 1958 to deliberate on its selection on the '121 over the newly proposed Bristol-Hawker Siddeley consortium's proposal.

In January 1958, the Bristol-Hawker Siddeley consortium unveiled its Bristol 200 design to the public. The consortium, with its combined expertise and resources, was able to send a sales team to the USA to discuss a potential order with Pan American. This proactive approach was seen as an attempt to overshadow the DH.121 by Bristol. There were even suggestions that the Bristol-Hawker Siddeley programme would proceed with or without the BEA order, should they secure '...20, 30 or 40' orders. The proposed Bristol 200 had an overall length of 121 feet 6 inches, a wingspan of 91feet, and was to be powered by 'three turbojets in the 13,000lb thrust class' (assumed to be the Rolls-Royce RB.141s). The aircraft had a range with its maximum passenger load (100 passengers) of 1,700 miles, a maximum gross weight of 120,000 pounds, and a maximum payload of 21,000 pounds.

De Havilland meanwhile had finalised its own amalgamation plans, minus Bristol, and called it the Aircraft Manufacturing Company (Airco). Revealed in January 1958, Airco was the revival of an old name that existed during World War One in which Sir Geoffrey De Havilland was the chief designer and which built the De Havilland DH1 to DH18. De Havilland was to have a 67.5 per cent shareholding with Hunting 22.5 per cent and Fairey 10 per cent, with the members represented on the board by four, two and one directors respectively. Handley Page had offered technical experience using its experience with high speed aircraft and tail design. Saunders-Roe was also pencilled in for sub-contract work on the '121.

The directors of Airco were Wilfred E. Nixon,

Chairman; Richard Fairey, Deputy Chairman; A F Burke, Managing Director; Charles P M Hunting, A S Kennedy, Francis E N St. Barbe and W A Summers.

Even by it's creation, considerable progress had been made towards the finalising of the specification and of design features, also in respect of contract negotiations with BEA. Production plans were in hand envisaging a high output rate to take care of world sales with early deliveries. Sales negotiations were in progress and technical sales teams had already gone overseas.

Aircraft Manufacturing Co. Ltd. had strong financial, technical, and productive resources to ensure the success of the project, whether for BEA alone or for a large production such as would be required if, as expected, the aircraft sold well in world markets.

The stumbling block over the selection of the source for BEA's new airliner seemed to be based upon fears that the De Havilland was not as strong in terms of size, assets and production capacity as the rival Bristol-Hawker Siddeley consortium, which through the Hawker Siddeley Group included Avro, Armstrong Whitworth, Gloster and Hawker. Therefore, although BEA favoured the De Havilland proposal the government apparently preferred the stronger Bristol consortium.

Hence the creation of the Airco consortium, which was primarily aimed at swinging government support away from the strong Bristol-Hawker Siddeley consortium to BEA's preference, the De Havilland group. At the end of January 1958, De Havilland went on record to state that *'the three Airco companies concerned have more than adequate financial resources to carry the risk of selling or not selling the DH.121, assuming that the BEA order was for 20 to 25 aircraft'.*

Bristol-Hawker Siddeley had been suggesting that De Havilland's negotiations for the order had

One suggestion put forward, but never adopted was a set of forward and rear airstairs.
[Photograph Courtesy of British Aerospace Hatfield]

involved discussion over progress payments that could amount to £10 million by the time of first deliveries. It was further implied that this substantial financial commitment could be lost should the programme fail, highlighting the significant financial implications of the Bristol-Hawker Siddeley consortium.

Following the completion of the DH.121's consortium, the final De Havilland proposal, a pivotal moment in civil aviation history, was put to the Minister of Supply on 23 January 1958. In the parliamentary civil aviation debate on 27 January 1958, Harold Watkinson stated *'the history of BEA's attitude was that to begin with, it favoured the Bristol concept, but after discussion and technical examination the final decision was in favour of the De Havilland design. I do not think that there was now any aircraft manufacturer who had not had a chance to associate himself with this order if he wants to. The final detailed proposals from the De Havilland group reached my Right Honourable friend and myself only this morning. They are being urgently examined.'*

In a House of Commons statement issued on 10 February, the Minister of Supply, Aubrey Jones, summed up the purpose of his cautious approach to the problem of the BEA order. Firstly he wished to ensure that the project would not involve financial liabilities on his department, partly because such liabilities had been heavy in the past, and partly because it was healthier for the industry to be more self-reliant. De Havilland's first proposal required government financial contribution. The proposal of 19 December had promised private financing among the other contractors with reservations about the volume of other Ministry contracts. However, the latest proposals were being considered to ensure that his department was protected against contingent liabilities. The alignment of home demand with potential foreign demand was also being examined.

The controversy seemed to be sown up when, on 12 February 1958, the Ministry of Transport and Civil Aviation (MTCA) announced that BEA was to begin final negotiations with Airco and Rolls-Royce over the acquisition of twenty-four DH.121s, plus twelve options. Accordingly, a Letter of Intent was signed, with deliveries scheduled to begin in early 1964.

However, the government also stated that it would 'wish to be satisfied that the whole project will be developed and manufactured as a private venture by the companies concerned, a stance that underlines the government's commitment to industry self-reliance'.

During 1958, BEA approached Smiths Industries and asked the company to develop an all-weather flight control system for its new jet airliner; the plan being that the aircraft would eventually be able to land automatically in all weathers, including the dense fog, which was a feature of smoggy Europe in the 1950s.

De Havilland were upbeat about the new consortium, as they said in an article in the April 1958 edition of De Havilland *Gazette: 'The Hunting and Fairey Companies had co-operated effectively with De Havilland over a long period in design, production and marketing projects on a worldwide scale, and the three companies undoubtedly muster the strongest and most penetrating world sales and servicing organisation in the British aircraft industry. They operate nearly twenty factories equipped with the most modern machine tools and technical facilities, and several design offices whose experience embraces every aspect of aircraft design, including the most up-to-date techniques affecting high-speed jet aircraft. The geographical proximity of the group factories is important to efficient and economical co-ordination.*

The project will benefit notably from the high-speed experience of the Fairey Company, whose Fairey Delta 2 held the world speed record at more than 1,100 miles an hour, and from this company's use of the Envelope Tooling Process in large-scale production.

Hunting Aircraft have had great experience building transport aircraft and has a production order for jet aircraft with the Royal Air Force. Nearly half of their output in recent years has been for overseas orders. The Hunting Group as a whole is a worldwide organisation with activities besides aviation in the shipping, oil and survey fields. These should be of great benefit in the promotion of overseas sales.

The full support of the Rolls-Royce Company will be applied to the project. The engines will be three Rolls-Royce RB 141s, a by-pass type of jet engine developed from the Conway but having an increased by-pass ratio to give even better fuel consumption. This type of engine is notable for its economy and quietness. The static thrust will be of the order of 12,000 pounds.

The Editor of the *Gazette* went on to speak in glowing terms about BEA: *BEA are the largest carrier of passengers outside the United States, and the main fleet serving their international network comprises British aircraft exclusively. For up to six years, BEA have operated a fleet of 20 Elizabethan aircraft* [the BEA fleet name for the Airspeed Ambassador] *built by the Airspeed Division of the De Havilland Company, and the Comet has been chosen to introduce jet operation on the BEA system. Aircraft Manufacturing Co. Ltd. are proud to be entrusted by British European Airways with this important new airliner.*

In the same article, the editor expounded in the then current state of the 121 design. *'The DH.121 is intended to be essentially a continental or inter-city airliner. It has been specified to provide fast, comfortable and economical travel, and to offer all the improvements in airframe and engine design, which are under development for maturity six years from now, when jet travel is likely to have become general for express services on continental networks, as it will on the trunk routes of the world.*

The requirement, as stated some time ago by the Chairman of British European Airways, Lord Douglas of Kirtleside, is to carry 70-80 standard-class passengers, or 95-100 passengers in high-density seating, on stage lengths of up to about 1,000 miles, and the maximum cruising speed is to be more than 600 mph. The basic design will embody a considerable measure of adaptability regarding stage length with capacity payload so that the D.H.121 will serve a variety of requirements, including those of overseas operators. Its adoption by several operators will be beneficial to them and the project as a whole.

Great emphasis is placed on achieving a high degree of economy and on the ability to operate from aerodromes of 6,000 feet in length. The DH.121 is designed to meet this requirement with operating costs comparable with the expenses for improved propeller-turbine aircraft that could be visualised for service in 1964.

Low operating cost on stages of a few hundred miles will make the D.H.121 suitable to replace Elizabethan, Viscount, Convair 330 and 440, Martin 404, etc., all of which, when carrying capacity payload, have stage lengths not more than about one thousand miles. There are approximately a thousand aircraft of this class in service or on order today was an indication of the world-market prospects for the DH.121.

Operators in this category, which accounts for something like two-thirds of the world's air traffic, place more importance upon short-range costs than upon maximum stage length.

In 1957, the average stage flown by passengers on international and domestic scheduled services of the world (excluding China and Russia), according to an ICAO statement, was 585 miles.

The DH.121 will carry its capacity payload on considerably longer stages than 1,000 miles if loaded to a higher take-off weight and with a longer runway than the 6,000 feet specified by BEA. This fact should extend the market for the type. Later, longer stages will be possible when engine development allows more thrust. The wing design affords a large fuel reservoir.

Regarding both take-off and landing run, the DH.121 will have excellent behaviour, fully adequate for the airport categories it intends to serve. It will have reverse-thrust braking.

The new company will now go out for export orders for the DH.121. There are excellent opportunities. Indeed, the DH.121 is designed to serve one of the largest air travel markets, and it will be based upon far more practical experience, as to both airframe and engine, than any contemporary jet airliner in its category.

Chapter Two

Does Size Matter?

On 12 February 1958, Sir Arthur Vere Harvey CBE, Conservative member of Parliament for Macclesfield, asked the Minister of Transport and Civil Aviation if he was now in a position to make a statement on the British Overseas Airways Corporation jet airliner to be ordered.

Mr. Harold Watkinson, the Minister of Transport replied: *I presume my hon. and gallant Friend means the BEA order. BEA will open negotiations this week with a new company in whichDe Havillands, Hunting Aircraft and Fairey Aviation will participate* (this was Airco). *Rolls Royce would develop and manufacture the power plant. The Government will wish to be satisfied that the whole project will be developed and manufactured as a private venture by the companies concerned.*

Final Ministry of Transport and Civil Aviation approval for BEA's Airco 121 order did not appear until later that year, when in Volume 592 of Hansard for the House of Commons, debated on Friday 1 August 1958 was under the heading *British European Airways (Jet Aircraft)'* it was reported that: *'Mr. Frederick Farey-Jones, MP for Watford (Con) asked the Minister of Transport and Civil Aviation whether he will make a statement on the ordering of new jet aircraft by British European Airways.*

Mr. Watkinson replied: *'The Government have now given approval for British European Airways to conclude a contract with the Aircraft Manufacturing Company Limited (Airco) for 24 DH.121 aircraft. These will cost about £29 million, and will be delivered between 1964 and 1966.'*

Harold Arthur Watkinson, 1st Viscount Watkinson, CH, PC (*b.*25 January 1910, *d.*19 December 1995) was a British businessman and Conservative Party politician. He was Minister of Transport and Civil Aviation between 1955 and 1959 and a cabinet member as Minister of Defence between 1959 and 1962. In 1964 he was ennobled as Viscount Watkinson.

Harold Watkinson, of course, was the Minister of Transport. The Minister had written to Lord Douglas on 30 July advising him that the Government agreed to the airline concluding the contract with De Havilland. The order for twenty-four aircraft valued at £29m, including spares and *Flight* magazine estimated the unit cost of the DH.121, allowing for spares, to be £1m each.

With all the contentions over the order now seemingly out of the way, and government approval awarded, the final contract signing could have been anticipated within a reasonably short period. Indeed, the Airco partners had made considerable progress with the preliminary design of BEA's new short-haul jet. The circumstances up to the final contract signing were not as straightforward as hoped.

BEA may have selected the De Havilland design as a basis for detailed negotiation, but an unexpected hitch occurred in the proceedings. In 1957, after the notorious White Paper on Defence, the Government had decreed that collaboration was the answer to all future projects. The BEA airliner, therefore, had to meet this requirement, and the Sir Humphrey Appleby's in Whitchall used it as a club to beat the firms into larger industry groupings. Bristol with chief designer Dr. (later Sir) Archibald Russell, was offering their type 200 with four Orpheus or BE-47 - the pure jet version of the Orion - while Avro had the type 740 tri-motor which closely resembled the Trident and was powered by 13,540 pound thrust Olympus 551s. A four-month delay was to occur in the decision on a manufacturer while the companies involved went through the most extraordinary mating and re-mating processes. To complicate matters, BOAC was going through its own selection

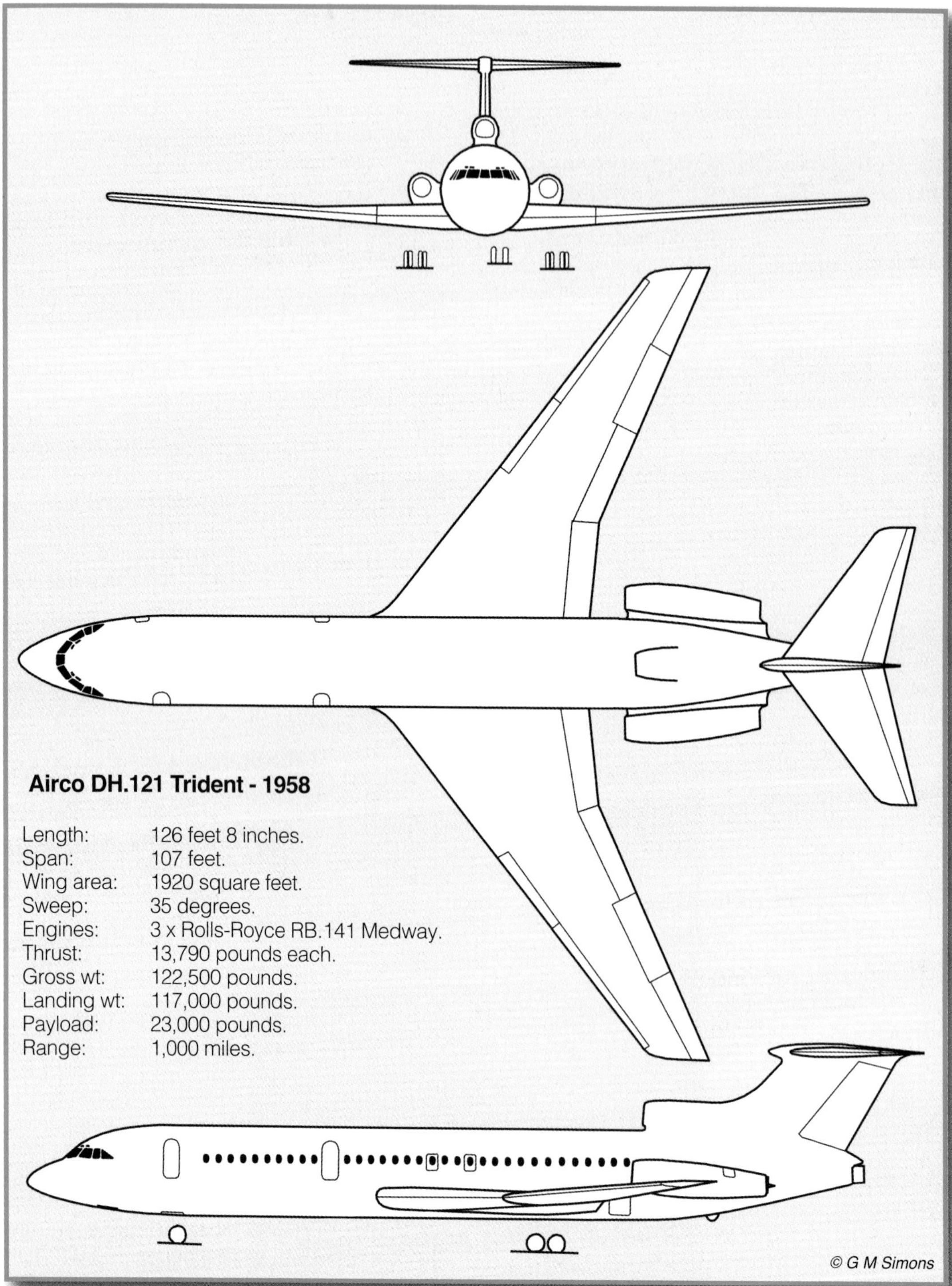

process to get a large four-engined jet, which later went to Vickers as the VC-10. Bristol appeared to have won the BEA contest, but the airline had strong leanings towards De Havilland as they were already considering ordering the Comet as an interim measure and wanted continuity of experience with the 121.

The De Havilland Board offered the Government a consortium with themselves as leaders building the fuselage, Bristol building the wings, and other companies such as Fairey and Hunting participating in a smaller way. Bristol was not at all keen and entered into separate negotiations with Hawker Siddeley for a united effort against De Havilland. By December 1957, Bristol and Hawker Siddeley had put forward proposals for a joint company to build the Bristol 200 with Rolls-Royce RB.121 engines. De Havilland replied with a mix of Saunders-Roe, Hunting, Fairey and possibly Handley Page.

In January 1958, an ad hoc committee of MoS, MTCA and BEA interviewed the contestants, and Bristol made it clear they were not going to go in with De Havilland. The in-fighting had now reached fever pitch, with the prize being a £30 million order from BEA and the possibility of an extensive overseas market. The high stakes of the competition added to the tension and excitement.

In late January, it was stated that a Bristol/Hawker Siddeley team had gone to the United States to offer the Bristol 200 to American operators and that they had been invited to see representatives of Pan American. De Havilland immediately retaliated by reporting that Pan American wanted talks with them on the 121 'as soon as it was possible for a meeting to be arranged.' On 4 February 1958, the Aircraft Manufacturing Company Ltd (Airco) was announced as the consortium to build the 121, consisting of De Havilland, Hunting and Fairey. A slight hitch occurred in the background when it was discovered that Airco was the registered name of a long-established aviation consultant in Jermyn Street, London. The Bristol/Hawker Siddeley team knew by this time that they were losing out, but they put on a brave face. Sir Matthew Slattery, Chairman of Bristol and Shorts, said that the BEA choice should be delayed to see whether the 200 or the 121 could get an export order. Pan American, he indicated, had been offered a 1,700-mile range type 200 tailored to its requirements and fitted with either American J57 or Olympus 550 engines. Shortly afterwards, Lord Douglas of Kirtleside replied that BEA wished to order the 121 and was awaiting Government approval. This was almost the last nail in the coffin of the Bristol 200.

Rolls-Royce was delighted as it could see initially 12,000 pounds and later 14,000 pounds of thrust from the 141 Medway engine. This thrust level would give them a new generation rival to the Olympus and American power plants in the same bracket, indicating a significant leap in engine performance. By the end of April, the general arrangement of the aircraft had been established and a first flight target was set at mid-1961. The De Havilland market research department happily forecast sales of five hundred and fifty aircraft in this category by 1965.

At the time, seating trends on airliners were far from clear and the 121 was to have had eighty seats in a 'standard' class five-abreast arrangement, making for an eleven-foot-nine-inch diameter fuselage. The emergence of the economy class was becoming understood, and the design was altered to a twelve-foot four-inch body diameter and six-abreast seating, giving one hundred and eleven seats. Britain was on the verge of building the right aircraft for the market and the success of the Viscount looked like being repeated.

Rear-Admiral Sir Matthew Sausse Slattery, KBE, CB, FRAeS (*b.*12 May 1902, *d.* 16 March 1990) was a British naval officer, military aviator and businessman. He was the managing director and chairman of Short Brothers and Harland, chairman of British Overseas Airways Corporation and latterly served as chairman of Hawthorn Leslie and Company. He was also a board member of Bristol Aeroplane Company and The National Bank. He is seen here in 1943, wearing his Rear-Admiral's uniform.

On 26 March 1959, BEA requested a meeting with De Havilland and Rolls-Royce, suggesting that it now thought the aircraft too large, as the corporation's market analysis foresaw a slowing of the rapid growth of recent years.

Following this, on 31 March, when discussing the size of both aircraft and engines, Sholto Douglas directed BEA's chief executive to write to both companies, *'...accepting the aircraft in its present form'*, but with reservations about the price. Debates on price continued over the following months, BEA suggesting it may have to reduce the number ordered.

On 28 April, the chief executive again expressed concern, supported by the commercial and sales department and the planning committee, that the aircraft might be too big. Following the meeting, the chief executive and the chief project and development engineer met with De Havilland and noted, *'...DH expressed great concern at the turn of events, especially after BEA had accepted the aircraft subject to price.'*

So it was that the whole programme was torn up and the 121's prospects all but ruined. BEA had been watching traffic trends very closely, and those for 1958/59 showed a significant dip in growth. Internal discussions and analysis led a BEA management committee meeting on 9 June 1959 to confirm that passenger accommodation would be reduced to seventy-five in a mixed first and tourist-class configuration, with a range of 1,000 miles at 600mph and a field length of 6,000ft. BEA thus asked the government to back the new, lower-rated Rolls-Royce RB.163 engine, which would become the Spey.

R. C. Morgan, BEA's chief project and development engineer, had summarised the implications of this turnaround in July. He noted how the move to the 10,100 pounds-thrust RB.163, a higher-bypass engine but scaled down from the envisaged initially 13,600 pound-thrust RB.141/ 3 Medway (both thrust figures would subsequently change, the Medway eventually achieving 17,000 pounds), to avoid an engine that was 'too big' for the now smaller aircraft would compromise the Trident's ability to operate with a full load to Athens, Moscow, Beirut and Tel Aviv. This was even the case with De Havilland's suggestion to achieve it by adopting a lower cruising speed, which would have undermined one of the aeroplane's key advantages, and BEA's proposal for a longer take-off run.

Morgan saw the RB.163 as having a 'fully stretched' thrust rating, and that '...no further

Above: Captain Sir Geoffrey de Havilland, OM, CBE, AFC, RDI, FRAeS (*b.*27 July 1882. *d.* 21 May 1965) was an English aviation pioneer and aerospace engineer. He was the founder and President of De Haviland Enterprise.

Above: Wilfred E Nixon, Chairman and Managing Director of De Havilland Holdings Ltd until 30 June 1959.

Below: Sir Aubrey Burke, Chairman and Managing Director of DH from 1 July 1959.
[AllCourtesy of British Aerospace Hatfield]

increase in performance could be obtained in the first two years'. He said this would additionally impact on the Trident's 'hot and high' airfield performance, and while the engine would fulfil BEA's requirement to make the Trident the fastest airliner in Europe at 606 mph estimated and 590 mph guaranteed , it would not meet the criteria to make it the quietest, *'...unless the bypass were increased'.* He concluded by recommending a small additional order for Trident 1Es to handle the lengthier routes and, in the longer term, to pursue the 1F, which became the 2E, a larger and longer-ranged derivative with more powerful Spey engines.

Instead of keeping calm and realising this was a temporary slippage, BEA panicked. The Trident, they argued, was far too big and could not be filled with passengers, therefore it had to be cut down in size, which also meant a smaller engine. This sudden change in size and power requirements emasculated the 121 in terms of size, power and range, significantly impacting its prospects.

Instead of doing the sensible thing and fighting the decision, the De Havilland Board under Aubrey (later Sir Aubrey) Burke meekly rolled over and submitted and even vetoed sales and market research department discussions with overseas airlines so that all could be concentrated on the limited BEA specification.

Publicly, De Havilland was of a similar opinion to BEA regarding the size of its aircraft and fully supported its customer's request. However, studies carried out by some of the Airco analysts revealed that, if anything, the DH.121 was smaller than ideal. Rumours circulated around Hatfield and elsewhere that the manufacturer apparently created a false document supporting the BEA opinion and contravening its own market studies. Seemingly, certain analysts in the company felt strongly about the whitewash and were almost sacked for refusing to sign the fabricated document.

This was to cost De Havilland worldwide sales and succeeding management a perpetual headache in trying to extend the 121's capacity and performance. It was to be six months before an agreement could be reached on a revised 121 for BEA with a scaled-down Medway, the RB.163, of 9,800 pounds of thrust.

Wind Tunnel Testing.

By late 1959 the wind tunnels at Hatfield had been fully occupied with tests on models of the DH.121 to provide the data required by the Aerodynamics and Design Departments. During this period, many different configurations were tested, and the final lines represented a blending of the often conflicting requirements of the many technical departments involved.

Some of the tests made during the early design stages of this project provided a good illustration of the part the wind tunnel could play in supplying the data necessary to the design team.

In the low-speed wind tunnel at Hatfield, the model characteristics during the take-off and landing conditions were studied together with the general static stability of the aircraft at low cruising speeds when the air compressibility effects are not pronounced. An accurate model of the complete aircraft with engine intakes, flaps and flying controls was erected in the nine-foot by seven-foot working section of the wind tunnel with the aid of three vertical struts attached to the mechanical balance below the working section.

When the airstream passed over the model, this balance automatically measured the three forces and moments. Therefore, it was possible to study the effects of various modifications or alterations to the design. The interference effects of various aircraft parts, such as the tailplane or engine nacelles, were investigated by testing the model with and without the parts. If the drag or interference measured was appreciably larger than expected, modifications were made accordingly.

Similar tests have been made to obtain the best arrangements for the double-slotted flap fitted to the aircraft, the optimum setting, and the relative position of the wing. The double-slotted flap configurations were obtained after numerous tests.

For the close study of the take-off and landing problems a large flat plate spanning the wind tunnel is placed below the model to reproduce the ground and measure its effects, which were fairly large when the aircraft was near the ground.

Unfortunately, in the wind tunnel, the model did not move relative to the ground as does the aircraft in flight, so the plate's boundary layer was thicker than in reality.

To reduce this discrepancy a slot is fitted to the ground board ahead of the wing so that most of the boundary layer was deflected underneath the ground plate where it does not affect the model.

A fair amount of the testing time in the low-speed tunnel was spent perfecting the aircraft's handling characteristics at the stall. The flow over the wing was studied either with an oil-white oxide mixture spread over the wing or with surface tufts, illustrating clearly when the flow becomes separated. Slight modifications to the planform or wing sections are sometimes necessary. Still, this is usually obtained by using fences or small spoilers fitted to the wing to induce the stall at the right time and position to prevent wing dropping or other objectionable characteristics when landing.

Concurrently with the low-speed wind tunnel programme described above, tests were made in the De Havilland transonic tunnel to develop a wing with a low drag at high Mach numbers and also generally to check the high-speed characteristics of the aircraft when cruising near the speed of sound.

For the wing development tests, half models fitted to the tunnel wall were used to have a model as large as possible in the two-foot by two-foot working section of this tunnel. Again, in order to remove the effect of the thick boundary layer of the side wall, a false wall one and a half inches away from the tunnel wall was erected, and the half model fitted to this. A circular strut connected the model to a strain gauge balance situated on the other side of the tunnel wall by which were recorded some of the forces and moments experienced by the model. Working closely with the Aerodynamics Department and reviewing the theoretical gain possible against the results obtained at all stages of this series of tests, a vastly improved wing was evolved.

Nine different wings were tested in all, and in some of the wings, as many as eight different modifications or configurations were tested. The results achieved showed the gain obtained during this extensive series of tests.

During the same period, tests were made on a large-scale model of the rear end of the aircraft to ensure that the benefits obtained by delaying the drag rise on the wing were not nullified by the drag in the tail region of the machine. Consequently, a similar series of tests was made to improve the overall drag of the model by reducing the interference of the engine units with the fuselage and the fin and by reducing the drag of the fin-tailplane junction.

The various modifications suggested by all the tests made in the De Havilland wind tunnels were finally incorporated in a larger, complete model of the three feet six inches span that was tested in the Aircraft Research Association's eight-foot by nine-foot transonic wind tunnel at Bedford.

This cooperative wind tunnel was owned by fourteen companies, of which the Aircraft Manufacturing Company is a shareholder. Tests made on this model have fully confirmed the results obtained on the smaller models at Hatfield.

As the detailed design proceeded, further tests were called for occasionally to check the aerodynamic effects of various modifications, which became necessary to ease the production problems and ensure that the high performance obtained during the earlier tests was not lost. The wind tunnel work thus proceeds until the aircraft is ready to fly.

As something of an aside...

The almost constant changing requirement - or should that be incredibly muddled thinking and dithering? - from both BEA and governmental departments on the Trident was not the first time this had happened. I feel I must mention, even as a very large aside, the ill-fated Fairey Rototyne as it reflects very similar thinking involved with both projects.

This was a 1950s British compound gyroplane designed and built by Fairey Aviation, intended for both commercial and military use. The Rotodyne featured a tip-jet-powered rotor that burned a mixture of fuel and compressed air bled from two wing-mounted Napier Eland turboprops. The rotor was driven for vertical takeoffs, landings and hovering, as well as low-speed translational flight, but autorotated during cruise flight with all engine power applied to two propellers.

During 1951 and 1952, BEA internally formulated its own requirement for a passenger-carrying rotorcraft, commonly referred to as the Bealine-Bus or BEA Bus. This was to be a multi-engined rotorcraft capable of serving as a short-haul airliner. BEA envisioned the type as typically flown between major cities and carrying a minimum of thirty passengers to be economical; keen to support the initiative, the Ministry of Supply sponsored a series of design studies to support the BEA requirement. Both civil and government bodies had predicted the need for such rotorcraft and viewed it as only a matter of time before they became commonplace in Britain's transport network.

The BEA Bus requirement was met with a variety of futuristic proposals; both practical and seemingly impractical submissions were made by several manufacturers. Amongst these, Fairey also chose to submit its designs and to participate in meeting the requirement; it produced multiple arrangements and configurations for the aircraft, typically varying in the powerplants used and the internal capacity; the firm made its first submission to the Ministry on 26 January 1949. Within two months, Fairey had produced a further three alternative submissions, centred on engines such as the Rolls-Royce Dart and Armstrong Siddeley Mamba. In October 1950, an initial contract for the development of a 16,000-pound four-bladed rotorcraft was awarded. The Fairey design, which was considerably revised over the years, received government funding to support its development.

Early in development, Fairey found that securing access to engines for its design proved difficult. In November 1950, Rolls-Royce chairman Lord Hives protested that the design resources of his company were being stretched too thinly across multiple projects; accordingly, the initially selected Dart engine was switched to the Mamba engine of rival firm Armstrong Siddeley. By July 1951, Fairey had resubmitted proposals for the Mamba engine in two- and three-engine layouts, supporting all-up weights of 20,000 and 30,000 pounds, respectively; the adopted configuration pairing the Mamba engine with auxiliary compressors was known as the Cobra. Following Armstrong Siddeley's complaints that it too lacked resources, Fairey also proposed using engines such as the de Havilland Goblin and the Rolls-Royce Derwent turbojet to drive the forward propellers.

Fairey did not enjoy a positive relationship with De Havilland; however, instead, they chose to use D. Napier & Son and its Eland turboshaft engine in April 1953. Following the selection of the Eland, the basic design of the rotorcraft, known as the Rotodyne Y, soon emerged; it was powered by a pair of Eland N.El.3 engines furnished with auxiliary compressors and a large-section four-blade main rotor, with a projected all-up weight of 33,000 pounds. At the same time, a projected enlarged version, designated the Rotodyne Z, outfitted with more powerful Eland N.El.7 engines and an all-up weight of 39,000 pounds, was proposed.

In April 1953, the Ministry of Supply contracted for the construction of a single prototype of the Rotodyne Y, powered by the Eland engine, later designated XE521 for research purposes. As contracted, the Rotodyne would have been the largest transport helicopter of its day, seating a maximum of forty to fifty passengers, while possessing a cruise speed of 150 mph and a range of 250 nautical miles. At the time of the award, Fairey had estimated that £710,000 would cover the costs of producing the airframe. With a view to obtaining regulatory approval as quickly as possible, Fairey's designers worked to meet the Civil Airworthiness Requirements for both helicopters and similar-sized twin-engined aircraft. A one-sixth-scale rotorless model was extensively wind-tunnel tested for fixed-wing performance. A smaller, 1/15th-scale model with a powered rotor was used for downwash investigations.

While the prototype was being built, funding for the programme reached a crisis. Cuts in defence spending led the Ministry of Defence to withdraw its support, pushing the costs onto any potential civilian customer. The government agreed to maintain funding for the project only if, among other qualifications, Fairey and Napier, through

The Fairey Rotodyne on the ground - it's size was particularly impressive. Note the lowered tops to the vertical fin to allow the rotor blades to 'droop' when at rest. *[John Stride Collection]*

their parent English Electric, contributed to the development costs of the Rotodyne and the Eland engine, respectively. As a result of disagreements with Fairey over policy matters, Dr Bennett left the firm to join Hiller Helicopters in California; responsibility for the Rotodyne's development was assumed by Dr George S. Hislop, who became the firm's chief engineer.

The manufacturing of the prototype's fuselage, wings, and rotor assembly was conducted at Fairey's facility in Hayes, Hillingdon, West London, while construction of the tail assembly was performed at the firm's factory in Stockport, Greater Manchester and final assembly was performed at White Waltham Airfield, Maidenhead. In addition, a full-scale static test rig was built at RAF Boscombe Down to support the programme; the static rig featured a fully operational rotor and powerplant arrangement, which was demonstrated on multiple occasions, including a 25-hour Ministry approval test.

While construction of the first prototype was underway, prospects for the Rotodyne appeared positive as there was interest in the type from both civil and military quarters. BEA was monitoring the programme's progress with interest; it was widely expected that the airline would place an order shortly after the issuance of an order for a militarised version of the rotorcraft. The American company Kaman Helicopters also showed strong interest in the project, and was known to have studied it closely as the firm considered the potential for licensed production of the Rotodyne for both civil and military customers.

Due to the army and RAF interest, development of the Rotodyne had been funded out of the defence budget for a time. In 1956, the Defence Research Policy Committee declared that there was no military interest in the type, which quickly led to the Rotodyne becoming solely reliant on civil budgets as a research/civil prototype aircraft. After a series of political arguments, proposals, and bargaining, HM Treasury authorised the continued work on both the Rotodyne and Eland engines until the end of September 1957. Among the demands made by the Treasury were that the aircraft had to be both a technical success and secure a firm order from BEA; both Fairey and English Electric also had to take on a portion of the development costs.

On 6 November 1957, the prototype performed its maiden flight, piloted by chief helicopter test pilot Squadron Leader W. Ron Gellatly and assistant chief helicopter test pilot Lieutenant Commander John G.P. Morton as second pilot. The first flight was originally projected for 1956; however, a delay was considered inevitable for an entirely new concept such as the Rotodyne.

On 10 April 1958, the Rotodyne achieved its first successful transition from vertical to horizontal flight and back to vertical flight. On 5 January 1959, the Rotodyne set a world speed record in the convertiplane category, at 190.9 mph over a 60-mile closed circuit. As well as being fast, the rotorcraft had a safety feature: it could hover with one engine shut down with its propeller feathered, and the prototype demonstrated several landings as an autogyro. The prototype was demonstrated several times at the Farnborough and Paris air shows, regularly amazing onlookers.

Throughout the world, interest was growing in the prospect of direct city-to-city transport. The market for the Rotodyne was that of a medium-haul 'flying bus': It would take off vertically from an inner-city heliport, with all lift from the tip-jet-driven rotor, then increase airspeed, eventually with all engine power transferred to the propellers while the rotor autorotated. In this mode, the collective pitch, and hence drag, of the rotor could be reduced, as the wings would be taking as much as half of the craft's weight. The Rotodyne would then cruise at about 150 kts to another city, such as London to Paris, where the rotor tip-jet system would be restarted for a vertical landing in the city centre. When the Rotodyne landed, and the rotor stopped turning, its blades drooped from the hub. To avoid striking the vertical stabilisers on startup, the tips of these fins were angled down to the horizontal. They were raised once the rotor had spun up.

By January 1959, BEA announced that it was interested in purchasing six aircraft, with a possibility of up to twenty, and had issued a letter of intent stating this, on the condition that all requirements, including noise levels, were met. The Royal Air Force had also placed an order for twelve military transport versions. New York Airways signed a letter of intent for the purchase of five at $2m each, with an option of fifteen more albeit with qualifications, after calculating that a larger Rotodyne could operate at half the seat mile cost of helicopters . However, unit costs were deemed too high for very short hauls of ten to fifty miles, and the Civil Aeronautics Board was opposed to rotorcraft competing with fixed-wing on longer routes. Japan Air Lines, which had sent a team to Britain to evaluate the Rotodyne prototype, stated it would test Rotodyne between Tokyo Airport and the city, and was interested in using it on the Tokyo-Osaka route as well.

The sole Fairey Rotodyne XE521 in flight . *[John Stride Collection]*

According to rumours, the U.S. Army was also interested in buying around 200 Rotodynes. Fairey was keen to secure funding from the American Mutual Aid programme, but could not persuade the RAF to order the minimum necessary 25 rotorcraft needed; at one point, the firm even considered providing a single Rotodyne to Eastern Airlines via Kaman Helicopters, Fairey's US licensee, so that it could be hired out to the US Army for trials. All Rotodynes destined for US customers were to have been manufactured by Kaman in Bloomfield, Connecticut.

Government financing had been secured again, on the proviso that firm orders would be secured from BEA. The civilian orders depended on the noise issues being satisfactorily addressed; the importance of this factor led Fairey to develop 40 different noise suppressors by 1955. In December 1955, Dr Hislop said he was certain that the noise issue could be 'eliminated'. The two most serious problems revealed with the Rotodyne during flight testing was the noise issue and the weight of the rotor system, the latter being 2,233 pounds above the original projection of 3,270 pounds.

In 1959, the British government, seeking to cut costs, decreed that the number of aircraft firms should be reduced and set out its expectations for mergers among airframe and aero engine companies. By delaying or withholding access to defence contracts, the British firms could be forced into mergers; Duncan Sandys, Minister of Aviation, expressed this policy to Fairey and made it known that the price of continued government backing for the Rotodyne would be for Fairey to virtually withdraw from all other initiatives in the aviation field. Ultimately, Saunders-Roe and the Bristol helicopter division were incorporated into Westland; in May 1960, Fairey Aviation was also taken over by Westland. By this time, the Rotodyne had flown almost 1,000 people for 120 hours in 350 flights and conducted a total of 230 transitions between helicopter and autogiro - with no accidents.

By 1958, the Treasury was already expressing its opposition to further financing for the programme. The matter was escalated to the Prime Minister, Harold Macmillan, who wrote to Aubrey Jones, the Minister of Supply, on 6 June 1958, stating that *'this project must not be allowed to die'*. Considerable importance was placed on BEA supporting the Rotodyne by issuing an order; however, the airline refused to procure the aircraft until it was satisfied that guarantees had been given regarding its performance, economy, and noise criteria. Shortly after Fairey's merger with Westland, the latter was issued a £4 million development contract for the Rotodyne, intended to see the type enter service with BEA.

As flight testing of the Rotodyne prototype proceeded, Fairey had become increasingly dissatisfied with Napier and the Eland engine, as progress in improving the latter had been less than expected. For the extended 48-seat Rotodyne to be achieved, the uprated Eland N.E1.7 would be required; of the estimated £7 million needed to produce the larger aircraft, £3 million would be for its engines. BEA was particularly supportive of a larger aircraft, potentially seating as many as sixty-six passengers, which would have required a still-far greater sum of money to achieve. Fairey was already struggling to achieve the stated performance of the Eland engine and had resorted to adopting a richer fuel mixture to get the necessary power, a side effect of which was to further aggravate the noticeable noise issue as well as reducing fuel efficiency. Unable to resolve issues with the Eland, Fairey opted to adopt the rival Rolls-Royce Tyne turboprop engine to power the larger Rotodyne Z instead.

The larger Rotodyne Z design could be developed to take fifty-seven to seventy-five passengers and, when equipped with the 5,250 shaft horsepower Tyne engines, would have a projected cruising speed of 200 knots. It could carry nearly eight tons of freight; cargoes could have included some British Army vehicles and even the intact fuselage of some fighter aircraft that would fit into its fuselage. It would also have been able to carry large cargoes externally as an aerial crane, including vehicles and entire aircraft. According to some of the later proposals, the Rotodyne Z would have had a gross weight of 58,500 pounds, an extended rotor diameter of 109 feet, and a tapered wing with a span of 75 feet.

However, the Tyne engines were also becoming underpowered for the larger design. The Ministry of Supply had pledged to finance fifty per cent of the development costs for both the Rotodyne Z and for the model of the Tyne engine to power it. Despite Fairey's strenuous efforts to secure support, the expected order from the RAF did not materialise — at the time, the service had no particular interest in the design, as it was more focused on nuclear deterrence. As the trials continued, both the associated costs and the Rotodyne's weight continued to climb; the noise issue persisted, although there were signs that silencers would later reduce it to an acceptable level.

While the costs of development were shared half-and-half between Westland and the government, the firm determined that it would still need to contribute a further £9 million in order to complete development and achieve production-ready status. Following the issuing of a requested quotation to the British government for 18 production Rotodynes, twelve for the RAF and six for BEA, the government responded that no further support would be issued for the project, for economic reasons. Accordingly, on 26 February 1962, official funding for the Rotodyne was terminated. The project's final end came when BEA declined to place its own order for the Rotodyne, principally because of concerns about the high-profile tip-jet noise issue. The corporate management at Westland determined that further development of the Rotodyne towards production status would not be worth the investment required.

Rivals Across the Pond

Airliner manufacturing and selling is not only a highly competitive business but also one that has produced its share of ironies. One of the more piquant of these is that back in 1932, when pilots of Boeing Air Transport Inc. were shown the outline specifications of the new Boeing 247 weighing 16,000 pounds and powered by two of the new Pratt & Whitney Hornet radials, they refused to accept the Hornet and stated that a 16,000 pound aeroplane was regarded as *'too heavy to land safely at several of the smaller airports'*.

The 247 was therefore scaled down to 12,000 pounds and re-engined with P. & W. Wasps, entering production for United Airlines, which had ordered no less than sixty, and other operators as a ten-passenger design. But although the 247 pioneered the modern piston-engined airliner formula, Boeing were not to reap the fruits of this enterprise. The scaling-down process and the large United order led Trans World Airlines to approach Douglas about a similar design, which resulted in the 14-passenger DC-2 and this - and even more so the 21-passenger DC-3 with a wider fuselage to meet American Airlines' requirements for sleeping berths - heavily outsold the 247 and eclipsed the name of Boeing as a major supplier of civil transports for the next two decades. Even at this stage, it can be seen just how much 'plurality of native user demand' (to use American jargon) - in the shape of a multiplicity of vigorously competing airlines - has benefited the US aircraft industry, just as it is easy to see how the lack of such plurality has hampered British airliner manufacturers.

Nearly three decades after the 247 was scaled down at the insistence of Boeing pilots, the De Havilland Trident was to undergo a similar process. Like the 247 in its day, the DH.121 (as it was initially known) introduced a new formula: that of the three-engined jet optimised for short/medium-haul stages and the then new concept of automatic landing. Like the 247, the British jet was to suffer a serious penalty in sales by being scaled down (mistakenly, as it turned out) for its sponsor and chief customer, BEA.

As we have already seen, the original DH.121 was a 111-passenger aircraft powered by three

14,000 pound static thrust Rolls-Royce RB.141s, and as such compared very closely in size with the Boeing 727-100 with engines of the same power and seating up to 119 passengers at thirty-four inch seat pitch; but the scaled-down and less powerful Trident 1C seated only 88 passengers in a typical BEA interior and like the 247 thirty years before suffered the fate of being heavily outsold by a slightly larger competitor with just that much more stretch in the basic design and the very important

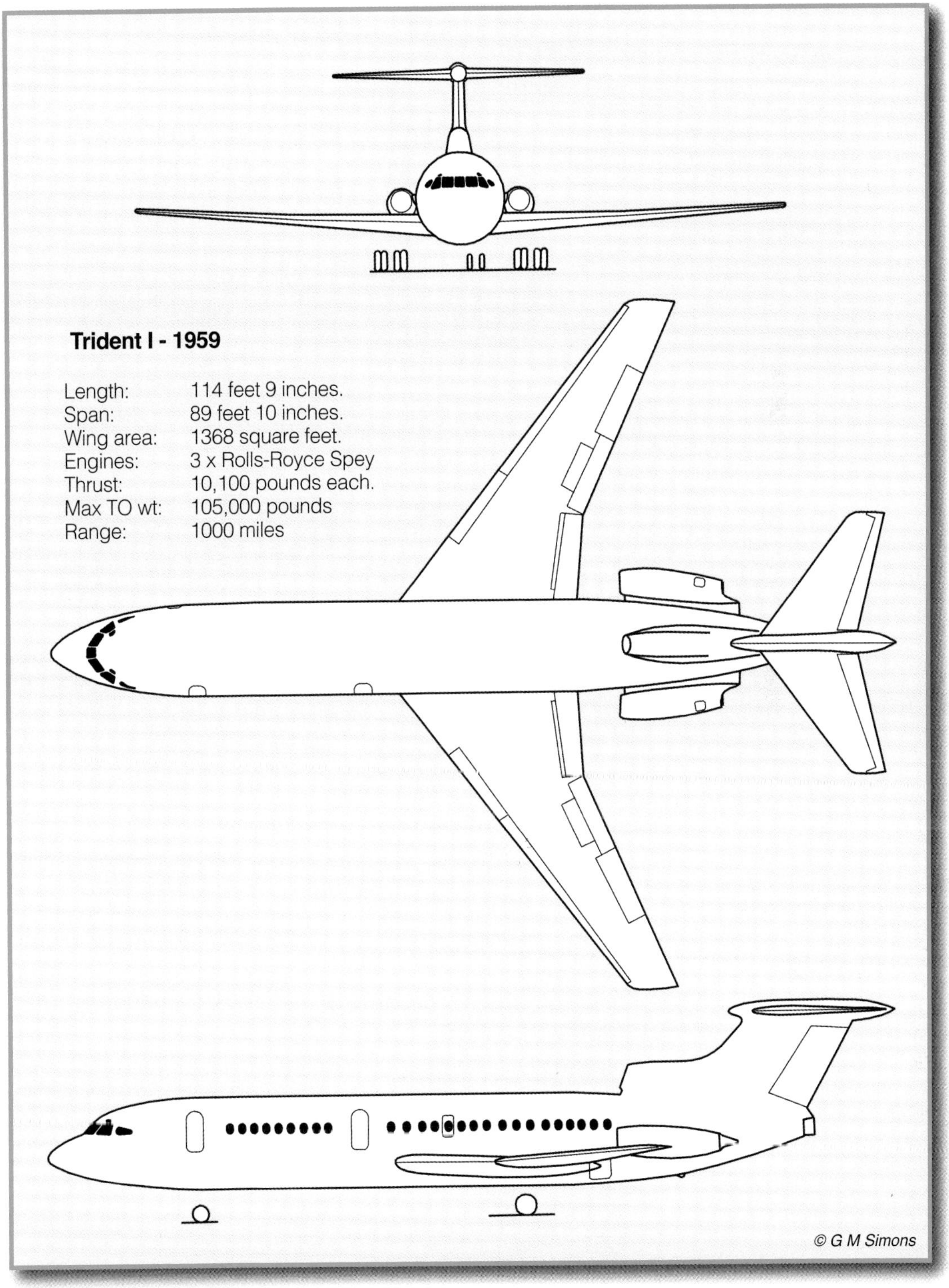

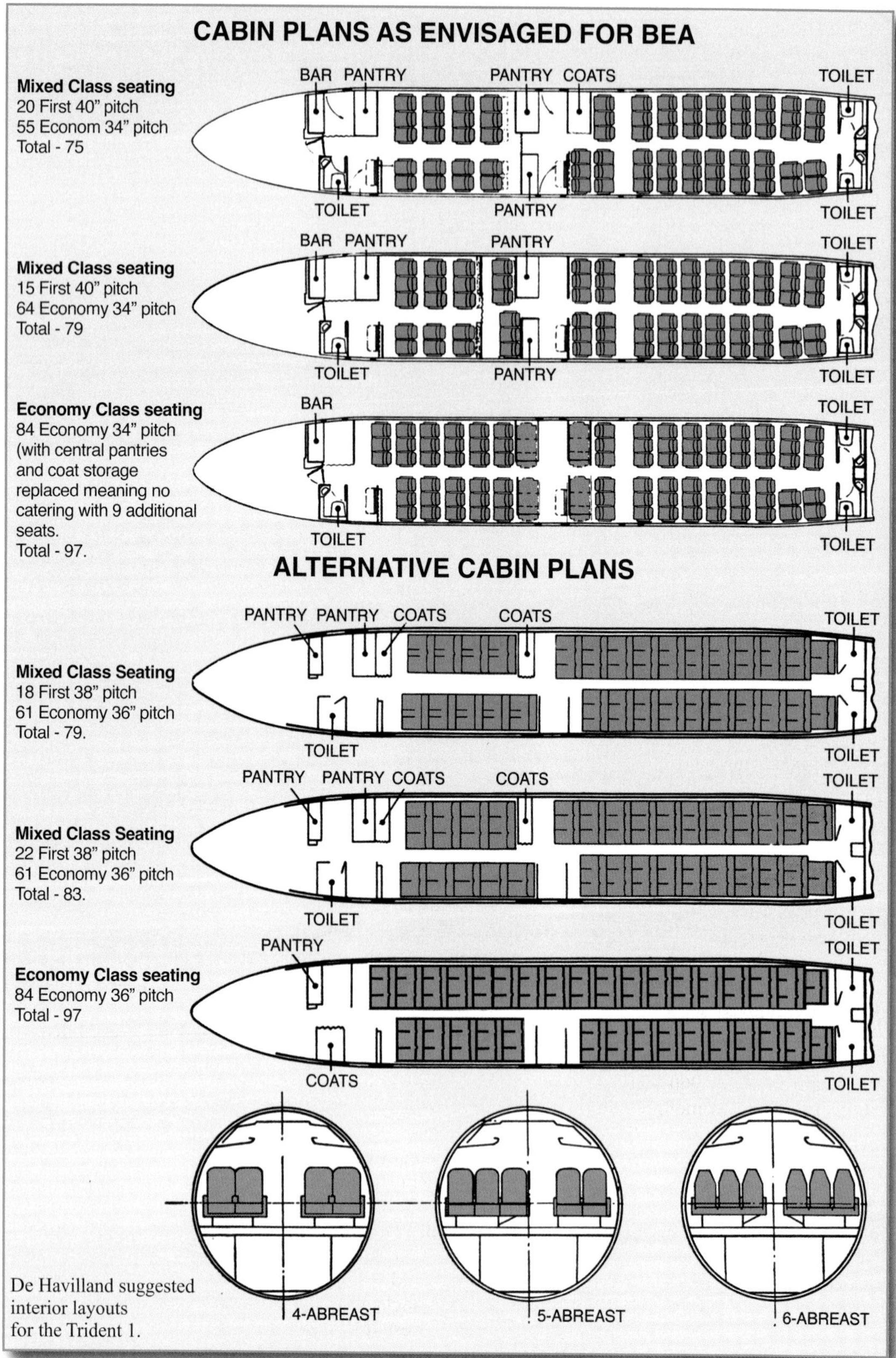

De Havilland suggested interior layouts for the Trident 1.

advantage of plurality, rather than the singularity of native user demand to ensure the most careful optimisation to the tough and demanding short/medium-haul role.

The Boeing 727 appeared as a very potent rival. The Seattle-based company had been doing extensive studies of the short-to-medium-haul field since 1956, but the concept did not achieve project status until 1959. Boeing took a much broader view than BEA and De Havilland and decided upon a layout with three Pratt and Whitney JT8D-1 engines of 14,000 pounds of thrust each, economy class seating for 119 passengers and a range of 1,900 nautical miles - was almost exactly the original plan for the DH.121!

The crowning piece of stupidity came following a visit to America by Lord Douglas of Kirtleside, then the Chairman of BEA. He had been to Seattle and had heard of the new Boeing project. Lord Douglas thought there was the possibility of collaboration with Boeing on the 121. He felt that as both the British company and the US manufacturer were studying trijet designs, especially as the former was significantly further along the development cycle, that it would make sense if they got together.

Boeing was eager to shore up customer demand by adding a short-to-medium-haul stablemate for its long-haul 707. It has never been clear who proposed collaboration with De Havilland on the DH.121, Some sources say it was Boeing, others suggested that on his return to the United kingdom, Lord Douglas of Kirtleside suggested to De Havilland that as both companies were developing three rear-mounted engined projects, they should get together and merge their efforts.

So it was that in early 1960 Boeing was invited to make a very close inspection of De Havilland's trijet research and the 121's design and performance. Indeed, it seemed that De Havilland apparently enjoyed showing the competition its design studies as Convair officials were also invited to study the DH.121. The compliment was returned by Boeing in May 1960 and four De Havilland engineers - Charles Timothy Wilkins OBE, FRAeS (chief designer), David R Newman (chief technician), John Wimpenny (senior aerodynamicist) and Peter Hall (sales manager) all visited Seattle. However, little or nothing of the US manufacturer's plans were revealed to De Havilland.

Instead of seeing the danger in the 'suggestion', De Havilland cow-towed to what their customer was thinking and reacted enthusiastically by promptly inviting a top-level team from Boeing to see everything on the 121 at Hatfield. Boeing was amazed but not unnaturally accepted with alacrity. So it came about that De Havilland solemnly handed all its research over to its rivals while at the same time barred the British media completely from the factory. The American company made some changes to its 727 design, including moving from a mid-set tailplane configuration, like the Caravelle, to a 'T-tail' set-up.

Without a doubt, this was as damaging to the Trident's prospects as the decision to downsize the aeroplane to fit BEA's revised specifications was that to share research and development findings with rival Boeing. Quite rightly, Boeing considered that if another company wanted to be foolish, there was no reason for them to follow suit! The results of this debacle could be seen for many decades.

The insight it had into De Havilland's trijet studies certainly influenced Boeing's design formats on aspects of the 727, and when the aircraft was formally launched at the end of 1961 - to the tune of eighty orders from Eastern and United - it bore a remarkable resemblance to the DH.121. However, the first 727 was not expected to fly until early 1963, apparently giving the DH.121 at least a year's head start on its rival.

Boeing's ultimate success with the was 727 stemmed not from its similarities to the Trident but from its differences: it allowed the company to recognise early on that the Trident to be underpowered and too small for the majority of major carriers, so Boeing refined their design into something that offered greater payload, power and range in its original format The 727-100, was a design which built in future stretch in the form of the -200.

While Boeing successfully caught up and overtook Hawker Siddeley's Trident, it would be the British manufacturer that tried to play catch-up later in the decade with the stretched-fuselage Trident 3, but the damage was already done.

Many of the airlines that had acquired large fleets of 727-100s would make the comparatively easy transition to the -200, cementing Boeing's by then insurmountable lead. The 727 entered commercial service on 1 February 1964, six weeks ahead of its British counterpart, and around 100 727s had been produced by the time BEA had taken delivery of its first five Tridents.

Hawker Siddeley sold a total of 117 Tridents - Boeing built 1832 727s, at the time a record for a western jet airliner.

Aviation cartoonist the late Chris Wren regularly featured in *'The Gazette'* including this full-page spread on aspects of the Trident.

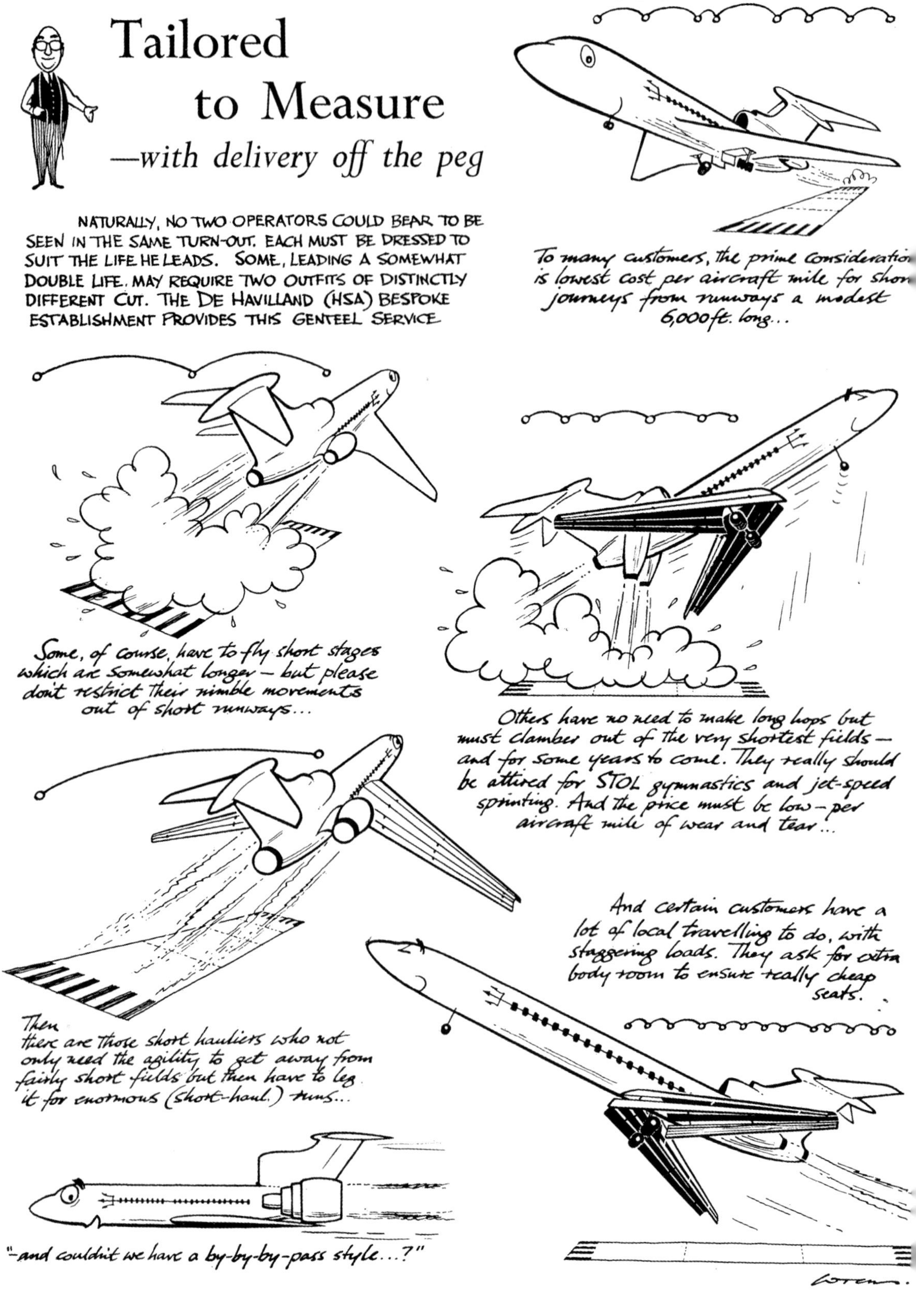

Chapter Three

Aerodynamics and Structure

The aerodynamic design of a transport aircraft is fixed by the functions it is intended to fulfil. For the purpose of this study, I will just look at the Series 1 Trident, after all, everything that came later was a result of this design!

When the Trident 1 design was begun, the aim was to provide a performance that would make it the ultimate subsonic short-range jet, able to remain in front-line service for at least ten years.

Maximum effort was concentrated on achieving low drag at high Mach numbers with good handling qualities to match. Comet experience had shown the value of good low-speed handling qualities, and so a continuous programme of wind tunnel and flight testing has been carried through to combine the requirements of high Mach number cruising speeds and an acceptable stall pattern, using, as far as possible, relatively simple and well-tried high lift devices.

A number of test facilities were used to carry out the aerodynamic development work for the Trident IE.

High Speed Wind Tunnels:

- De Havilland high speed wind tunnel (two feet by two feet).
- Aircraft Research Association high speed wind tunnel (eight feet by six feet).
- Royal Aircraft Establishment high speed wind tunnel (eight feet by six feet).

Low Speed Wind Tunnels:

- De Havilland low speed wind tunnel (nine feet by seven feet).
- Avro low speed wind tunnel (nine feet by seven feet).

National Physical Laboratory compressed air tunnel (high Reynolds number - six foot diameter jet).

Special Engine Rigs:

- De Havilland intake rig for quarter-scale models.
- Rolls-Royce Derwent tunnel for quarter-scale models.
- Rolls-Royce intake rig for full scale models.
- Rolls-Royce thrust reverser rig.

Flutter Test Wind Tunnels:

- Blackburn Aircraft high speed wind tunnel.
- National Physical Laboratory high speed wind tunnel.
- Handley Page low speed wind tunnel.

Flight Development:

- Trident 1 used for development of slats.

Over four thousand hours of tunnel testing were conducted on the Trident design, and an additional ninety three hours of flight testing were spent developing the IE slat. In all cases, the extensive model investigations were guided by parallel theoretical work so that the maximum worth was achieved from each hour of testing.

Numerical methods were programmed to solve the theoretical equations that specified the wing geometry and sections, the fin, the tailplane and its functions, the rear fuselage shape, and the engine intake profiles.

High Speed Design.

To obtain the best high-speed performance from a given wing geometry, it was necessary to obtain the best sectional design for the required cruise and maintain the drag rise qualities of the section over the full span of the swept wing. This involved maintaining the sweep of the isobars on the wing surface right up to the fuselage side - an aim which could be accomplished by body waisting, wing planform changes, wing section changes or some combination of all three. Attention was focused principally upon wing section changes as it was estimated that this would involve lower weight, lower drag and smaller penalties than drastic wing planform changes. Body waisting was regarded as a matter to be considered only as a last resort.

An extensive series of eight models was tested with many ad hoc variants, the development being carried out mainly in the De Havilland high-speed tunnel. The aerodynamic design of these models was based upon the work of Dr Dietrich Küchemann and his collaborators at the Royal Aircraft Establishment. This work provided an excellent framework and an essential starting point for the test programme, but the ad-hoc development phase was an inescapable part of the task - particularly when balancing the need to maintain the isobar pattern with various practical requirements. Foremost among these was the desire to have the joint between the stub and outer wings normal to the line of the stringers and to have flat surfaces over a substantial part of both sides of the root section. The latter would allow the dihedral kink in the wing skins at the body side to be formed on normal press equipment, thus saving a wing joint and a significant amount of weight.

As a result of the effort devoted to maintaining the drag rise characteristics of the ten per cent thickness/chord ratio, thirty-five degree swept wing, a gain in drag critical Mach number of 0.75, over the simple datum case with no root treatment and the outer wing thickness/chord ratio maintained up to the body side, was achieved. This gain was equivalent to over fifty m.p.h. at 20-25,000 feet.

About half this total gain was directly associated with the section modifications near the root while the remainder came from improvements in the basic wing section based on the work of H H Pearcey at the National Physical Laboratory.

Some of the half models used in developing the Trident wing. Half models were used to obtain the best Reynolds number in the Hawker Siddeley high-speed tunnel and had the added advantage that they could be modified more quickly when changes were necessary. *[De Havilland Aircraft Co.]*

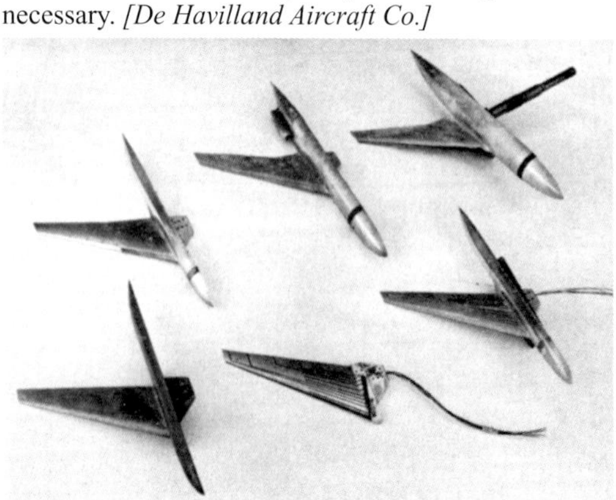

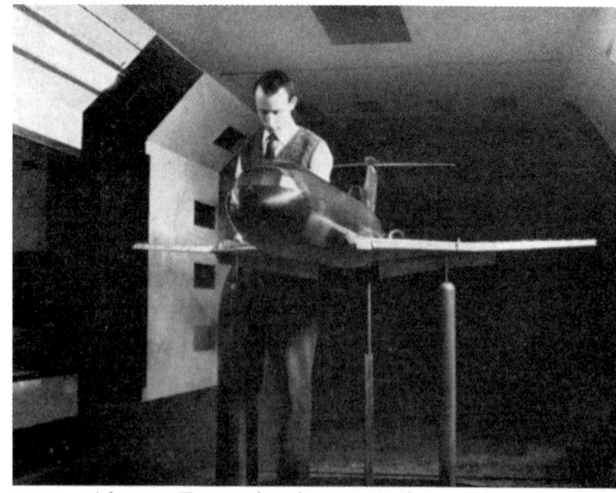

Above: Extensive low-speed tunnel research has backed up each phase in the development of the Trident's high-lift devices. This IE model is shown being used for development work associated with the leading-edge slat.

Below: An early model mounted in the Aircraft Research Association's eight foot by six foot high-speed wind tunnel.
[Photographs Courtesy of British Aerospace Hatfield]

This work involved the concept of 'peaky' wing pressure distributions for high-speed flight.

Mr Pearcey's philosophy aimed at deliberately creating a supersonic region of flow at the nose of the aerofoil, thus making some of the increased suctions actually suck the aerofoil forward, while at the same time the suctions over the aft face of the aerofoil were reduced. Compressibility drag rise was thus reduced in two ways. The manner in which this was effected was as follows. Consider a wing travelling through the air at some high subsonic speed just above the initiation of the compressibility drag rise but less than 1.0 Mach.

Under these conditions, the flow was supersonic on part of the wing and therefore, in the flow around the aerofoil, there must be a boundary between this supersonic region and the general subsonic flow known as the sonic line. Now, the high suction peak near the nose of this type of wing was generated by a series of expansion waves emanating from the aerofoil surface immediately behind this sonic line. When these expansion waves reached the sonic line, they were reflected as weak compression waves. These compression waves, in turn, reduce the suction behind the peak and give a modified pressure distribution, resulting in a reduction in the final shock strength and drag.

The section modifications and wing twist to maintain this pressure distribution were derived from Dr. Küchemann's work, as already mentioned.

This work provided an excellent framework and an essential starting point for the test

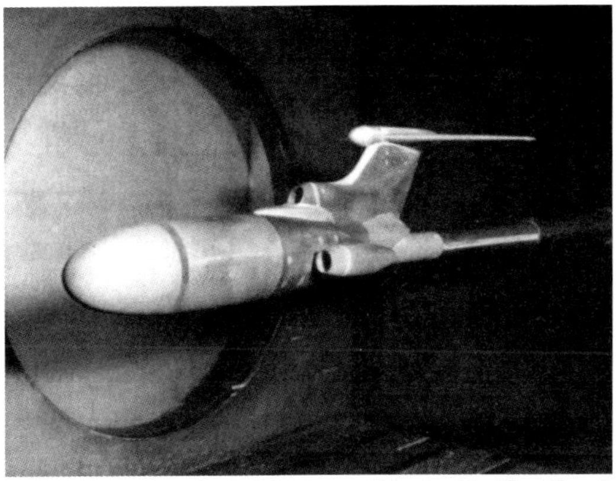

Above:A rear-end model mounted in the De Havilland high-speed tunnel.

Below: One of the fifth-scale half model of a Trident in the low-speed Hawker Siddeley wind tunnel.
[Photographs courtesy of British Aerospace Hatfield]

programme but the ad hoc development phase is an inescapable part of the job, particularly when solving the compromises of maintaining the isobar pattern while meeting various practical requirements. Foremost among these was the desire to have the joint between the stub and outer wings normal to the line of the stringers and to have flat surfaces over a substantial part of both sides of the root section. The latter would allow the dihedral kink in the wing skins at the body side to be formed on normal press equipment, thus saving wing joint and a significant amount of weight.

As David Newman of De Havillands said: '*We found during the course of this development programme that we gained a total improvement in drag critical Mach number of 0.075 over the simple datum case with no root treatment and the outer wing thickness chord ratio maintained up to the body side. About half of the total gain was directly associated with the section modifications near the root, the remainder coming from improvements in the basic wing section based on the work of H H Pearcey at the National Physical Laboratory.*

The benefits of this development program are most strikingly shown in the high value of the cruising speed for minimum operating cost (around 585 mph).

All the development testing done in our own tunnel used half-models of the wing and fuselage. Half-models were used to get the best Reynolds number (around 0.8' x 10^6) in a rather small two foot by two foot working section tunnel. It also meant only half the work of modifying the shapes when necessary. A good deal of useful experience was gained in the process'.

Confirmatory tests of the final configuration were made in the ARA cooperative industry tunnel at Bedford, giving a Reynolds number of 3.5 x 10^6 , and the agreement on drag rise between the two sets of tests is very good indeed. In both tunnels, observations of surface flow patterns were made by painting the models with an oil mixture, and these were of particular value during the development phase of the job.

David Newman again, speaking in 1962: '*More recently we have made and tested a complete model of the aircraft in our own tunnel, the main purpose being an insurance measure to have available a ready tool for exploring any difficulties arising during the flight programme'.*

Achievement of the high drag rise/Mach

number was assisted by having a clean wing, uninterrupted across the span except by a single fence at forty-six per cent semi-span.

High-speed flight tests with the Trident 1 have confirmed a drag rise similar to tunnel predictions and that trim changes up to the maximum design 0.95 Mach number were extremely small. Also, successful low-speed flight development has been achieved without any modifications to the leading-edge shape.

It was of interest to note that the wing dihedral angle was not determined by aerodynamic considerations, but by fuel system requirements - to ensure that there was not an excessive amount of unusable fuel in the wing tanks.

With respect to the low-speed aspects, a leading-edge device of some sort was essential, as in most other transports having similar wing sweep.

A simple hinged droop was chosen for its adequate maximum lift coefficient to meet the design requirement, while being a simpler, easier anti-icing mechanism than a slat.

The closing plate that fills the gap between the wing and the leading edge in the deflected position has been carefully designed to preserve a smooth contour.

At the trailing edge, conventional double-slotted flaps averaging twenty-nine per cent of the wing chord are used. Outboard of these, split ailerons were fitted initially, the inner half being always in operation while the outer portions were brought into use when the flaps were deflected. This arrangement was chosen to give adequate lateral control without the use of spoilers (with which we had no direct experience). However,

Photographs of Trident airframe testing are pretty thin on the ground, even poor quality ones such as these.

Above: A Trident fuselage centrre-section and wings are about to be placed in the testing jigs.

Left: Testing the rear fuselage and fin.
[Photographs courtesy of British Aerospace Hatfield]

schemes to bring the airbrakes into use as a backup lateral control were evolved (initially as an insurance measure), and these proved to be so attractive that the outer aileron will not be used on production aircraft, the inner one being enlarged somewhat, and the control mechanism was arranged to bring in the spoiler/airbrakes after about ten degrees of aileron deflection.

The other major high-speed test programme concerned the development of the external shapes of the rear fuselage, side pod, centre intake, and fin tailplane fairing. These are regions with considerable potential for unfavourable interference effects. A great deal of tunnel test time was spent in arriving at the final solution, much of it being done on a partial model of the rear fuselage and tail.

To ensure adequate control at dive demonstration, Mach numbers close to unity, an all-moving tail was chosen for longitudinal control. The control jacks operated directly on the tailplane, and what appeared to be an elevator that was, in fact, a flap geared to the tailplane by a mechanical linkage similar to that of a servotab.

The Trident 1E Wing

The higher maximum lift coefiicient of the Trident 1E has been achieved with the minimum compromise to the excellent high Mach number performance of the Trident 1. The same design methods and aerodynamic principles used in developing the basic wing were applied to extend the wing leading edge forward and to design the leading-edge slats to achieve the required maximum lift coefficient.

The Rear Fuselage and Tall

The advanced wing design had to be matched by a high standard of performance from the rest of the aircraft. Another major high-speed test programme, therefore, concerned the development of the external shapes of the rear fuselage, the side pod and centre intakes and the fin-tailplane fairing. A rear-end model was used in conjunction with theoretical methods to blend together the aerodynamic interference effects in this region of the aircraft. This stage of the development had to be integrated with the low-speed tunnel investigation, which ensured that the engine intakes were outside the influence of the fuselage boundary layer.

Final confirmatory tests were carried out on a complete model in the Aircraft Research Association eight foot by six foot high-speed wind tunnel.

Low Speed Design -
High Lift Devices and Flying Controls

From the outset, a leading-edge lift device was considered essential. For the Trident 1, a simple hinged droop was chosen because it provided adequate lift for the design requirements and was lighter and easier to anti-ice than a slat. To give the improved aerodrome performance necessary for the Trident 1E, the wing span was extended by five feet, the flap span and area increased, and the droop of the Trident 1 replaced by a large slat.

With this change to the leading edge, the wing planform was changed by extensions of three per cent chord at the tip, two per cent chord at mid-span and fairing at zero at the root. There were four sections of slats on each side, driven by irreversible ball-bearing screw-jacks in a similar manner to the droop of the Trident 1. The discontinuity at the inboard end of the slat (seventeen per cent semi-span) was faired by a simple Kruger flap, which operated with the slat.

At the trailing edge, conventional double-slotted flaps averaging thirty-five per cent of the wing chord were used.

The inboard end of the IE ailerons has been moved eighteen inches outboard to permit an increase in the span and area of the outer sections of the flaps. The chord of the IE flaps has also been increased to make maximum use of the ground clearance available.

Immediately outboard of the flaps were the ailerons, which were arranged to operate in conjunction with diflerential spoiler movement after approximately the first fifteen degrees of aileron deflexion. The spoilers were fitted ahead of the outboard flaps and also operate in unison as airbrakes. Ground lift dumpers were fitted forward of the inboard flaps.

A flight development programme was successfully completed, with IE slats fitted to the fourth. Trident 1 aircraft which proved that:

1. The reduction in stalling speeds expected for the Series 1E has been fully achieved.
2. The handling qualities at the stall were excellent and fully up to the standard required.

Handling at the Stall

The stall development programme was aimed, successfully, not only at achieving the required minimum speeds, but also at producing handling qualities which would enable the approach speeds used for determining the Flight Manual performance to be obtained consistently in airline service. As a result of setting this high standard, considerable wind-tunnel and Trident 1 flight testing was carried out to achieve a natural 'square' nose-drop at the stall.

The actual modifications made to the Trident 1 configuration were relatively minor (i.e., small Kruger flaps inboard of the droop, and vortex generators on the droop sealing plate). Numerous flight results showed clearly that there were no pitch-up tendencies prior to the stall, and there was a natural nose-drop at the stall, on the final production configuration of the Trident 1, at all flap settings.

Initial stall development work for the Trident 1E was satisfactorily completed using the fourth Trident 1 fitted with a fixed leading-edge slat, and

Right: Work proceeds on the first batch of DH.121 fuselages at Hatfield.

Below: Nearing its final form the mock-up of the trident flight deck shows the cockpit arrangements as derived by Airco to suit the requirements of British European Airways. *[Photographs courtesy of British Aerospace Hatfield]*

it was expected that no further development work will be necessary with the first 1E.

As both the Trident nose-drop and buffet were not very pronounced, it was decided to fit, in addition to the usual stick-shaker for pre-stall warning, a pitch augmenter of 'stick-pusher'. The stick-pusher was fitted into the tailplane circuit, and for the Trident 1, it pushes the control column forward with a force of eighty pounds when the aircraft reached an incidence of seventeen degrees with droop down and one hundred and fifteen degrees with droop up in slow approaches to the stall. Similar angles were expected for the Trident 1E with slat 'out' and 'in'. In fast approaches to the stall, the stick-pusher operated earlier as a function of pitch rate, with a maximum lead of three degrees of incidence. This lead was varied by signals from a pitch gyro.

The action of the stick-pusher was very definite, and the recovery from the stall was very positive regardless of the rate of approach into the stall. The height loss with the stick-pusher operating was no greater than for manual control. Thus, the Trident offers excellent stall recovery characteristics. The stick-pusher had been designed to achieve a high degree of reliability in the correct operation at the stall, and what was probably more important, adequate safeguards have been provided to prevent inadvertent operation at any other condition.

Engine Intakes

As already mentioned, the design of the external shape of the tail section for high speed required an extensive programme of wind tunnel testing. Considerable effort was also expended to ensure that the centre engine intake produced satisfactory flow at the engine face in all flight conditions. At an early stage in the design, Rolls-Royce ran an engine in simulated flow conditions representative of high incidence and yaw with satisfactory results, and flight tests have since confirmed the accuracy of the design estimates.

Measurements of total head distribution at the face of both the pod and centre engines were made over the full range of operational flight conditions to ensure that pressure distributions are conducive to a long fatigue-free life for the engine.

The centre engine intake was designed from an early stage for a mass flow considerably greater than that needed for the Spey Mk. 505 engine of the Trident 1 and more than sufiicient for the demands of the Spey Mk. 511 engine of the Trident 1E, and only minor modifications have been required to accommodate the greater length of the Spey Mk. 511.

Centre engine surge was experienced during early flight testing of the early prototype Spey Mk. 505s. This was cured by a minor modification to the intake lips, together with engine modifications that have been incorporated to improve engine performance during normal engine development. Rolls-Royce ran a Spey Mk 505 engine, which was aerodynamically to production standard, behind a production centre intake up to take-off rpm.' in cross winds of 35 kts., with no surge. Aircraft with production engines have operated without surges during take-offs and landings with crosswinds of up to 30 kts.

As a result of this development work, the only area in which care was needed to be exercised when certain engines are throttled back at high altitudes. In these conditions, the pod engines had to be throttled first, or a slight surge may occur on the centre engine. Flight trials shown that this precaution was unnecessary when using engines with a slightly increased surge margin. Later production engines will have a better surge margin with no performance penalty. This was confidently expected to make any precautions unnecessary.

Flying Controls

The Trident employed fully powered flying controls on all surfaces, operated hydraulically. There was no reversion to manual control. The reasons for this choice was as follows:

Manual controls have proved to be unsatisfactory at Mach numbers in excess of 0.90 and virtually impossible above 0.95m This was because the rearward movement of the shock waves, as Mach number increased, results in a reduction of the effectiveness of tab and main control at the same time as an increase in control hinge moment. There could also be a tendency for controls to buzz, and up-floating of manual ailerons, which may add to handling difficulties. As these problems increased with increasing Mach number, a manual arrangement for the primary control system could seriously limit the development potential of a new aircraft in the speed range being considered. Also, while it was possible to design a satisfactory manual system for a small aeroplane, the hand loads become very high on an aircraft the size of the Trident, and for this reason, power assistance becomes necessary for at least the tailplane, rudder and spoilers. Mixed systems employing powered control on these surfaces, together with manual control of elevators and ailerons, provided a reasonable standard of control with the power systems operating up to Mach numbers in the range 0.90 to 0.95, but give a poor standard of control with the power system inoperative.

These considerations lead to the conclusion that a fully-powered primary control system was desirable on the Trident, which had an initial design cruising 0.875 Mach, later raised to 0.88. If, next, a fully powered standby system of the same type as the primary system was chosen in preference to having manual reversion, then the desirable aerodynamic characteristics of the primary system are retained, and the following advantages added:-

1. The feel characteristics were the same whether on primary or standby systems. If a failure of the primary system occurred at a critical stage in flight, the pilot did not find himself in control of an aircraft which was different to handle.
2. Similarity of handling characteristics on main and standby systems reduced pilot training time.
3. Control surfaces were replaceable without it being necessary to make a test flight to check aerodynamic balance.
4. The benefit of development work carried out on the type of powered system chosen applied to both primary and standby systems, whereas with power plus manual reversion, two different types of systems are have to be developed and maintained.
5. Without manual reversion, aerodynamic and mass balancing can be eliminated, with a consequent saving in weight.
6. No control locking devices are required.

Consideration of these factors, combined with fifteen years of satisfactory experience in the performance and reliability of hydraulically-operated, fully-powered controls, without manual reversion on the Comet, and on the Sea Vixen all-weather fighter at speeds in excess of M1.0, led Hawker Siddeley to decide on a fully powered system for the Trident.

The full reasons for the subsequent choice of a triplex system -one where three separate sub-systems, each with its own pump, reservoir, lines, valves and jacks worked in unison all the time to power banks of three jacks at each primary control surface - were given in the 'Aircraft Systems' article. Briefly, however, the main advantage was that a triplex system was fail-safe, since with all three systems working continuously, no hurried change-over was necessary if one system fails, and control was maintained uninterrupted. The defective system was subsequently depressurised at a convenient time. Jack sizes are chosen so that full control over the flight envelope was available with only two systems working. Should a further system have to be shut down for any reason, the one remaining set of jacks will still provide sufficient power for control of the aircraft, including landing. Since the first flight of the Trident in January 1962, experience gained in development flying and in airline service has shown that the choice of a powered triplex flying control system has been fully justified.

Flight Simulator.

Hawker Siddeley are convinced that simulation and assessment of aircraft flying characteristics during the design stage was an essential part of modern aircraft design. A simulator was coupled to the full-scale Trident hydraulic systems and flying control rig some time before the aircraft's first flight. This enabled pilots to assess the handling characteristics of the aircraft on the rig, and suggestions made by them were incorporated in the design of the flying control system. The handling characteristics of the Trident in flight were very close to those experienced with the simulator and were very much better than was usually the case with a new aircraft. A television tube display was used to provide visual realism for flying. The simulator was also being used as an important tool in the work required to complete the development of the flight control system for fully automatic landing. Test pilots experienced with the Trident make an essential contribution to this simulator work by giving critical appraisals of simulated automatic landings, which. they have monitored on the display.

Engineering of Flying Control circuits

Component design was aimed at providing high system integrity and good accessibility, and at eliminating the possibility of incorrect assembly during servicing. The effect of wear has been carefully analysed, and component testing has been conducted under all representative environmental conditions. Automatically retained bolts are used wherever it was necessary to ensure continued safe operation with the nut and split pin missing. A complete fault analysis, incorporating an analysis of misrigging, negative g eflects, incorrect emergency drill, disconnections, servo

No, not a flight simulator, but Hatfield's Trident test facilities include this full scale hydraulic rig, for checking, fault-finding and endurance running of the flying controls and undercarriage systems. Linked to it was a computer which could feed, amongst other test information, complete automatic landing programmes into the rig in support of flight test development.

Below: Aileron controls on the test rig illustrate the Trident's hydraulically powered triplex system, giving three wholly independent 'live' sources of power control. The rig has enabled every conceivable type of failure to be simulated, for verification of the fai/-safe qualities of the Trident control system.

[Photographs courtesy of British Aerospace Hatfield]

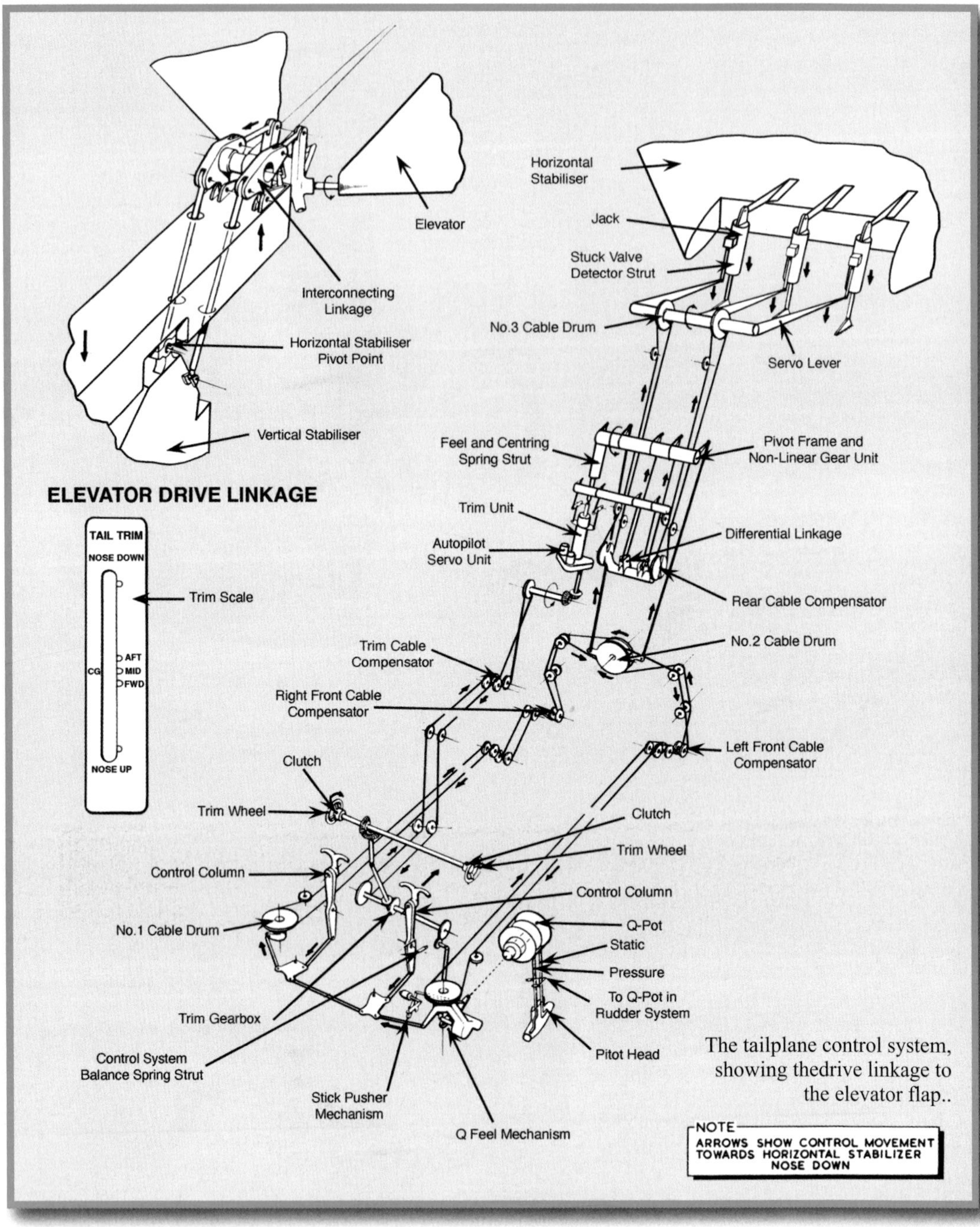

The tailplane control system, showing thedrive linkage to the elevator flap..

unit valve malfunction and feel failure, has been carried out using both the functional test rig and the actual aircraft.

Flying Control Circuits.
High-lift flaps and a leading-edge slat have been used to achieve a high maximum lift coefficient. The high-lift flaps provide a large pitching moment, and this, combined with the large C of G. range required with a rear-engine layout, demands a powerful pitch control for take-off and landing manoeuvres.

Design studies of the low-speed case and the requirements for control at high Mach numbers led to the all-moving tailplane with a slotted trailing-edge flap. The trailing-edge flap was actuated by a simple mechanical link to the tailplane, providing a high negative CLT for takeoff and landing but with little movement at high speed. With this flying-tail arrangement, the tailplane was directly coupled to the stick. And there are no elevators which could be moved independently from the tailplane.

Feel was provided by a Q pot, together with a centring spring strut, and to achieve pilots' recommendations of stick forces and stick movements over the wide speed range, a system dividing control between stick and trim circuits was used. The term 'Q pot' is the aero abbreviation for dynamic pressure which is used to adjust control feel.

At any trim setting, full stick movement, fore and aft, results in tailplane movement over approximately three-quarters of the full range of tailplane angle. The trimmer selects both the datum and the sector of the tailplane movement over which the stick has authority. It was a design safety requirement that it must be possible to fly between sequences of the flight profile without change of trim setting; for example, the transition from landing approach to overshoot could be made without trim adjustment.

The autopilot operated the trim system, and full trimmer movement 'stick free' produces full tailplane travel, which was required by the autopilot for the auto-flare manoeuvre. Since the trim system movement changes the stick-free datum, autopilot operation was clearly indicated to the pilot by stick movement.

In addition to the normal stick-shaker for prestall warning, the Trident was fitted with a pitch augmenter or 'stick-pusher', which comes into operation automatically at the stall. The stick-pusher produces nose-down pitch, at an incidence dependent on the rate of approach to the stall, by applying an eighty pound load to the control column. Should a stall be induced in a manoeuvre, the pusher will operate sufficiently before the stall to ensure adequate recovery. The device was engineered with full protection against malfunction.

Tailplane Operation.

The control system consisted of duplicated main input circuits and a trim circuit, was a simple mechanical system providing the proper feel characteristics, trim arrangements and autopilot input. The duplication of the main input circuit meets FAA requirements, and either branch could operate all or any of the tailplane jacks.

The DH.121 production line at Hatfield. Closest airframe to the camera is the prototype, later to be registered G-ARPA. *[Photograph courtesy of British Aerospace Hatfield]*

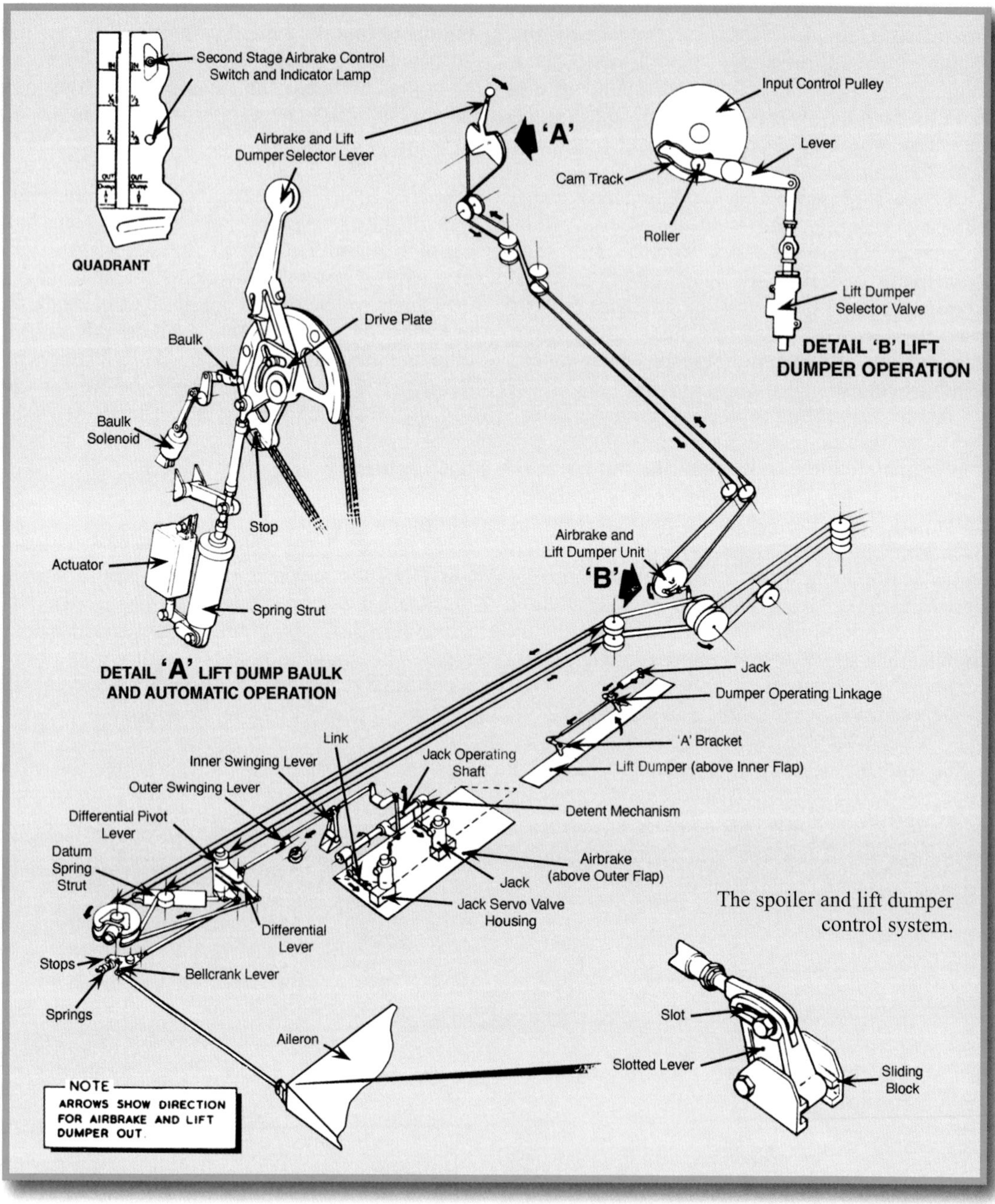

The spoiler and lift dumper control system.

The stick input was linked to a Q-pot located beneath the flight compartment floor. Whenever the stick is moved from the trimmed position, the Q pot loaded the stick with a force proportional to both Q and to the stick displacement. The stick trimmed position was thus governed by the Q-Pot. The input from the stick to the non-linear linkage was constrained by feel for the system and accurate position the tailplane. The datums of the Q-Pot and the centring spring strut, which provided the spring strut, are adjusted together by the trim circuit. The non-linear linkage was a simple device for providing gearing curves of the right shape. The circuit then continued through the differential lever and the 'stuck valve' detector struts to the control valves on the three tailplane jacks.

In the extremely unlikely event that a jack valve should seize, the function of the 'stuck valve' detector struts was to give a warning of which hydraulic system was affected so that appropriate action can be taken.

The trim input was by a chain-driven screwjack, operated by a handwheel on each side of the central control pedestal. The trim circuit also operated another screwjack, which kept the Q-Pot operating lever in line with the Q-Pot piston rod throughout the trim range, so that the trimmed position of the stick always corresponded to the neutral position of the Q-Pot.

There are two inputs from the trim screwjack to the main control circuit: one via the centring spring strut governing the stick trimmed neutral position; the other by a duplicated mechanical linkage to the differential levers, and this selected the sector of tailplane movement corresponding to the particular position of trim.

The input of the two autopilot servos (with provision for the addition of a third servo if the autopilot is upgraded to a triplex level) is effected through the trim circuit system, so that when the autopilot was disengaged, the aircraft was always left in trim. When under autopilot control, magnetic preload increased, the breakout force in the centring spring strut, so that it acted virtually as a rigid member over the range of loads likely to be injected by the autopilot. The control column, therefore, movesd with the tailplane, and the pilot was aware of the autopilot's behaviour. When the autopilot is engaged, a solenoid-operated clutch disengages the trim wheels, removing flywheel effects. The trim position indicators, however, continue to give a proper indication of trim at all

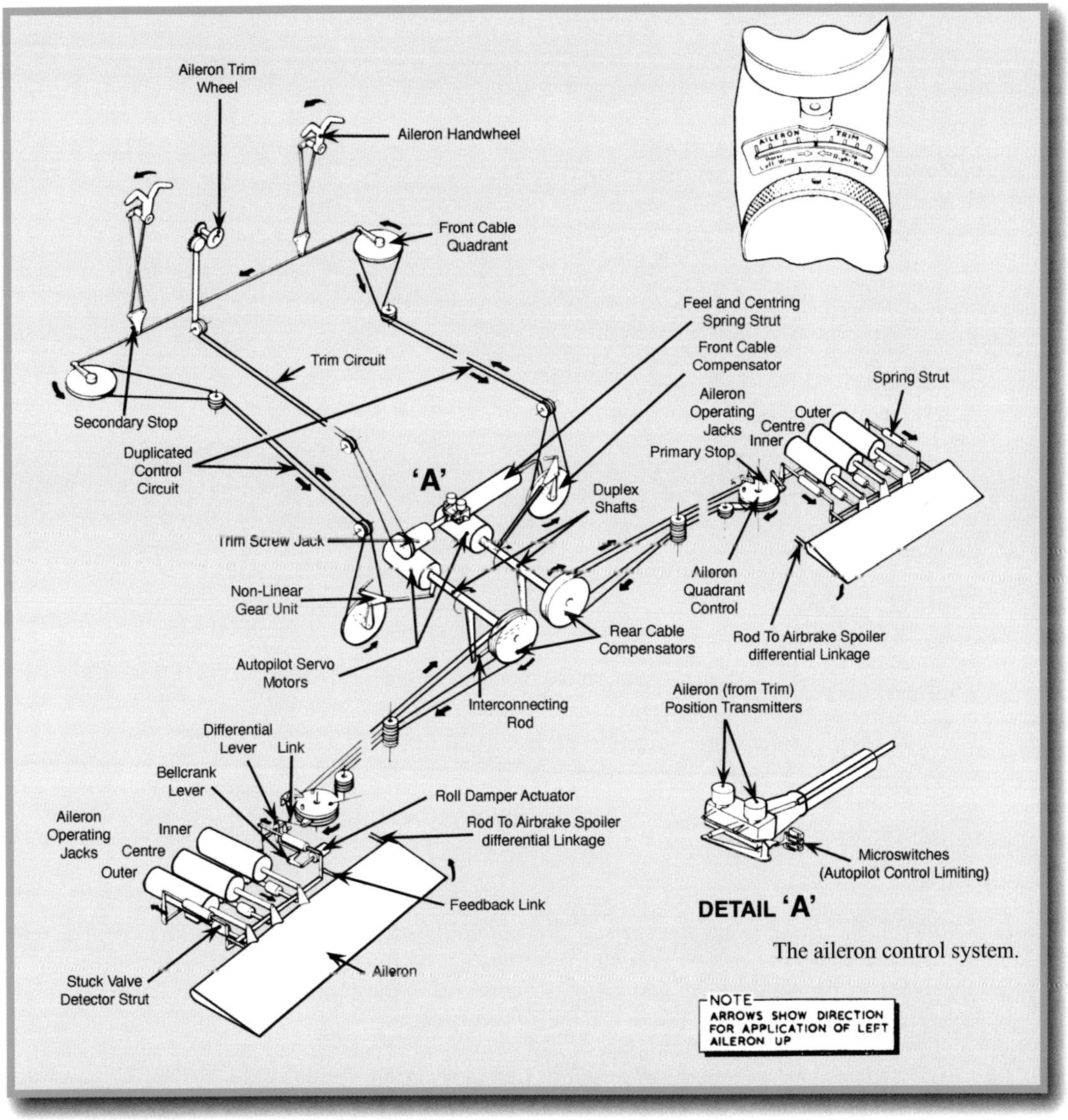

The aileron control system.

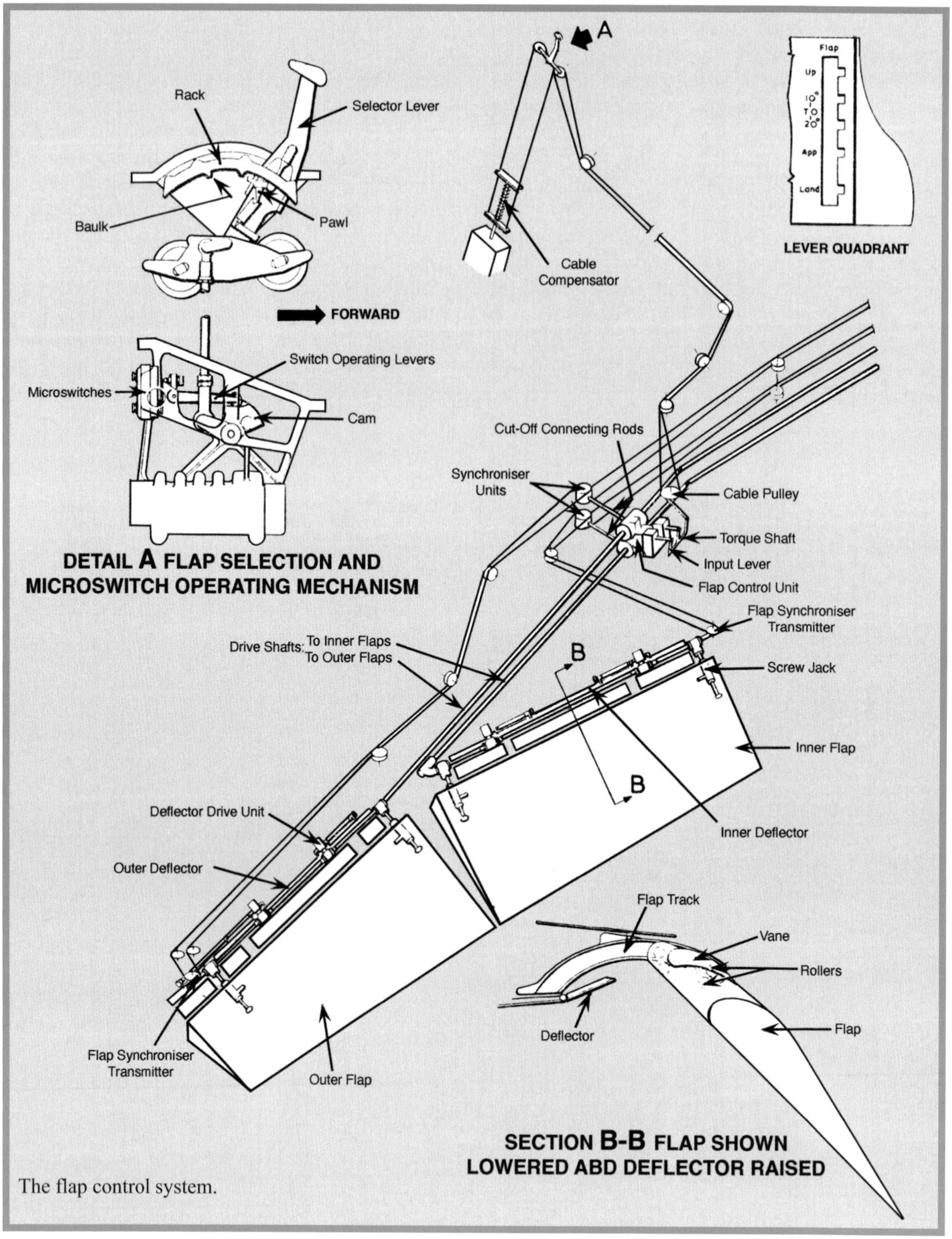

The flap control system.

times, whether the autopilot is engaged or not. In addition, there is a tailplane position indicator on the pilot's main instrument panel. The normal method of disengaging the autopilot is to use the cut-out button on the control column, but it is possible to disengage in an emergency by pushing or pulling the control column with a force greater than the normal force. This overrides the magnetic preload in the centring spring strut. Switches are incorporated to cut out the autopilot, recouple the trim handwheels and release the magnetic preload in the centring spring strut.

The stick-pusher consists of a pneumatic ram, linked to the tailplane circuit by a simple mechanism which does not displace the ram during normal control movements. The ram is actuated by engine bleed air, stored in a reservoir and controlled by two solenoid-operated valves connected in series in the supply line.

The valves are automatically controlled by two independent circuits, each of which receives two main signals: one indicates aircraft incidence, and the other indicates the rate of approach to stall. Incidence is sensed by two probes that protrude, one on each side of the fuselage. The incidence probe signals are automatically adjusted to account for the leading edge slat's extended or retracted position. The complete system is inhibited above 250 knots IAS and below 50 knots IAS by speed switches, and while the aircraft is on the ground, by switches on the nose landing gear.

Operation of the stick-pusher would only occur if both control circuits were in agreement when the appropriate angle of attack was reached, since both control valves had to be open before air could pass to the pneumatic ram. If a spurious signal in one circuit caused one of the valves to open, a warning was given to the pilot enabling him to cut out the complete stall recovery system. The ram applied a force equivalent to eighty pounds at the control columns, causing nose-down movement of the aircraft, until the incidence fell below that at which the stick-shaker would operate, when the control valves closed and the control force returns to normal.

Should the nose-down force on the control columns remain after the aircraft has recovered from the stall the pilot disengages the system by operating a stall recovery override lever on the centre console.

This operated the manual override valve, which vents the air to the pneumatic ram and thus equalises the air pressure on either side of the ram piston. For the remainder of the flight, automatic stall recovery would not then be available. The manual override valve must be reset on the ground.

Test switches are incorporated to allow the system to be checked on the ground.

Aileron and Spoiler Control

Powerful control over the roll axis is provided by fully-powered ailerons operating in combination with the differential action of spoilers. The differential action of the spoilers is superimposed on any previous selection by the pilot of the spoilers as airbrakes.

The ailerons alone are sufficient for rolling control at high speeds and high Mach numbers. The first fifteen degrees approximately aileron movement, therefore occurred without differential movement of the spoilers. The lateral control reversal speed is expected to be at least 105 knots EAS above design diving speed, and this will be confirmed by test flights.

Particular attention has been paid to control at approach speeds in turbulent crosswinds, and pilots' comments indicate that plenty of control power is available in these conditions. It is in crosswind landings and take-offs that the differential action of the spoilers becomes most important, as the ailerons alone do not provide sufficient rolling moment for extreme crosswinds.

The aileron control system incorporates spring feel and non-linear gearing. The spring feel is provided by a centring spring strut, and the non-linear unit is, as in the other control circuits, a simple duplicated one.

A mechanical link prevents over-sensitivity of control at high speeds while ensuring appropriate control movements at approach speeds. A roll damper is fitted to improve lateral handling characteristics in turbulent conditions.

The airbrakes had a range of settings controlled by a gated quadrant. The pilot can select maximum airbrake at any speed, as the operating jacks are designed to stall before the resulting aerodynamic loads on the airbrakes exceed the design limit. The pilot, therefore, has no airbrake angle limits to remember and can select full airbrakes, knowing that the maximum permissible braking effect will be applied.

Secondary airbraking can be obtained by lowering the main gear, which can be selected down independently of the nose gear for this purpose. After landing, lift dumping in the region of the outer flaps is provided to the full airbrake position.

Aileron and Spoiler Operation.

Control inputs from the stick are carried by a simple mechanical circuit to a non-linear linkage, which is situated beneath the cabin floor at the wing centre section. The input is restrained at this point by the centring spring strut. Drive to the aileron jack control valves was then via a duplex torque tube, duplicated cable circuit, duplex lever linkage and stuck valve detector struts.

The aileron trim handwheel was mounted on the central control pedestal, and a mechanical position indicator was located alongside it. The trim input to the control circuit was through a chain-driven screwjack and the centring spring strut. A change in trim, resulting in a new aileron circuit trimmed to the neutral position, would be reflected in the stick position.

The autopilot servo input was injected into the circuit after that of the non-linear link and the trim input.

Position transmitters are fitted at the ailerons to enabled the autopilot to sense the total aileron deflection, including the deflection due to trim. A further pair of position transmitters was located at the centring spring strut, which measured control movements from the stick trimmed neutral position and enabled the yaw damper to coordinate turns. Also located at the centring spring strut were cut-out switches, which prevented excessive aileron from being applied if there is a roll channel runaway, when the autopilot is operating in the simpler mode.

The two spoilers were positioned on the upper

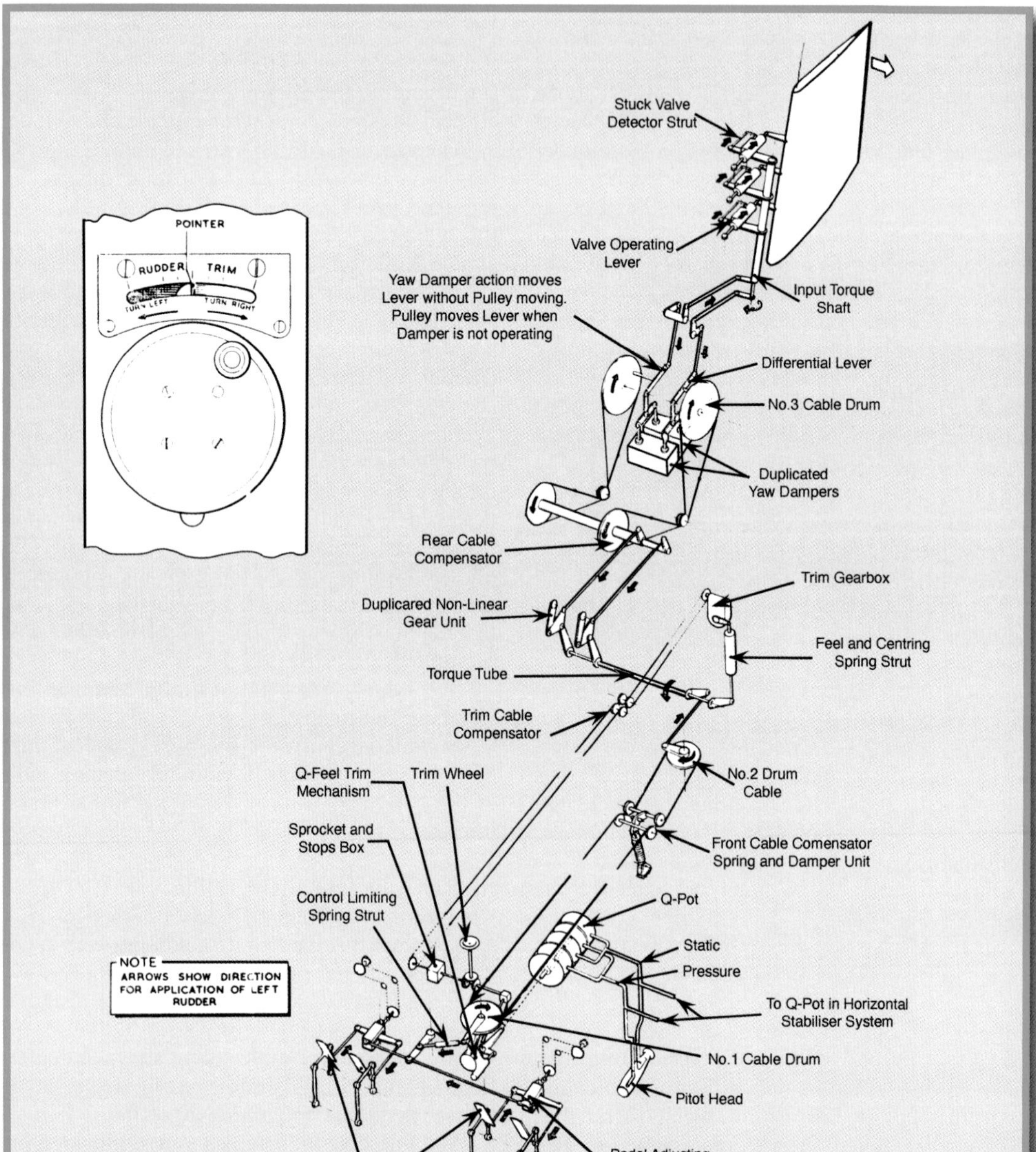

T
[De Havilland Aircraft Co.]

surface of each wing ahead of the outboard flaps. Operation of the airbrake selector lever in the flight compartment resulted in symmetrical spoiler extension, so that the spoilers could be used as airbrakes in flight, and as lift dumpers, over the outer flap region of the wing, after landing. The control quadrant was gated over the range of airbrake settings. Movement of the airbrake selector lever into the last position in the gate, beyond the full airbrake position, extended the two lift dumpers located ahead of the inboard flaps.

The input from the airbrake selector lever was by a single cable circuit to the centre section drum; from there to the most outboard pulley in each wing, the circuit consisted of duplicated cables. The remainder of the circuit, from the outboard pulley to the spoiler jack control valves, via the differential lever and the two detent mechanisms, consisted of a rod-and-lever mechanism. The detent mechanisms were spring-loaded devices, each transmitting operating movement to one jack control valve. If a valve seized, movement of the input circuit would cause the corresponding detent mechanism to 'crack', to permit normal operation of the input circuit to the other jack.

The connecting rod, which fed aileron movement to the spoiler circuit through a non-linear unit, was joined to a simple slot and pin assembly, so that differential spoiler movement did not occur till after the first fifteen degrees of aileron deflection.

Further aileron deflection, from fifteen degrees to the maximum aileron angle, causes the spoiler angle on the same wing as the upgoing aileron to increase by up to ten degrees. Thus, with zero airbrakes, maximum aileron causes one spoiler to extend ten degrees. With maximum airbrake selected (thirty-eight degrees), maximum aileron deflection will cause the angle of one spoiler to increase to forty-eight degrees.

Rudder Control

Rudder control by a triplex system of jacks provided a reserve of power during normal operation. This is because adequate control must be provided with only one system working. The critical case is for a crosswind landing. In this condition, at least three-quarters of full rudder travel can be applied by two jacks at 120 knots.

At high Mach numbers, the use of maximum jack thrust would induce rudder angles which would result in high aerodynamic loads on the fin and high g loads on the airframe. The maximum rudder angle which can be obtained is therefore reduced, as speed increases, by the combined action of a breakout spring strut and the artificial feel in the rudder input system.

The rudder control system incorporates a mechanical non-linear linkage similar to that used in the tailplane circuit, providing a reasonable amount of rudder pedal travel at high speed without excessive pedal travel at approach speeds. The feel is by a pot and a centring spring strut, and the datums of the pot and the spring strut are determined by the trim.

The duplicated yaw dampers adjacent to the rudder jacks provide Dutch roll damping and coordinate turns, made by the pilot or autopilot, from information sensed in the aileron control circuit. Pilots' comments indicate that with yaw dampers coupled, there is no tendency to Dutch roll. At high speeds, the aircraft is easy to control without the yaw dampers, though they make control easier in turbulent air. The yaw dampers are automatically cut out during kick-off drift manoeuvres when the pilot makes a control movement with the rudder pedals.

Rudder Operation.

The duplication in the rudder control system is provided by the trim circuit. Interconnected adjustable pedals are linked to the main input circuit through a breakout spring strut.

This strut will transmit up to a certain fixed pedal load, but further loading beyond this merely 'cracks out' the strut. On removal of the load, it returns to its original length. Thus, the strut will only transmit pedal movement to the main input cable until the pedal force resulting from the artificial spring feel and q-feel loads equals the breakout load. Pedal movement beyond this point produces no further rudder movement.

This prevents the pilot from making rudder movements which would cause excessive aerodynamic loading of the airframe.

The breakout spring strut is connected to a lever and pulley, which operates the main input single cable circuit. The q-feel piston is connected to the same pulley via a duplicated chain, the q-feel lever and the q-feel trimming mechanism.

A connecting rod and lever mechanism carries movement from the aft pulley of the single cable input circuit to the duplicated non-linear linkage, and thence to the duplex torque tube. The trim circuit also feeds motion into the duplex torque tube through the centring spring strut and duplicated non-linear linkage.

The trim circuit input was by a handwheel on

the control pedestal, and controlled the position of the centring spring strut via a chain-driven worm box. A change in trim setting, therefore, resulted in a new rudder pedal trimmed neutral position. The trim circuit was also linked to the Q-feel trim mechanism. This ensures that the trimmed neutral position of the rudder pedals corresponds to the neutral position of the Q-feel by adjusting the position of the Q-feel lever.

From the duplex torque tube, the input was carried to duplicated differential levers by rod, lever and cable circuits. Duplicated yaw dampers gave equal input to common links connected to the differential levers. The use of equal input links ensured that, in the event of a damper runaway, the remaining damper could fully compensate, so that the net yaw damper input to the differential lever was nil. Subsequent adjustment of the trim after the runaway, even if the faulty damper remains at the limit of its travel, restores control through the remaining yaw damper circuit over half the normal input range.

The purpose of the differential levers is to combine the inputs from the stick and yaw dampers to give a single output to the jacks. Output from the differential levers passes to the

A Trident 1C fitted with leading-edge slats in place of it's droop, that was used to establish the general performance of this wing configuration to complement wind-tunnel research on 1E and 1F wing design. *[Photograph courtesy of British Aerospace Hatfield]*

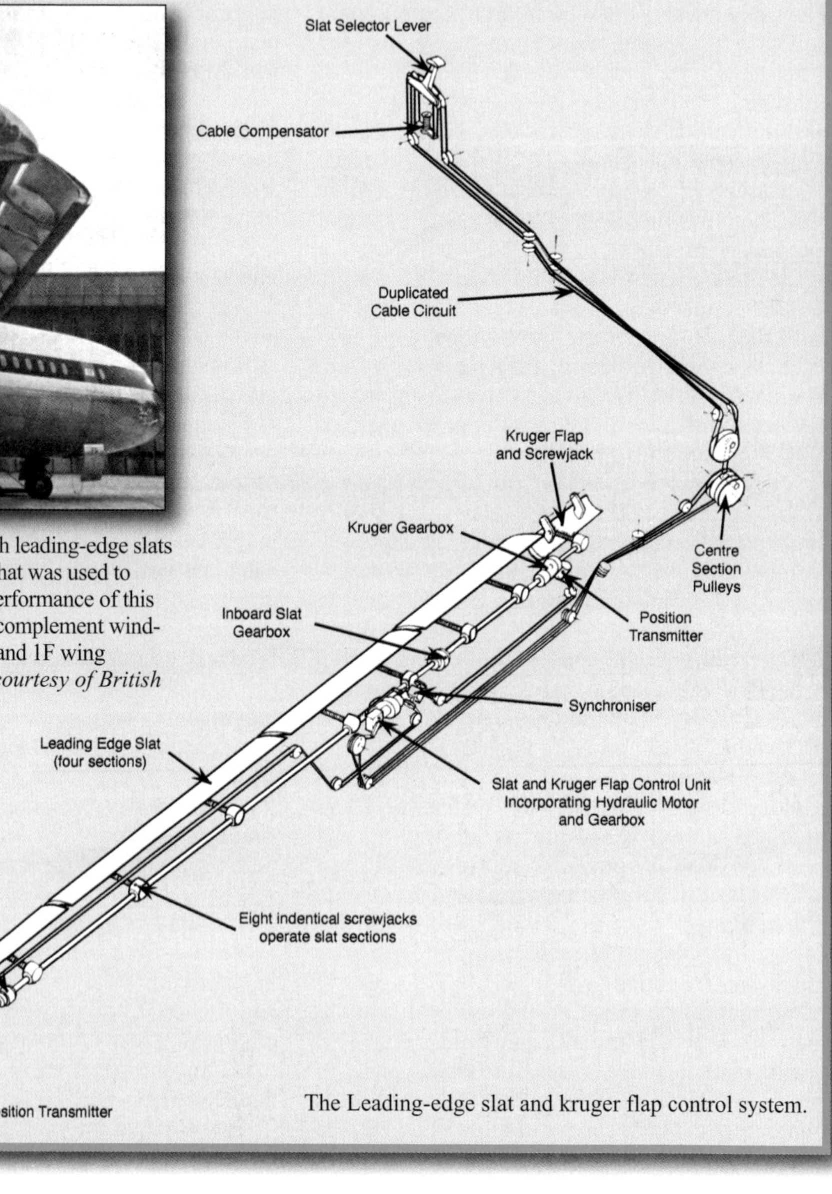

The Leading-edge slat and kruger flap control system.

three jack control valves via rod and lever mechanisms, and 'stuck valve' detector struts similar to those used in the tailplane and aileron circuits.

Subsidiary Controls.
The aircraft was fitted with two pairs of double-slotted flaps, which combine a large flap area with a rearward extension that increases the effective wing area by five per cent. Slats were fitted to the leading edge of the flaps, and these, together with movable lower shrouds, established a smooth flow from the slots and from the wing upper surface. The flap operating mechanism was of clean design and was contained within the wing profile to ensure maximum aerodynamic efiiciency.

A leading-edge slat was fitted in order to augment the high maximum lift coefficient associated with double-slotted flaps and to raise the angle of attack at which the stall occured. A small Kruger flap, inboard of each leading edge slat, avoided the discontinuity which would otherwise occur when the slat was extended.

Lift dumpers were automatically operated immediately after touchdown to spoil the flow over the inner sections of flaps, and so supplement the air-brakes, which also extended automatically to spoil the flow over the outer sections. Their combined function was to reduce the total wing lift as soon as possible after touchdown, which, by increasing the vertical load on the wheels, permitted a greater effort to be applied, and hence shortened the landing run.

Flap Operation.
The double-slotted flaps were divided on each wing into inboard and outboard surfaces. The flaps were powered by two hydraulic motors located at the left wing root. One motor was coupled to the inboard pair of flaps, the other to the outboard pair. The flap selector lever had five gated positions and was connected to the control units on the hydraulic motors via a cable circuit. Movement of the flap selector lever resulted in simultaneous operation of the hydraulic motors, which lowered the flaps and automatically stopped at the pre-selected position. The drive from the hydraulic motors to the recirculating ball screw jacks at the flap surfaces was via a system of torque shafts and bevel gears.

Each section of the flap was supported by a pair of steel tracks mounted on the primary wing structure. When the screwjacks are extended, the rollers mounted on the flaps follow the tracks, extending the flaps outwards and downwards. The fixed slats, fitted to the flap leading edge, lay within the shroud profile when the flaps are retracted.

Separate layshafts, driven from the main input torque shafts, rotate edthe lower deflector shrouds so that they move upwards during the initial stages of flap movement to modify the underwing profile, so permitting smooth airstream entry into the slots.

With the flaps in any position, 'no back' ratchet devices incorporated in each screwjack ensure that the flap drives are irreversible, and do not move as a result of aerodynamic or any other external loading. When the flaps are in the fully retracted position, a notch in the end of each flap track

Not the best of images, but interesting nevertheless. The double-slotted flaps are shown in their fully-extended positions. Ahead of the inboard flap is the lift dumper and ahead of the outboard flap, the spoiler. The aileron is to the left of them at maximum angle. design. *[Photographs courtesy of British Aerospace Hatfield]*

engages with a peg attached to the flap structure, providing a positive lock. Scrapers incorporated in the screwjacks cleared the threads of ice.

Simple mechanical circuits, attached to both inboard and outboard pairs of flaps, prevented asymmetrical flap operation. On the inner pair of flaps, a drive from the gearbox of each inner screwjack motor was a closed-loop cable that rotated an input pulley in a simple bevel-gear differential unit. This unit consisted of two bevel gears and an idler, arranged to provide a flap synchronising mechanism.

Symmetrical flap movement caused the cable loops to rotate the bevel gears in opposite directions at the same rate. Under these conditions, the idler revolved on its bearing, but was not displaced. Asymmetrical flap movement caused the bevel gears to rotate in opposite directions but at differing rates, and this would immediately cause displacement of the idler as well as rotation. This displacement was then transmitted through a linkage to operate a hydraulic cut-off on the appropriate flap drive motor. The cable loops received their input signals from pulleys driven at the extreme ends of the flap drive system on each side, downstream of all main drive shafts and screwjacks. These pulleys were therefore in a position to sense asymmetric failure of any part of the drive system, and to transmit this information to the synchronising unit and motor cut-off. A similar synchronising circuit was provided for the outer pair of flaps.

Leading Edge Slat Operation.

The leading edge slat was operated by a system of torque shafts and screwjacks similar to that used for flap operation. There are, however, separate hydraulic motors for left and right wing slat surfaces, mounted midway along each wing on the front spar. Each motor is connected by torque shafts to nine screwjacks, eight of which are identical and operate the four slat sections in pairs, while the ninth operated a small Kruger flap at the wing root. The slat was selected to UP or DOWN positions by a gated lever in the flight compartment, and control of the hydraulic motors was by a duplicated cable circuit to the wing centre section, where it divided into separate circuits along the left and right wings.

A synchronising circuit operated on each wing and ensured that if any asymmetry develops within the system on either wing, that system will be automatically shut off. Each synchronising circuit comprises two cable drums operated by the slat torque shaft, one inboard of the innermost slat jack, and one outboard of the outermost slat jack. Drum signals were transmitted via cable circuits to a receiver unit adjacent to the control unit; if the two signals differed, the receiver unit operated a hydraulic shut-off valve in the control unit. The receiver units operate on the same principle as the flap synchronising mechanism.

Between-wing asymmetry of the slats, which would result from one motor being cut off, could only occur while extension or retraction of the slats is taking place, that is, at speeds of 225-250 knots. At these speeds, the asymmetric slat has a negligible effect on the trim, and on receiving a warning of failure from the control warning

Specifications of materials used in the Trident structure

Component	British Material Spec.	Broad USA Equiv
Wing		
Top Skin	DTD.5060	7075S
Stringers	DTD.5074	7075S
Bottom Skin	DH.Spec.	2024S
Stringers	L.64	2024S
Front and Centre Spars:		
Booms	L.65	2014S
Webs	DTD.746	2104S
Rear Spar:		
Outboard Booms	L.65	2014S
Outboard Webs	DTD.746	2014S
Inboard Integral Machining	DH.Spec.	2024S
Fuselage		
Skin of pressure cabin and majority of airframe	DTD.710	2024S
Skin of unpressurised rear portion	DTD.746	2014S
Fuselage Stringers	DTD.746	2014S
Wing Spar Frames	L.65 DTD.746	2014S
Fin Spar Bulkhead		
Integral Machining	DH Spec.	2024S
Build-up Structure	DTD.746	2014S
Fin		
Majority of Structure	DH.Specs	2024S
Tailplane Pivot fitting: forging	S.99	
Tailplane		
Centre Section Box		
Integral Machining	DH Spec.	2024S
Skins	DTD.710	2045S
Stringers	DTD.746	2014S
Landing Gear and Flap Tracks Main and Nose Gear legs, and Flap Tracks are machined from 84-ton steel forgings.	DTD.73C	

system, the pilot can motor the one leading edge, which is still functioning correctly, to the same position as the failed one, as indicated by the slat position indicator.

It is impossible for a slat with a drive shaft or motor failure to retract accidentally to its UP position, because the 'no back' locks in the screwjacks make them irreversible.

A sealing plate provides a positive seal between the inboard leading edge slat section and the wing when the slat surface is extended. This is linked to the retraction within the slat section at the UP position.

Kruger Flap Operation.

The Kruger flap operation is by a single screwjack connected to the inboard end of the leading edge slat torque shaft, so that the Kruger flaps are automatically raised or lowered when the slat was selected UP or DOWN. Each Kruger flap pivots on two hinges. Anti-icing to the same standard as for the rest of the stub wing leading edge was provided.

Lift Dumper Operation.

The lift dumpers are located immediately forward of the inboard flaps and are powered by single hydraulic jacks. When the airbrake selector lever was moved rearward beyond the full airbrake position, the lift dumpers are extended. This will normally be done automatically by means of an electric actuator, mounted on the front face of the central pedestal in the flight compartment. Pre-selection of the automatic circuit must, however, be made by the pilot before landing. Automatic LIFT DUMP was pre-selected by lifting the airbrake lever, which causes the lever to disengage from the gate and engage the linkage to the electric actuator.

There are two breaks in the electrical circuit which must be closed before the actuator will move the air-brake lever to LIFT DUMP. A break was made by selecting the landing flap. The second break was made when both main gear oleos are compressed. As the lever was automatically moved rearward by the actuator, the spoilers are fully extended first, followed immediately by the lift dumpers. A mechanical baulk prevents inadvertent LIFT DUMP selection in flight, and this was also only released when the main gear oleos are compressed. The operation of the lift dumper selector valve was by a cam and roller mechanism incorporated in the airbrake input pulley at the wing centre section.

Provided the airbrake lever was selected to automatic operation, the spoilers and lift dumpers will be automatically retracted when the flaps are raised to the take-off position.

Testing.

A full-scale hydraulic and flying control rig, coupled to a flight simulator, was being used for functional testing, fault analysis, endurance testing and investigation of autopilot performance. In addition to the rig tests, further tests are being carried out.ed out on a production aircraft, in flight and on the ground. One aim of these tests was to obtain data on the hydraulic system, including the flying control jacks, to verify the validity of the duty cycles currently applied to these units in the fatigue tests. This information was obtained using pressure transducers in the circuits and strain gauges on the

Below left: The main wing torsion box of a trident IC - that of a Trident 1E differs only in minor detail.
Below Right: The wing centre-section structure - highlighted by under-exposing the surrounding structure in typical De Havilland fashion - showing the front and rear spars and the spanwise baffles of the centre fuel tank. The wing root ribs mark the beginning of the wing sweep.*[Photographs courtesy of British Aerospace Hatfield]*

jacks. A further aim of the tests was to confirm that the available power was consistent with the required hinge moments on the control surfaces.

Structure.

The structure of the Trident 1, and later the IE, , being designed for operations from hot and high airfields, needed more wing area and higher maximum lift coefficients to improve aerodrome performance. Thus, the design work was aimed at developing the high lift devices and wing section to give the required low speed performance with the minimum loss of high speed capabilities. The success of the slat development has been confirmed by extensive flight trials on a modified Trident 1 fitted with slats.

The centre engine intake posed its own aerodynamic problems, which were tackled through a thorough investigation using quarter-scale models, followed by full-scale checks of the most promising designs. Subsequent flight tests on the Series 1 Trident proved the validity of the design solution.

The Trident was designed with the objective of achieving freedom from fatigue cracks on the primary structure, during the operational life of the aircraft. Additionally, in areas where the fail safe concept could be applied, the design aim was to provide multiple load paths and/or crack stoppers so that in the event of any one member failing, the remaining structure could sustain at least limit loads for a longer period than the interval specified between major inspections of the structure. In the places where it was not possible to apply the fail safe concept, that was on flap and slat tracks, tailplane hinge fitting, engine mountings and landing gear, a substantial margin of safe life was provided.

The Trident's design objective of a primary structure free from fatigue cracks throughout its operational life was achieved through unique design features. Stress levels were deliberately kept low, and materials with a slow rate of crack propagation were chosen. The structure was designed with straightforward and continuous main load-carrying elements, minimizing joints and cut-outs. Redux bonding was used throughout the aircraft, reducing the number of holes drilled for bolts and rivets and thus minimizing stress concentrations.

A meticulous survey of all the critical loading cases was conducted with particular emphasis on calculating the dynamic responses of the aircraft structure using extensive computer programmes. This thorough approach ensures the Trident's design was robust and reliable. These techniques were applied to both design ultimate and fatigue loading conditions. In addition, aircraft engaged on the flight test programme were fitted with strain gauges and accelerometers which measured loadings on the aircraft to verify design conditions, and to calibrate loads applied to the fatigue and static strength test programmes.

Above: Trident 1C wing bottom skin panels. Those of the Trident 1E were similar in principle.

Below: The front spar of the extension wing showing the horizontal spanwise crack-stopper and the reinforcing for a slat jack cutout. This was Reduxed to the spar web and provided continuity of fail-safe design.
[Photographs courtesy of British Aerospace Hatfield]

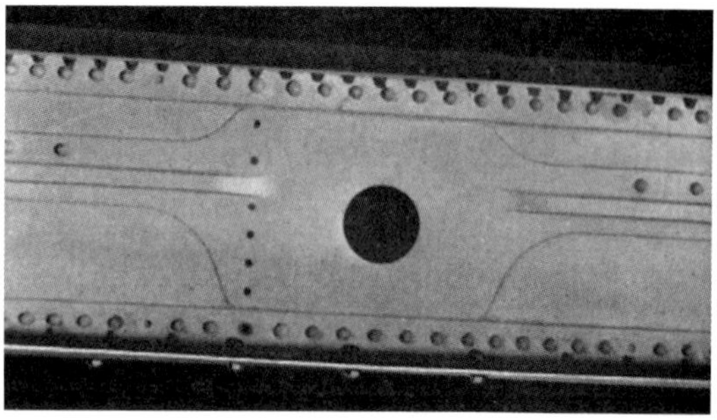

Materials

To achieve a long airframe life free from fatigue damage, aluminium-copper alloys were used in all parts of the structure of the Trident which were subjected to fluctuating tensile stress. Aluminium-zinc alloys were used only for the top skins and stringers of the wing, where the fluctuating stresses are, compressive in normal flight, and the higher strength of these alloys could be used to advantage.

Redux

This was a thermo-setting structural adhesive used extensively in the Trident structure to bond stringers and reinforcing to wing and fuselage skins and stiffeners to the webs of spars and ribs.It became the generic name of a family of phenol–formaldehyde/polyvinyl–formaldehyde adhesives developed by Aero Research Limited (ARL) at Duxford, UK, in the 1940s, subsequently produced by Ciba (ARL). The brand name is now also used for a range of epoxy and bismaleimide adhesives manufactured by Hexcel. The name is a contraction of 'Research at Duxford'.

Devised at ARL by Dr. Norman de Bruyne and George Newell in 1941 for use in the aircraft industry, the adhesive is used for the bonding of metal-to-metal and metal-to-wood structures. The adhesive system comprises a liquid phenolic resin and a PVF (PolyVinylFormal) thermoplastic powder.

By using Redux, many holes were avoided, which would otherwise be necessary for bolts and rivets, and the number of local stress concentrations in the structure was correspondingly reduced. Structures having Redux bonded stringers and stifleners also possess markedly better crack-stopping properties than those with riveted, bolted or integral stiffeners.

Wings were built alongside the fuselages at Hatfield. *[Photograph courtesy of British Aerospace Hatfield]*

Right: Details of Window reinforcing, sealing and assembly on the Trident.

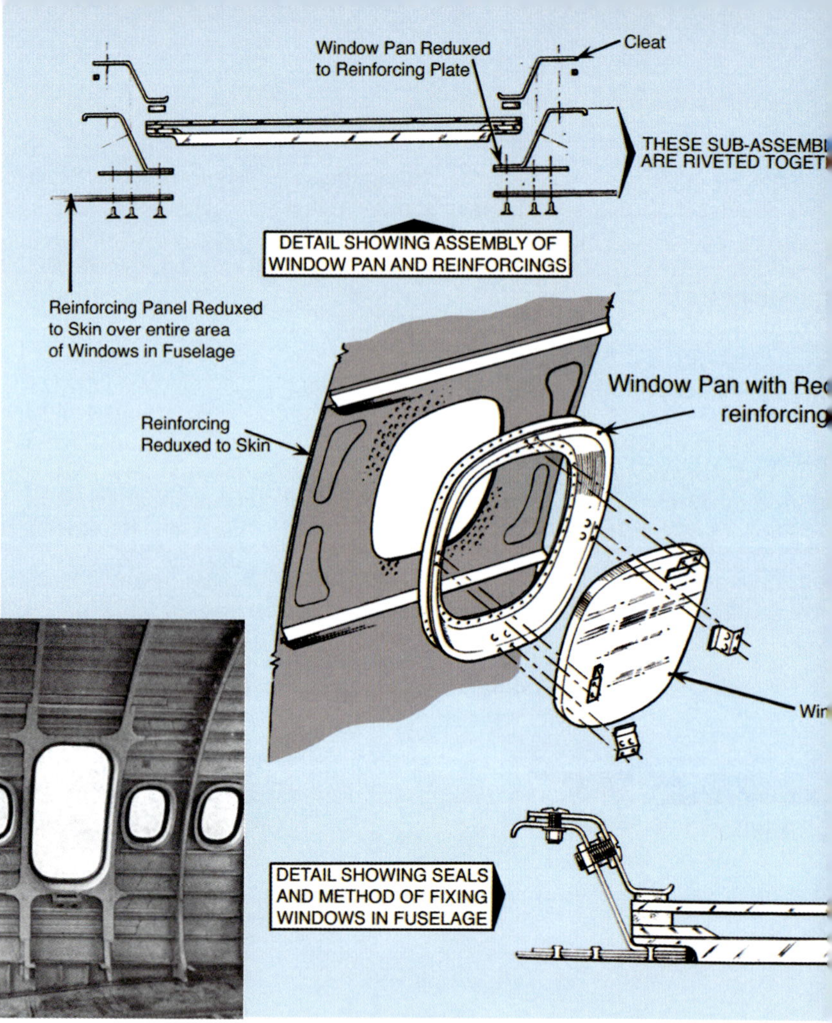

Below: Skin and Frame reinforcing around the Escape hatch cut-outs and adjacent windows was by contour-machined plate riveted to the main skin. To the left of the picture may also be seen the duplicated main rear spar frame fittings.*[both De Havilland Aircraft Co.]*

Extensive use of Redux is, therefore, complementary to the design aim of providing a fail-safe structure.

Redux adhesive had a long history of successful use by the De Havillands, mainly for bonding stringers to skin on wings, fuselages, tailplanes, and fins. It had been used on Doves, Herons, Sea Vixens, and Comets before its use on the Trident. The maximum life of any one of these aircraft had been achieved by a Dove which entered service in December 1947 and was still in service in the mid-1960s. The many Reduxed joints incorporated in all these aircraft have successfully withstood the test of operational service.

Repairing bonded structures was no more difficult than repairing riveted structures; in fact the technique was exactly the same and was carried out by riveting.

External patches were either riveted or bolted through stringer flanges and thus took advantage of the reinforcing which was inherent in the fact that the stringer flange was Reduxed. If the crowns of stringers were damaged, capping stringers were fitted which were also riveted or bolted through the flanges. All repairs were to ensure that structural reliability was unaffected.

Structural Features - Wing

The main wing box was continuous from wing tip to wing tip, and comprised of a six-cell centre section box extending across the fuselage, a two-cell box from the wing root out to forty per cent of the semi-span, and from there a single-cell box to the wing tip. The entire wing box was sub-divided to form integral fuel tanks.

The leading edge surfaces on each wing comprised a slat in four sections, extending over the entire leading edge, except for the inboard two feet, the discontinuity at the wing root being faired by a small Kruger flap.

The gap between the fixed wing and the trailing edge of the inboard slat section was sealed by a light spring-loaded plate.

The trailing edge surfaces comprised inboard and outboard sections of flap, together with associated vanes and deflector plates, ailerons, airbrakes and lift dumpers, all of which were mounted from the structure aft of the rear spar.

Centre Section

The centre section of the wing extends across the width of the fuselage and serves as an integral fuel tank. It was bounded by the front and rear spars, the top and bottom wing skins and the root ribs of the wings was and was divided into six sections by five intermediate baffle beams.

Between the root ribs, the five chordwise beams provided no full-depth ribs and stability in compression. These also support the cabin pressure floor formed by the top skin of the wing over the area of the centre section. The front and rear spars and the root ribs formed the fuel tank walls, which were machined from thick plates with a lattice of integral stiffeners.

Provision for inspection of the centre section was made by a reinforced manhole in the centre of each baffle web, entry to this crawlway being gained through a single cut-out in the bottom skin.

Wing Skins

The number of cut-outs in the bottom skin of the wing as a whole was reduced to a minimum, and only four manholes were necessary in each stub wing for inspection purposes. A complete interior inspection was possible by providing removable panels in the ribs adjacent to each maintenance hole. In the extension wing, where the wing was thinner, it was necessary to provide a maintenance hole in each rib bay, but by positioning these in a straight line, only one stringer was interrupted. All the wing skins were taper-milled from thick plate and pocketed out to leave landings where the stringers and rib booms were attached. The stringers, Reduxed to the skin panels, were made from top hat section extrusions having sloping sidewalls and a flat crown, which reduces in thickness spanwise. The stub wing skins were split into two panels with a joint along the centre spar. The top skins were continuous spanwise from the centre line of the aircraft out to Rib 8. The bottom skins were similar but for a small panel forty-eight inches wide, inserted between the front and centre spars, and symmetrically disposed about the aircraft centre line. The skin joints thus created at tweny-four inches either side of the centre line were used to accommodate a double-curvature dihedral break which existed only over the forward part of the wing. On the bottom skin rear panels, and on the forward and rear panels of the top skins, the wing root dihedral break was formed by a straightforward bend.

Both top and bottom rear skin panels were continuous in a chordwise direction across the rear spar to form the top and bottom skins of a short box cantilevered aft of the spar and designed to carry the rear trunnion of the main landing gear leg. This trunnion was integrally machined in a heavy forging, forming an extension of Rib 5 behind the rear spar. The forward trunnion was a separate fitting bolted to the rear spar. The wing skins were 0.270 inches thick on the top and 0.370 inches thick on the bottom, where they crossed the rear spar in the region of the cantilever box.

Below left: The nose section of the fuselage provided an excellent standard of visibility with large cut-outs while maintaining high standards of structural integrity, with a strength factor of three on pressure throughout.

Below Right: The top fuselage structure in the region of the rear main frame shows the duplication of the frame structure and the attachment of the stringers to the butt strap, which surmounts the frame. Note also the integral reinforcing around the holes in the frame for air conditioning ducts.

[Photographs courtesy of British Aerospace Hatfield]

Spars

The front and centre wing spars and the outer part of the rear spar comprised booms machined from extrusions and webs with vertical stiffeners Reduxed to the face, which lies inside the main box. On the opposite face, a single spanwise stringer was Reduxed to the web at one-third of the spar depth up from the bottom skin. These stringers extend across the entire span and were provided to act as crack stoppers in the unlikely event of a crack developing in the web. On the front spar, the crack stopper also forms the reinforcement around holes for the slat tracks and jacks.

The inner part of the rear spar from Rib 1 to Rib 5 was machined from a thick billet and had integral booms, stiffeners, and crack stoppers. Extruded top and bottom booms were bolted back-to-back with the integrally machined section of the rear spar, and the rear spar bottom boom was a fully duplicated member across the centre section and outboard to the main landing gear boxes at Rib 5.

The shroud structure in the triangle between the rear spar of the wing and the leading edge of the flaps was supported by a light false spar that passed across the rear of the landing gear mounting box.

The Trident's design and manufacture aimed at producing a fail-safe structure with a long, crack-free life. The wing and tail skins were machined out of thick plate on a profile mill. The template to be followed was overhead, with the stylus following the shape while the milling cutter machines the plate below.
[Photograph courtesy of British Aerospace Hatfield]

Above left: Showing the change in structure between the nose fuselage (on the left) which has closely pitched frames and no stringers and the forward part of the main fuselage (on the right).

Above right: The large double webbed bulkhead and the pressure dome at the rear of the fuselage. The deep transverse beam across the bulkhead carries at its extremities the attachments for the forward pair of cantilevered side engine mounting beams.*[Photographs courtesy of British Aerospace Hatfield]*

Ribs

All wing ribs which formed the fuel tank boundaries were machined from thick plates with a lattice of integral stiffeners. Other ribs have plate webs with extruded booms and stiffeners assembled to the webs by bolting, Reduxing or riveting.

Leading Edge Slats

Each slat section was operated by twin screwjacks and runs out on curved I-section tracks machined from titanium forgings and guided by rollers mounted on the fixed leading edge structure. Slat 1 (the inboard section) and Slat 2 slide operate on twin tracks, Slat 3 on four tracks, and Slat 4 on three tracks. The tracks themselves and their attachment lugs were designed as safe-life parts, ensuring the reliability and safety of the aircraft. The slat ribs on which the tracks were mounted each comprise two members machined from the plate and bolted back-to-back, which provide full duplication of load paths. The operating jacks pick up on the slats on similar mounting ribs and were attached to the fixed wing structure by safe-life steel gimbals in which stress levels have been kept low.

The slats consist of chemically milled skins reinforced by flanged spars, stiffeners and ribs. Slat 1 had two main spars, while the outboard sections each have a single main spar. The slat spars were heat-resistant material to withstand the thermal effects of anti-icing air whose input temperature was approximately 200 degrees C. Provision was made for the thermal expansion of the slats by swinging links at the attachment points of all slat tracks except the one chosen to locate each slat laterally. Closely-pitched light diaphragms and riblets between the mounting ribs maintain the slat skin shape.

The screwjacks and rollers for the slat tracks were mounted on the fixed leading edge structure behind the slats. The tracks and jacks pass through suitably reinforced holes in this fixed structure, and fuel tank sealing was provided at the points where they pass through the front spar by light titanium cans bolted onto the back of the spar. Access doors beneath track and jack mounting ribs were provided throughout the span.

Trailing-Edge Surfaces

The moving trailing edge surfaces were mainly constructed from skins riveted to spars and ribs. The flap and aileron skins were chemically milled to leave additional thickness along the rivet lines attaching ribs and spars.

Each section of flap was run out on two curved rails machined from steel forgings, which guide rollers mounted in the flap structure. The rails themselves were considered safe life components, but in their attachments to the main wing structure full duplication of load path was provided. The flap structure had three main spars and one intercostal nose spar. The flap vane was mounted on seven blades, projecting forward from the nose of each section of flap, and was a light member of conventional construction having two spars. Deflector plates were positioned in the bottom shroud skin ahead of the flaps, and these were of honeycomb construction approximately 0.750 inches thick. A narrow-chord lift dumper was provided over the span of the inner flap to reduce the total wing lift remaining after touchdown on landing, and thus give earlier wheel adhesion to the runway for braking. It was simple single-cell plate structure.

A spoiler/airbrake was situated forward of the outer section of flap. This component, built of plate and pressings, had four spars, and was designed to increase drag and reduce lift, aiding in the aircraft's descent and landing.

The ailerons were single-cell structures of orthodox construction, attached to the wing by six hinges on each surface.

Fuselage

The fuselage of the Trident comprises a pressure shell extending back to the side engines, and a tail fuselage which was designed to carry the engines, fin and tailplane.

The pressure shell was designed to work at a normal operating pressure of eight to twenty-five pounds per square inch. It contains the flight compartment and passenger cabin above the floor, and below floor level there were the forward equipment bay, and forward and rear freight holds.

There were unpressurized cutouts for the nose landing gear, wing centre section, main landing gear wheel wells, and centre extension tank. The extreme nose of the fuselage was formed by a fibreglass radome which was partly solid laminate, partly honeycomb, and which houses the weather search radar. Between the radome and the front pressure bulkhead there was a very short section of orthodox built-up structure.

The doors in the pressure shell were all of the inward opening plug type and comprise: two passenger entry doors on the left side of the fuselage forward of the wing, an emergency exit on the right side of the fuselage forward of the

Redux bonding was extensively used in the DH.121 Trident airframe to reduce riveting hole stress concentrations in the attachment of reinforcing members to skins and to give a reliable, easily repaired structure.
[Photographs courtesy of British Aerospace Hatfield]

wing, a forward freight hold door and a rear freight hold door. In addition to these doors two Type 3 emergency exits were provided on each side of the fuselage over the wings.

The fuselage pressure shell was a semi-monocoque structure of circular cross-section. It was twelve feet one and a half inches outside diameter. The skins have a minimum thickness of 18 s.w.g. (Standard Wire Guage for the non-engineet, or 0.048 inches) and were stiffened by hat section stringers at an average pitch of six and a half inches with 'Z' section frames at an approximately twenty-inch pitch. Redux bonding was used to attach stringers to skins throughout the pressure shell. There were no stringers in the nose section of the fuselage.

Windows of a modified elliptical shape were positioned between the frames in the passenger cabin, at twenty-inch pitch, so that passengers will have an adequate view whatever seating pitch was used. There were no structural bulkheads in the passenger cabin, thus giving the operator maximum flexibility of interior layout.

Cutouts in the Pressure Shell

The reinforcings around all cutouts were designed to achieve a satisfactory life free from fatigue cracks under repeated pressure loading, and have a static strength factor of at least three, as compared with the Airworthiness Registration Board's (ARB) minimum allowable factor of two, so that at normal operating pressure working stresses were kept low. The structure, in addition to the skin, had also been designed to fail-safe requirements and was capable of carrying operating pressure loads should failure of the skin panel occur due to damage.

Various types of reinforcing were employed around cutouts. In an area where there was a large cutout such as an entry or luggage bay door, the cutout was made in a thick one-piece panel to which the door pan and additional structure were riveted, and which was then inserted in the pressure shell and riveted to the adjacent skin panels. The thickness of the insert panel was reduced by chemical milling away from regions of high stress.

This type of reinforcing had the additional advantage that in the event of severe damage to the edge of the door, the entire panel could be removed and replaced without the necessity to cut through adjacent fuselage structure.

Above the wing centre section, the escape hatch and window cutouts were reinforced by an additional inner machined panel riveted to the inside of the outer skin, to which the window pans were Reduxed. Over the remaining parallel portion of the fuselage, cabin windows were reinforced by a Reduxed doubler inside the skin, to which was riveted a local reinforcing plate and Reduxed window pan assembly.

In the double curvature region of the rear fuselage, a thick side panel was provided to which the local reinforcing plate and window pan assembly was riveted. The skin panel was chemically milled away from the cutout region.

It was standard practice to treat all surfaces which have been either chemically or mechanically milled by 'Vacu' or 'Vapour' blasting, the fatigue strength of the component being thereby maintained.

Canopy

The canopy enclosing the flight compartment exemplified the practice with regard to cutouts and was designed throughout to a strength factor of three. The main canopy transparencies by Triplex Safety Glass Co. Ltd. were four-ply laminations of glass and vinyl, and the three centre panels were maintained free of ice by an electrically-heated gold film sintered on the inner face of the exterior lamination. The remaining transparencies have similar electrical heating.

The strength of the windshield had been established by ground testing for resistance to damage by bird impact. A complete canopy specimen was mounted on a carriage and accelerated to speeds of over 400 m.p.h. in a series of test runs, so that each panel in turn struck a stationary suspended bird carcass weighing four pounds.

The canopy structure comprises two large 9 s.w.g. (0.144 inch) chemical milled skin panels drop-hammered to shape, joined along the centre line of the fuselage and extending down below the level of the cockpit coaming.

There were two horseshoe-shaped rails extending around the cockpit above and below the windows, radial stiffeners in the roof which join on to window pillars, horseshoe-shaped frames below the windows and a tie bar across the fuselage forward of the instrument panel. Angle sectioned steel window pans were riveted to the skin around each window, and adjacent vertical flanges of the pans were riveted to a 'V' section steel member to form, with the skin, a composite window pillar. If the skin component of the pillar should fail, the remaining members could sustain at least 1.33 times the normal working load without failing.

Nose Fuselage

Behind the flight compartment was a short section of fuselage containing the front passenger entry and front emergency exit doors, the nose landing gear bay and in it a provisional bay for airstairs. This section was largely built of thick chemically milled skins, frames and longerons, but without stringers. The nose gear retracts sideways across the fuselage, thus making a transverse cutout in the pressure shell rather than a longitudinal one. The more critical conditions for this part of the fuselage were due to pressurization. Since the stresses due to pressurization were greater in the hoop direction than the longitudinal, reinforcing of a transverse cutout could be provided for a lower total weight than on a longitudinal cutout. A large underfloor forward equipment bay beneath the flight compartment was one of the benefits arising from sideways retraction of the nose gear. Another was that the roof of the nose gear bay forms a convenient unpressurized space where airstairs could be stowed, and could be extended through the side of the fuselage directly below the forward passenger entry door. By making provision to stow the airstairs outside the passenger compartment, this door was left completely unobstructed for use as an emergency exit.

A pressurized tunnel runs through the nose gear bay on the left side which connects the forward freight hold with the forward equipment bay. The forward trunnion for the nose gear was mounted on the tunnel backed by two diaphragms inside the tunnel. The rear trunnion, and a forging to pick up the retraction jack and the sidestay were fitted to the rear bulkhead of the bay.

Main Fuselage

The cylindrical part of the fuselage forward of the wing conforms to the general description of the pressure shell given earlier. Passenger floors throughout the cabin comprise skin panels stiffened by top hat stringers and supported on transverse floor beams at each frame station. In the area of floor over the unpressurized main landing gear wheel bays and A.P.U.bay, the passenger floor was separated from the pressure floor by an air space two-and-a-half inches deep. This air space helps to insulate passengers from direct contact with skin panels exposed to low ambient temperatures.

The centre section of the fuselage was built integrally with the centre section of the wing. The pressurization boundaries are: the front spar, top skin of the wing, extension of the rear spar web above the top skin, the pressure floor over the main landing gear bay and the rear bulkhead of that bay. Heavy spar frames were built above the front and rear spars of the wing, and above the rear pressure bulkhead of the main gear bay.

Duplicated load paths were provided in the frames and in their respective connections to the wing spars. The rear spar frame, for example, comprises two channel section extrusions placed back to back and surmounted by a butt strap. It was connected to the rear spar by two very large fittings machined from plate.

Higher shear loads were developed in the fuselage skin in the region of the wing and the side panels were 14 s.w.g. (0.080 in.) thick between front and rear panels. Two heavy longerons carry bending loads from the rear fuselage across the cutout formed by the main gear wheel bays, and diffuse these loads out into fuselage skin and stringer structure below the wing centre section.

The design of the rear part of the pressure cabin between the wing and the pressure dome was similar to that of the front fuselage. However, due to the greater shears and bending moments that the rear fuselage had to sustain, it was of heavier construction and employs more chemically milled panels, so that greater thickness could be provided locally where required.

Tail Fuselage

The tail fuselage extends rearwards from the end of the passenger compartment, and contains the pressure dome, engine mounting structure, two fin spar bulkheads and the stub fin. To the rear of the dome the fuselage shell comprises 18 s.w.g. skins to which were riveted lipped 'Z' section stringers. Riveting was used throughout the tail fuselage in preference to Reduxing because the complex shape of the skin does not lend itself to economical Redux press tooling.

The fin and tailplane loads were distributed into the tail fuselage by two very stiff fin spar bulkheads, each of which had a large central cutout for the centre intake duct, and also to give access to the rear equipment bay.

The fin had a stub section which was built integrally with the fuselage between the bulkheads. It comprises chemically milled skins, ribs and riveted stringers which collect end loads from stringers in the upper fin and diffuse them out into the fin spar bulkheads, so that at the base of the stub fin all bending loads were taken by these bulkheads.

The upper part of each spar bulkhead was made of two integrally machined panels placed back-to-back, thus providing fail safe duplication of both webs and booms. At other points in the spar bulkheads where it was not practicable to use integral machinings, the booms were duplicated and crack stoppers were Reduxed to the web.

Forward of the stub fin, the fuselage torque box, between the fin front spar bulkhead and the forward engine mounting bulkhead, was closed by a horizontal diaphragm extending between these bulkheads in the upper part of the nacelle of the centre engine intake.

Engine Mountings

One of the advantages of rear mounted engines was that they could be positioned so that the planes of the turbine disks pass behind the pressure cabin and fuel tanks, as was done on the Trident. A burst turbine disk was a very rare occurrence; in twenty million hours of civil experience of Rolls-Royce gas turbine engines there had been only one case of a disk failure - and that in an early series Dart engine. Nevertheless, in spite of the unlikelyhood of turbine disk failure, all possible precautions have been taken to minimize the effects of such a failure, should it occur. Multiple load path structure minimizes the possibility of structural failure.

Each of the cables or pipes of the multiplexed control, hydraulic and electrical systems were separated from other cables or pipes of that system where they pass through the planes of the turbine disks of the side engines, so that a disintegrating disk was unlikely to cause complete failure of three flying control, hydraulic or electrical systems, or sever the fuel lines to both remaining engines. A burst turbine on the centre engine could cause damage only if a fragment passes through the fifteen degree arc which was subtended by fin structure above the engine.

Almost at the rear end of the passenger compartment a large double webbed bulkhead was provided to carry the forward mountings of the side engines and to take re-distribution loads, caused by the change in fuselage cross section, from circular forward of the pressure dome to a double-lobed shape in the tail. The bulkhead was formed by two webs two inches apart. A deep transverse beam across the bulkheadcarries at its extremities the attachments for the forward pair of cantilevered engine mounting beams.

Above this beam there was a very deep stiff arch from the top of which a frame was grown to surround the centre engine air intake. Below the beam the construction was similar to that of a duplicated normal frame.

The bulkhead was fail safe by virtue of duplicated load paths throughout. The pressure dome was built in one unit with the engine mounting bulkheads and was stiffened by a grid of top-hat stringers riveted to the skin in a vertical direction on the forward face, and horizontally on the rear face.

The support structure for the rear pair of cantilever mounting beams for the side engines was formed by a transverse beam of triangular cross section, built on to the sloping face of the front fin spar bulkhead. The beam was built up from plate and booms and was fail safe.

The two pairs of arched cantilever beams, which were bolted on to the extremities of the forward and rear engine mounting beams in the fuselage, were machined from steel forgings and were safe-line components.

The engines were each attached to the airframe at three mounting points. To achieve interchangeability of engines in the three installed positions, five pick-up fittings were provided on each engine. These fittings comprise a trunnion on each side of the inter-compressor casing capable of transmitting load in any direction, two lugs between the trunnions on the upper half of the casing and a rear suspension lug on top of the by-pass casing above the rear bearings of the engine.

On the side engines the attachment points to the front cantilever beam were the inboard trunnion and a single link to one of the lugs on the upper part of the compressor casing. The rear cantilever was bolted at its outer end to the rear suspension lug on the engine. Thrust was transmitted from the engine into the mounting through the front inboard trunnion only. A tubular steel strut carried the forward and reverse thrust loads, from the trunnion, diagonally back into a fitting at the root end of the rear cantilever mounting beam, from which they were diffused forwards into the sfuselage skin by a heavy stringer.

Mountings for the centre engine were cantilevered off the fin rear spar bulkhead, and picked up on both trunnions of the engine and on the rear suspension lug. The trunnions were carried by tubular steel mountings, comprising a tripod on the left and a bipod on the right. A short box constructed of light alloy, titanium and stainless steel extends from the rear fin spar bulkhead over the top of the engine, to carry the attachment to the rear suspension lug. All thrust loads from the centre engine were transmitted into the structure by the trunnions, the rear suspension pick-up being designed to transmit vertical loads only. From the trunnions, the tubular forward mountings transfer the thrust load into horizontal shear diaphragms which then diffuse them out into the fuselage shell.

All engine mountings were designed to withstand forward decelerations of at least 12g in those directions which would allow a less securely mounted engine to enter the passenger compartment.

Fin and Rudder

The requirements of the tailplane pivot design were the upper part of the fin structure. At the upper rear corner of the fin, a heavy steel forging bolted to the fin skins carried the taper roller bearings on which the tailplane pivoted. Concentrated loads from this fitting were diffused into the fin by a fail-safe combination of a thick taper milled skin and a grid of stringers, machined in one piece from a solid billet and then Reduxed on to the skin. The stringers radiate from a thick platform at the pivot fitting and extend in one piece down to the base of the fin.

At the base, they flared out to form part of a multiple load path joint between fin and stub fin. Fin spars had machined booms and webs with Reduxed crack stoppers. Ribs followed wing practice. A chemically milled double-skinned leading edge circulated anti-icing air. Between the rear spar of the fin and the rudder, there was a space in which the three rudder jacks and the yaw dampers were mounted. The three jacks were positioned between four rudder hinges, with two further hinges at the top and bottom. The rudder comprised a single spar and 20 s.w.g. (0.036 inch) skins riveted to close-pitched ribs, but there were no spanwise stringers or stiffeners. The ribs were even more closely pitched at the bottom of the fin as a precaution against noise damage, and mushroom head rivets were used.

Tailplane

At the tailplane's centre was a stiff box with components machined from the thick plate. This precision-engineered box collects the air loads from the tailplane and feeds them as concentrated loads into the tailplane pivot fitting and the three control jack pick-ups at the front end of the box. The precision of this design ensures optimal performance, instilling confidence in the system.

Outboard of this box, the structure was similar to the wing's. There were spars at fifteen per cent and seventy per cent chord. Spar webs have Reduxed crack stoppers at mid-depth. Hat section stringers of 14 s.w.g. material at the root were step-tapered by chemical milling to 20 s.w.g. at the tip. The stringers were Reduxed to skins chemically milled to thicknesses varying in steps from 16 to 20 s.w.g. Plate ribs were used with cutouts to allow the stringers to pass through. A double-skinned leading edge of plain skins, separated by spacers, forms the anti-icing duct.

At the trailing edge of the tailplane, there was a slotted flap, which was geared to move in a fixed relationship to the tailplane by a system of links. The linkage of the flap control system was duplicated to operate left and right flaps separately, providing a high level of redundancy. Torque links interconnect the two flaps, ensuring complete duplication of the load path. This redundancy was a testament to the system's reliability. Each flap had a single spar with skins reinforced by a one-piece Reduxed doubler extending over spar rib and trailing edge boundaries. Attachment to the tailplane was by four hinges on each side, and each surface was mass balanced at its outer end.

Main Landing Gear

The landing gear was conventional, comprising two main load-bearing units and one steerable nose unit. The main gear units had four tyres abreast, as this layout permitted a small turning circle without serious tyre scrubbing, and also paid large dividends with regard to stowage. The main gear legs were twisted through almost ninety degrees and increased in length by six inches during retraction; this affected the neatest stowage of the wheels within the fuselage and gave a track of over nineteen feet. There were no external bulges underneath the fuselage enclosing the landing gear.

The nose gear was hinged at a position offset from the fuselage centreline to allow it to be stowed transversely in the fuselage. The nose gear bay occupied the minimum fuselage length, leaving ample room for a large electrical bay below the floor of the flight compartment. The transverse nose gear bay also had structural advantages and, further, was suitably positioned and large enough to accommodate an air-stairs unit.

The landing gear was hydraulically operated, but had free-fall capability with mechanical backup for emergency operation. Operating times were approximately ten seconds for retraction or

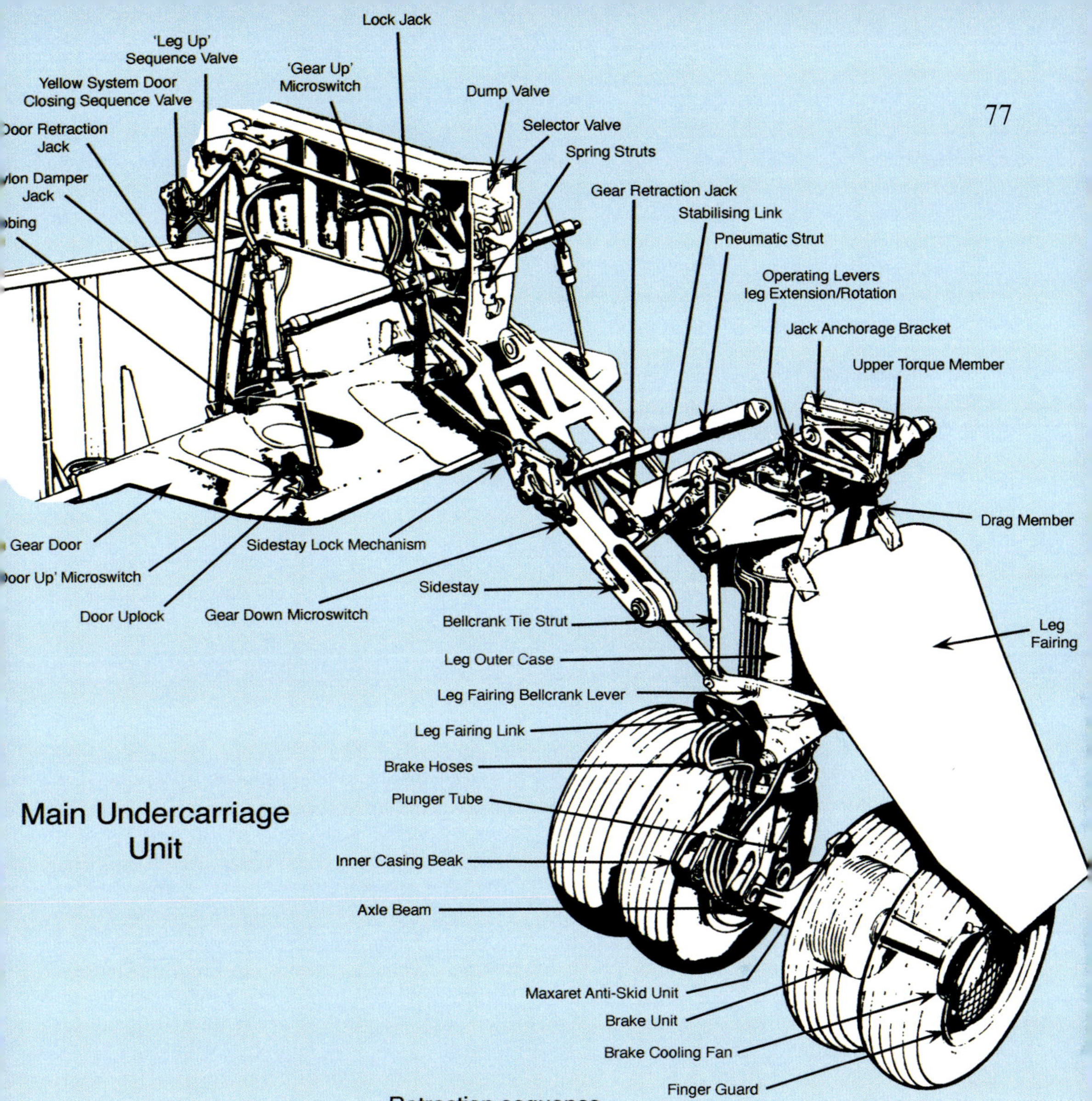

Retraction sequence

extension. The main gear could be extended as an independent air brake at speeds below 300 knots.

Each main gear unit consisted of two twin-tyred wheels, mounted on a common axle which was lever-suspended and linked to an oleo plunger moving in a cylinder. The support structure, locks and operating rams for the door and leg were conventional. An unusual feature of the design was a helical cam mechanism within the top of the leg. Full movement of this cam twisted the oleo unit and hence the wheels through almost ninety degrees, and also changed the length of the leg by six inches.

The cam, in the form of two helical slots, was cut into the inner wall of the two concentric cylinders. A pin, fixed diametrically in the outer cylinder, passed through two rollers running in the slots. Thus, lengthwise movement between the two cylinders caused rotation between them, which was controlled by the pin and rollers in the helical slots.

The outer cylinder formed the outer casing of the main gear leg. The casing was pivoted at its upper end in trunnions forming part of the wing structure, and at its lower end was stabilised by the side stay. The retraction jack operated on the upper end of the casing. The inner cylinder was an integral part of the top of the oleo. Lengthwise movement between the cylinders was actuated by a lever linking the wing structure to a thrust bearing at the top of the inner cylinder and only occurred during extension or retraction of the leg.

At the final stage of extension, the inner cylinder engaged a Curvic coupling; all vertical and torsional loads imposed on the extended leg were carried by this coupling, not by the cam mechanism.

The main gear leg outer casings could be interchanged between the left and right wings due to the redundant lugs provided.

Power for the normal operation of the main gear was supplied by the No. 1 (Green) hydraulic system. The operating lever was on the flight compartment central control pedestal. In the retracted position, the wheel axle of each main gear lay parallel to the aircraft longitudinal axis. On selecting 'gear down', the door and leg were released and fell under the control of jacks, which prevented the wheels from fouling the door. A sequencing valve operated when the leg was fully extended and closed the door. A spring-pneumatic strut assisted in locking the leg in the down position. During the latter stages of the extension, the helical cam mechanism twisted the wheels through almost ninety degrees; this shortened the leg by six inches, and the Curvic coupling was engaged in the final part of the movement.

On selecting 'gear', the door opened, the leg was retracted, and the door closes. During the early stages of retraction, the helical cam mechanism causes the wheels to twist almost ninety degrees while the leg lengthened by six inches, this set the gear in the correct attitude for stowage.

The choice of the four-tyre-abreast main gear layout was made because design studies show it was superior to a twin-wheel or bogie layout, particularly in reducing fuselage stowage space.

By designing the gear so that in the retracted position the wheel axle lay parallel to the fuselage axis, the frontal envelope presented by the wheels was smaller than that for a corresponding bogie. Consequently, it was possible to enclose the wheels inside the fuselage cross-sectional envelope, without blister fairings. In addition, the length of bay required in the fuselage was thirteen inches less than that for a bogie unit. The pressure floor above the bay was therefore shorter, which effected a saving in structure weight and also releases twenty-eight cubic feet of underfloor volume for inclusion in the rear freight bay. A bonus arising from the mechanism used to twist the wheels was that the length of the leg was increased by six inches during retraction. This allowed the mounting points of each main gear unit to be six inches farther outboard than would otherwise be the case, giving an increase of five per cent in the track without increasing the height of the aircraft above the ground.

If the No. 1 (Green) hydraulic system failed, there were two alternative ways of releasing the main gear so that it fell free. The first enabled a changeover to be made to the No. 2 hydraulic system, while if both No. 1 and No. 2 systems failed, so the gear could be allowed to fall freely after manual selection.

If the leg failed to lock into position with the normal air pressure of 150 pounds per square inch in the pneumatic strut, the pressure could be increased to 800 pounds per square inch from an air bottle supply. The air bottle and its controls were in the rear freight bay. A mechanical gear position indicator in the bay showed when the gear was fully locked down.

Nose Landing Gear

The nose gear was a twin wheel unit with oleo-pneumatic springing and hydraulically powered steering and retraction. An unusual feature of the gear was that it was mounted so that the leg was offset by twenty-four inches from the centre line of the fuselage, and retracted sideways into a transverse slot in the fuselage shell.

The twin nose wheels were splined onto an axle which revolves in bearings in the axle barrel. This axle had shoulders between the bearings so that if the axle fails only one wheel was lost. The nose gear is conventional in its system of oleo springing and steering. A baulk prevents the tow-bar being connected until the torque linkage to the steering jack was disconnected. There was then no limitation on the towing angle.

Extension and retraction of the nose gear was normally powered by the No. 1 (Green) hydraulic system, selected by the same lever which operates the main gear. The door was sequenced to close in the last stages of leg retraction, whilst in the case of extension, the rate of fall of the leg was controlled to prevent it fouling the door. A spring strut assisted in locking the leg into position.

An emergency lever manually released the leg up-lock and relieved all nose gear hydraulic pressure. The door fell open, the leg fell free and the spring strut locked the gear into position. If the

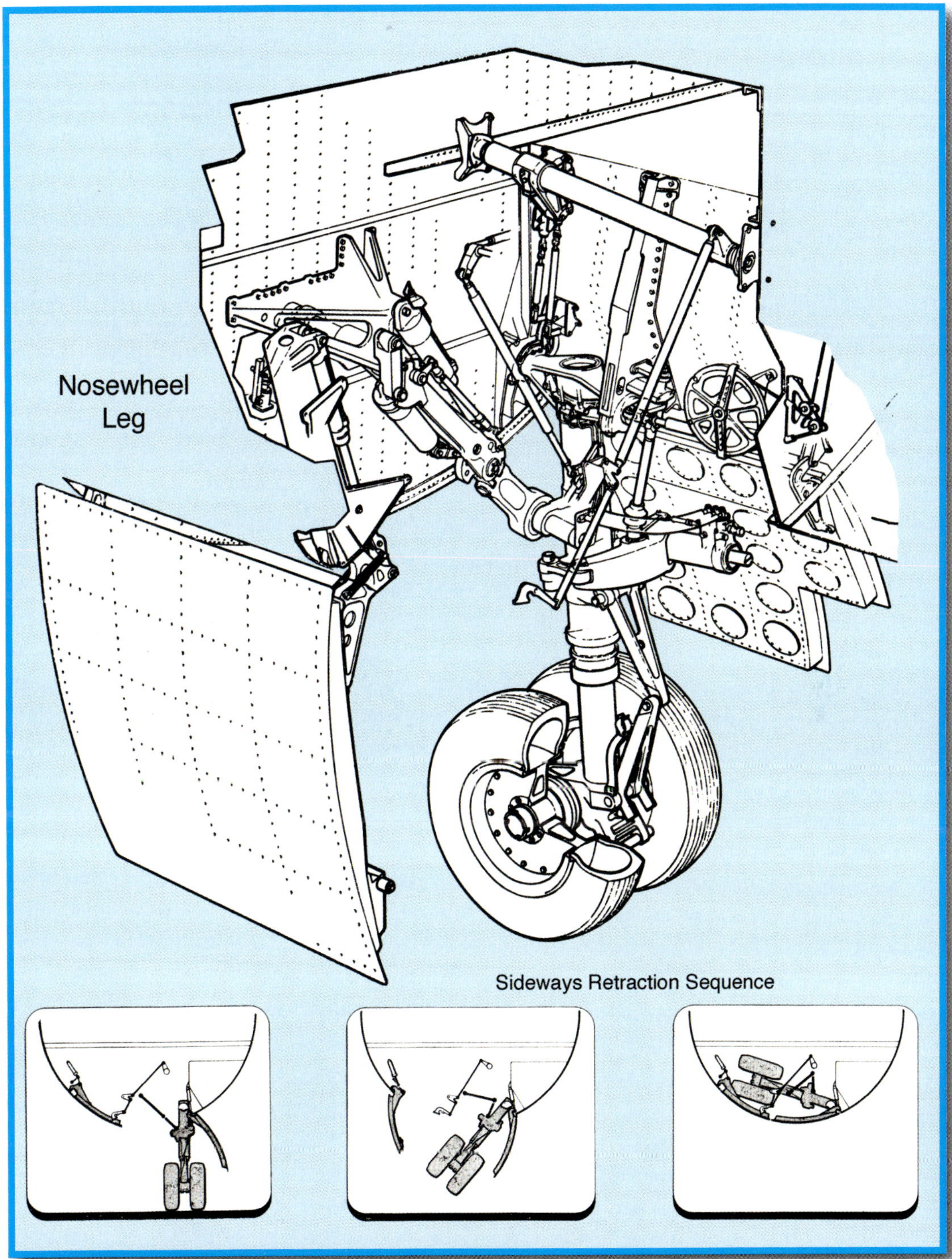

Dangling the Dunlops! A series of pictures showing the undercarriage of the Trident, with the offset nosweheel in prominence. The red-painted underside of the wings of the BEA scheme is also noticable.
[Photographs courtesy of British Aerospace Hatfield]

free fall was incomplete, the leg could be wound down by a screw jack located in the equipment bay to the rear of the nose gear bay. Access was through a hatch in the floor.

The minimum radius of turn was the same when turning left or right, compensation for the offset nose gear being made by limiting the angular travel to sixty-four degrees to the left and sixty-two degrees to the right. The steering was powered by a jack mounted on the nose leg, and controlled from the flight compartment by steering wheels at both pilots' positions. The steering was self-centring and incorporated a spring strut to absorb control movement not immediately acceptable to the steering jack.

As with the main gear, the choice of an unusual type of nose gear was made for several good reasons. On orthodox gear which retracted into a longitudinal slot in the fuselage, the small segments of underfloor space which were formed on each side of the slot were wasted from the viewpoint of equipment or freight, because of the difficulty of access. By retracting the gear sideways into a transverse slot, as on the Trident, only three feet of fuselage length was taken up, which leaving ample space for a large electrical bay below the floor of the flight compartment. The transverse slot saved weight by requiring less reinforcing than its longitudinal counterpart.

Other advantages have resulted from locating the transverse nose gear bay directly beneath the forward passenger door. The two frames which diffuse loads from the nose gear into the fuselage also serve as edge members for the passenger door cut-out, giving further weight economy. Also, the roof of the bay can be used to stow the airstairs; this avoids encroaching on valuable cabin space and leaves the doorway clear for use as an emergency exit.

Having decided to adopt sideways retraction of the gear, it was necessary to offset the leg by twenty-four inches from the centre line of the fuselage, in order to achieve enclosure within the boundaries of the underfloor cross-section. The offset had no adverse effects.

A simple lever controlled the landing gear and incorporates a solenoid baulk, connected to weight switches in the main gear to prevent 'gear up' selection while the aircraft was on the ground. A trip lever was provided; however, to cut out the solenoid, the baulk should be switched in if the gear fails to operate after take-off.

A switch on the control pedestal adjacent to the airbrake selector lever allowed the pilot to extend the main landing gear as a second-stage airbrake without extending the nose gear.

In conjunction with thrust reversers on the side engines, large fan-cooled Dunlop multiple-disk brake units on each main gear wheel provided powerful, progressive braking. The normal braking system, using No. 2 (Yellow) hydraulic system, operated five brake cylinders on each main wheel, controlled through Maxaret anti-skid units. A completely separate braking system using No. 1 (Green) hydraulic system and an independent set of brake cylinders provided back-up, but operated without anti-skid protection.

The No. 1 (Green) hydraulic system incorporated an accumulator, which was dedicated solely to the brake circuit and stored sufficient energy to provide six full brake applications. For towing and parking, Green system fluid was used, and the accumulator was kept charged by a small d.c. electrically driven pump operated from the aircraft battery. In an emergency landing without engine power, the accumulator was provided

adequate braking, but without anti-skid protection.

The brakes were toe-operated by rocking the rudder pedals. Selection of normal or emergency braking was controlled by a three-position lever mounted on the throttle pedestal. In the forward normal position, the lever selected the Yellow hydraulic system. The centre position selected the Green hydraulic system. To apply the parking brakes, the lever was moved fully rearwards.

Auxiliary Power Plant

The auxiliary power unit (APU) was mounted in the extreme tail of the fuselage, a unique design that showcased the aircraft's complex structure. It was carried by a tubular mounting supported on the centre engine mounting box and cowling structure.

The jet pipe and its fairing were cantilevered aft from the APU itself. Deflector plates in the jet pipe direct the efflux upwards and away from the tail unit.

The auxiliary power unit in the Trident 1, the first civil airliner to use a British APU, was a Bristol Siddeley Artouste 514 installed just behind the rear spar in the ventral fuselage between the main landing gear wheel bays. In the Trident IE, the auxiliary power unit was relocated behind the centre engine support box at the rear of the fin spar bulkhead between the centre engine and the rudder. This repositioning was primarily driven by several drawbacks associated with the ventral fuselage location. The noise level from the APU was higher than anticipated, and hot exhaust gases were being ejected into the vicinity of ground crews.

The Artouste 514 APU was fitted to the Trident .1 and 1C, while the Trident IE had the Bristol Siddeley Artouste 520. The engines were

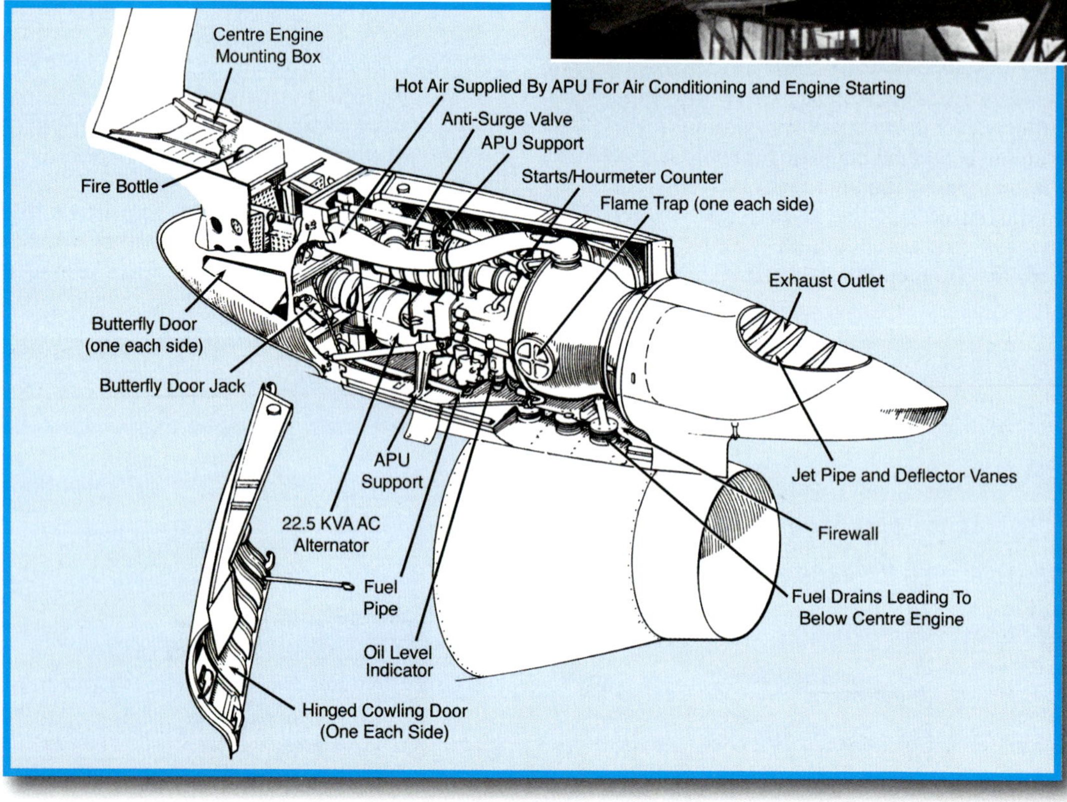

Above: Under the tail of the Trident was the rear equipment bay, with built-in steps, giving easy access to hydraulic services, ground intercom and air charging points.

Previous page: The Bristol Siddeley Turbomeca Artouste auxiliary power unit, made the Trident independent of ground power sources. The aft mounting resulted in low noise level and the exhaust is well away from the passenger and freight doors. *[Photographs courtesy of British Aerospace Hatfield]*

essentially similar with minor differences in intake, exhaust and accessories. The following description applies to the Artouste 520 in the Trident 1E.

The main requirements of an airborne APU for airline service were reliability, dependability, safety, low installed weight, ease of maintenance and low cost. Fuel consumption was not of major importance, as the amount consumed was small compared with the main engines' demands. The Artouste 520 installed in the Trident IE gives the aircraft complete independence from external ground power sources, particularly important for an aircraft intended for short-to-medium-haul operations from smaller airports. The Artouste was a gas turbine engine comprising a single-stage centrifugal compressor driven by a two-stage axial turbine and an annular combustion chamber with centrifugal fuel injection. Compressed air for aircraft services was bled from the combustion chamber casing, and an auxiliary gearbox was provided for an a.c. generator. The Artouste 520 could deliver 120 pounds per minute while driving a generator to provide 22.5 kVA of electrical power.

The APU was started from the aircraft's internal battery and provided three services normally obtained from a ground unit, namely: (i) the supply of low-pressure air for main engine starting, (ii) the supply of air for cabin air conditioning, and (iii) the supply of electrical power, from which the hydraulic system could also be operated.

Fuel for the APU was fed from the inboard right wing tank via a 28-volt d.c. booster pump and was selected by a solenoid-operated valve, controlled from the flight compartment APU panel.

Three attachment points, one above the engine and one on either side, support the APU. The right side-mount carries loads in all directions: the left-side mount vertical and horizontal loads, and the top-mount horizontal loads. A removable tray fits under the engine.

To install or remove the APU, a simple gantry was used in conjunction with a mini hoist. The gantry consists of an I-beam and two tubular side supports. Once the APU had been raised by the mini-hoist, it was swung through ninety degrees connected to the I-beam trolley, released from the mini-hoist cable and then slid into position, the I-beam acting as a support rail until the unit was secured by its mounting pins. It was estimated that complete removal and replacement of the APU would take one hour.

The APU change unit weighs 460 pounds. The intakes were at the base of the fin and consist of two butterfly doors in the blister fairings, on either side of the centre engine mounting box. These doors were spring-loaded in the open position and will only close when the compressed air jacks, one of which was connected to each door, were supplied with high-pressure air bleed from the main engines. A solenoid valve in the bleed air supply to these jacks prevents this from happening when the APU was switched on. Air was drawn from the blister fairings through flanged holes in the sides of the centre engine mounting box. The rear of this box serves as a plenum chamber. Two silenced bell-mouth intakes then feed the air into the twin silenced APU intake ducts. The plenum chamber had silencing pads in the centre and on the front and side walls. Cooling air for the alternator was taken from the forward part of the centre engine mounting box.

A microswitch on the main gear leg cuts off the electrical supply to the APU, which in turn cuts off the fuel supply whenever the oleo was not compressed, and thus stops the unit should the aircraft take off with the APU still running.

The exhaust outlet was in the topside of the rear cone of the APU 'bullet'. Deflector vanes in the exhaust pipe direct the jet noise and fumes rearwards and upwards away from the ground.

Controls for the APU include a flight compartment control panel and an APU cut-out switch at the refuelling control panel and an instrumentation and control panel in the rear equipment bay with overheat, fuel flow over-temperature and over-speed indicators, a governed speed switch, jet pipe temperature gauge, oil pressure gauge, oil level gauge, r.p.m gauge and emergency stop switch. In addition, instrumentation mounted on the APU itself recorded the number of starts and the number of hours ran.

A fire warning system using Graviner Firewire was provided. A single shot two pound BCF fire bottle (non-toxic) linked to switches on the APU panels in the flight compartment and equipment bay was provided for fire extinguishing.

The hot part of the unit (combustion and turbine casing) was encased in a flameproof canister which was ventilated by the suction of the exhaust, the air being drawn in from the space around the APU, thus providing a flow of cooling and ventilating air. The two intakes to this canister were fitted with flame traps to prevent flames from a blow-back getting into or beyond the area around the APU. The normal operating temperature between the APU and the fairing was forty degrees Celsius.

The 22.5 kVA a.c. generator, identical to the main unit ran through a gearbox on the front of the APU. Another gearbox drives the accessories for the unit itself, i.e. fuel pump, oil pump, centrifugal switch and tachometer generator.

Fuel System

The Trident 1E fuel system, designed to operate on either kerosene or JP-4, had a straightforward layout with few controls. Five integral tanks, comprising four in the wings and one in the centre section, gave a total of 5,880 Imperial gallons, of which 2,000 Imperial gallons were contained in the centre tank. (Total fuel capacity of the Trident 1C was 4,960 Imperial gallons, with 1,160 Imperial gallons in the centre tank.) Each wing's inner tank had slightly more than twice the capacity of the outer.

Independent feed arrangements were such that each inner tank fed its corresponding side engine, and both outer tanks together feed the centre engine. This configuration, once established for takeoff, was maintained throughout short flights and during the latter part of long flights. On long flights, there would be fuel in the centre tank, which was used exclusively during the early part of the flight.

Common feed was selected by setting the two-position cross-feed valve control to the 'Common' position. The selection of tanks was then made by supply pump switches. A separate on/off ontrol valve permitted the centre tank to be isolated.

A jettison system was available for all Trident variants as an optional extra, since it was not required under British Civil Airworthiness Requirements.

Refuelling and offloading were simplified by a Load Limit Control System, which automatically controlled the operation according to instructions preset on the refuel control panel. Provision was made for overwing refuelling of the inner and outer wing tanks. All tanks, or any one, could be drained completely, or alternatively, fuel transferred from one tank to another, by the power drain system in conjunction with an external hose.

Two independent content gauging systems were fitted: a capacitance system for general use and non-drip magnetic indicators (as used in later versions of the Comet 4 Series) for ground checking. Both systems were substantially free from aircraft attitude errors.

Vent/surge tanks formed part of the venting system and prevented fuel from spilling onto the ground or in flight. All the space between the wing spars, inboard of Rib 19, was used for tankage. A centre-section tank was formed between the wing root ribs, with a 400 Imperial gallon extension behind the rear spar, and each wing was subdivided into an inner and outer tank (Ribs 1-8 and 8-19, respectively).

The internal structure divided each tank into a series of anti-surge compartments, with clack valves to maintain one-way flow towards the pumps. To permit fuel levelling, either prior to the use of magnetic level indicators or during overwing refuelling, the clack valves in each inner and outer tank could be opened by a manually-operated trip mechanism.

Each tank contained two electrically-driven centrifugal supply pumps. These were housed in a reservoir, formed by the surrounding structure, which maintained the local fuel level during sudden changes of attitude.

The reservoir for each inner tank was continuously replenished by a jet pump drawing fuel from outside the reservoir and energized from both main pumps, so that loss of any one main pump had no effect on the system. Each inner tank main pump also activated a jet pump, which scavenged fuel from the vent/surge tank and returned it to the inner tank.

Supply pumps each incorporate three hermetically-sealed overheat switches (one in each a.c. phase), any one of which will sever supplies to the pump in the event of overheating. All spanwise wing tank piping was enclosed within the tanks. Pumps were encased in individual isolating chambers and may be changed without draining the tanks.

Isolating valves in the feed lines were unnecessary on wing tanks, as they always contain fuel at the end of a flight. However, an isolating valve was provided for the centre tank to prevent air from being sucked into the fuel system in the highly unlikely event of suction feed only being in operation.

Internal tank surfaces were protected against corrosion by anodic treatment followed by two coats of chromate etch-primer, the tank joints being sealed with a Thiokol-type compound. Water drain points were provided at the lowest points in the tanks. Tank design ensures an extremely small residue of undrained fuel.

Independent feed was from the centre tank or from both outboard tanks to the centre engine, and from each inboard tank to the corresponding side engine. Lateral symmetry was maintained by a simple mechanical proportioner ensuring that equal volumes were drawn from each outboard tank. By-pass valves, incorporated into the proportioner, provide unrestricted flow in the event of mechanical malfunction and permit selection of supplies from an individual outboard tank.

Individual manually-operated low-pressure cocks, one for each engine, one for the cross-feed system and another for the centre tank, control the flow to the engines. The two-position cross-feed cock interconnects all supply lines, permitting selection of independent feed, or, in conjunction with the booster pump switches, any configuration of common supplies. Non-return valves situated in

G-ARPG closest to the camera, with other Trident 1s behind.*[Photographs courtesy of British Aerospace Hatfield]*

the pump outlet lines prevent cross-feeding from one tank to another.

During normal independent feed conditions, the two electrically-driven supply pumps in each tank feed fuel to a mechanically-driven backing pump mounted on each engine, which in turn delivers it to the engine's high-pressure pump. Failure of a single supply pump causes no embarrassment whatsoever. With failure of both supply pumps, engine manufacturer's requirements were fully met up to 6,000 ft. under the most adverse conditions, for example, hot unweathered JP.4 fuel, maximum rate of climb, full take-off power, etc. At altitudes exceeding 6,000 feet, the backing pump still confers a high degree of protection against the adverse conditions mentioned above. For example, no engine malfunction was expected up to 30,000 feet with cool fuel, or up to 20,000 feet with warm fuel, for example, JP-4 at 20 °C. In all flight conditions, other than take-off, the two booster pumps in any one tank can, by themselves, supply the demands of all engines simultaneously. A.c. supplied to the tank pumps were diversified so that the loss of a single busbar affected no more than one pump per tank.

Supplies to the centre engine did not enter the fuselage pressurized section but passed through an external pipe enclosed in a vented fairing running from the right wing root to the engine area. Where side engine feed lines passed beneath the rear cabin floor, they were encased in jointless vented conduits.

Fuel for the auxiliary power unit was taken from the right inner tank via a manually operated isolation valve and an electrically actuated supply valve, and through an external pipe in the right wing root fairing. A self-priming, electrically driven gear pump downstream of the valves ensures that APU pressure requirements were met under all conditions, and also permitted initial priming of a dry system.

The capacitance contents gauging system provided continuous flight compartment indication of all tank contents and also supplied contents information to the refuelling/offloading pre-selector; the latter was electrically independent of the contents gauging system and could in no way impair its functioning. The system was substantially unaffected by aircraft attitude.

The capacitance system comprised several electrically paralleled capacitor units per tank connected to individual tank gauges in the flight compartment.

The magnetic level indicators provided an independent physical check of tank contents on the ground without fuel drip. One indicator in each was provided for the centre and inner tanks. Two indicators were provided for each outer tank, the inboard ones were used for tank contents up to 480 Imperial gallons and the outboard ones for higher fuel contents. All magnetic indicators were so located that aircraft attitude changes have no

The fuel load required was pre-selected at the Refuel Control Panel in the right main gear bay. Intake of fuel was then automatically controlled. *[Photograph courtesy of British Aerospace Hatfield]*

Above: for gravity fuelling four overwing points were provided.

Below: Through two underwing pressure couplings, all tanks could be filled in fifteen minutes. Fueling for a one thousand mile stage took around five minutes. *[Photographs courtesy of British Aerospace Hatfield]*

significant effect on their accuracy. Prior to using magnetic indicators, the fuel levellers had to be operated.

A water injection system was designed to restore full take-off thrust in high ambient temperatures, and could be fitted as an optional extra for operators who fly regularly under particularly adverse conditions of airfield altitude and temperature.

Operation of the system was fully automatic after initial selection by the pilot, and the design of the system was such that failure of one engine had no adverse effect on the operation of the other engines.

Water was fed by gravity from a 145 Imperial gallon water tank in the stub fin to an air-driven turbine pump, which delivers water to the engines. Comprehensive instrumentation and safety devices were fitted, and well-proven components were used.

An accurate one-sixth scale model wing was used to confirm certain vent system and fuel transfer design principles. The model was also used in conjunction with a digital computer to develop the capacitance gauging system so that it was substantially unaffected by changes in aircraft attitude. The compactness and manoeuvrability of the model permitted the simulation of a comprehensive range of aircraft attitudes and altitudes, both inside and outside the company's high altitude test chamber.

Electrical System

The electrical power installation comprised a primary 115/200 volts, 400 c.p.s. three-phase, constant frequency a.c. system, obtained from the outputs of three a.c. generators, and a nominal 28-volt d.c. system derived from the primary system. Both systems fed multiple distribution bus-bars and utilized the aircraft structure as neutral or earth return.

The complete installation, from generators to distribution bus-bars, was designed to function as three isolated electrical channels, thus providing three independent sources of supply to preserve the integrity of a triplex autopilot system, eventually to be incorporated as a fully automatic landing feature. Special attention was paid to safety requirements in that the circuits were designed to 'fail safe', and the layout of the electrical installation, both physically and electrically, ensures that no single fault could affect more than one electrical channel.

Constant frequency a.c. systems, in comparison with d.c. and frequency-wild systems, had many advantages, among which were a far higher degree of reliability, a more efficient power transmission and a considerable weight saving in electrical components and cabling. The latter point was emphasised when comparing the weight of the Trident electrical installation with that of the Comet 4B. Although a direct comparison was not possible, it was significant that the equipment on the Trident weighs 750 pounds less, yet the power output was increased by 12 kVA. The improved transmission efficiency and reduction in cable weight was of paramount importance in the Trident, where the generators were installed on the engines at the rear of the aircraft, and the control and distribution components were in the nose.

A great advantage of constant frequency a.c. was that it permits the use of squirrel-cage induction motors. These had no brushes or electrical connections between rotor and stator, and thus, the problems associated with brush gear were eliminated.

The A.E.I. generators, installed one per engine, were driven by Hobson constant speed drive units (CSDs) and give a maximum continuous power output of 67-5 kVA with a five-minute overload rating of 100 kVA. The constant-speed drive units maintaied the generator speed at 8,000 r.p.m.,+/- one per cent above engine speed, varying from ground idling to maximum take-off r.p.m. under steady-state conditions. During transient conditions of load and speed change, the variation does not exceed fifteen per cent.

The aircraft electrical loads were divided between the a.c. and d.c. distribution bus-bars in such a manner that the loss of one a.c. bus-bar or one d.c. The bus-bar would not significantly affect aircraft services. Additionally, in the event of one channel sustaining a generator or constant speed unit malfunction, switching arrangements were included to re-allocate the bus-bars equally between the two remaining serviceable generators. The No. 2 a.c. bus-bar was split to assist this aim.

In the extremely unlikely event of complete failure of all three generators, both a.c. and d.c. bus-bars could be supplied from a 24-volt 25 Ah lead-acid battery. The a.c. bus-bar fed from the d.c bus-bar via a static inverter, the output of which was a single phase, 115 volts, 400 c/s supply, rated at 400 continuous. The battery was capable of maintaining the a.c. and d.c. vital services for a period exceeding thirty minutes. This was where the battery efficiency was eighty-five per cent.

An auxiliary power unit was installed as standard equipment in the aircraft to provide complete independence, if desired, from external ground power sources. The APU was equipped with a power-generating system similar to the main generating systems, the generators and control units being interchangeable; the aircraft thus carries its own spares. The APU also supplied cabin air conditioning and engine-starting air.

To enable the aircraft services to be operated from a.c. or d.c. ground supplies, two external supply plugs were fitted in the nose of the fuselage.

The APU generator and the a.c. ground supply was controlled by static control units in conjunction with control contactors; the contactors were electrically interlocked so that only one could operate at a time.

The a.c. and d.c. bus-bars were contained in the main distribution panel together with associated fuse and circuit breaker sub-panels. The fuse-holders were of the self-indicating type, having an

In the foreground is a nose and front fuselage section, awaiting further assembly to the centre section and rear.
[Photograph courtesy of British Aerospace Hatfield]

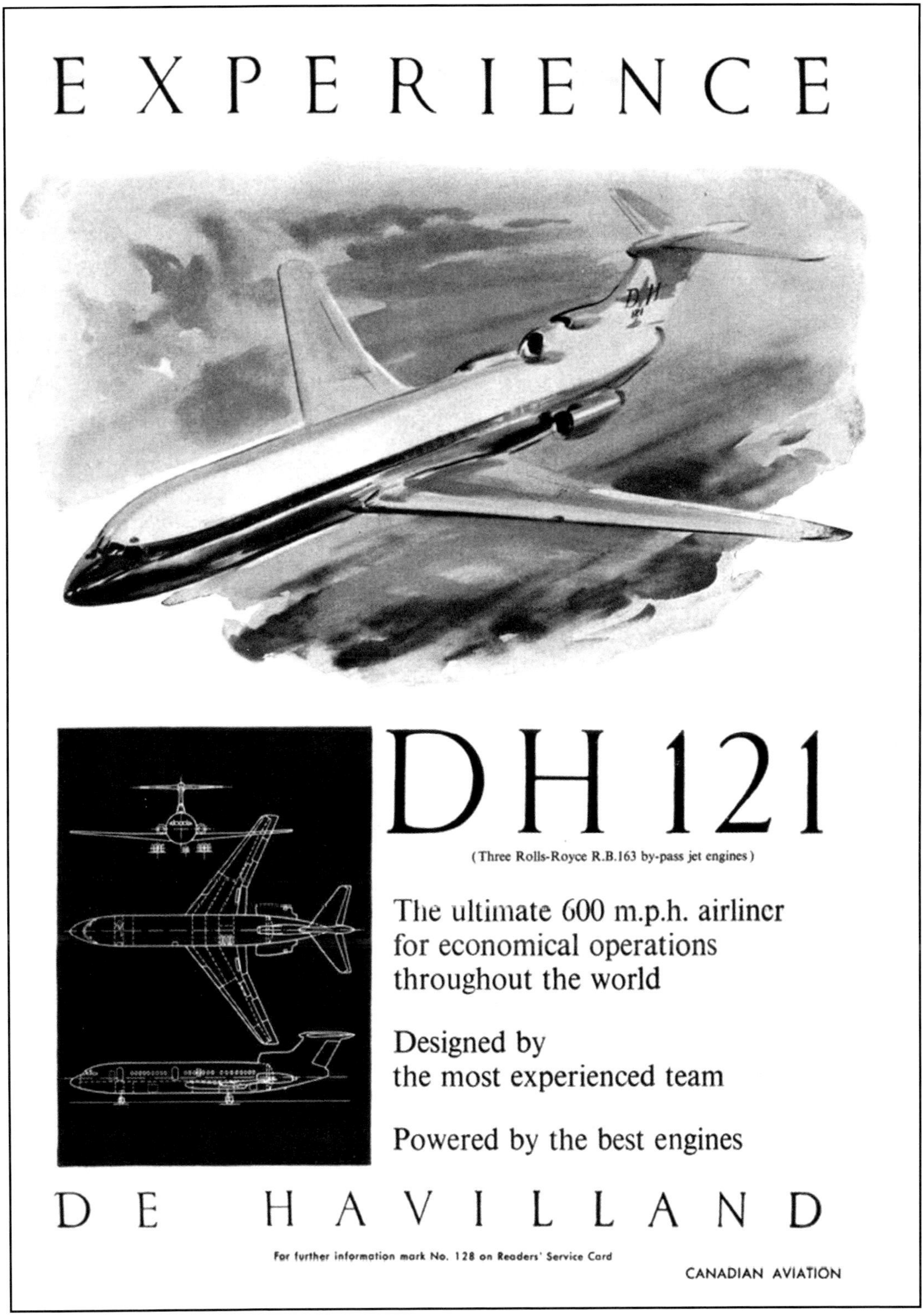

A De Havilland Canada advert for the embrionic Trident, again with the DH.121 on the fin.
[De Havilland Aircraft Co.]

integral lamp which lit up when the fuse was blown. The thermal circuit breakers, supplied by AEI, could be operated manually to make or break a circuit by the operation of a single trip /reset button and were 'trip-free'. Three-phase a.c. thermal circuit breakers with a single trip /reset button give short-circuit and overload protection. This type of circuit breaker opened all three phases simultaneously.

The AEI generators were brushless, blast air-cooled machines embodying integral d.c. exciters. Built-in permanent magnets provide the initial excitation flux for the exciter rotor, the windings of which were in series with a silicon diode rectifier bridge and the generator field windings. The a.c. output induced in the stator windings by the rotating field was subsequently rectified and fed back to the exciter field windings to increase the excitation flux and thus the build-up of generator voltage.

The rotor bearings of the generators were lubricated with oil fed from the engine, thus prolonging their service life. A bearing life of 3,000 hours was anticipated with an eventual generator overhaul period of 5,000 hours.

The generators were cooled by ram air in flight and by engine-bleed-induced air during ground running, so that full power could be taken under either condition. A mercury switch incorporated in each generator casing operated to light an associated warning lamp if the stator internal temperature exceeded 172-178 degrees Celsius.

The Hobson constant speed drive units (CSDs) were hydro-mechanical units mounted on each engine wheel case and driven by the engine auxiliary drive. The drive was coupled to the CSD and transmitted via two differential gear trains and a variable ratio hydrostatic fluid power transmission to drive an output shaft at a constant speed of 8,000 r.p.m.; the output shaft was in turn coupled to the generator drive.

The use of the differential gearing system allowed the greater proportion of the power to be transmitted mechanically. The maximum proportion of power transmitted hydraulically was twenty per cent, which occurred at a point in the centre of the engine speed range, but under cruise conditions was only ten per cent. This allowed a low working pressure of five hundred pounds per square inch at cruise, without incurring excessive rates of fluid flow, thus retaining the quiet, smooth operation normal to low-pressure hydraulic systems. Additionally, within the engine's normal cruising r.p.m. range, the pump of the hydraulic system unloaded and idles at a working pressure of fifty pounds per square inch. These features promote a high standard of reliability and permit an overhaul life of 2,000 hours.

Hydraulic System

There were many reasons for the choice of a fully-powered flying control system for the Trident, not the least of which was the experience on the Comet. On a powered flying control system, it was necessary, for safety reasons, to have two complete hydraulic systems operating the power control jacks, with one or more backup systems. This arrangement was used on the Comet, and if one system fails, the pilot changes over to the other. Experience of such an arrangement, which was by no means unsatisfactory, led to the conclusion that it would be simpler on the Trident to fit an additional complete system and to make all three systems work together, thus eliminating the need for pilot change-over from one system to another in the case of a failure.

This idea of using three hydraulic systems

The Dowty drop-out Ram Air Turbine which provided emergency hydraulic power during flight in the enevent of a complete engine failure.
[Photograph courtesy of British Aerospace Hatfield]

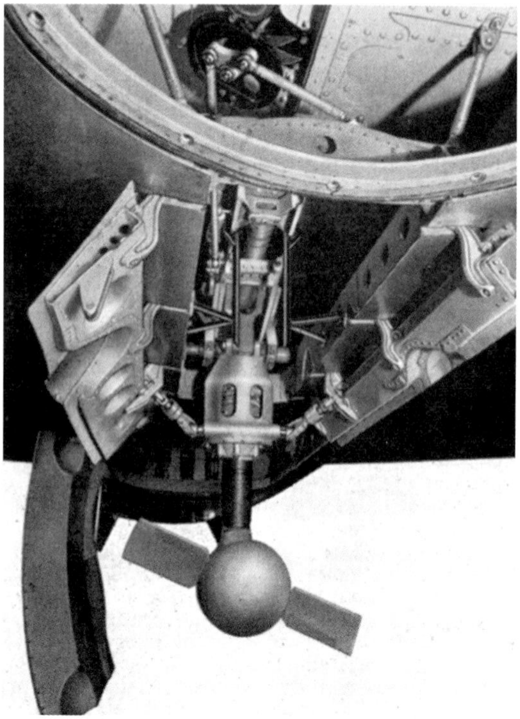

Something of a mystery picture. Clearly a Trident, but one with a number '2' on the radar nose. The ground handler giving the pilot the 'thumbs up' is also unusual, for he should be showing him the ground locking pin for the nosewheel to demonstrate that it has been removed. A press photo perhaps? *[De Havilland Aircraft Co.]*

working in unison - a triplex system - was further sustained by the three-engined layout of the aircraft, whereby the basic sources of hydraulic power could be independently provided by a pump on each of the three engines. A triplex system, i.e. three separate sub-systems working continuously together - each complete in itself with its own pump, reservoir, lines, valves and jacks - differed fundamentally from a triplicated system, in which only one of the separate power sources was working at any one time. It was chosen before automatic landing was considered for the Trident, and thought to be the most satisfactory and elegant arrangement for powered control operation, whether or not automatic landing equipment was going to be fitted.

On the Trident, if one system fails, the two remaining systems provide full control throughout the flight envelope, making the arrangement inherently fail-safe. If any two systems fail, the remaining system provides adequate power for all normal manoeuvres, including landing. Back-up was provided by two electrically driven pumps and one air turbine-driven pump, which could feed any one of the three systems. Operation of general services was confined to two systems. One of these operates the service normally, with a secondary system available in case of failure.

The systems use Monsanto Skydrol 500A fluid, chosen for its reduced fire risk and its worldwide availability. A system pressure of 3,000 lb./sq. in. was used as a compromise to permit the use of relatively small-sized components without the sealing problems associated with higher pressures. The selected pressure also results in longer fatigue lives and overhaul periods than components operating at higher pressures. All the systems were self-bleeding, except the wheel brakes, for which bleed points were provided.

All the hydraulic components were located outside the pressure cabin, the majority behind the rear pressure dome, and most of the remainder in the main and nose landing gear wells and beneath the centre section fuel tank. Hydraulic jacks were situated adjacent to the surface they operate, and windscreen wiper components were forward of the front pressure bulkhead.

Stainless steel tubing was used for both pressure and return lines, except for some return lines having no transient pressures, where, to save

The bare bones of a Trident - the interior without all the trimmings. *[De Havilland Aircraft Co.]*

The Trident had 700 cubic feet of underfloor freight space. The forward hold (425 cubic feet) was loaded on the right side of the aircraft, the rear hold on the left. Both holds had upward hinging plug-type doors, easily operated by one man.
[Photographs courtesy of British Aerospace Hatfield]

weight, light alloy tubing was used. The type of steel chosen has good flaring qualities, and extremely close inspection control was maintained, thus virtually eliminating the possibility of splitting due to internal scores coinciding with flares and bends. Banjo-type connections were not used, as they have been found to be prone to fatigue and seal failure. For reliability, flexible hoses were used in preference to swivel couplings wherever possible. Pipes through the pressure cabin were routed behind the freight bay walls, their connections being either contained by structure or boxed in and vented overboard.

Self-sealing disconnect points were employed at the connections to the engine-driven pumps and also at ground test and reservoir fill/drain points. Particular attention was paid to the design of the systems to ensure accessibility of connections and ease of removal of components for overhaul. Components were tested and developed to provide overhaul lives of not less than 3,000 flying hours. The design aim was to achieve fatigue lives of components, pipes, and pipe couplings of at least 30,000 flying hours.

The power supplies required to operate the aircraft's hydraulic systems were as follows. Three pumps were engine-driven, each pressurising one of the three simple and completely independent main systems, coded No. 1 (Green), No. 2 (Yellow), and No. 3 (Blue). These pumps were driven by No. 1 (Left), No. 2 (Centre) and No. 3 (Right) engines respectively. Two other pumps provided a standby power source should any of the three main pumps fail. These two pumps were electrically driven by individual a.c. motors and were normally used for ground testing of all hydraulic services on the aircraft. A further pump, also electrically driven, by a d.c. motor provided a second standby supply to the wheel brakes and power for towing and parking. Finally, a drop-out air-turbine pump provided another source of power for any one of the three main systems in the unlikely event of the stoppage of all engines. The three main systems, although completely separate and independent, had basically similar power circuits. For descriptive purposes, therefore, they may be considered together.

Each system incorporated its own reservoir, containing one to eight Imperial gallons of fluid. These reservoirs were located in the rear equipment bay outside the pressure cabin and were therefore pressurised to prevent aeration of the fluid causing cavitation at the pump. The air for this reservoir pressurisation was tapped from the high-pressure air supply from each of the three engines, with a further tapping being taken from the APU air supply for the initial period prior to engine starting. All air was reduced to 25-35 pounds per square inch before entering the reservoir through a filter and a non-return valve, both inward and outward relief valves being incorporated on the reservoir. For maintenance purposes, the inward relief valve could be manually depressed to release residual air pressure.

Each reservoir contained a fluid-level sight-glass as well as transmitters for flight compartment indication of fluid contents and temperature. The reservoir could be pressure-filled with hydraulic fluid through a self-sealing coupling, which also served as a drain point.

Fluid from the bottom of the reservoir passed through a suction filter, where it was filtered to ten microns before entering the suction side of the engine-driven pump. These were of the variable-displacement, constant-pressure type and could supply approximately sixteen and a half gallons per minute at cruise conditions.

Pressure fluid from the engine-driven pump was filtered down to five microns through a pressure filter, which incorporated a tell-tale indicator to show the presence of any blockage. A tapping from the line downstream of the pressure filter fed a full-flow relief valve, which limited system pressure to 3,500 pounds per square inch should a fault in the engine-driven pumps cause it to go to full stroke. The valve, in this case, will open to relieve fluid pressure back to the reservoir and will reseat at 3,150 pounds per square inch.

Fluid from the outlet of the pressure filter passed through the power on-off valve and out to the various components of the system. A tapping in the line downstream of the power on-off valve led to the system accumulator. Four such accumulators were installed, one for each of the three main systems and a fourth reserved purely for the wheel brakes. Each accumulator incorporated a pressure gauge and an air charging connection and initially inflated with air to 950 - l, 000 pounds per square inch.

Each power-on/off valve was controlled by one of the three levers in the flight compartment roof above the pilots, and when operated to shut down the system, it connectsed the system and accumulator pressure lines back to the reservoir.

The lever incorporated a warning lamp which lights if a jack actuating a flying control surface suffers a stuck input valve, or the hydraulic fluid temperature rises above 90 degrees Celcius approximately, or the hydraulic fluid pressure drops to 1,250 pounds per square inch.

The warning was repeated on the relevant section of the Central Warning System panel and also at the Caution/Alert flashing lights. Movement of the control lever to shut down the faulty system automatically cancelled the warning light in the lever, except in the case of a stuck valve.

Fluid for the electrically powered standby system was taken from any one of the three main system reservoirs through tall stack-pipes, thus ensuring that any fluid loss in the Standby system could exhaust the fluid supplies for the main systems. The Standby system fluid from each reservoir was piped to the three system selector valves, controlled from the flight compartment by a single lever. A cam arrangement ensured that only one system could be selected ‘on’ at a time. From these valves, the fluid passed to the inlet side of both pumps. Two small pumps were used in preference to one larger pump, so that electrical loads on start-up could be reduced by switching them ‘on’ one after the other. These pumps were of the variable-displacement type, and were each driven by an a.c. electric motor, the electrical supplies being arranged so that they were unaffected by the loss of any one engine. With two engines lost, one pump still remained available. Non-return valves prevented a casing leak on one pump from causing fluid loss to the other pump.

The pressure supplies from the two pumps joined together and enter the pressure filter, with filtration down to five microns. The supply then splits into three to enter each system selector valve. The operation of any valve would direct the Standby system pressure into the selected system through non-return valves. These ensureed that the main system fluid caould not be lost through a fault in the Standby system and also that certain emergency services could be operated by the Standby system using main system fluid taken through the reservoir stack-pipes. Thus, a leaking component operated under emergency would only lose main system fluid down to the stack-pipe level.

Self-sealing disconnect points were tapped into the pressure and suction lines of the Green, Yellow, and Blue systems, so that they could function singly or together by a ground hydraulic rig.

The drop-out air turbine system consisted of a single, variable displacement pump driven by an air turbine, dropped out into the airstream by the release of a simple mechanical linkage. It provided hydraulic power during flight in the event of complete engine failure, resulting in the loss of the three main systems and the standby system.

A pressure regulator and starting valve ensured that the turbine windmilling speed was built up before the pump came on load. The pump suction and pressure lines were tapped into the standby system lines, thus allowing operation of any of the three main systems on selection of the system selector valve lever. A small generator fitted into the hub of the air turbine provides electrical anti-icing of the unit from the moment windmilling speed was obtained.

From De Havilland *Gazette* No.115 of February 1960 comes this: *'RAPID PROGRESS WITH BRITAIN'S 'UNSUPERSEDABLE' SHORT-HAUL JET AIRLINER: Airco D.H. 121 structure tests were well underway at Hatfield. The first large component, the fuselage nose section with cockpit canopy, was undergoing static and fatigue pressure testing in one of the Hatfield water tanks. When this picture was taken, the nose section with strain gauge attachments had just completed its first proof-pressure test at eleven pounds per square inch, one-and-a-half times the normal working cabin pressure. Now progressing was a fatigue test representing 40,000 flights each of one-and-a-half hours. This is equivalent to 60,000 hours of flying or about 20 years of service for a short-haul airliner. The present tests are part of a series covering other major components of the aircraft which will precede the proving of a complete airframe in a specially-constructed water tank'.*
[Photographs courtesy of British Aerospace Hatfield]

A plan view of G-ARPB in flight, showing the scarlet wing surfaces.
[Photographs courtesy of British Aerospace Hatfield]

The purpose of the wheel brake pump system was to provide pressure to the wheel brakes for towing and parking. The d.c. electrically-driven pump obtained its fluid from the bottom of the Green system reservoir, the outlet from the pump being controlled at 3,000 pounds per square inch by a relief valve. From the relief valve, the pressure supply was used to inflate the wheel brake accumulator, the capacity of this accumulator being sufficient to provide six full braking applications. Both the Green main system and brake pump system inflated this accumulator through non-return valves. The outlet from the accumulator goes directly to the wheel brake control valves.

For towing and parking, the pump was operated by the aircraft's internal battery to inflate the brake accumulator. Selection was via a spring-loaded switch that released when working pressure was reached.

Structural testing

The structural test programme for the Trident was evolved from the extensive experience gained in the development of the Comet 4 that grew out of the unforeseen metal fatigue problems with the Comet I. The methods then devised have been elaborated to cover the more severe structural requirements demanded by the long service life and high cruising speed of the Trident.

The Trident 1 was initially analysed in full by methods which had previously been confirmed as reasonable and correct on the Comet 4. This analysis began in 1957 and used the most modern methods and high-speed computer techniques.

In 1959, a structural test programme was started whose object was to confirm the theoretical work; not only to establish by itself that the structure had satisfactory strength, stiffness and minimum fatigue life. Initially tests were confined to small laboratory specimens used to explore and develop the main features of the design. Subsequently, larger components, and finally major assemblies, have been tested to confirm the correctness of the design calculations.

In the testing of major assemblies, the policy was to conduct fatigue and static strength tests on the same specimen, so that the related effects of these two factors on the structure as a whole were properly represented. The use of separate specimens for fatigue and static strength tests, while simpler and more convenient, could be seriously misleading, and it was only by the use of single specimens subjected to tests throughout the whole range, and in the right order, that the structure could be shown to have adequate static strength at the end as well as at the beginning of its working life.

A complete production airframe was being used for the main tests, sub-divided into a number of large specimens. Each specimen had been built with additional structure from the next adjoining assembly so that there was an overlap between specimens. Local effects at the boundaries of each specimen were absorbed in the overlap, and do not

May 1962, and De Havilland Canada promotes the De Havilland Trident.
[De Havilland Aircraft Co.]

affect the area which was under examination. The main test specimens were as follows:

- The nose fuselage including the canopy.
- The main fuselage up to the pressure dome, together with the complete wing.
- The fin and tail fuselage extending forward of the pressure dome.
- The tailplane.
- The pressure dome.
- The main landing gear assembly.
- The nose landing gear assembly.
- The engine mountings.
- The tailplane pivot assembly.

There was an adequate number of strain gauges on each main test specimen to measure stress distributionsand peak values and so to substantiate the theoretical calculations.

The test programme was designed to confirm that each specimen meets the requirements for static strength, stiffness, minimum fatigue life and fail-safe characteristics, where these were applicable.

The pressurised fuselage of the Trident with the complete wing attached to it was being tested in a water tank, as was the pressurized part of the tail fuselage specimen. The tank tests could be used to confirm fail-safe characteristics by showing that the structure in a cracked state had satisfactory strength and stiffness. The great advantage of testing full-scale structures as opposed to small specimens was that all portions of the structure were correctly loaded and any potential fatigue areas were brought to light; unknown effects of loading frames and rigs being eliminated. Moreover, because the tank fatigue test conditions so closely represented those occurring in actual service, the areas of the structure on which to concentrate during inspection will be emphasised by the tests.

Fail Safe Structure

The primary structure was designed for a minimum crack-free fatigue life of 20,000 flights, each of one and a half hour duration. To establish this life a minimum of double this value, 40,000 flights, will be accomplished on test in the water tanks. Loading spectra in all fatigue tests were based on varying amplitude loads with adequate allowances for scatter of loadings.

The test programme was divided into eight stages, the first four of which are, in fact, sufficient to obtain a Certificate of Airworthiness.

Stage 1. Stiffness tests - resonance and some stiffness tests were carried out on the first Trident before the first flight.

Stage 2. Static strength tests to cover the first flights of the first two Tridents. These tests were to 50 per cent of the ultimate design load, not enough to affect the fatigue life of the specimens.

Stage 3. A fatigue test to the equivalent of 10,000 flights, each of one and a half hour duration. During each flight cycle loads were applied to simulate taxiing and landing loads, ground-air change of loads, a spectrum of gust loading, and cabin pressure reversals.

Stage 4. Static-strength tests to proof loads of 67 per cent of the ultimate design load in critical cases.

Stage 5. Further fatigue tests up to a total, including Stage 3, of 40,000 flights of one and a half hour duration. These tests apply to the parts of the main airframe structure which were designed on fail-safe principles. As described later, safe-life parts were tested to a longer life because of the larger scatter factors which must be applied.

Stage 6. Static strength tests beyond proof load. These tests were to at least 75 per cent of the ultimate load in critical cases.

Stage 7. Fail-safe testing, including the effects of 'accidental' damage inflicted on the structure, for a further 20,000 flights, making a total of 60,000 flights in the fatigue test programme. Proof loads were applied after every 5,000 flights, and stiffness tests were carried out at the end of the stage.

Stage 8. Ultimate static strength tests.

By January 1964, the progress made in the test programme was as follows :

- The nose fuselage including the canopy: all tests completed satisfactorily.
- The main fuselage up to the pressure dome, together with the complete wing: Stages 1 to 6 completed satisfactorily.
- The fin and tail fuselage extending forward of the pressure dome: Stages 1 to 6 completed. Stage 7 was proceeding, and a total of 45,000 flights had been completed satisfactorily.
- The tailplane: Stages 1 to 7 completed satisfactorily. This specimen will proceed eventually to bird impact tests.

Six Trident 1s together!

Clockwise, starting top left:
G-ARPA, G-ARPC, G-ARPF unknown, G-ARPE. All of the aircraft appear to be in BEA colours, while Papa Echo also wears a rooftop design of a trident, incorporated into the aircrafts type name as a logo. An enlargement of the design is shown left.
[Photographs courtesy of British Aerospace Hatfield]

- The pressure dome: All tests completed satisfactorily, including fatigue tests to 100,000 cycles, fail-safe demonstration tests and static strength tests to ultimate loads.

Safe Life Parts

In the case of parts which it was practicable neither to duplicate nor to design to be fail safe, and which were therefore designed on safe life principles, fatigue tests were extended to at least six times the service life required of the component, and in many cases to more than this, depending on how closely the actual service loads could be predicted and represented. The fatigue tests on the engine mountings, for example, extended to the equivalent of 180,000 flights, a factor of nine. The number of safe life parts were been kept to the absolute minimum.

By January 1964, the progress made in testing the safe life parts was as follows :

- The main landing gear assembly: The main landing gear as designed was a cantilever type, and structural tests began on such a landing gear to prove that the static strength and fatigue life were both satisfactory. The landing gear was a safe life part for which a life factor of six was taken.

All tests in Stages 2 to 5 were completed to a total of 60,000 flights, and the specimen was then modified to include the levered suspension unit. A further programme of static strength and fatigue tests was under way to confirm that the modified design was fully satisfactory. To date 3,000 flights (out of the target of 60,000 flights) have been completed.

- The nose landing gear assembly: Fatigue tests to a total of 120,000 flights and static strength tests to ultimate load have been completed satisfactorily.
- The engine mountings: The engine mountings have undergone the following tests satisfactorily :—
- Fatigue tests: 180,000 flights.
- Static strength tests to proof load.
- Static strength tests to ultimate loads.
- The tailplane pivot fitting: Fatigue tests were continued to a life of 1,680,000 flights - the equivalent to eighty-four times the aircraft life. Strength tests to proof load and to ninety per cent ultimate load were also completed satisfactorily.

Extensive use of strain gauges was made throughout the test programme to measure stress distributions and peak stresses in the test specimens. The results of the strain gauge analyses were in good agreement with the theoretical work and have confirmed that the stress analysis was soundly based and accurately carried out.

Additional Testing for the Trident IE

There were no fundamental differences in structure or structural principles between the Trident IE and the Trident l; the changes in weight, speed and geometry were all minor. Consequently, the repetition of full-scale static, fatigue, stiffness and resonance tests on the Trident lE airframe was not necessary. A number of tests has, however, been carried out on the few components new to the Trident lE - for example the leading edge slats - and tests on existing specimens were extended, wherever it was felt that additional test evidence of satisfactory strength, stiffness and fatigue life was desirable.

Flight testing - Structural Aspects

To confirm the external loads used in design and structural testing of the Trident Series I, a standard production aircraft was used for flutter tests and for flight measurements.

The structural aspects of the flight test programme may be considered under three main headings, and by February 1964, the progress achieved was as follows:

- Flutter tests: Completed satisfactorily.
- light load measurements - to confirm design loads.
- Completed satisfactorily - to confirm fatigue loads.

Flutter Tests

The object of these tests was to justify flutter clearance up to the design diving speed boundary.

The test programme involved some thirty test flights centred round three altitudes of 10,000 ft., 25,000 ft. and 30,000 ft., mainly in level flight, with shallow dives to reach the highest Mach numbers.

Continuous vertical and lateral vibrations of the structure were induced by two 400 lb. hydraulic inertia exciters mounted in the fuselage nose and in the tail near the fin root. Excitations ranged from 21 to 35 cycles per second. Instrumentation consisted principally of fifteen accelerometers mounted at chosen points in the structure, which fed data into multi-channel recorders, with selected data telemetered to the ground while the tests were taking place. The data were analysed using vector plots, with twenty-two vibration modes followed throughout the flight tests.

These tests confirmed the damping characteristics derived in the design calculations and showed that the margins between flutter speed and diving speed were adequate.

Flight Load Measurements to Confirm Design Loads Steady Flight Tests

The object of these tests was to confirm the external load data used in the design stage.

Measurements were made during pull-ups, turns, and side-slips, over a range of speeds and Mach numbers, including the following: Symmetric tailplane loads, with airbrakes open and closed, for various C of G positions; tailplane rolling and yawing moment; fin loads; wing lift slope; flap loads, with main landing gear up and down; control surface hinge moments; rates of roll, to confirm aileron reversal margin.

Instrumentation for these tests used mainly

Facing Page: Trident 2 to the sun - one of the many BEA travel posters designed to attrach the holidaymakers to European sunspots.

BEA
Trident Two

electrical resistance strain gauges, calibrated on the ground before each relevant flight. The measured loads compared well with the design loads.

Confirmation of the design loads for the Series I droop leading edge was obtained by deriving normal and chordwise forces from records of pressure distributions around the droop and sealing plate, for various drroop alnd flap angles, over a range of speeds down to the stall.

Flight Load Measurements to Confirm Fatigue Loads

The gust cases were the critical design cases for the wing, tail unit and, to a certain extent, the pressure cabin of the Trident. The essential feature of the loads on the structure due to gusts was that they were transient in nature and depended upon the stiffness and dynamic characteristics of the structure, and aerodynamic damping effects.

The main objects of these tests were therefore:

- To check the dynamics of the wing and tail and to measure tail loads.
- To deduce which natural modes of vibration of the aircraft contribute significantly to the 'over-swing' loads in the structure.
- To measure the gusts encountered during the tests.
- To measure the effect of the autopilot response and yaw damper on loads in turbulence.
- To provide information on rigid body pitching and yawing effects on the loads on the structure.

The instrumentation consisted principally of accelerometers and strain gauges feeding into twenty-five recording channels, together with an aural track to record speed, altitude, weight, weather conditions and so on.

The aircraft was to be flown in rough air conditions up to the design cruising speed and Mach number. The analysis of the gust data would compare the loads due to the measured gust with the loads predicted for this.

A counting accelerometer - or 'fatigue meter' - was fitted to each Trident to record the accelerations ('bumps') at the centre of gravity (C of G) throughout the aircraft's life. This provides a full history of the frequency and magnitude of the C of G accelerations, for regular comparison with the corresponding data used in the structural fatigue calculations in the design stage.

Runway Tests

High speed taxiing tests were carried out with the object of measuring the magnitude and frequency of accelerations on the landing gear and fuselage structure, to check design assumptions and to ensure that a high standard of passenger comfort was provided.

Acoustic Tests

The object of these tests was to confirm that an adequate sonic fatigue life will be obtained. With all three engines running simultaneously at maximum r.p.m., continuous recordings of strains at various points in the tailplane, elevator and rudder will be made, from which peak alternating stresses, root mean square alternating stresses and panel frequencies were derived and compared with those used in design.

Additional Testing for the Trident 1E

The flight load measurements made on the Trident Series 1 have been completely satisfactory and confirmed the design data extremely well. Thus flight load measurements for the Trident IE, which were no fundamental structural differences from the Trident 1, could be restricted to those detail aspects of the aircraft which were different; in particular the leading-edge slats, the revised flaps and ailerons and the tail-mounted APU.

Confirmation of the design loads for the leading-edge slats were already been obtained from flight tests with the fourth Trident I, which was fitted with a fixed slat with the same aerodynamic characteristics as that on the Trident IE. Pressure distributions on the slat were measured under a full range of operating conditions to cover the design cases, and the measured loads have been used as the basis for the design loads.

Other flight load measurements which will be made on the Trident IE include the following:

- Symmetric tailplane loads, with airbrakes open and closed, for various C.G. positions; rates of roll, to confirm the reversal margin of the revised ailerons; aileron hinge moments; loads on the new A.P.U. mountings, measured by accelerometers on the A.P.U. itself and/or by strain gauges on the A.P.U. mountings.
- In addition, flutter tests for the Trident IE will be made, consisting of stick jerk tests with instrumentation fitted to give additional confirmation of the damping characteristics derived in the design calculations.

Chapter Four

Engine

The DH.121 initially had a unique and interesting engine arrangement. Its three engines were mounted at the aircraft's rear, providing a clean, efficient wing and a quiet passenger cabin. Two engines are cantilevered out from the sides of the aft fuselage; the third is in a virtually faired pod behind all the major structures.

Why were three engines chosen for the 121 and mounted this way? The main factors were the engine arrangement's economy, including aerodynamics, and engineering considerations.

Before deciding where the engine should be mounted on the 121, detailed studies were conducted to compare the relative merits of the various mounting arrangements. In the event three engines were chosen, which necessarily eliminated some layouts due to asymmetric trust consideration in the rearrangement, the layout was divided into three parts. The *De Havilland Gazette* of February 1960 explained:

1. Safety.
The three engines are well spaced from one another, which means that should a compressor blade be ejected from an engine, there is no likelihood of it being sucked into a neighbour, or should a fire occur in one engine, there is no possibility of the controls of another being affected. The centre engine was particularly well fire-protected, based on De Havilland's experience on truly buried engines of the Comet.

The area around this centre engine is divided into two zones, each with its own fire-sensing and protection systems, and the engine itself is mounted with duplicated attachment points: one set on the side, the other on the top.

The planes of the side-engine turbine discs are clear of all major structure, while for the centre engine, it is only within fifteen degrees of the centre line that the rear fin spar or a small section of the tailplane could possibly be damaged by a disintegrating disc.

In the normal attitude on the runway, the side engine intakes are ten feet up, well clear of stones and debris, and in the take-off condition, the lowered flap will provide complete protection. In a wing-pod-mounted configuration, the ground-clearance case is difficult, particularly for an

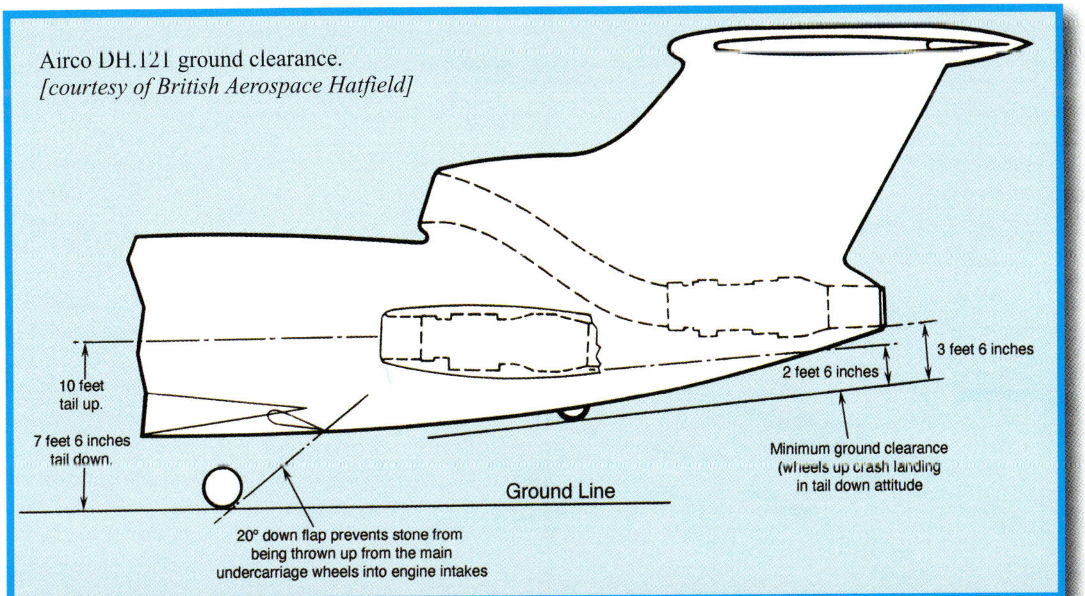

Airco DH.121 ground clearance.
[courtesy of British Aerospace Hatfield]

aircraft of 121 size operating from some smaller airfields with narrow grass- and gravel-verged taxiways. During a belly landing, all engines still have ample ground clearance.

In a crash, the deceleration experienced at the rear of an aircraft tends to be much less than at the nose. If a crash were severe enough to break the 12 G engine mountings on the 121, it would hardly have been a survivable one for passengers in the first place, but the centre engine, in this case regarded as the critical one, must break through two fin spars, two engine mounting bulkheads and the pressure dome before it could possibly enter the cabin.

2. Servicing Aspects

All the engines are easily accessible. The side-engines are obviously so - they have cowling doors opening sideways and upwards, exposing the undersides where all the accessories are placed. The centre engine is accessible through large doors that hinge downwards, allowing a man to stand up alongside the engine within the rear fuselage, fully protected from the weather. Engine removal is very simple. Hoists are inserted through doors in the fuselage sides above the engines, and the engines are then lowered to their trolleys. An engine change will be completed in two hours. There is plenty of space in this rear fuselage for stowing ancillary equipment, which can be easily inspected and maintained.

Possible noise-damage areas are reduced to a minimum on the 121. There are no costly wing under-surfaces or flaps within the engine noise cones. The only areas within the side engines' cones are non-structural ones, and precautions are being taken to ensure that these are suitably resistant to damage. In addition,the RB.163 gives low jet velocities so that the noise pressures are approximately thirty per cent. lower than those generated by jet engines now in service.

3. Operational Aspects

In the event of an engine failure, there will virtually be no swing for the pilot to control because the engines are mounted near the aircraft's centre line as opposed to the long lever arm of the underwing pod arrangement. In this respect, the 121 continues the beneficial tradition of the Comet - in both aircraft, it is easy for the average airline pilot to achieve the optimum performance after failure of an engine. It will also be easy to ferry the 121 on two engines to one of a few major bases where spare engines will be held.

Air brakes are provided on the wing, and the undercarriage may be lowered to increase drag, but the use of reverse thrust on the two side engines in the air instead of lowering the undercarriage is being actively investigated.

In the past, criticism has been levelled at aircraft with rear-engine layouts, with a large mass placed aft of the wing, because it would prove difficult to maintain a suitable centre of gravity when loading the aircraft.

Particular attention has been paid to this potential problem on the 121. The aircraft has been given a full fifty-inch centre-of-gravity range, compared with that found in much larger aircraft with wing-mounted engines.

4. Integration with total design

A detailed description cannot be made of the blind landing and system design of the 121. These were both outlined in the Gazette for October, 1959. The three-engined arrangement fits naturally with the design requirements for three separate hydraulic and electrical systems to operate continuously in parallel, providing the reliability necessary for an automatic blind-landing system.

The three-engine arrangement also allows for a very simple fuel system. Each wing has two tanks, the outer one half the volume of the inner one. The outer tanks feed the centre engine, the

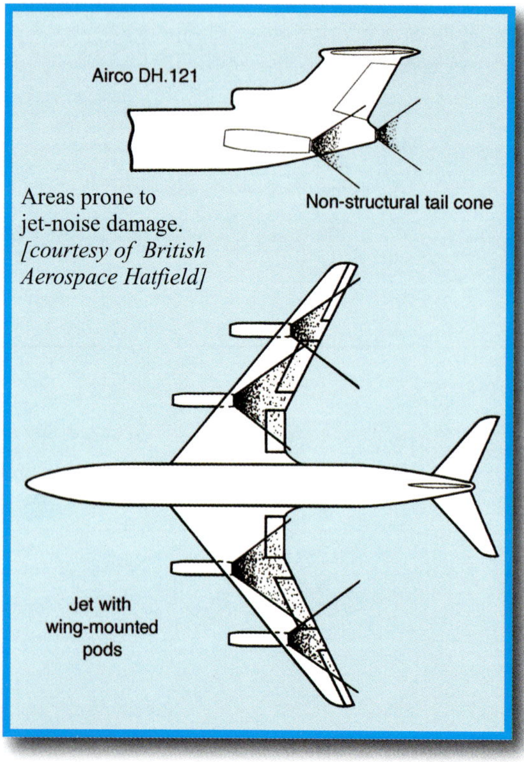

Areas prone to jet-noise damage. *[courtesy of British Aerospace Hatfield]*

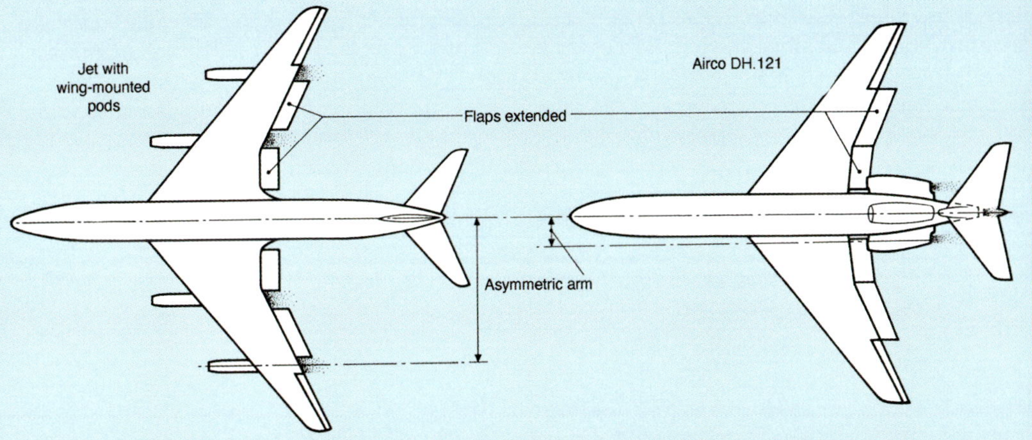

Engine-out handling in relationship to flaps and engine position.
[courtesy of British Aerospace Hatfield]

inners each feed a side engine, and, with equal tankage volumes, no fuel management is necessary. The disposition of these tanks is such that little change of trim arises from the use of fuel.

The third engine is provided only for a small increase in frontal area, and the top intake, very aerodynamically efficient both internally and externally, is used to add strength to the rear fuselage. Fuselage and wing weights are admittedly a little higher with a rear-engine arrangement, but in compensation, the wing has no engines to spoil airflow. The whole aircraft probably weighs 4 per cent. more than its podded equivalent, but with its clean wing, with uninterrupted flap, it shows a 4 per cent. A better maximum lift coefficient so that the two aircraft have the same size. But only the aircraft with the rear installation can benefit from the use of three engines.

The simplicity gained with three engines is not accounted in formula costs, any more than is experience, but it is these factors which, when combined with very advanced aerodynamic and structural design, will give the Airco DH 121 outstanding operational economy.

All of this was coloured by the design requirements that were to be met; initially, it was a high-speed short-haul jet airliner designed for outstandingly good economics. Broadly, the performance required was that the aircraft could easily operate from six thousand foot runways, with docile low-speed handling qualities, and travel at six hundred mph over stage lengths of about one thousand statute miles, with full reserves, carrying a payload of eighty or so passengers and their baggage.

These aims represented no less than the ultimate in speed and economy for short-haul operation. The aircraft had a simple structure designed to have a long fail-safe life, which would reduce the operator's expense by providing trouble-free service.

Considering engine costs alone, it was found that in buying a given package of thrust, it paid to buy as few and as large units as possible. For example, taking representative and comparable quotations from engine manufacturers, one engine of 15,000 pounds static thrust would cost £76,500, two 7,500-pound units would cost no less than £109,000. Many of the recurring overhaul expenses similarly varied with engine size. From this point of view, the twin-engined aircraft appeared to offer a real advantage over three or four engines, but this is not the only consideration.

It could be shown that the two engined aircraft had advantages up to about four hundred miles range, while four engines were perhaps better for ranges of two thousand miles or more. Between these limits. there was however, a big region where three engines had the advantage, and this was the target area for which the Trident had been designed.

In short- and medium-haul operations, an aero engine was subjected to a greater frequency of full-power cycles; these operations imposed more exacting conditions on an engine than long-haul service. For this reason, it is essential to appreciate that Rolls-Royce could call on many millions of hours of experience with short- to medium-haul operation designing the Spey.

The Spey was a two-shaft by-pass engine with a pressure ratio of more than 16 to 1 and a by-pass ratio of 1 to 1. It had a four-stage axial low-pressure compressor (or five stages in the later versions), which passed up to two hundred and eight pounds of air per second and had a pressure ratio of up to 2.5 to 1. A two-stage low-pressure turbine drove it. The air from this compressor was divided equally, half going through the high-pressure compressor, the combustion zone and the turbines. The other half passes into the by-pass

The location of the three Spey engines, showing their mounting points.
[courtesy of British Aerospace Hatfield]

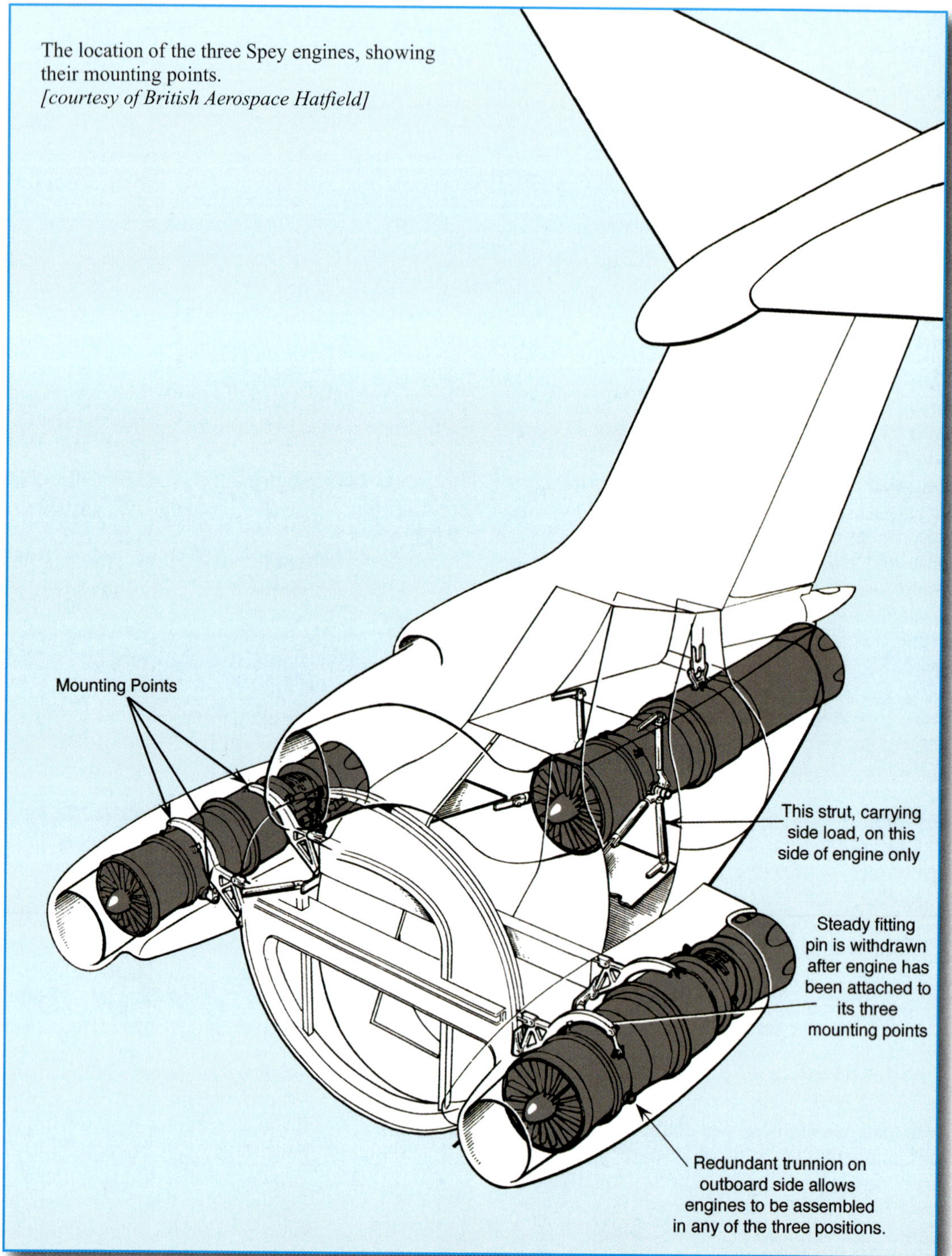

The Spey on build in the Rolls-Royce experimental assembly shop. The Spey has a by-pass ratio of unity, that is the airflow through the low-pressure compressor splits equally between the high-pressure compressor and the by-pass duct. In this view the by-pass duct has yet to be fitted.
[Photograph courtesy of British Aerospace Hatfield]

duct, after which it was mixed with the turbine exhaust gas and discharged through the final nozzle. The axial high-pressure compressor had twelve stages and was driven by the two-stage high-pressure turbine with a pressure ratio of 6.5 to 1. The combustion zone contained ten straight-flow flame tubes.

The design of the RB.163 Spey began in July 1959 following the extensive revisions to the DH 121 configuration. At that time, the RB.141 Medway, the fifteen thousand pounds thrust engine initially designed for the DH 121, was under manufacture, and it was decided to continue with its development to provide a support programme for the Spey. Initially, the Spey was conceived as a direct scaled-down version of the RB.141 with a basic thrust rating of ten thousand pounds.

The first Spey ran on the test bed on 31 December 1960, and by the end of June 1961, seven engines were running, and over five hundred hours of testing had been completed. On 12 October of that year, two Speys installed in the inboard nacelles of modified Vulcan B1 bomber XA902 flew for the first time. Altogether, eighty-eight engine hours were flown in the Vulcan. By the end of 1961, ten Speys had completed two thousand one hundred hours of bench and flight testing. On 9 January 1962, the first Trident made its maiden flight, and thereafter, Spey flying experience began to build up rapidly as further aircraft entered the programme.

Development testing of the Spey took a wide variety of forms: covering regular sea-level test bed running; environmental testing in fully-equipped Trident pods; one hundred and fifty hour type tests and modification approval tests; cyclic endurance testing at high flame temperatures; testing under simulated flight conditions in the Rolls-Royce altitude test facility, including anti-icing trials to full ARB/FAA icing schedule. Tests which would have normally occupied six months or more using a flight test aircraft were satisfactorily completed in two weeks. The Spey was also subjected to extensive tropical handling trials, various rig tests on components, and complete engine assemblies.

In the August 1961 edition of the De Havilland *Gazette,* reporting on the rollout of the first Trident at Hatfield on 4 August 1961, the editor paid particular attention to the engine arrangement.

The intake for the central engine affords the opportunity for a very stiff rear fuselage, extending into the fin, with the all-moving tailplane as its endplate. This intake effectively increases the depth of the fuselage structure, making for extra stiffness against both torsional and bending stresses. All this looks right.

The central engine itself is at the tail-end of the fuselage, so structural and fire aspects, and, of course, noise damage, are exceedingly well looked after, while servicing and engine-changing facilities are excellent. The cowling doors are large, the engine accessories are conveniently grouped and four men are intended to change the central engine in two hours.

The two side engines look higher above the ground than one expected, well away from the dangers of stones, and are further protected by the wing flaps. The segments of their reverse thrust are arranged so as to be clear of the tailplane and to prevent stones being blown into opposite engines. Although well separated the engines are relatively close inboard from the point of view of lever arm, ensuring very good handling qualities in the case of asymmetric and reverse thrust.

The editor went on to say that the Spey engines had been announced in the Autumn of 1959, and was progressing well in establishing itself as a leading low-economy engine in the 10,000-pound thrust class specifically suited for the coming generation of short/medium-haul jet transports. The editor also provided much more information that had been previously published.

'Following selection of the engine to power the De Havilland Trident aircraft for British European Airways and world markets, the Spey has been selected to power the new BAC One-Eleven twin-

Access to the power plants. This photograph demonstrates effectively the manner in which the rear engine configuration has been designed with a maximum number of access panels and cowling doors to facilitate servicing and maintenance. *[Photograph courtesy of British Aerospace Hatfield]*

Three of the four man team changing a Spey on a Trident 1. The engine is suspended from a lifting hoist attached to the upper rear fuselage of the Trident and is hand-wound up into position.
[Photograph courtesy of British Aerospace Hatfield]

engined short-haul transport, which is in a different category.

Rolls-Royce earlier this year received a development contract from the Ministry of Aviation for the military version of the Spey.

Design work on the Spey was initiated in September 1959 and the first engine ran at the end of December last year. Seven development Speys were soon running and experience on these quickly built up. Over 450 hours had accumulated by June, approximately 120 hours of this time being on one engine which completed a 60-hour endurance test. This experience is backed-up by the more extensive development testing on the earlier RB.141 from which the Spey is derived.

From the considerable running time on nine RB.141 engines since November 1959 valuable experience had been gained which almost in its entirety is directly applicable to the smaller-scale Spey. This enabled improvements to be incorporated in the Spey in advance of its own development, .

Typical of the manner in which the RB.141 has facilitated progress with the Spey has been the series of tests on the engine simulating the compressor entry flow conditions occurring with the centre air intake on the Trident. From this it was possible to go direct to test bed running of the Spey fitted with the complete centre intake duct and entry cowl of the Trident. Both the Spey and the RB.141 have been evolved from the Rolls-Royce Conway by-pass jet on which some 300,000

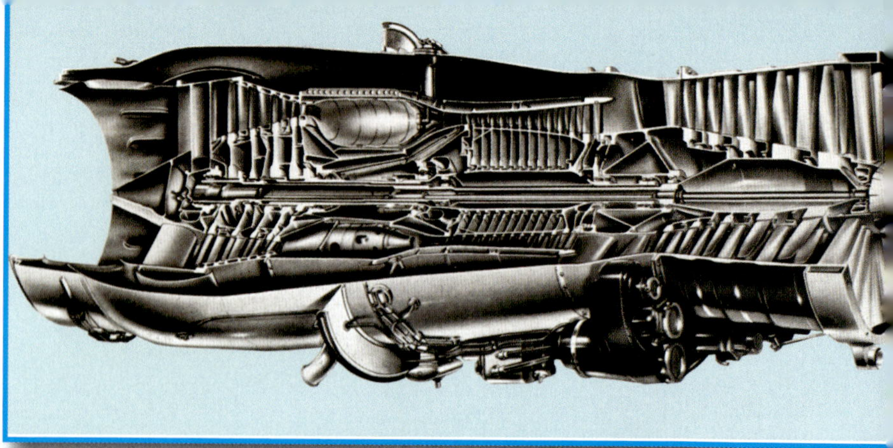

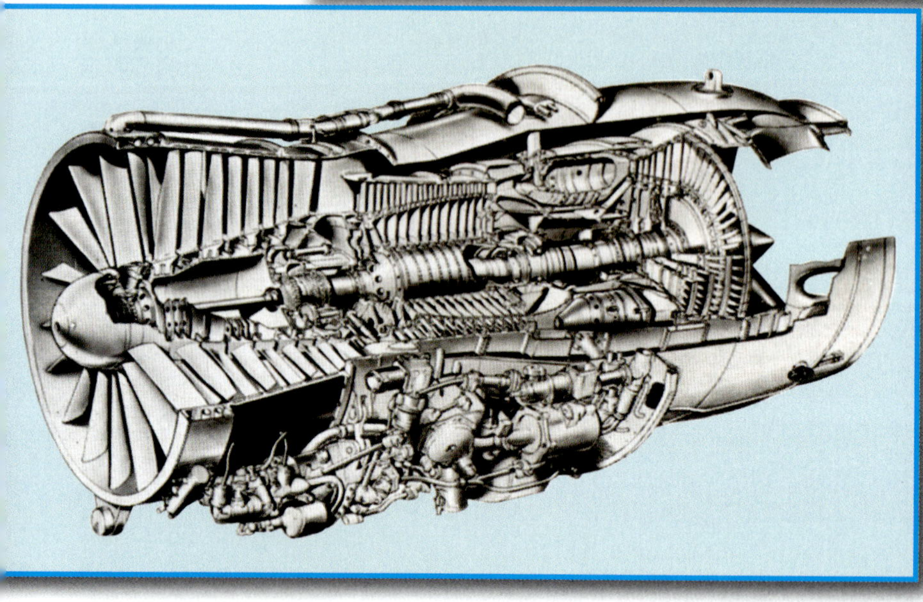

Two sectional views of the Rolls-Royce Spey as it appeared in the De Havilland *Gazette.* Allegedly this was the first time the internals of this new engine had been revealed to the public.*[Photograph courtesy of British Aerospace Hatfield]*

hours in airline and military operation have accumulated.

Among the new design features of the Spey on which development effort is being directed are the fuel-control system, the low-pressure compressor spool and the by-pass air/engine exhaust mixer. The control system, designed by Rolls-Royce on fresh principles, is aimed at producing a less dirt-conscious, less leak-prone system of the speed-selection type. The L.P. compressor carrying four stages of rotor blading, is of simple drum construction, and strain-gauging tests have been performed to determine blade operating stresses. (This form of compressor construction is used also on later Conway engines.) The mixer has individual chutes which direct the by-pass air into the turbine exhaust, thus ensuring a high degree of mixing of the two streams to achieve a lower mean exhaust velocity. This has a beneficial effect on the engine's specific fuel consumption.

A large part in the Spey's development programme is testing of the engine in the Rolls-Royce altitude test facility. Here the engine has to be subjected to the full range of conditions of the Trident's flight envelope.

Also, static testing is undertaken on a Spey powerplant complete with a Trident production-standard pod, thrust reverser and noise suppressor nozzle. This is installed on a special test stand at the Company's Flight Test Establishment at Hucknall, Notts. More than 125 hours engine testing had been completed on this by June. During August 1961 two Speys are to commence test flying in an Avro Vulcan and, following initial ground-running trials in the Trident, engines will be provided for the prototype flight trials of the aircraft which are scheduled to start during the winter.

The civil and military Spey engines are being developed to an integrated programme. This provides for a total of 14 bench development engines, in addition to engines used for flight development and endurance testing. The military contract for the Spey covers initial development work and supply of prototype engines. A production contract is being negotiated.

In December 1962, performance testing of the

Spey-25 began. It was the most powerful civil version of the Spey to date and offered ratings up to 11,400 pounds thrust for take-off. It was this engine, together with the Spey -2 and -2W, which in November 1962 became the subject of official financial support - with the overall development costs of the three variants being shared equally by Rolls-Royce and the British Government. The availability of these higher-rated Speys greatly enhanced the operational flexibility of the Trident. The Spey -25 was derived from earlier versions of the Spey, and by adding a fifth stage to the rear of the low-pressure compressor and making some complementary changes to the turbine blading, the increase in thrust over the earlier Speys was achieved with no increase in operating temperature.

The Spey -1 received full ARB/FAA certification in 1963 and entered airline service in British European Airways' Trident 1 airliners in April. Engine components underwent intense cyclic testing in rigs and engines to establish their service life. It was the standard practice with a Rolls-Royce civil engine; testing of this type ensured that component lives were always kept well ahead of those reached in service.

The Spey -2 variant was similar to the Spey -1 but had a turbine of the type developed for the Spey -25. It has completed a declared type test to ARB/FAA approval. It also completed a 150-hour ARB modification approval test.

The Spey-2W completed its type test with water injection in April - this feature restored take-off power on a hot day. Water is sprayed into the combustion chambers at twenty-three gallons per minute during the take-off phase. The process was entirely automatic since, after initial selection, the pilot obtained water injection by opening the throttle. The declared type test on the Spey -25 was completed in April on the American Airlines One-Eleven engine at an initial rating of 11,000 pounds thrust. A Spey -25 rated at 11,400 pounds thrust was rapidly produced and was ran with water injection with good results. Spey-25 engines were ordered to power the Trident 1E airliners of Kuwait Airways, Iraqi Airways and Pakistan International Airlines.

The engines underwent a five hundred-hour endurance test and then one thousand hours of endurance testing to a schedule based on a typical short-haul airliner flight plan. These tests were carried out to a typical airline schedule and included the use of thrust reversers.

The two side engines of the Trident's three-engine configuration were fitted with thrust reversers, and noise suppressors could be fitted to all engine exhaust units if required, but these were not included in the standard specification.

The centre engine was mounted within the envelope of the rear fuselage but is behind and below the fuselage and tail primary structure. The pod installations have been designed and

Seen at the 21st SBAC display at Farmborough was this display of small and large models flanking a huge globe, demonstrating the worldwide operations of 68 Comets in service or on order for early delivery and the many opportunities for the first fast economical shorthaul Trident airliner which had been offered for service from 1963. *[Photograph courtesy of British Aerospace Hatfield]*

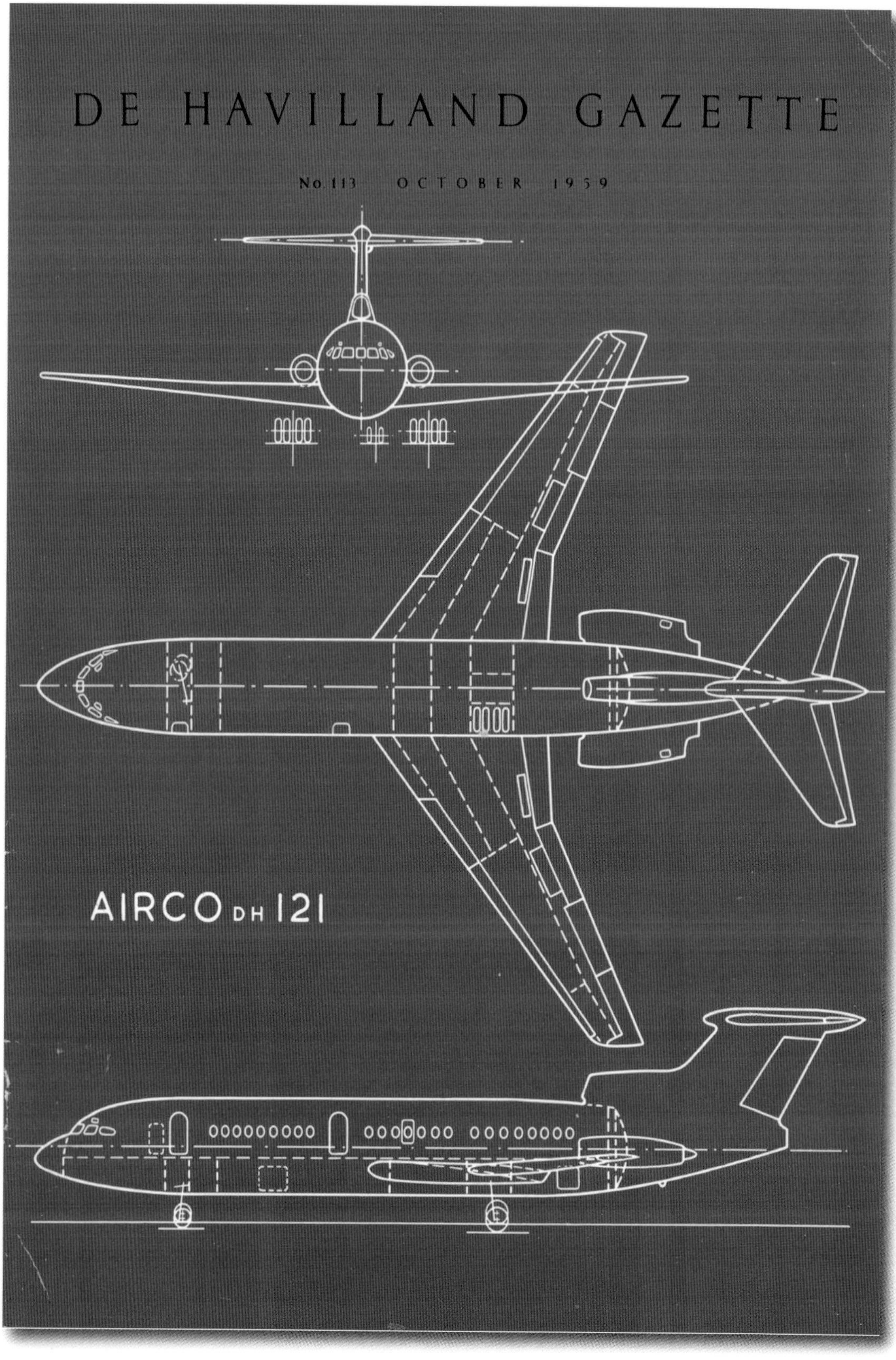
DE HAVILLAND GAZETTE
No. 113 OCTOBER 1959
AIRCO DH 121

The roll-out of Trident G-ARPA at Hatfield on 4 August 1961.
[Photograph courtesy of British Aerospace Hatfield]

developed by Rolls-Royce, which manufactures them as complete units ready for assembly on the aircraft. All three engines have their combustion, turbine and tailpipe sections to the rear of, and clear of, the pressurized portion of the fuselage. In the event of an asymmetric engine failure, the rear-mounted engines give a very small yawing moment, yet the three intakes are well separated, reducing the possibility of a failure in one engine affecting another.

Each engine is attached to the airframe at three points, but mounting details differ slightly between the three power plants. Interchangeability of the engine in the three installed positions is achieved by providing each engine with five 'pick-up' points. The fittings comprise two trunnions, one on each side of the compressor casing, two lugs integral with the top of the compressor casing, and a rear mount. The centre engine mountings utilize both trunnions and the rear mount. The side engine mountings use one trunnion, lug, and rear mount.

The pod installations divide the cowlings into five groups: upper sections, cowling doors, air intake, rear fairing assembly, and thrust reverser fairings. The upper sections are fixed to the engine mounting beams. Four hinged cowling doors are attached to the upper sections. The air intake assembly is bolted directly to the engine face, and the rear fairing assembly is bolted to the rear of the thrust reverser. Thrust reverser fairings are added in four sections after the engine has been installed.

Previous page: The striking front cover of the No. 113 October 1959 De Havilland Gazette, one of the few times the phrase AIRCO DH.121 appeared in print.
[courtesy of British Aerospace Hatfield]

The centre engine was enclosed in the rear fuselage fairing. Access was provided from below by four doors, and there was sufficient room inside the cowling for access all around the engine. There was a hatch in the bottom of the centre intake duct to facilitate inspection of the front stages of the engine compressor. The hatch was linked to the high-pressure fuel cock of the centre engine so that the engine cannot be started when the hatch is open, nor the hatch opened once the engine is running.

An engine change could be made on the centre installation in just over three-and-a-quarter hours by five men and on the pod installation in three-and-a-half hours by five men, using a complete power plant prepared for the particular installation in each case. These measured times include one hour's running to check the engine after installation but not the time taken to position the Trident for the run.

Careful design, influenced by Comet experience, minimized the risk of fire and overheat conditions in the power plants. Providing adequate ventilation and fireproof bulkheads reinforced primary protection inherent in separating the three engines. The type of engine further reduced the likelihood of fire. The high by-pass ratio meant that half the total mass flow of air entering the engine passed through the by-pass duct. This annular duct completely enclosed the hot parts of the engine since by pass air was not mixed with gas from the main part of the engine. The engine had a very cool outer case with a surface temperature between 100 and 120 degrees Celsius. depending upon ambient conditions.

The first tri-jet meeting! Both machines are seen during respective sales tours to the Far East. On 9 October 1963 Boeing 727-100 N7003U and Trident 1C G-ARPE met for the first time at Karachi. Just visible on the fuselage roof of the Trident is the Trident Arrow' logo, seeming applied just for this tour.
[John Stride Collection]

Graviner pyro-electric Firewire gave instant warning of engine fire or engine bay overheating. Overheat conditions in the side engine pod fillets and rear equipment bay, which could be due to leakage of hot air from the anti-icing or air conditioning systems, were detected by heat-sensitive resetting switches. A Graviner methyl bromide fire extinguisher system provided two discharges into any engine until it reached the tailpipe.

To prevent ice formation on engines and their intakes, each engine and its intake has a self-contained thermal anti-icing system, which was selected and controlled independently of the airframe anti-icing system.

For the podded engines, hot air is tapped from the final stage of the high-pressure compressor and was circulated around the engine face manifold and the lip of the air intake. A portion of the flow to each manifold passes down the centre of the hollow inlet guide vanes and then returns up the vane to the manifold. A small portion of the flow is fed from the vanes to anti-ice the centre bullet fairing, from which it is exhausted into the primary airstream entering the engine.

The centre engine and its intake lip had a similar ice protection system, but due to the greater length of the centre intake, an additional sub-system was incorporated to protect the portion of the intake between the lip and engine face were described in paperwork as the centre intake trunk.

During the starting cycle, each engine is accelerated to a self-sustaining speed in approximately eleven seconds by a Rotax air-driven turbine starter driving the high-pressure compressor. This starter has most of the advantages of the solid propellent turbo starter (of which it is a direct descendant) without its disadvantages. Several thousand turbochargers are in service now, and the functional reliability of their basic components has been proven over a long period.

Starting air supplies derived from the auxiliary power unit mounted in the aircraft or a ground source such as a mobile air compressor or air bottles may be fitted into the aircraft system at any pressure up to 235 pounds per square inch. Each starter air valve reduces the pressure to approximately 28 pounds per square inch. Without any alternative supply, the engines could be started by taking air from another Trident whose engines are running. It could be achieved by coupling the ground supply connections with a suitable pipe and manually overriding the non-return valve at this connection on the aircraft that was supplying the air.

Chapter Five

‘The Other Bits!’

The basic layout of the Trident flight compartment was designed to facilitate the eventual introduction of a fully automatic landing system, ‘Autoflare’ being the initial step towards this concept. Close collaboration was maintained from the project stage with the pilots and engineering staff of airlines specialising in short- and medium-haul networks. The result was a flight compartment that was simple, spacious, and adequately met the operational safety requirements of a high-speed civil airliner designed for all-weather utilisation.

Principal among the features which arose from new thinking in design was the neat, uncluttered appearance. The use of small ancillary instruments allowed the main panel to be occupied by presentations primarily concerned with flight path control and navigation. The area and positioning of windshields, direct vision panels, and ‘eyebrow’ windows complied with the latest BCAR and FAA vision requirements.

To facilitate maintenance, instruments fitted on the flight compartment panels were designed for front-of-panel removal.

The aircraft was intended for three-crew operation. The third crew member could position himself at the aircraft services panel or on the centre line of the aircraft facing forward, to suit the operational situation. A detachable stowable seat, that could be occupied at take-off and landing, was provided for a supernumerary crew member behind the Captain’s seat.

The Captain’s and co-pilot’s seats were adjustable for height and tilt, and move forward and rearward on rails. The third member’s seat was a swivel type with height adjustment, and also mounted on rails for the operational reasons previously mentioned.

An optional fourth crew member’s or check captain’s seat could be fitted in place of the supernumerary crew member's seat. It was mounted on rails and may be moved to a position near the aircraft centre line, facing forward.

Installed on the main instrument panel, the Central Warning System display was a new feature in flight compartment instrumentation, and indicated the location of a fault by means of illuminated notices on a central panel. In conjunction with red and amber ‘attention-getting’ flashing lights, positioned in front of the Captain and co-pilot, and at the aircraft services station, the system which was at fault was identified in a bank of eight red and fifteen amber windows. The degree of urgency of crew action required was graded by the two colours; a red notice demanded immediate action and an amber signified that attention was necessary.

Having identified from the Central Warning System display the system in which a failure had occurred, the nature of the failure was then traced by reference to the detailed warning indications on the aircraft services panel and on the hydraulic and HP fuel cock levers, allowing appropriate action to be taken. The system had sufficient display capacity to cover every aircraft system, and any number of warning devices could be fitted in each system to initiate a warning to its own window on the panel.

The Central Warning System provided an initial alert and was complementary to the normal system warnings and indications displayed throughout the flight compartment.

The pilots’ instruments were displayed on four panels mounted at a common ten-degree slope. These were the under-shroud panel, the centre panel and the Captain’s and co-pilot’s panels. The under-shroud panel was designed to display the essential instruments and controls for navigation. It contained two Flight Control System radio input switches, a VHF navigation controller and time of flight/elapsed time clock on either side.

The engine instruments, consisting of ten ‘two-inch’ presentations, grouped within a distinctive white outline, occupy the centre position on the panel. Below them were the ‘reverse-unlocked’ warning lights, and above them, space provision for water injection indicators.

The weather radar display was placed on the left of the panel, and below this was the roll and

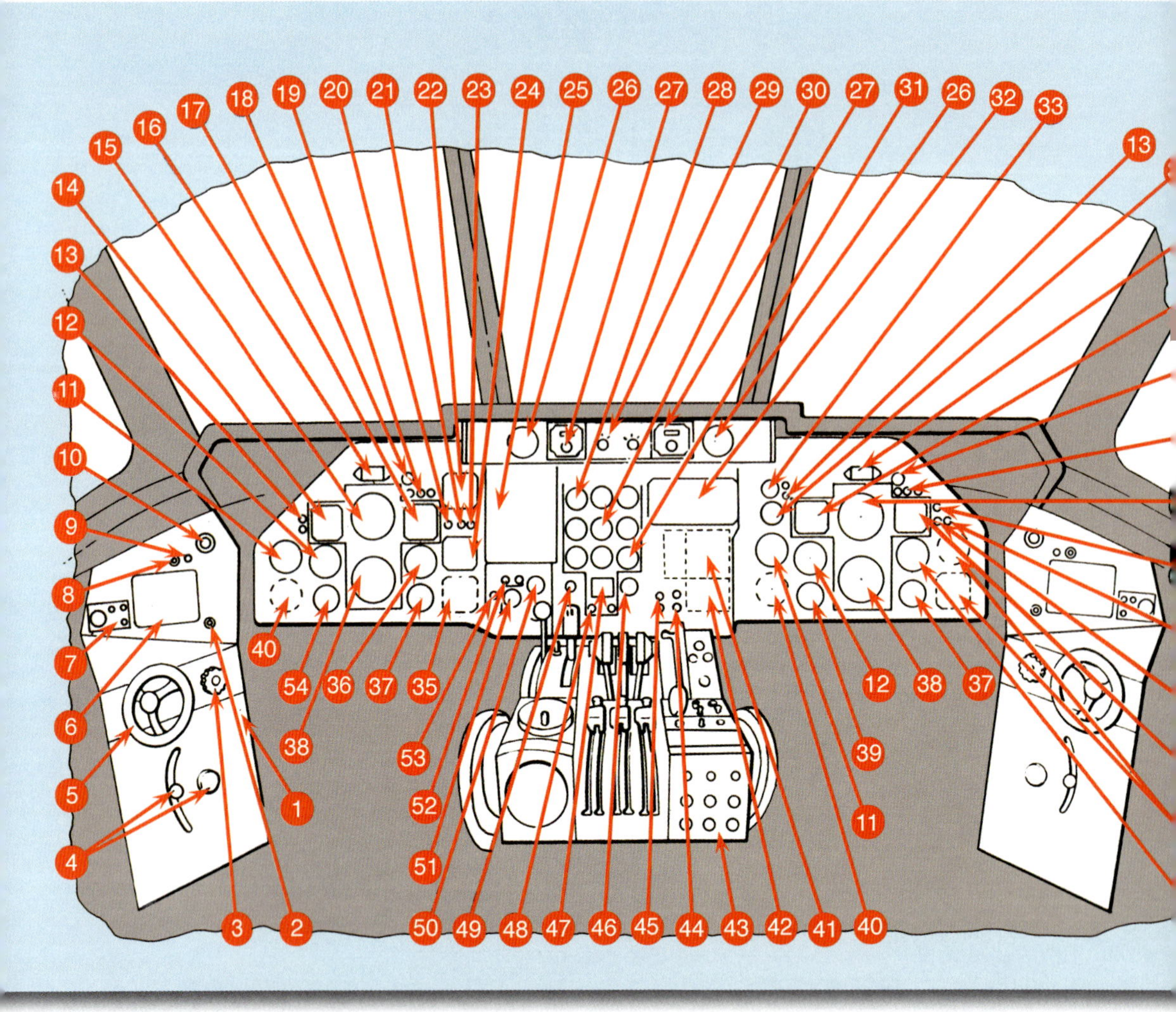

1 Pilots Side Panel.
2 Compass Light Control.
3 Rudder Pedal Adjuster.
4 Pilot's Warm Air Control.
5 Nose Gear Steering Wheel.
6 Communications Station Box.
7 SelCal Selector.
8 Chart Light Control.
9 Chart Light Switch.
10 Cold Air Outlet.
11 RMI.
12 Machmeter.
13 Stall Recovery Lights.
Top Fail.
Bottom Operate.
14 Airspeed Indicator.
15 Attitude Director.
16 Autopilot Mode Indicator.
17 Altimeter.
18 Height Acquire Warming Light.
19 ILS Localiser and Marker Lights.
20 Flight Level 100 Warning Light.
21 Central Warning System 'attention-getting' Alert Light.
22 Standby Horizon.
23 Central Warning System 'attention-getting' Caution Light.
24 Standby Altimeter.
25 Weather Radar Display.
26 Elapsed Time Clock.
27 VHF Navigation Controller.
28 Turbine Gas Temperature Instrument x 3.
29 Flight Control System Radio Imput Switches.
30 Engine RPM Indicators x 3.
31 Thrust Indicators x 3
32 Central Warning System Display Panel.
33 Slat Position Indicator.
34 Flap Position Indicator.
35 Landing Indicators (provision)
36 Vertical Speed Indicator.
37 Turn and Slip Indicator.
38 Flight Compass.
39 Cabin Altitude Indicator.
40 RMI (provision for extra Indicator).
41 Doppler Computer Display (provision).
42 Space for Rudder Drift Indicator.
43 Control Pedistal.
44 Lift Dumper Position Indicators.
45 Airbrake Position Indicators.
46 Outside Air Temperature.
47 Engine Syncroscope.
48 'Reverse Unlocked' Warning Lights.
49 Tailplane Position Indicator.
50 Brake Pressure Gauges.
51 Engage and Trim Indicator.
52 Yaw Damper Engaged Indicators.
53 Roll Damper Engaged Indicator.
54 Accelerometer.

yaw stabiliser 'engaged' indicators, the engage and trim indicators and the brake pressure gauges. The Central Warning panel was to the right of the engine instruments, and below it was space provision for either a Doppler computer display or a radar drift indicator. Other instruments, displayed at the bottom of the centre panel, were the airbrake and lift dumper magnetic indicators, the tailplane position indicator and the outside air temperature gauge.

The Captain's and co-pilot's instrument panels contained flight instruments of the Smiths Flight Control System. Manometric information was supplied to each group by two air data computers fed from independent pitot/static inputs. Flight compass and attitude director instruments operated on the roller-blind principle, and their displays were designed to provide increased clarity for all-weather operation.

The co-pilot's layout differed in that it contained, in addition to the Flight Control System instruments, a cabin altimeter and the slat and flap position indicators. The autopilot mode indicator and warning lights were similar to those on the Captain's panel. Provision was made for two landing indicators on the right side of the panel. These panels were illuminated by floodlighting and pillar lighting, as needed.

Captain's and co-pilot's side panels were basically similar, each housing a nosewheel steering control, rudder pedal adjustment, compass, instrument panel lighting dimmer switches, chart light switch and dimmer, communications control equipment and SelCal selector. A switch panel for the towing and parking brake hydraulic system was located at the Captain's position. The co-pilot controled emergency landing gear selection, the flight system and the essential services circuit breaker panel. A hot air regulator and cold air outlet were installed in both positions, and adequate stowage was provided for manuals, pilots' torches, flight logs and charts, sun visors, cups, etc.

The Aircraft Services Panel was located behind the co-pilot and was designed so that essential switches and controls were accessible from the co-pilot's seat. During the en route phase, it was normally monitored by the 'third man'. In keeping with the overall instrumentation in the flight compartment, rationalisation of controls and instruments were followed wherever possible. The layout comprised eight sub-sections for the smoke detection, oxygen, fuel, engine functioning, hydraulic, electrical, pressurization and air conditioning, engine and airframe anti-icing systems.

A roof panel was recessed into the flight compartment canopy to provide maximum headroom at the pilot's position. This panel was tiered in three sub-sections down towards the top of the windshield. The rear sub-section carried the hydraulic systems selectors, warning lights and switches as well as the navigation console, auxiliary power unit, engine starting, engine/airframe de-icing and E2B compass switches. The centre sub-section was occupied by radio supplies master, landing and taxi, and cabin notices switches, while the forward sub-section contains the switches for flight compartment window and windshield heating, and the internal and external lights.

Positioned immediately to the rear of the centre instrument panel was the pedestal on the right of which was the landing gear selector lever with the leg position and door warning lights on an adjacent panel. The panel also carried the controls for tailplane trim, aileron trim, rudder trim, airbrake and lift dumper selector, parking brake and toe brake hydraulic changeover selector, throttles (with auto throttle disconnect and reverse thrust levers), leading edge slat lever, flap lever, high pressure and low pressure fuel cock levers, as well as warning lights and switches associated with these systems.

A console formed a centralised panel for navigation, communications and flight system controllers and was a contributing factor towards the clean appearance of the flight compartment.

Pilots' instrument panels were illuminated by combinations of edge, pillar, and flood lighting. For daylight and storm lighting, fluorescent white floodlighting were used at a set level of brightness. Controllable incandescent white was used for night operation mixed with a small fixed amount of red to avoid harshness. A separate circuit provided incandescent white for emergency standby lighting.

Plasteck panel illumination was installed on the centre pilots' panel, the radio controller console, the aircraft services panel, and the roof panels. A lamp on each control column was directed at the Captain's and co-pilot's flight compasses, and a spotlight was installed in the roof at the two positions. Light for the pedestal was provided by a roof floodlight. General lighting of the compartment was provided by a single roof lamp, with floor lighting concentrated around the four seats. Landing gear safety pin stowages and the crew wardrobe were spotlighted when the general compartment lighting was switched on at the entry door. This lighting could be switched off at the roof panel when the crew were seated.

The fuselage of the Trident was designed so that the interior may be furnished to meet operators' individual requirements. The passenger accommodation was unobstructed by permanent bulkheads of any sort, allowing complete freedom to vary seating layouts. There were two passenger doors on the left side of the fuselage forward of the wing, and a smaller door for galley servicing on the right side. Freight was accommodulated in two spacious holds, one forward and one to the rear of the wing.

The fuselage was soundproofed and insulated by airtight bags containing fibreglass, which were laced to the structure by nylon cords. Cobex transparent sheeting between bags and cords restrained the bags and ensured free circulation of conditioning air in the inter-wall space. Soundproofing was also fitted behind the trim panels on passenger doors and in the freight holds.

In the flight compartment, fibreglass was used for the canopy, roof trim, side trim and wardrobe panels, and were bolted to the supporting structure. A fixed curtain was fitted at the forward end of the aircraft services panel, and a sliding curtain was provided at the front of the wardrobe. PVC material covers the floor, and a PVC foam underlay can be supplied if required. The door separating the flight compartment from the passenger cabin was panelled with rigid plastic and was frangible to allow forced opening in an emergency.

In the passenger cabin, soundproofing was concealed by an interior trim lining of fibreglass cloth with PVC finish, assembled in sections for ease of removal. The window trim panels were made of fibreglass and trimmed with PVC. Each panel incorporated ball-headed studs, which engaged spring clips on the trim support structure. The bottom of the panel rested on a skirting extending throughout the cabin length, and a locating plate on the panel that slid over an air conditioning duct which protruded from the skirting. Air flowed along the skirting, out of the duct into the trim panel, and entered the cabin through a metal grill above the panel and also through perforations in the underside of the hat-rack. Removal of a window trim panel was very simple: the top of the panel was pulled away from the cabin wall, releasing the studs, and the panel was then lifted clear of the skirting.

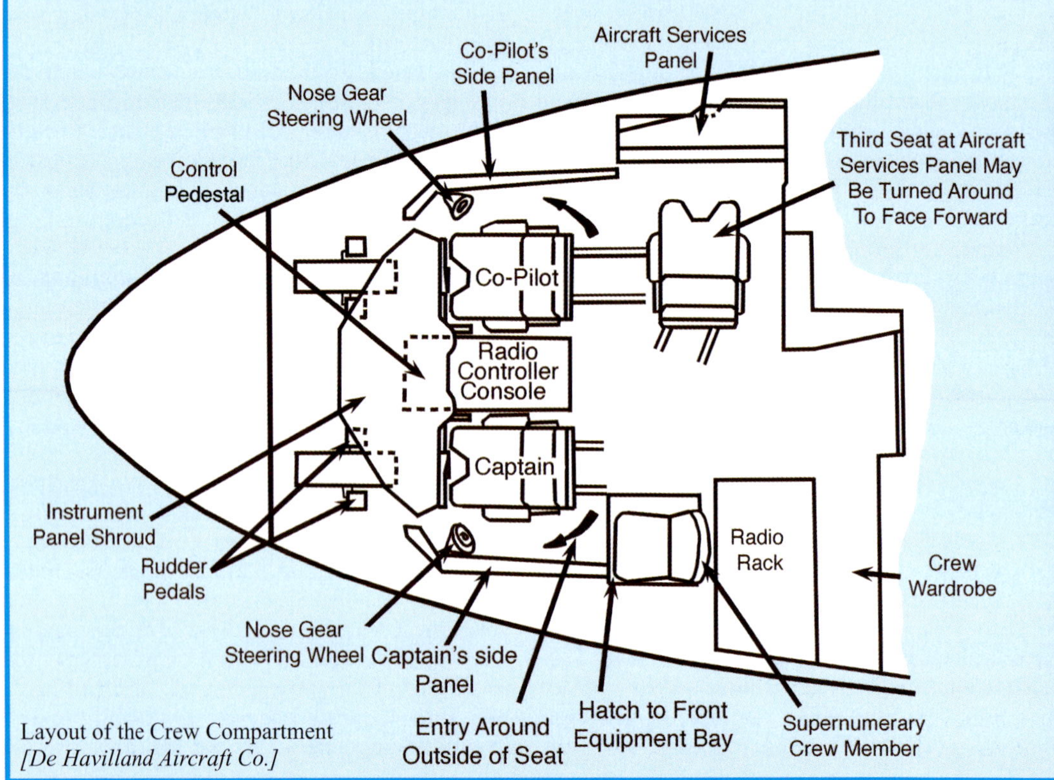

Layout of the Crew Compartment
[De Havilland Aircraft Co.]

northeast's Trident G-AWYC wore this striking yellow scheme, a paint-job that dramatically faded in the sunlight and ended up looking decidedly anaemic at times. *[Kirk Smeaton Collection]*

Windows, each measuring thirteen and a half inches by ten inches, provided a good view, and their close pitching at twenty-inch intervals allowed an operator complete freedom to vary seating layouts without depriving any passenger of a window. Each window was of cavity construction, consisting of two perspex panels, separated by and bonded to both a perspex and a thick rubber ring. Gallery piping connects breather pipes at each rubber ring to the air conditioning system. Each window was fitted with two smoked plastic blinds that extended as eyelids to meet halfway up the window. This system provided protection from both direct sunlight and sunlight reflected by the wings. without totally obscuring the window.

The decor of the cabin, trim and vestibules was styled by Charles Butler Associates of New York. Interior colour schemes, furnishings and material for bulkhead facings were dependent on the customer's choice.

A wide variety of cabin seating layouts was possible as there were no permanently fixed bulkheads anywhere in the entire length of the passenger cabin. Seats were mounted on rails, which permitted seat pitch variations in one inch increments. Each seat was adjustable for tilt, and carried an armrest ashtray, a newspaper pocket and an individual table.

A removable rigid bulkhead with a curtained doorway divided the first- and tourist-class cabins. It could be placed in virtually any position in the passenger cabin, giving a wide variety of possible mixed-class layouts.

The Trident had two freight holds, one immediately forward of the wing, the other behind it. Each hold was pressurised but not ventilated, though provision was made for ventilation of the front part of the forward hold so that it could be adapted to carry livestock. The holds were metal-lined.

Flush-fitted lashing rings were permanently attached to the floor, walls and roof at every alternate frame position in both freight holds. They were located so that the nylon sheet freight curtains could be strung vertically across the hold at the alternate frame positions. Stowage was provided for spare sheets in each hold.

Large entrance hatches with sills only four feet six inches above ground level facilitated freight loading and therefore faster turnaround. Usable freight hold volume was 425 cubic feet in the front and 275 cubic feet in the rear hold, giving a total of 700 cubic feet at a density of twelve pounds per cubic foot.

Ground Handling

To achieve high utilisation during intensive operations on short- or medium-haul route networks, the Trident had been designed to keep aircraft turnaround times t as low as possible. With this requirement in mind, many features were built into the Trident to facilitate ground handling and to reduce the time spent on the ground at intermediate stops.

Integral airstairs (optional) and an auxiliary power unit reduce the demand for servicing equipment to a minimum. The APU provided electrical power - which could, if required, be used to power ground testing of the hydraulic system via the standby pumps - and also air for air conditioning and engine starting. If necessary, the APU could also be used to provide warm air for airframe defrosting. The unit, which was started electrically from the aircraft battery, thus gave the aircraft complete independence from ground power supplies.

Two large passenger entry doors, both forward

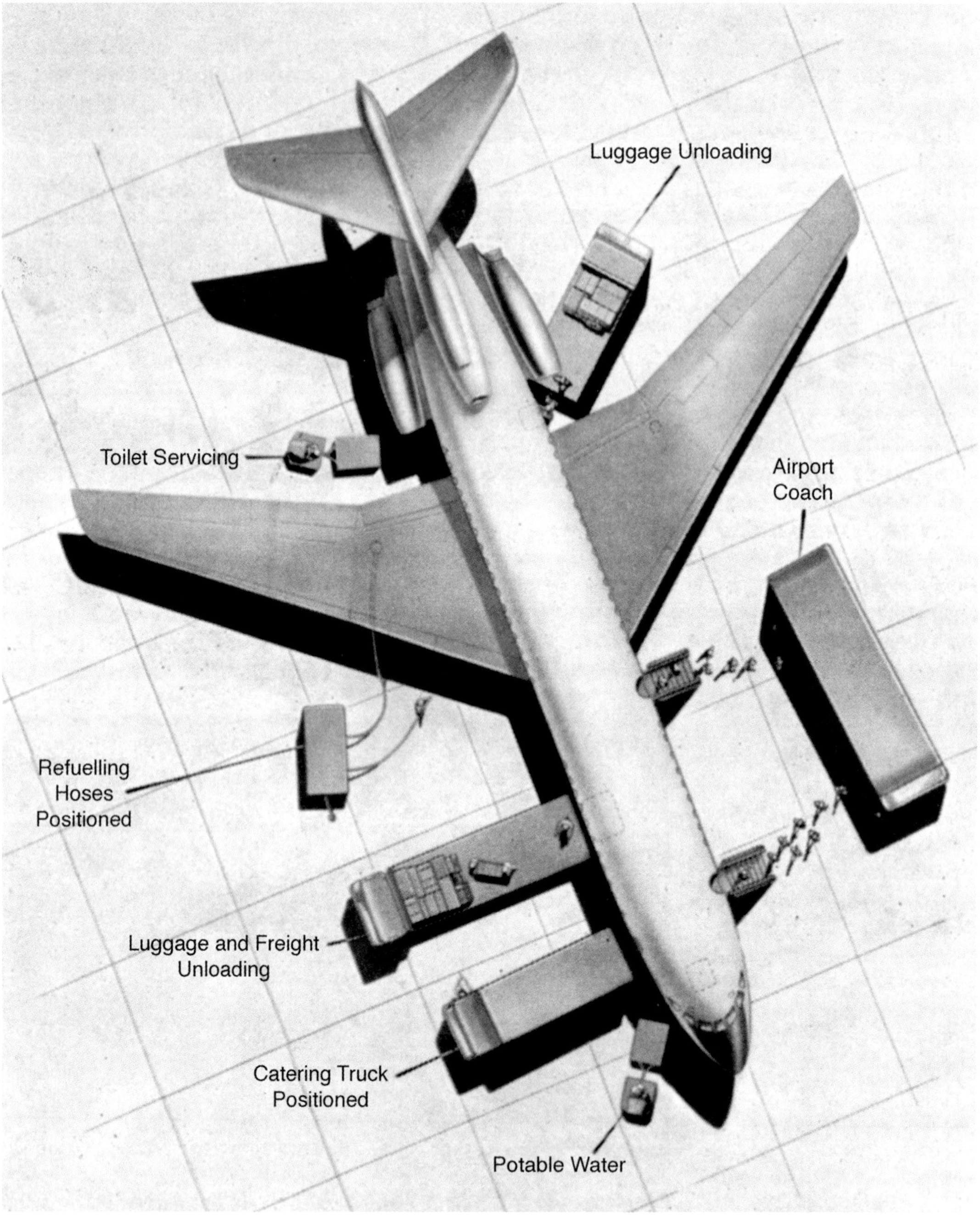

The normal arrangement of ground support vehicles parked around a Trident during turn-around.
[artwork courtesy of British Aerospace Hatfield]

of the wing on the left-hand side of the aircraft, expedited passenger boarding. At the same time, the forward galley could be serviced through a door opening directly into the galley area, on the opposite side of the aircraft. Two large freight doors, well separated from passenger entry and galley service doors and conveniently arranged for side loading, permit rapid handling of freight and passengers' luggage.

All normal turnaround replenishment points and controls were located so that servicing personnel do not need to enter the aircraft, and no special tools were required. Toilet and water service points were designed to prevent delays caused by icing. Refuelling and offloading were controlled automatically from a panel in the right-hand main landing gear bay, giving the operator a clear view of refuelling operations. All toilet, water and fuel servicing points can be reached from the ground.

A Bristol Siddeley Artouste 520 auxiliary power unit installed in the Trident IE gave complete independence from external ground power sources. The APU operated only when the aircraft was on the ground and supplied air for engine starting, air conditioning, and electrical power for all services. The APU could also be used to supply air for externally defrosting the aircraft. A three inch diameter coupling in the fuselage skin adjacent to the rear equipment bay door was provided for the connection of a ground conditioned air unit as an alternative to the APU. By connecting a long, flexible pipe to this coupling and overriding the non-return valve embodied in it manually, the normal direction of flow can be reversed, and air supplied by the APU to the aircraft side of the coupling can be tapped for defrosting purposes.

The flight compartment and passenger cabins were able to be cooled to 78° Fahrenheit on a 100° Farenheit day with forty-six per cent relative humidity, or heated to any desired temperature in the range 60-80° Fahrenheit on a cold day, using air from the auxiliary power unit or a ground air conditioning unit.

The air was passed into the normal air conditioning gallery and was temperature-controlled and distributed in the normal in-flight manner. Ground pressurisation test points were located in the nose gear bay.

The APU was equipped with a generating system to meet the requirements of the aircraft's electrical system services on the ground and thus dispensed with the need for any electrical ground supplies.

A ground supply point for the connection of either 200/115-volt a.c. or 28-volt d.c. Ground supplies were provided on the lower right side of the fuselage nose, for use when the APU was not being run.

The oxygen system charging point was located inside the front freight hold door and was positioned to give minimum interference with baggage handling. The system employed three storage cylinders and had a charging pressure of 1,800 pounds per square inch. A contents gauge was provided alongside the charging point.

The hydraulic reservoirs, containing Skydrol 500A, were located in the rear fuselage equipment bay and were pressure-filled and drained via Avery couplings. The hydraulic accumulators were also installed in the rear equipment bay with easy access for air charging. Self-sealing couplings for each of the three systems were located immediately inside the rear equipment bay door and were provided for the connection of ground

For ease of turn-around, De Havilland offered built-in air-stairs.
[artwork courtesy of British Aerospace Hatfield]

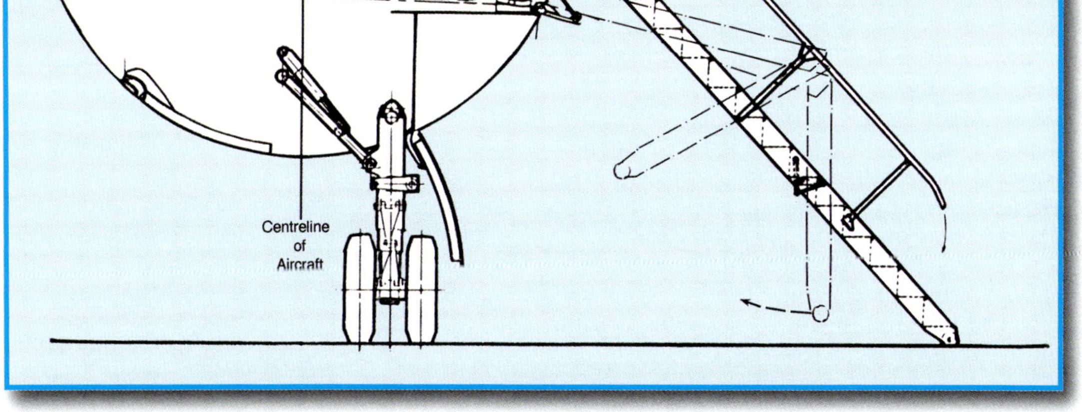

test rigs for checking all hydraulic services on the aircraft.

Water/waste servicing provisions vary with system configurations to meet operators' requirements. Fresh water fill and drain, and waste water drain servicing points were grouped inside the fuselage at the forward equipment bay and rear freight hold doors. The rear servicing point was positioned to give minimum interference with baggage loading. Standard couplings were used with 'stow-away' pipes, which enable connections to be made outside the aircraft. The valves were controlled at the servicing points, and access doors were arranged so that the valves cannot be inadvertently left open. The tank full indication was provided by overflow from outlets incorporated into the charging connections. Toilet drain and sluice points were installed beneath each toilet and were accessible via flush doors on the fuselage side.

Engine starting utilises compressed air from the auxiliary power unit, ground power unit or air bottles according to the particular operator's specification. The remaining two engines can be started from any one running engine.

Each engine had its own self-contained lubrication system. The oil-filling point was at the lower left side of each engine, with provision for both pressure and gravity filling. Oil levels can be checked without opening the engine bay doors. Large doors beneath the centre engine and the outer engine pods give full access to the engines. All engine accessory units were grouped beneath the engines.

Fuel

Pressure refuelling and suction offloading was accomplished through a coupling on the underside of each wing. Each point supplies fuel to the wing tank in which it was installed. The centre tank was supplied from the right-hand coupling.

The fuel load required in each tank was set by the ground operator on the load limit control at the refuel control panel in the right-hand main gear bay, and the quantity of fuel was then automatically controlled by the amount selected. Tank capacity filling was terminated by float switches within the tanks. Blow-off valves prevent excessive pressure from building up in the tanks. The refuelling rate at fifty pounds per square inch was five hundred imperial gallons per minute. An aircraft with empty tanks could be completely refuelled in fifteen minutes, determined by the time taken to fill the inner tanks.

Offloading was effected through the refuelling points by selecting 'OFFLOAD' on the refuel control panel and the refuelling vehicle. A typical offloading can be accomplished in about thirty minutes using a suction of seven pounds per square inch at the aircraft coupling. Alternatively, by using the aircraft's fuel pumps, fuel can be offloaded through the power drain coupling located in the centre engine bay at a rate of hirty-five gallons per minute from each tank.

The refuel/offload system piping was protected from any excessive surge pressures that may arise by relief valves that open at eighty pounds per square inch. Provision was also made for offloading by gravity without using electrical power from the aircraft.

Over-wing filling points were provided for the wing tanks. Fuel levellers in each wing were provided to open clack valves and allow the fuel to find a common level within the tank's inter-compartments. Two independent systems were provided for gauging tank contents - a capacitance system indicating in the flight compartment and at the refuel panel, and a magnetic level indicator system for use during ground servicing. Both systems were substantially unaffected by aircraft attitude. The magnetic system consists of one indicator each for the centre and inner tanks and two indicators for each outer tank. These indicators permit an independent physical check of tank contents on the ground without fuel drip. When using this system, the fuel levellers must be operated first.

Towing and Taxiing

Hydraulic nose wheel steering and multi-disc brakes on each main wheel give the Trident excellent manoeuvrability under engine power. Steering was controlled from either of two handwheels, one on each pilot's side panel, and the standard of visibility from the flight compartment was such that each pilot can see the wingtip on his side. Towing or pushing was accomplished by a tractor, having a tractive effort of approximately 3,400 pounds with a towbar attached to the base of the nose gear leg.

The nose leg was designed so that the towbar can only be connected when the torque links were disconnected. This automatically disconnects nose wheel steering and allows the aircraft to be steered directly by the towbar. When towing, the nose wheels can be turned through any angle, limited only by the height of the tractor. A light-weight folding towbar was been specially designed to be

A truly stunning picture of G-ARPN banking away from the camera.
[Photograph courtesy of British Aerospace Hatfield]

air-transportable. The unit incorporates shear pins to protect the aircraft structure, and was fitted with pneumatic wheels. Other towbars were also available. The aircraft incorporated a small electric d.c pump, operated by the aircraft battery, to provide hydraulic power for brake application during towing and parking. In an emergency, the aircraft could be towed rearwards using a bridle attached to lugs on the main gear legs. Low-intensity Nav./Park lights were fitted and supplied from the battery under towing or parking conditions.

Lifting and Shoring

The main jacking points were located, one aft of the nose gear bay and one outboard of the main gear bay under each wing. A 10-ton tripod jack was used at the nose point, and a 40-ton tripod jack at each wing point; international standard jack pad adaptors were used at all three points. The maximum jacking weight was 106,000 pounds.

For wheel changes, each landing gear can be jacked individually, using an eight to ten ton bottle jack on an integral jack pad on the nose gear, and a thirty ton bottle jack with a special adaptor fitted to the main gear axle barrel. The maximum jacking weight for wheel changing was 130,000 pounds..

Those components which cannot be conveniently manhandled have built-in slinging points for the attachment of hoisting gear. Built-in attachment points for Minihoist lifting gear make the Trident independent of aerodrome crane facilities even for engine or APU changes.

Airstairs

The Trident airstairs were an efficient alternative to the standard airport ground stairs and will be particularly useful for short-haul operators making transit stops, as passengers will be able to disembark immediately without awaiting the arrival of ground stairs. The airstairs were a sturdy but relatively lightweight structure which can be installed for an additional weight of 370 pounds. The stairs extend below the forward passenger door at an angle of forty-five degrees. and stow in the roof of the nose gear bay, below the pressure floor. In this position, they do not obstruct the passenger doorway in either the normal or emergency exit functions.

The main structure consists of three main parts: (i) a chassis, (ii) an upper stair of nine treads, and (iii) a folding lower stair of four treads.

Spare Parts

Information on spare parts planning and procurement was presented in accordance with ATA Specifications 100 and 200. ATA Spec. 100 currently in widespread use provided a universally accepted means of listing spare parts consistent with the operating and engineering manuals. ATA Spec. 200 lays down a procedure to cover all aspects of spares planning and procurement. This procedure may either be incorporated using the operator's individual system of spares tabulation, or using a semi-automatic system supplied by Hawker Siddeley. The latter, which stores up-to-the-minute spares information on Integrated Data

Processing Punched cards (this was pre-digital days, remember?!) that had the advantage of being highly accurate and saving time and labour.

Only nine different lubricants were used on the Trident - four being used in day-to-day maintenance and the other five being required during overhaul.

Who supplied what

Due to meticulous record-keeping by De Havillands and pride in using British suppliers, we know in great detail which long-gone companies and organisations provided materials and equipment for the Trident. The paperwork listing reads something like a Browns Brothers Aircraft parts catalogue.

About twenty tons of James Booth Aluminium Ltd. material went into each Trident, all material being completely ultrasonically tested and control-stretched for stress-relieving purposes. The materials provided were Dural G (DTD 5090), Aldural G (DTD 5100) and Dural S (DTD S010 and 5020).

Firth-Derihon Stampings Ltd. supplied a number of drop-forged components for Trident applications. In particular, two of their main contributions were the turbine disks and compressor wheels produced in vacuum remelted FV.535 and FV.448 - these and other drop forgings were supplied to Rolls-Royce for Spey production.

A range of non-ferrous rivets was supplied by Clevedon Rivets and Tools Ltd., while Lentern (Aircraft) Ltd. manufactured special bolts and supplied a range of parts. Tubing in Tungum alloy was provided by Yorkshire Imperial Metals Ltd. at the instruction of Tungum Co. Ltd.

Fine Tubes Ltd. supplied seventy per cent of the stainless steel tubing for the Trident, a great deal of which took the form of hydraulic pipes for flaps and undercarriage. Heli-coil screw thread inserts by Armstrong Patents Co. Ltd, in addition to being used in the Rolls-Royce Spey engines, were incorporated in more than twenty important points in the Trident, including the flying controls, refuelling manifold, centre-section wing structure, and tail bumper mounting arm.

Alcan Industries Ltd. supplied Alclad sheet in Alcan GB-24-ST3 and Alcan GB-B26SWP alloys

John Cunningham hands over the log-book of G-AVFC to a representative of BEA . Note the slightly different style of font for 'Trident Two'. *[The late John Stride Collection]*

A close-up of the main undercarriage unit, showing the mechanism. *[The late John Stride Collection]*

for the fuselage. As far as the wings and tailplane were concerned, the majority of the stringers were extruded in Alcan GB-B26SWP and Alcan GB-C77SWP alloys. A certain amount of the internal portions of the wing were in the Alcan GB-B26SWP and the Alcan GB-24ST plate. The tailplane was manufactured on a sub-contract from Fairey Engineering, Stockport, and for this, Alcan Industries supplied a plate in Alcan GB-B26-SWP alloy for the top skin and in Alcan GB-24ST for the bottom skin.

Aluminium and magnesium alloy castings were provided by Sterling Metals Ltd. for the control systems, airframe, landing gear, cabin installations and other accessories. In all, Sterling produced some two hundred different parts for the Trident, which were produced principally by the sand and shell mould methods.

Various types of extrusions, sheet and plate in high-strength aluminium alloys, as well as a number of forgings for the Spey, such as stator casing, ram mounting bracket, turbine and compressor blades, and other forgings in titanium, were supplied by High Duty Alloys Ltd.

T. J. Brooks (Leicester) Ltd. delivered standard aircraft bolts in the cold forged and bar turned conditiontion as well as various types of ESNA lightweight-stiffnuts such as reduced hexagon, 12 point, fixed and floating anchor nuts.

English Steel Forge and Engineering Corporation Ltd. produced from steels of their own, manufactured forged steel components for the undercarriage and airframe in Vibrac V.45 (En. 26) and Hykro V (DTD.730) qualities. These included: axle beam, inner casing, flap tracks, main leg inner and outer casings, plunger tube, axle barrels, main gear axles, torque links, upper high ends, main body upper stay, upper torque member, cam head, rings for main gear leg, axles, drag stay, cam roller bolt and attachment pins.

The use of plastic coating on alloy components of aircraft control mechanisms was then a recent development, of which extensive use was made on the Trident. The principal coatings used were Nylon RP.95 and, to a lesser extent, PVC Vylastic RS.60. These coatings were specified not only for their extreme wear-resisting properties, but also for their ability to effectively eliminate corrosion of

A tyical London Heathrow scene in the early 1970s with three Tridents 'on stand', with G-ARPW closest and a BOAC VC-10 in the background. *[The late John Stride Collection]*

the magnesium and aluminium alloys. Both of these coatings were applied by Plastic Coatings Ltd., working closely in conjunction with the aircraft manufacturers to the Hawker Siddeley Spec. DHA/517 and in accordance with their own A.I.D. approved Spec. PCL/l, Plastic Coatings Ltd., applied these coatings with special equipment, ensuring that the temperatures involved had no adverse effects on the highly-stressed alloys. These nylon coatings were applied to many parts of the control mechanism, including magnesium servo control drums, aluminium alloy elevator sling assemblies, mild steel cable guide brackets, and numerous pulleys used in the aileron control cable runs. In the pilots' cabin, nylon coating was extensively used on throttle levers, brake selectors, and hand grips. The nylon coating was also applied to aluminium or magnesium substrates, and in some cases the nylon was treated with a special finish to give a matt, non-reflective surface on the Flight Deck.

Over two hundred Glacier DU dry-bearing components were incorporated into each Trident, in fuselage controls, airstairs, tail unit controls, and other control systems. Glacier DU bearings were also incorporated in the Rolls-Royce Spey engines. Glacier DU components were designed to operate entirely without lubrication over a wide range of temperatures and under conditions where lubrication would be either impracticable, impossible or undesirable.

F.P.T. Industries Ltd. supplied a number of small components, including stringer seals, sealing clamp blocks, intake sealing rings, anti-vibration mountings, water tank covers, and numerous sealing rings. These were precision mouldings from specially compounded synthetic rubbers to withstand a wide temperature range range, in addition to being oil-, fuel- and ozone-resistant.

Standard aircraft parts, including bolts, washers, screws, pipe unions, and nuts for the Trident, were supplied by Brown Bros. (Aircraft) Ltd. Precision Rubbers Ltd., and Metalastik Ltd., manufactured a number of components for the airliner, including window and other packings, door seals, radio seals, bushes, and flexible hose as well as 'O' seals and other rubber components for the engines.

Rapp Metals Ltd. supplied a range of aluminium alloys (L59, L61 manganese alloy sheet, L72 copper alloy clad sheet, DTD 5020 plate, L64 and L65 bar, L34 aluminium bar, L56 and L62 tubing), carbon steels (S14, S93B, S92 bar, S511, S514 sheet, T35 and T45 tubing), alloy steels (S96 and S98B-nickel-chrome-molybdenum steels) and stainless steels (SI 10, S80, S124 bar, S520, S521 sheet, T55 and DTD 743 tubing).

Polypenco Ltd. provided three main materials for three different applications. The first was Fluorosint material used for piston rings for a light-weight actuator used in the air conditioning supply system. The second was a Polypenco Nylon 66 plate, which Hawker Siddeley machines into cable clamps used on the various electrical runs. Finally, Polypenco Fluorocarbon TFE (PTFE) was also used in sheet and tube form for machining into rings used in various items of equipment throughout the Trident.

The Unbrako Socket Screw Co. Ltd. Hi-Torque Fastener was employed on the Trident. This has a

safety on board see pages 1, 2 and 3
sécurité à bord voir pages 1, 2 et 3
sicherheit an bord siehe seiten 1, 2 und 3
BEA
BRITISH EUROPEAN AIRWAYS
for you to keep
gardez cette brochure
bitte mitnehmen
about your flight
votre vol
ihr flug
BEA

novel head recess which was accurate in form and diverged outward from the centre. It was undercut at the sides where driving torque was applied, thus locking the driver in the recess. This configuration presents maximum bearing for driving thrust.

Materials for decorative purposes were supplied by John Cox and Son Ltd. VT.1266FR/PTV.9363 was a stretch fabric that has been specially designed to trim right around and into the windows in lieu of the normal hard frame as this material was an excellent sound deadener. The same colour and grain has been developed in VT.1327 quality material to be used on the panels where it was unnecessary to get around tight curves or trim into windows - the object being to reduce weight. VT.1234FR/6856 was used on the top of the fuselage, and Vynair 8/9822 was a porous material to cover vents and speakers. Two other Vynides were used on the aircraft. All these materials were manufactured especially for John Cox by CI (Hyde) Ltd. and all were fire resistant.

The C F Taylor Group of Companies was making a substantial contribution to the Trident programme. They were producing water tanks in stainless steel for the Trident I aircraft, while prototype tanks in titanium alloy were currently being fabricated for later versions. Ducting in stainless steel carrying hot air for anti-icing purposes was manufactured and supplied, fitted with fibreglass insulation and a retaining stitched jacket. C. F. Taylor also formed the fin skins which were milled from solid, the forming being carried to shape the metal to fin aerofoil shape. Another item produced was a heat exchanger intake duct assembly in light alloy. On the plastics side, passenger window surrounds, hat racks, and roofing decor panels were produced in glass-fibre-reinforced plastics, as were ducting for the air conditioning system.

The Trident 1E main undercarriage units were designed by the De Havilland Division of Hawker Siddeley Aviation and were manufactured by the Lostock production factory of Hawker Siddeley Dynamics.

Each Trident main leg carried four wheels fitted two to each axle and arranged ‘line abreast’. The legs retracted sideways and inward into the fuselage. To accomplish this, the legs rotated through ninety degrees and, at the same time, the leg was lengthened by a cylindrical cam mechanism built into the top of the oleo.

The nose undercarriage, main and nose retraction gear and general hydraulic equipment for the Trident were designed by Lockheed Precision Products Ltd., who drew on their considerable experience with the Comet and Caravelle, and, in order to ensure absolute reliability and maximum fatigue life, instituted one of the most comprehensive test programmes to which their equipment had been subjected. For example, the nose undercarriage assembly was fatigue-tested, without failure, for a simulated 180,000 flying hours to give a safe life of 30,000 flying hours. The test programme, however, was not applied solely to major assemblies such as the nose undercarriage, but covered every one of more than 75 units supplied by Lockheed.

Dowty Seals Ltd. supplies main undercarriage and nose-leg shock absorber seals and a wide range of precision seals and mouldings in a variety of plastics and rubbers for use in fuel, hydraulic and pneumatic system, powered flying control systems, etc.

For cooling the braking system after landing, a 9.5 inch three-bladed cast aluminium alloy impeller was mounted in each of the main wheels. These impellers, by Airscrew- Weyrac Ltd., were supplied to Dunlop Rim and Wheel Co., for a duty of 600 cubic feet per minute of air through the braking system was obtained at 7,200 r.p.m.at 0.2 absorbed h.p.

Two Saunders Valve Co. Ltd. SP valves were fitted in the fuel system as well as flap and plate-type non-return valves at various points in the system - one of the plate type being a component of the auxiliary power unit. A feature of the flap-type non-return valve was its ability to permit greater flow efficiency by virtue of the high lift to the operating flap. A total of fifty Saunders valves were incorporated in each Trident - twenty-six of these units being installed in the fuel system, including the compact motorised spherical plug type, also multi-way versions of this same valve.

The Hobson booster pump type 436, Mk. 2, was installed in a Hobson canister type 443, Mk. IA. Apart from this item, Hobson was also supplying the fuel flow proportioner type 440, which was fitted in the pipelines leading from the outer port and starboard wing tanks to the centre engine nacelle.

A wide range of fuel systems equipment had been designed for the Trident by Flight Refuelling Ltd. including fuel level indicators, refuelling/defuelling valves, transfer valves, and float switches.

All the important items of equipment supplied by Rotax and Lucas Gas Turbine for the Trident were fitted to the Rolls-Royce Spey engines. Rotax supply the pneumatic (low-pressure) engine starter and a twelve-joule high-energy ignition unit for each engine, together with various valves and solenoid units throughout the aircraft. Lucas supplies the CASC system (combined acceleration and speed control) for the engines.

The primary control surfaces of the Trident - the all-moving tailplane, the ailerons, and the rudder - were power-operated by three Fairey hydraulic jacks located adjacent to the surfaces. Each surface was positioned by three jacks working in parallel and operating continuously side-by-side. Three sources of hydraulic power were provided by a pump on each engine, with a fourth and independent power supply provided by a Dowty ram air turbine for the remote case where all three engines fail.

Other Trident components produced by Fairey Engineering include four micro-filters - three (of 14 gallons per minute capacity) mounted on the rear bulkhead to serve the triplejacks (one per system), and the other was in the nosewheel bay to protect the emergency/ auxiliary electrically-driven hydraulic circuit.

H M Hobson Ltd. were supplying the type 392 and type 421 droop power control units for the Trident 1 as well as slat controls for the Trident IE. Hobson also provide the couplings and shafting of the droop control system which transmit power from the droop control unit to the ball screw jacks to lower or raise the wing leading edge. The ball screw jack type 422 provided the means of translating the rotational output from the droop control unit into a linear movement to extend and retract the wing leading edge droops, and consists basically of a bevel pinion, bevel gear, screw and nut with a 'no-back' mechanism to ensure irreversibility. The Hobson units type 482 function as brakes in the droop shaftings.

The Hobson flap control unit type 377 was basically a hydraulically-driven power control for operating the wing trailing edge inner and outer flaps and was essentially a twin unit. Habson couplings and shaftings transmit the power from the flap control unit to the type 378 ball screw jacks to extend or retract the flaps and to the flap deflector drives type 433 to lower or raise the deflector surface. Ball screw jacks type 378 provide the means of translating the rotational output from the flap control unit into a linear movement to extend and retract the flaps. Other Hobson items include flap position transmitters type 390 and 513, and reduction gearbox type 379 and 512.

An Engel and Gibbs temperature-sensitive switch unit was fitted into the main hydraulic tanks and was manufactured in stainless steel, and the normal setting was ninety degrees to make contact on a rising temperature and operate warning lamps, and relays should the temperature of the system rise above the safety level.

The Emergency Passenger and Crew Oxygen System was supplied by The Walter Kidde Co. Ltd. This system automatically supplies both passengers andcrew with oxygen in the event of a loss of cabin pressure.

Damic Controls Ltd. have produced, especially for the Trident, two new oxygen valves - one being a master control valve SDV.543 with the necessary slow opening characteristics and fireproof metal-

Another Heathrow view! BEA Maintenance Base, Olympic Airways 720 and a BEA Trident.
[The late John Stride Collection]

to-metal seating, made throughout in stainless steel, while the other was a charging valve DC.53, which was flanged having a length of B.S.P. (British Standard Pipe) left-hand thread on the charging end. Other Damic components in the Trident were a number of charging valves, type DC.47, for the control of DTD.585, and air.

The electrical power system for the airliner was designed, developed and manufactured by Associated Electrical Industries Ltd. and was the first all-British constant frequency a.c. power system with brushless self-excited a.c. generators driven through Hobson constant speed drives. The control equipment makes extensive use of static devices and incorporates modern semiconductor techniques.

In addition to three a.c. Generators driven by the aircraft engines, there was a fourth driven by an auxiliary power unit. Although the generators were not normally operated in parallel, provision has been made for parallel operation, if required. Each generator was rated at 22-5 kVA, 3-phase, 400 c.p.s., 200 V.

The bearings provide the limiting factor for overhaul life with brushless a.c. generators (there being no brushes to wear), and to obtain maximum life, they were lubricated with engine oil. The use of oil-lubricated bearings for aircraft generators were pioneered and have been fully proven in service with Comet 4 aircraft.

Direct current power supplies were provided by three self-cooled transformer rectifier units, each rated at 3 kW, 28 v.

The AEI magnetic amplifier control unit contains no moving parts and, with the use of silicon rectifiers and of a potting technique, was completely free from any adverse effects introduced by changes of environment.

Right from the initial stages, Leach relays were selected for the Trident, and each aircraft goes into service with approximately 100. They fall into three basic types - a 2-pole 10 amp. relay, a 4-pole 15 amp. relay and a 3-pole 10 amp. time delay relay. They were made in two variations to operate from two different supplies- -28 volt d.c. and 115 volt 400 cycles a.c. The 2-pole and 4-pole relays have a wide variety of applications in circuit control throughout the aircraft. The time delay relays were set with delay times of 400 millisec., 1 sec. and 8 seconds, respectively, for three different functions. Leach relays for the Trident were now supplied from Leach's manufacturing plant in Germany and Switzerland through their UK representatives of FieldTech Ltd.

Sperry Gyroscope Co. Ltd. manufactures 27 units for the Smiths Flight Control System, as well as Vickers engine-driven pumps and ancillaries for the hydraulic systems of the Trident. All units of the flight control system have been designed for ease of changeability, and all the instruments were suitable for solid mounting conditions. No recalibration or re-adjustment of any system was necessary when a functional unit has been changed, and all the units will meet British and American Civil Airworthiness requirements.

The complete attitude system was manufactured at Sperry, and the majority of the manometric repeater instruments, the direction gyros and their mountings and part of the flight director system. Thus Sperry contributes at least three-quarters of the basic instrument displays, together with their sensing gyros without of which the Trident would not be able to fly.

The attitude system consists of three vertical reference units, two attitude directors, two attitude director display amplifiers, two rate gyro units and one yaw rate gyro unit, together with the associated mounting tray necessary for housing these gyro units. Each vertical reference unit provided the aircraft attitude in pitch and roll, to

Trident Three G-AWZM in the full 'British' scheme. *[The late John Stride Collection]*

LUCAS

QUALITY EQUIPMENT FOR AIRCRAFT AND GAS TURBINE ENGINES

Every eleven seconds, throughout the twenty-four hours of the day, somewhere in the world an aircraft takes off, or lands, relying on Lucas Equipment — a vital contribution to the dependability, efficiency, safety and comfort of your flight.

JOSEPH LUCAS (INDUSTRIES) LTD · BIRMINGHAM AND LONDON · ENGLAND the autopilot, flight director, basic attitude displays and the Ekco weather radar, in the form of synchronous and proportional a.c. signals.

Terminations manufactured by Aircraft-Marine Products (Great Britain) Ltd. include: Nylobond terminations of tin-plated copper with a pre-insulation sleeve of nylon material; heat-resistant termination of nickel-plated copper, which was used for high-temperature applications involving Tersil and Efglas cabling: butt connectors - tin-plated copper with an overall nylon insulation; and Certi-seal splice specifically designed as a moisture-proof splice forjoints in critical circuits. All these A-MP terminations give the constant reliability of the crimped type of joint connector with the added advantage of insulation support for the cable, thus providing first-class electrical and mechanical connection. The use of nylon insulation ensures compatibility with all aircraft fuels and lubricants, including Skydrol ester-based hydraulic fluid.

The following Honeywell Controls Ltd. micro switches were fitted to the Trident: EN-type environment-proof switches on the landing gear; EN and XE switches on the Smiths autopilot; hermetically sealed switches on the throttle box; a number of toggle switches on the cockpit control panels; and EN and SE switches on the stick-pusher system.

A total of seventy-seven Sangamo Weston Ltd. instruments were fitted to the Trident, including twenty temperature indicators, twenty-seven resistance bulbs, and four d.c. voltmeters, three d.c. ammeters, two d.c. milliammeters, two position indicators, one a.c. voltmeter, one frequency meter, one accessory box, two position transmitters, three TGT indicators, three hydraulic contents indicators, three adjustment spools, three

Something of a mystery as to the location! It is certainly a picture of Trident G-ARPE being inspected by BEA staff, but I cannot work out where it is. I suspect it is the old North Side of Heathrow, looking out over Runway 28/10 Right in the near foreground towards the eastern maintenance area certainly there is a Lockheed Constellation in the top right! *[The late John Stride Collection]*

The door hinge design on the Trident 1C was unique - later marks had the 'up and over' style that were still plug-in, but gave better use of available space.
The galley is seen on the right hand side, while cabin staff seating is behind the door. The hatch in the floor was not usually open for passenger boarding!
[Photograph courtesy of British Aerospace Hatfield]

thermocouples, one miniature homing indicator, and one dual position indicator.

An Engel and Gibbs temperature-sensitive switch unit, fitted with a sprung head which keeps it in direct contact with the alternator field windings, gives over-temperature warning of these windings. The unit was capable of adjusting itself to manufacturing differences and has a normal setting of 175 degrees Celsius to make contact on a rising temperature and thus operate warning lamps and relays.

Uni-Tubes Ltd. PTFE conduit was first proved on the Comet airliner. On the Trident, flexible conduits from half to one and a half inches in diameter were used to convey cables to the alternator and other equipment on each of the three Spey engines where fuel, oil and high temperature were likely to be encountered; in the undercarriage bay and on the undercarriage legs to connect with micro switches and brake cooling blowers where corrosive hydraulic fluids were accompanied by repeated flexing and exposure to the airstream when the landing gear was extended.

Each Trident airliner required something of the order of thirty miles of electrical cabling of various types. Of this quantity, British Insulated Callender's Cables Ltd. supply a considerable percentage. Among the types of cables supplied were Tersil, Nyvin and Efglas cables, including screened and sheathed variants; general wiring cables as well as extensionand multi-way cables for instrumentation and flight test purposes. BICC were also providing special cables for the wiring of the autoland and flight control systems manufactured by Smiths Aviation Division.

All cables in the Trident were tied and fixed in position by means of Ross, Courtney and Co. Ltd. nylon Ty-Rap cable ties and straps. Ty-Raps have been employed for two main reasons: the very high quality of the finished cable work when using this method and the considerable saving of time during assembly.

Batteries for the Trident have been supplied by Pritchett and Gold and EPS Co. Ltd. and were from their standard Dagenite ED range. Consisting basically of two 12-volt blocks, which were fitted into a robust corrosion-resistant aluminium container to protect them from mechanical damage, the batteries each have an output of twenty-five amps per hour at the one-hour rate of discharge and weighing fifty-three pounds.

In the early stages of the Trident project, it was decided that the primary responsibility for the air conditioning supply system should be assigned to a single contractor. The broad outlines of the system and the design philosophy would be discussed, and following mutual agreement, and subject to continued liaison, the system contractor would continue largely on his own right up to the point where the aircraft was established in full passenger service. The task was given to De Havilland Propellers Ltd., which was at the time operating as a virtually independent group, on the basis of competitive tendering. Although this company has now become part of Hawker Siddeley Dynamics, the Trident system was being manufactured and supplied under the original contractual terms and obligations.

The system chosen for the Trident uses direct high-pressure engine bleed. It was important to achieve high performance with the absolute minimum installed weight and, though high-pressure bleed does on the face of it increase the engine fuel penalty, the choice made has been amply justified, bearing in mind the economics of this short-haul aircraft. The system was far simpler than could have been achieved by other means, and where complexities have been introduced, this has been done to make the system as safe as any low-pressure system and to allow it to continue operating under certain failure conditions. The safety consideration was important, since the bleed air could reach pressures up to 225 lpounds per square inch at temperatures up to 500 degrees Celsius. With high-pressure air available under almost any flight condition, the system's performance was outstanding. In addition, an auxiliary power unit was carried in the aircraft, and it was used for ground cooling when an air bleed was led directly into the two supply circuits. Thus, excellent cooling performance was achieved on the ground as well.

Normalair supplied a number of components for the Trident's air conditioning and pressurisation systems. These include a combined safety and inward relief valve, a 6-in. dump valve, ground pressurising connections and non-return valves of various types. The company was also developing a vapour cycle cooling system for the Trident to provide a greatly improved standard of ground conditioning efficiency. This equipment will be fitted to the aircraft currently on order for Pakistan International Airways and consists primarily of an electrically driven freon system. This system was used to cool recirculating cabin air when the aircraft was on the ground, during take-off, and up to an altitude of 400 feet. At this altitude, the main conditioning system takes over to provide normal cabin air.

This Normalair system was based on a number of components that have been fully proven in service trials with the VC.10. It was available as an option for operators wishing to maintain comfortable cabin conditions at all ambient temperatures, but cannot be installed in aircraft fitted with the auxiliary power unit in the ventral fuselage position, as a freon condensing unit was fitted there.

Two Saunders motorised SP valves with a combination of auxiliary switch boxes and terminal blocks were used to control the air flow to the radio bay and animal bay (for aircraft carrying livestock). A number of Avica Equipment Ltd. gimbal joints, ‘V’ flange couplings and support clips were installed throughout the Trident on high-pressure ducting for the air conditioning, anti-icing and engine starting systems, together with stainless steel bellows expansion joints and metallic hoses. There were more than 50 gimbal joints and 180 ‘V’ flange clamps on each Trident aircraft.

The Trident radio and radar installations have been designed to allow the widest possible flexibility of choice of both British and American equipment. Consequently, although British units were employed in the basic design, the type of equipment fitted can be readily varied to suit airline requirements. With the minor exceptions of the radio altimeters, equipment and controller sizes for radio and radar installations conform to ARINC spec. No. 404 and wiring conforms to ARINC spec. No. 406. Suppressed aerial systems were used wherever possible and were sited to obtain the best polar diagrams and to avoid mutual interference. All projecting aerials were sited away from the fuselage top surface, thus avoiding a hazard to the centre engine.

Navigation aids were integrated with the flight system to permit a fully automatic landing and to ensure a level of accurate position fixing and track keeping compatible with the high-density areas in which it was expected the Trident will operate. Trident was for BEA was equipped with Decca Doppler type 62 equipment providing information to a ‘distance to go’ indicator and to the flight system with provision for a navigation computer for use with a pictorial navigation display.

The Trident IC incorporates a single air traffic con- trol transponder while allowance was made for the fit- ment of an altitude encoder unit. Provision was made in the IE for such an installation. In all Trident VOR/ILS facilities, a dual Marconi 260 installation provided duplicated ILS localizer and glide slope receivers, with provision for a third localizer to meet the Autoland case.

A dual Marconi AD 360 system provided two medium-frequency automatic direction-finding receivers (ADF). Radio magnetic indicators (RMI) containing integral compass heading amplifiers were used with the ADF and VOR/ILS systems to indicate aircraft bearing relative to two radio navigation beacons. For the Autoflare and Autoland installation, provision was made for the Standard Telephones and Cables STR.40 low-range radio altimeter in triplicate, with the low-range height function being passed through the flight system to three landing indicators. The STR.40 was fully transistorised except for the transmitter output valve. Each piece of equipment consistsed of the main unit containing the transmitter, receiver, amplifier and counter circuits; two aerials; and an ‘in-flight‘ test delay unit. The main unit was fully sealed and normally operates with inert gas. The test delay unit represents a fixed, known altitude and was

COMET
VISCOUNT
VANGUARD
and now Trident
BEA CHOOSE CASTROL
The Rolls-Royce engines of the Trident, like those of the Comet, Viscount and Vanguard in service with BEA, are lubricated with Castrol. The same brilliance of research which produced the lubricant for the Tridents' engines, is devoted to every Castrol product. That is why Castrol motor oil is notably in advance in technical development. That is why every British motor manufacturer approves Castrol. It is *safe* for all engines. That is why each year more British motorists ask for Castrol by name than for any other oil.
Castrol
MOTOR OIL

Conversion of BEA pilots to Tridents, photographed here in the circuit at Stansted, has proved uncomplicated. In this picture the training captain (right-hand seat) has shut down two engines. BEA 's Tridents are flown by three pilots, known as captain, P2 and P3 (centre): the P3 seat slides on rails and can be placed at the systems panel or behind the pedestal, so that all three pilots can look forward for full monitoring during take off, climb and approach. The map display seen in the centre of the panel is part of the Decca 62 Doppler system.
[Photograph courtesy of British Aerospace Hatfield]

switched into the circuit by the pilot to check the system's accuracy while in flight. STC have designed, sited and manufactured the majority of the aerials installed in the Trident. STC also supplies the fully transistorised audio distribution equipment type SA 10 and the associated loudspeaker amplifier SA ll, used to provide intercommunication between members of the flight, cabin, and ground crews for the Trident 1 and lC.

STC HF (long distance) radio communication was provided by the I00 channel 100-watt communication equipment type STR l8Cl covering the band 2-8 to 18-1 Mc/s. An Elliott intercommunication system has been selected as standard equipment for the Trident IE, and this makes use of audio selector control boxes type ESB-3|L or ESB-32C, amplifier EAM-33B, cockpit loudspeakers ESK-32A, central amplifier EAM-33C, ground crew jack boxes EJA-37A and pre-amplifier EAM-38A.

Very high frequency (VHF)communication facilities were provided by two Marconi AD.l60 installations. The Marconi selective calling 'Selcal' decoder unit was fed by HF and VHF communication signals, as selected by the Selcal controllers, to obviate the need for continuous ground-station monitoring by the crew.

Airborne weather radar in the BEA Tridents was the subject of close liaison between Hawker Siddeley Aviation and Ekco Electronics since the early design stages of the aircraft. The standard equipment was Ekco Type E.l90 transistorised airline system single display, in which radar units sixty-two pounds in weight and require only 325 VA a.c. power. The Ekco transmitter/receiver was a short ATR unit mounted just behind the forward pressure bulkhead, allowing a very short waveguide run. The radar indicator was mounted centrally in the instrument panel. It provided a 180 deg. Sector PPI display of turbulent cloud formations for all ranges up to 150 miles in the path of the aircraft. Similarly, it displays a PPI map of the terrain illuminated by the one hundred and eighty degree sweep of the antenna.

Kuwait Airways and Iraqi Airways have ordered an alternative E.190 installation which uses the above system together with the Ekca drift indicator, which was also mounted in the instrument panel.

Early in the discussions, between Smiths Aviation Division and De Havilland relating to the location of the Smiths' Automatic Multiplex Landing system, which had been designed to meet ATEC 201 specifications, Cementations (Muffelite) Ltd. were called in to discuss how best to provide an effective and reliable isolating system.

Certain specific problems were encountered, space was at a premium both vertically and horizontally, and the volume of equipment to be mounted necessitated shelves of considerable length, and the shelves had to support relatively heavy loads. It was apparent also that each mounted in the Isolating System would carry a load in excess of the capacity of any standard aircraft isolator, and also that a relatively stiff mount would be necessary to reduce sway space.

After examining the forcing frequencies and the other factors determining how the equipment should be mounted, Cementations (Muffelite) Ltd. put forward an isolating system which satisfied all the specified requirements, the system being based on the use of a specially modified version of a standard isolating mount. Only four mounts were used for each shelf.

In addition to supplying the isolating system for the standard shelves, Cementations (Muffelite) Ltd. supplied standard air-damped isolators for electronic equipment mounted elsewhere in the aircraft, including the vertical reference units supplied by the Sperry Gyroscope Co. Ltd.

Saunders spherical plug valves were fitted in the toilet effluent system and a further thirteen two-way and four multi-way valves were employed in the water and wastewater systems.

Eagle Transfer Ltd. were providing Hawker Siddeley with transfers for use for numerous identification purposes on the Trident, and BEA were also using transfers from this Company at many points of identification and instruction.

All twenty four Trident for BEA were equipped with lightweight pantry equipment supplied by GEC (Industrial Heating) Ltd. One item was a rapid boiler which boiled a gallon of water in just seven minutes.

Apart fom the impeller by Airscrew-Weyroc for brake cooling, two other types of fan were supplied for the Trident. The first was a 4.5 in. diameter HEBA-type centrifugal fan mounted on the forward bulkhead beneath the pilots' cabin to cool the radio equipment.

This fan was precision cast in aluminium alloy and gives a duty of 200 cu. ft./min. at 2-8 in. s.w.g. when running at 7,700 r.p.m. absorbing 0-15 hp. on 220 v. 400 cycle electrical supply. The second application involved two Airscrew 3.5 in. diameter single-stage axial flow fans with guide vanes, which extract air from the galley. Precision-cast in aluminium alloy, each unit gives a duty of 150 cu. ft./min. when running at 1,100 r.p.m., absorbing 0-16 h.p. The electric motor was housed in the stator ring - the fans being arranged in ducting passing through the galley and each weighing three and a half pounds.

Torrington aircraft needle bearings NBF 614 Y.1 were employed on the flap trolley bearings a side being used -while other Torrington bearings used were needle thrust bearings type NTA 24 35 on the undercarriage and other needle bearings on the landing gear doors.

Avimo Ltd. were supplying fuel line pipe couplings, pressure heads and 'Q feel pitots. The type MR.8610C and MR.8615C fuel line couplings were designed specifically for the Trident and accommodated an angular misalignment between pipes of at least eight degrees and a variable gap between pipe ends of 0.05 inches to 0.35 inches The types G17, G21 and G22/150/27 pressure heads were all of the pitot-only type; static pressure was obtained by separate static vents on the aircraft. The only difference between these three heads was their mounting orientation. The heads have a 150 watt heater in the pitot and another 100-watt heater in the mast. They were made almost entirely from high thermal conductivity copper and have excellent anti- icing properties. The Avimo 'q' feel pitot type QP 121 was an instrument designed to supply air pressure, proportional to the speed of the aircraft, for the purpose of operating the 'n' feel system used in conjunction with the aircraft controls. The type QP 122 was being developed for use on later Trident versions. It was essentially like the QP 121 but has been re-shaped aerodynamically to produce less drag.

Skyhi Ltd., a subsidiary of Zwicky Ltd., has manufactured double-ram tripod jacks for use with the Trident - these jacks have a built-in locking device that enables the aircraft's weight to be sustained for long periods without risk of failure.

Skyhi was also incorporating its Air-Draulic unit on a number of jacks for BEA for use with Tridents.

The Trident carries a large number of components manufactured by Bells Asbestos and Engineering Ltd. Of particular interest were the Janitrol Duct Couplings, which were incorporated in the aircraft's de-icing system by means of stainless steel mating flanges. A wide selection of Bells' products, for example, silicone/glass flexible bellows and hoses, flexible non-metallic Neoprene hose and silicone/glass connecting sleeves, was also fitted in the air conditioning and air distribution systems of the Trident. All three of the Rolls-Royce Spey engines also incorporate bulkhead and cowling seals manufactured by Bells

Tools, Ground Equipment and Test Rigs

All aspects of this range of equipment have been studied by specialist ground equipment engineers. Their study covered all vendor-supplied equipment as well as that made by Hawker Siddley. As a result, 'special to type' tools have been kept to a minimum, all equipment was simple, safe and robust, and every tool has been thoroughly tested and proved suitable for the job, whether the work was done in the hangar or in the overhaul shop.

Electrical Test Sets

The Trident electrical test sets were designed with the aim of reducing man-hours by simplifying the form of individual sets and tests that they were to carry out. Thus, the sets were mostly specialised in their applications, but this was valuable advantages with regard to safety and operational speed.

Flight Control System Test Equipment

Up to the arrival of Trident, aircraft have only used simplex autopilots, and the check-out for this single-channel type of the flight control system had involved a fairly complicated, labour- and time-consuming procedure. The method involved using a test set that the service engineer connected to the system's various units. Test sequences were then followed according to instructions on a maintenance sheet. The procedure required two skilled men to complete the tests satisfactorily.

The check-out procedure for the Smiths S.E.P.5 flight control system in the Trident was based on an entirely new approach, made possible through the introduction of a triplex autopilot for automatic landing. The basic principle of this check-out procedure was to test each channel of the three - channel system by reference to the other two channels. The only essential test apparatus required to do this was a simple signal generator weighing approximately six pounds, which was permanently fixed in the aircraft. No additional test equipment needed to be plugged into the flight control system since the signal generator gave all the required test conditions merely by selection of the appropriate switch.

In order to reduce the time taken and to demand the minimum skill for this simplified procedure, the check-instructions were given aurally via Smith's Aural Diagnostic Inspection Equipment, or 'SADIE'. Instead of reading the instructions given in a maintenance manual, the engineer listened to instructions played on a tape player and received on the aircraft intercom. headset. Special features of the tape player, which has a four-track tape, enabled the engineer to follow through a full check-out in about twenty minutes if there were no faults, or to request the necessary initial fault tracing instructions, should faults be found. This was done by the engineer pressing a YES switch as each test proved satisfactory, or a NO switch if a test did not give the correct result. A REPEAT switch could be pressed to repeat an instruction. Further reference to a small file of fault tracing cards could be called upon by the taped instructions, where a diagram or written instruction was discovered to be more explicit. The tape player, measuring eight inches by five inches by five inches used six inch by three inch by half-inch thick tape cassettes that were small and light enough to be permanently carried on the aircraft, together with the cards. This was just at the time when Phillips were bringing out their compact cassette recorder at the Funkausstellung (Radio Exhibition) in Berlin, Germany.

The benefits of this new checkout procedure will be far-reaching. It was possible for the Trident flight control system to be fully checked at any airport, since the equipment can be carried on the aircraft. The unnecessary removal of serviceable equipment was greatly reduced because the instructions given by 'SADIE' followed through a carefully planned procedure that eliminated opportunities for guesswork in fault tracing while leaving no doubt as to the location of the failure. This was achieved by reducing the time required by up to seventy-five per cent compared to conventional methods.

Chapter Six

Autoflare and Autoland

The Trident was uniquely designed to introduce a system that allowed completely automatic landings. Based on the multiplex principle, the aircraft's automatic control systems ensured uninterrupted performance during and after a failure, setting it apart from other systems.

When BEA signed its original contract with De Havilland for the DH.121 in 1958, part of the agreement stipulated that *'if, during the service life of the aircraft, automatic landing guidance facilities become available, then additional facilities can be added to provide automatic landing through the autopilot or flight director. It is required that automatic flare-out should be provided from the outset.'*

The Trident was to be the first airliner to be designed from the start to have the eventual ability to land automatically, enabling it to operate into airports in 'zero zero' weather conditions - that is, zero decision height and zero visibility. In 1958, Smiths Industries was contracted by BEA to develop the Autoland equipment for the new aircraft.

Before proceeding further, it would be good to consider what is 'Weather Minima' and what is the ICAO Measurement definitions:

Category 1 : Operation down to a decision height of 200 feet with a visibility of more than 2,600 feet.

Category 2 : Operations down to decision height of between 200 feet and 100 feet with visibility between 2,600 feet and 1,200 feet.

Category 3A: Operation to and along the runway with an external visibility during the final stage of landing down to 700 feet (with a decision height of 65 feet).

Category 3B : Operation to and along the runway down to a visibility of 150 feet, which is sufficient only for taxiing (decision height of 12 feet)

Category 3C : Operation to and along the runway with no external visibility (no decision height).

The automatic landing system, developed by Smiths Aviation Division, allowed the aircraft to operate in weather conditions of minimal visibility and significantly enhanced safety. The minimum visibility distance was set at about fifty yards, ensuring the safety of passengers and crew.

Particular attention was paid to the overall safety problems involved, and the Trident's automatic landing system resulted from a meticulous integration of the electrical, radio, autopilot and flying control systems. This careful engineering of all the components from the earliest design stage ensured the system's reliability.

In the late 1950s, the only automatic landing experience was conducted by the Blind Landing Experimental Unit (BLEU) at RAE Bedford, where a modified English Electric Canberra was used to perform automatic landings. The somewhat crude system used 'Leader Cables' that provided directional guidance and were laid on both sides of the runway, extending several hundred yards beyond the airfield boundary. The programme was aimed at a military rather than a civil requirement, with little attention paid to redundancy and the safety of the system.

As the Trident's design evolved, Smiths was working on the Autoland system. During the late 1950s, modified Vickers Varsities and a De Havilland Comet 2E were allocated to the BLEU at Bedford to assist with the development of automatic ILS-coupled approach and landing using Smiths 'multiplex' autopilot systems. (ILS stands for Instrument Landing System, which guides aircraft to runways in low-visibility conditions.)

ILS was a more sophisticated ground-based system that transmitted two radio beams, the 'Localiser' and 'Glidepath'. The former was a radio beam transmitted from the end of the runway to give lateral, or 'centreline', guidance; the latter was a radio beam transmitted from the side of the runway at three degrees to provide guidance on the correct angle of descent to the runway. The level of both its low altitude accuracy and its reliability was at the time not considered high enough to allow the safe use of ILS in civil airliner landings, let alone 'Blind Landing' in low visibility.

However, using onboard radio altimeters below one hundred and fifty feet to allow automatic flare-outs would overcome the ILS's low-altitude inaccuracy. 'Autoflare' was therefore to become the first phase of the Trident's 'Autoland' ability, with the plan that the aircraft would be introduced into service with this facility.

Why 'Autoflare' for the Trident?

Progress towards fully automatic 'autoland' was approached cautiously and in stages, ensuring thorough testing and development. By 1964, the aircraft entering service were fitted with equipment for automatic flare-out - known as 'Autoflare'. This was the automatic control of approach airspeed and automatic throttling back of the engines just before touch-down - termed 'Autothrottle'. This equipment was used to gain experience in automatic control of the aircraft in close proximity to the ground, representing the first stage leading to automatic landings.

This system, which would be a totally new concept to aircrew, involved the pilot, using the ailerons, keeping the aircraft lined up with the runway whilst the autopilot performed the flare-out. Meanwhile, there was a concerted push to develop more accurate and reliable ILS localiser equipment, improve runway lighting, and introduce a visibility-measuring system to enable full-blown Autoland to become a reality.

What is Autoflare? In the late 1950s, it was a new word coined to describe the control of the aircraft by automatic equipment through the flare-out, or that part of the landing between the end of the steady approach path and the wheels touching the runway, which is carried out by changing the pitch attitude of the aircraft by moving the elevator. By definition it excludes automatic control of the ailerons or rudder, but includes automatic control of approach airspeed and throttling back of the engines prior to touchdown.

The need to control the approach and landing automatically had arisen for two main and quite separate reasons:

(i) The primary goal of the Autoflare system was to significantly enhance the safety of the

A diagrammatic presentation of the airborne and ground equipment was necessary if civil aircraft were to operate safely in various weather conditions. It could be seen that both ground and airborne equipment were essential once the visibility falls below three-quarters of a mile and that any reduction in minima below those in use today (200-foot ceiling and half-a-mile visibility) could only be achieved by automatic control of the aircraft together with the best visual aids. It is, of course, possible to operate in very low visibilities under manual control provided that the local runway visibility was raised by some device such as Fog Investigation and Dispersal Operation (FIDO), but up to that time, the installation and operational costs were too high for an economic return.

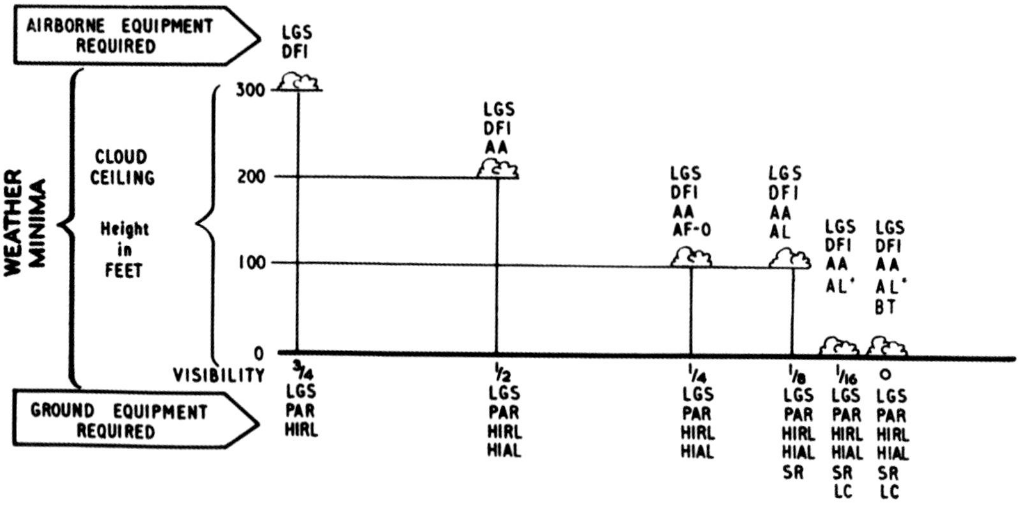

AIRBORNE EQUIPMENT

- **LGS** Localizer and Glide Slope Receiver
- **DFI** Director Flight Instrumentation
- **AA** Automatic Approach
- **AL** Automatic Landing (with a failure survival capability
- **BT** Blind Taxying

GROUND EQUIPMENT

- **LGS** Localizer and Glide Slope Transmitter
- **PAR** Precision Approach Radar
- **HIRL** High Intensity Runway Lights
- **HIAL** High Intensity Approach Lights
- **SR** Surface Radar
- **LC** Leader Cable for Taxying

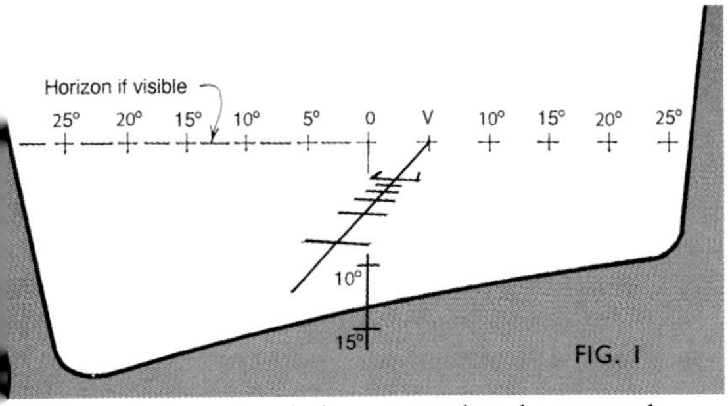

FIG. I

Figure 1 shows the aiming errors when the approach lighting is visible. The aircraft is displaced about 200 feet to the right of the centre line and is heading 5º left. It is on a glide path of 1 in 20.

Figure 2 shows height and aiming errors when nearly all the runway is visible and there is an horizon. The only difference in the shape of the three images is the convergence of the edges and the ideal length, 'Y' which represents zero height error. Changes in pitch, attitude and head position do not confuse the height indication, i.e., visual guidance at this height is very much better than at contact height (500 feet). The aircraft is at a height of 200 feet, the glide-path is 1 in 20, the visual range is 11,000 feet, and 8,000 feet of runway is visible. The runway is 200 feet wide. Airspeed and angle of approach are assumed to be constant.

Figure 3 shows height and aiming errors when only the runway is visible and there is no horizon. Note that the only difference in the shape of the three images is the convergence of the edges which becomes greater when the height is reduced. The apparent length of the runway cannot be used as a height indication because the length seen depends on the visibility. The distance, x, of the image above the cut-off line depends on pitch attitude, height, air-speed and head position, and various combinations of these can give a picture which, in the absence of the horizon, is indistinguishable from the correct one. With a sloping cut-off line as shown, a cross-wind will make it even more dificult to judge whether x has the correct value. The aircraft is at 500 feet, the glide-path angle is 1 in 20 and the visual range is 11,000 feet, with 2,000 feet of runway visible. The airspeed and angle of approach are constant.

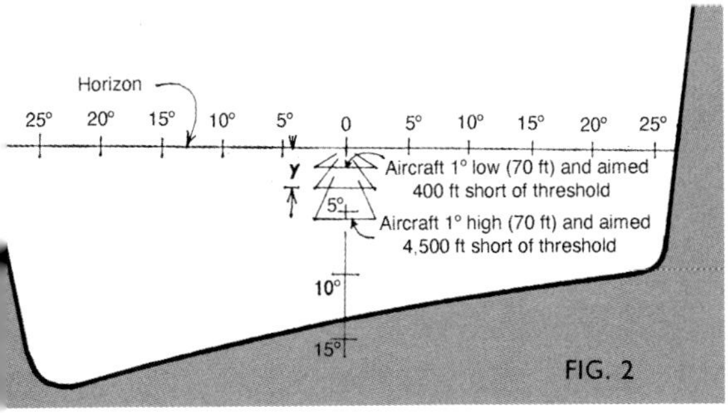

FIG. 2

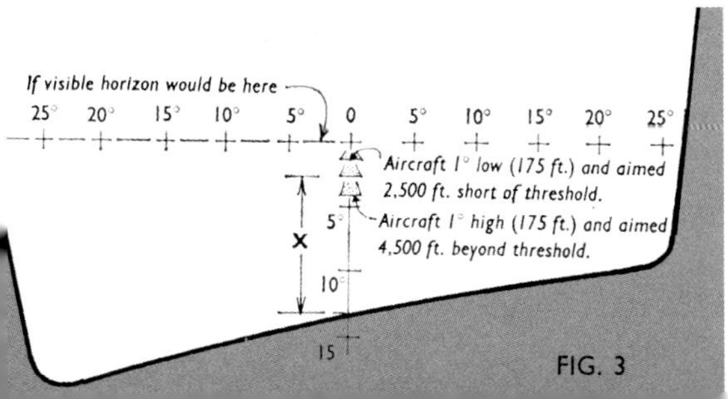

FIG. 3

approach and landing phase of flight.

(ii) The Autoflare system also played a crucial role in enhancing operational regularity, especially in adverse weather conditions.

However, it was apparent at an early stage of the Trident design investigation that it would not be possible to go in one step from 'manual' approaches and landings to the routine use of fully automatic equipment capable of landing the aircraft in 'zero-zero' weather which required only to be monitored by the flight crew - some interim standard was necessary which would both contribute to safety and at the same time instil confidence in the flight crew in the ability of equipment safely to control the aircraft close to and onto the ground.

Unfortunately, in the period 1946-1958, forty per cent of all airline fatalities occurred during the approach and landing. During that period, transport aircraft were designed and produced with higher approach speeds, increased size and weight and handling problems associated with swept-back wings and jet engines, and yet, with the reduced weather minima which have also been achieved, in 1959, forty per cent of all fatalities on the US domestic airlines were again to be found in that last phase of flight, with as many incidents associated with good weather conditions as with bad.

Edward Spence Calvert (1902-1991) of the Royal Aircraft Establishment (RAE) suggested that the failure rate for the task of making a visual approach was dependent on the approach speed, the acceleration which the pilot was willing and able to apply during a corrective manoeuvre, and 'K', an index representing the goodness of the visual information. Although approach speeds had been rising and the manoeuvring acceleration falling as aircraft have got larger and heavier, these was hitherto been counteracted by improvements to the visual aids, i.e., by increasing 'K'.

There was, however, a limit to this improvement which could well be reached when runways had been equipped with visual aids then being developed.

The Trident was a short/medium-range aircraft of relatively small size and weight, with a moderate approach speed and powerful hydraulically operated lateral and longitudinal controls. It had proved possible to provide a standard of control which would further reduce the failure rate for the approach task. It was to be expected, however, that the aircraft would

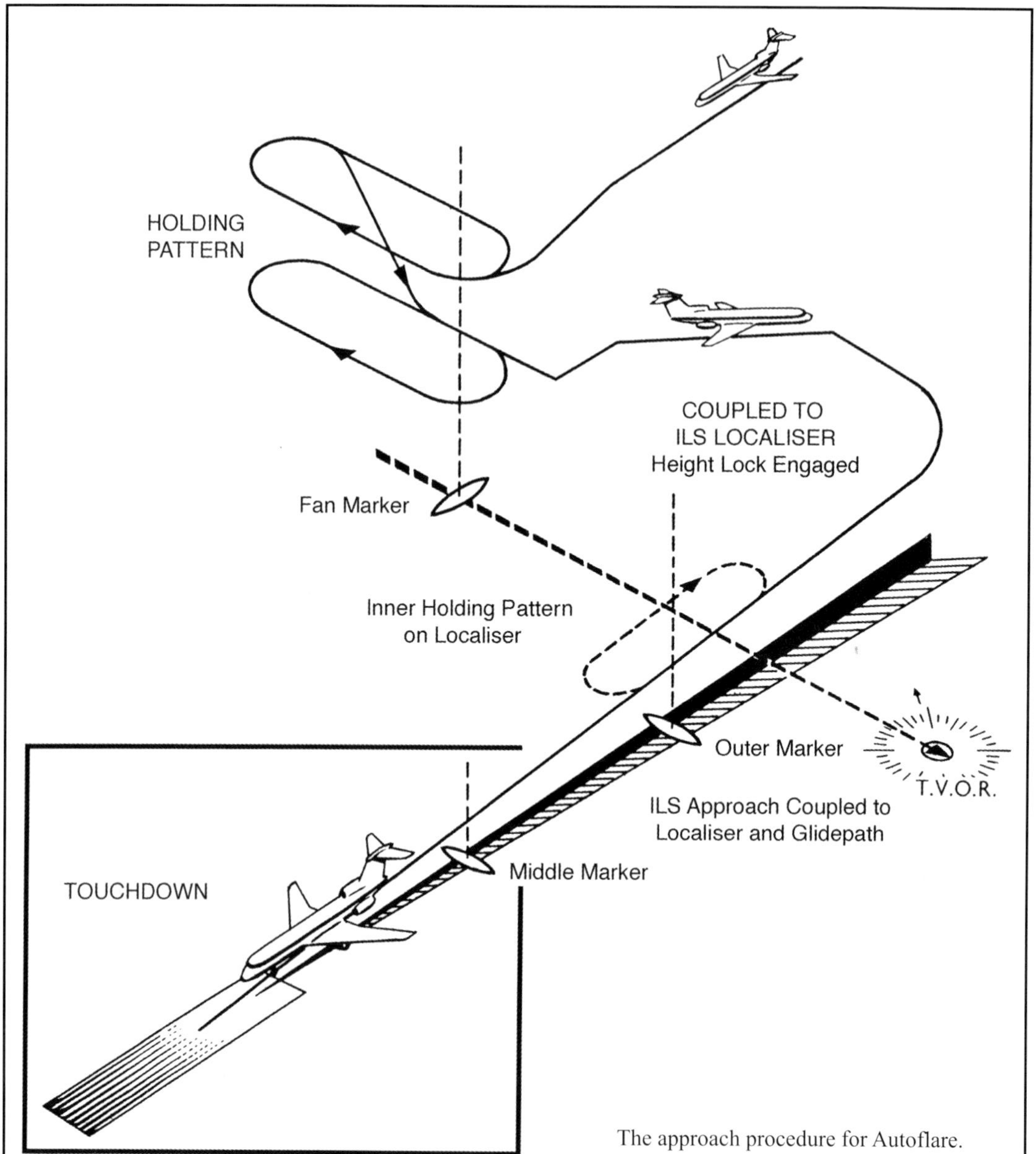

The approach procedure for Autoflare.

frequently operate into airfields where visual aids were not of a high standard, and there would also be a need to operate in really bad weather when visual aids could supply sufficient information on their own.

Although the primary objective must always be to provide the utmost in safety and regularity, it was also becoming increasingly important to airlines that none of its fleet should sustain even minor damage through a misguided approach or landing, resulting in an aircraft being 'taken off the line'.

Why was the pilot finds accurate path control difficult during the approach and landing, particularly in the vertical plane? The path which the pilot should follow during an approach was defined by the intersection of the glide path plane and the centre line of the runway, but the visual indications associated with the two planes differ in two important respects which were inherent like visual guidance derived from ground patterns.

First, if the aircraft was correctly lined up with the runway, this was indicated by the centre line of the runway or approach pattern being perpendicular to the horizon. Alignment was also indicated by symmetry about the centre line. Since small departures from symmetry were immediately and easily recognized without special training, pilots find that quite small lateral errors could be quickly recognized as soon as one crossbar of the approach lighting or the runway itself comes into view.

In contrast, displacement above or below the glide path merely results in vertical extension or compression of the image. Correct positioning was indicated not by symmetry but by comparing the actual image and an ideal image in the pilot's mind. Because the differences were small even for large displacements from the glide path, the pilot must concentrate all their attention on making this difficult mental comparison, and fatigue or additional stress may seriously impair the accuracy he achieves and greatly increase the probability of a serious misjudgment. Furthermore, progressive reductions in visibility remove more and more of the upper part of the image and increasingly mask the apparent change in the shape of the approach or runway picture.

Secondly, an error in heading relative to the runway was shown by the continuous apparent rotation of the ground features in a clockwise or anticlockwise direction depending on whether the error was to the right or the left of the runway centre line but in the vertical plane there was no simple connection between the angle of descent and the apparent movement of the ground. The result of these two differences was that a pilot could detect and correct minor lateral errors without difficulty but finds it difficult to perceive large height errors and corrects them only after an appreciable time lag.

At this time, in good visibility conditions the pilot could be given additional vertical or glidepath-guidance information by such devices as the Australian Precision Visual Glidepath or the RAE-Thorn Visual Glidepath Indicator. In poor visibility the visual glidepath cannot be seen until too late, if at all. Although it was possible to project on to the windscreen a synthetic picture of what the pilot would see if the visibility were good and therefore, theoretically, provide sufficient information for him to continue to fly the approach as though he were doing a normal visual task, most attempts to date have resulted in heavy and complicated electronic and optical dsvices which in themselves were liable to failure and occupy large areas in a very congested part of the flight deck.

So in poor visibility neither the ground visual aids nor artificial simulation of them within the cockpit were yet suitable to supply the pilot with sulficient information of his position relative to the

The Autoflare and Autoland System on the Trident.

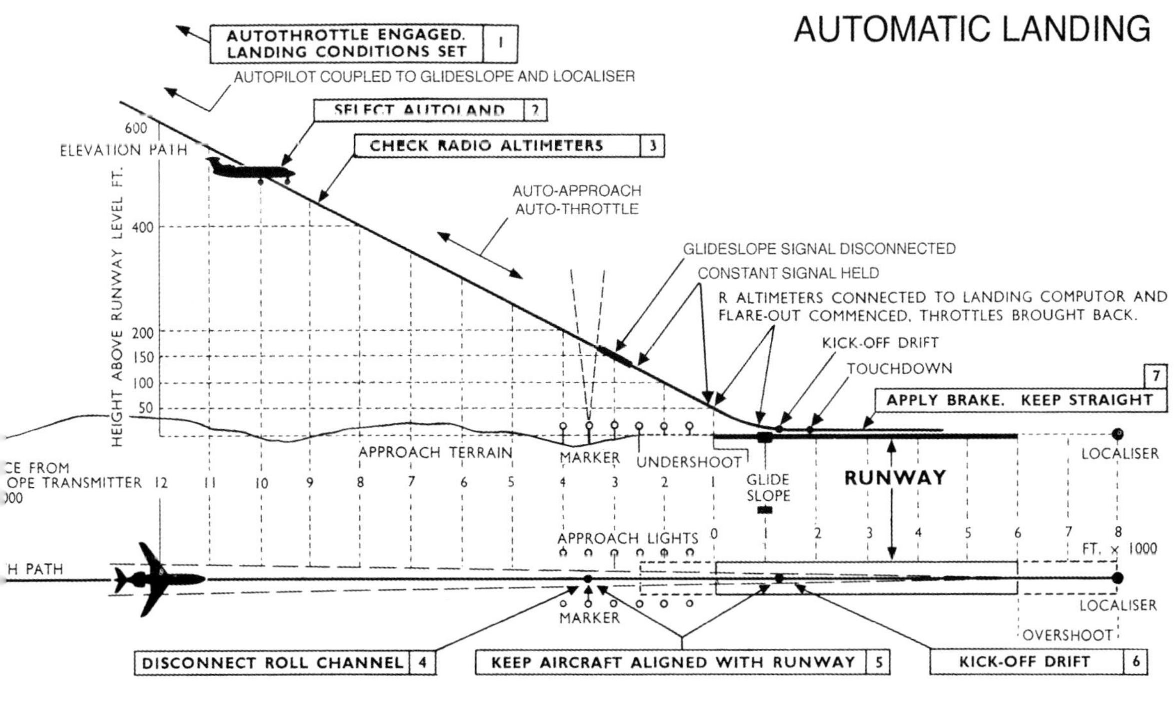

desired approach path, also, the pilot's task was more difficult in the vertical plane than the horizontal. When automatic control down to the ground was available, a real benefit in both safety and regularity could be achieved by first introducing Autoflare.

The method proposed for Autoflare of the Trident was to take advantage of the ground aids already installed at reasonably well-equipped airfields, and of the autopilot, which was an essential airline requirement for providing automatic control during climb, cruise, descent and that part of the approach down to two hundred feet or so, and to extend the automatic approach down to ground level, initially in the vertical plane only.

As was written at the time, *'Not until more airline experience was available will it be known if it was economically worthwhile to be able to operate in 'zero-zero' weather, but considerable economic benefit will inevitably be derived by an airline which could safely operate in a minimum of one-sixteenth of a mile, particularly if its competitors were unable to do so'.*

Autoflare, as the first step towards complete automatic landing, strongly emphasised safety. The design requirement for automatic equipment during a blind landing was that it should not fail to operate correctly more often than once in ten million automatic landings. To meet this standard, new principles in the design of autopilots and flight instrument systems have been adopted, such as the 'multiplex' principle developed by Smiths Aviation Division for the Trident and the SEP.5 Flight Control System. This underscores the significant progress in aviation technology and the unwavering commitment to safety.

Success or failure may, in reality, depended on the degree of confidence that the flight crews had, or acquire, in the system and their ability to monitor its performance and take over when necessary.

The Proceedure.

Let us look at a typical task a crew faced at the end of a flight into a hypothetical airfield likely to be served by a Trident. The airfield has a 6,000-foot runway with an undershoot of 1,500 feet and an overrun of 2,000 feet. It was equipped with a two-and-a-half- to three-degree glidepath transmitter, a localiser transmitter, marker beacons, approach and runway lights, and the facilities of a medium-sized modern airport. The pilot must control the aircraft so that it flies down the glide slope and localiser beams, and a flare-out and touchdown must be executed smoothly and accurately. During all this, the speed must be accurately controlled despite disturbances from gusts and changes to the flight path and aircraft configuration.

With Autoflare, control of the aircraft's pitch was transferred from the pilot to the autopilot and its associated equipment. The important difference between past practice and that proposed for the Trident lies in achieving safe automatic control of the aircraft below about 200 feet, a height at which a coupled approach is at present terminated partly due to the failure characteristics of autopilots, and partly to the limitations inherent in using the glide slope beam at close quarters. A good glide-slope beam was usable down to about 150 feet, but below this, additional equipment is normally required to complete the descent along the glide path and perform the flare-out and touchdown. The Trident system was based on the Blind Landing Experimental Unit method, which used radio altimeters to measure height above ground and the rate of change of height, and fed these quantities into a flare computer.

As can be seen, a height of 150 feet corresponded to a horizontal distance of some 3,000 feet from the glide slope transmitter, and although the desirable point to transfer to radio altimeter control was that at which the glide slope signal must be disconnected, the ground at 3,000 feet from the glide slope cannot be assumed always to be level and at the same height as the touchdown point.

It is therefore necessary to prevent the aircraft from being controlled down a path that can be materially affected by the terrain beneath, to defer using the measured radio height until over the undershoot area, which can be seen to correspond to a height of about one hundred feet. So there is a very short period during which the aircraft descends from about one hundred and fifty feet to about seventy feet, during which the autopilot's control function is to hold the same average attitude it has maintained down the approach path to that point. Below about seventy feet, the radio altimeter's output is fed to the landing computer, and signals are generated to perform the flare-out, touchdown, and throttle back.

The multiplex principle was applied to each main control channel whenever a high standard of safety and reliability was required. It had to be established throughout those systems in the aircraft that contribute to the automatic control performance - the electrical system, radio receivers, and other equipment items. A multiplex channel comprises two or more independent but similar sub-channels. Each could achieve its objective alone and suffice as a conventional single-channel autopilot. In a multiplex channel, all the sub-channels were used both collectively and simultaneously to provide continuous 'redundancy'; this also ensures that the complete system was in use during nominal operation. Thus, when a failure occurs, the faulty sub-channel was switched out rather than a changeover being initiated to an alternative system, which had not until that moment been in full operation.

After a malfunction, a triplex channel automatically reverted to a duplex level, and automatic control was maintained without interruption. Thus, it was suitable for a fully automatic landing system with failure survival capability.

A duplex channel automatically disengaged both sub-channels after a malfunction without any disturbance to the flight path of the aircraft. It was possible to arrange for the re-engagement of one-half of the duplex channel after a failure since the aircraft was adequately safeguarded by other means against a runaway fault of the single channel.

It should be noted that the multiplex principle need only be applied to those parts of the system which have critical safety requirements, for example, control of the flare or landing manoeuvres. It was normal practice to use a single source of information for the height or speed locks.

The initial equipment standard for Autoflare was based on a duplex autopilot which could easily be raised to a triplex level at a later date.

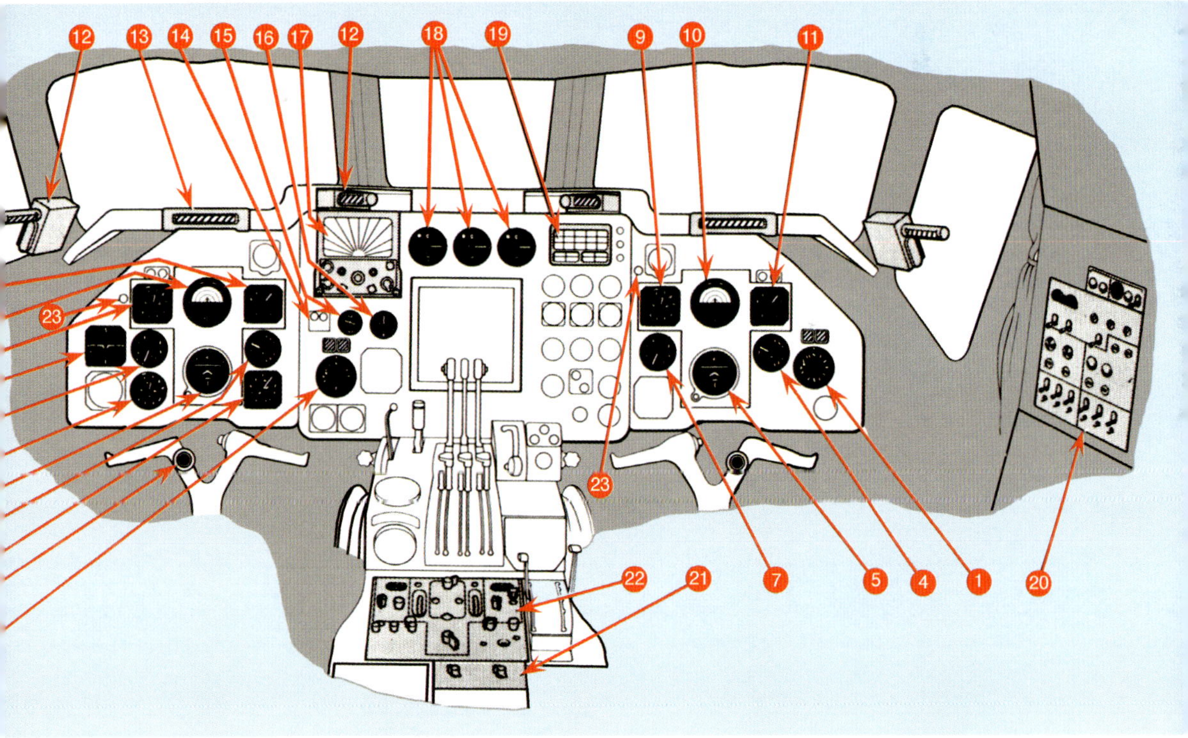

The Flight Deck layout of Smiths Flight Control System instrumentation in the Trident as specified by BEA.

1. R.M.I.
2. Instinctive cut-out.
3. Altimeter (standby system).
4. Vertical speed indicator.
5. Flight compass.
6. Airspeed indicator (standby system).
7. Machmeter.
8. Artificial horizon (standby system).
9. Airspeed indicator.
10. Attitude director.
11. Altimeter.
12. P.V.D. pitch command unit.
13. P.V.D. bank command unit.
14. Height lock indicator and height acquired warning light.
15. Autopilot engage and trim indicator.
16. Turn and slip indicator.
17. Weather radar display.
18. Landing indicators - radio altimeters.
19. Central warning system display panel.
20. Flight control systems test panel.
21. Radio selectors.
22. Flight controllers.
23. Speed lock.

The equipment comprised the following:
A duplex autopilot.
A roll damper and a duplex yaw damper.
A duplicate compass system.
A triplicate attitude reference system.
A duplicate air data system.
A single flight director system.
A single Para Visual Director system.
A duplex automatic throttle control system.
A triplex radio altimeter installation.

As Autoflare assumed the automatic control of the aircraft in the pitch axis, and manual control by the pilot in the roll and yaw axes, a landing cannot be attempted in very low visibilities because the human pilot might be unable to keep the aircraft aligned with the runway or kick off the drift due to crosswind.

Thus, for an Autoflare landing, the pilot will have sufficient visibility to take over (should the autopilot disengage) and complete the landing

Block diagram for the Smiths Flight Control System as fitted to the BEA Tridents. Note the now unusual spelling of the word computer (computor) - something that was standard at the time.

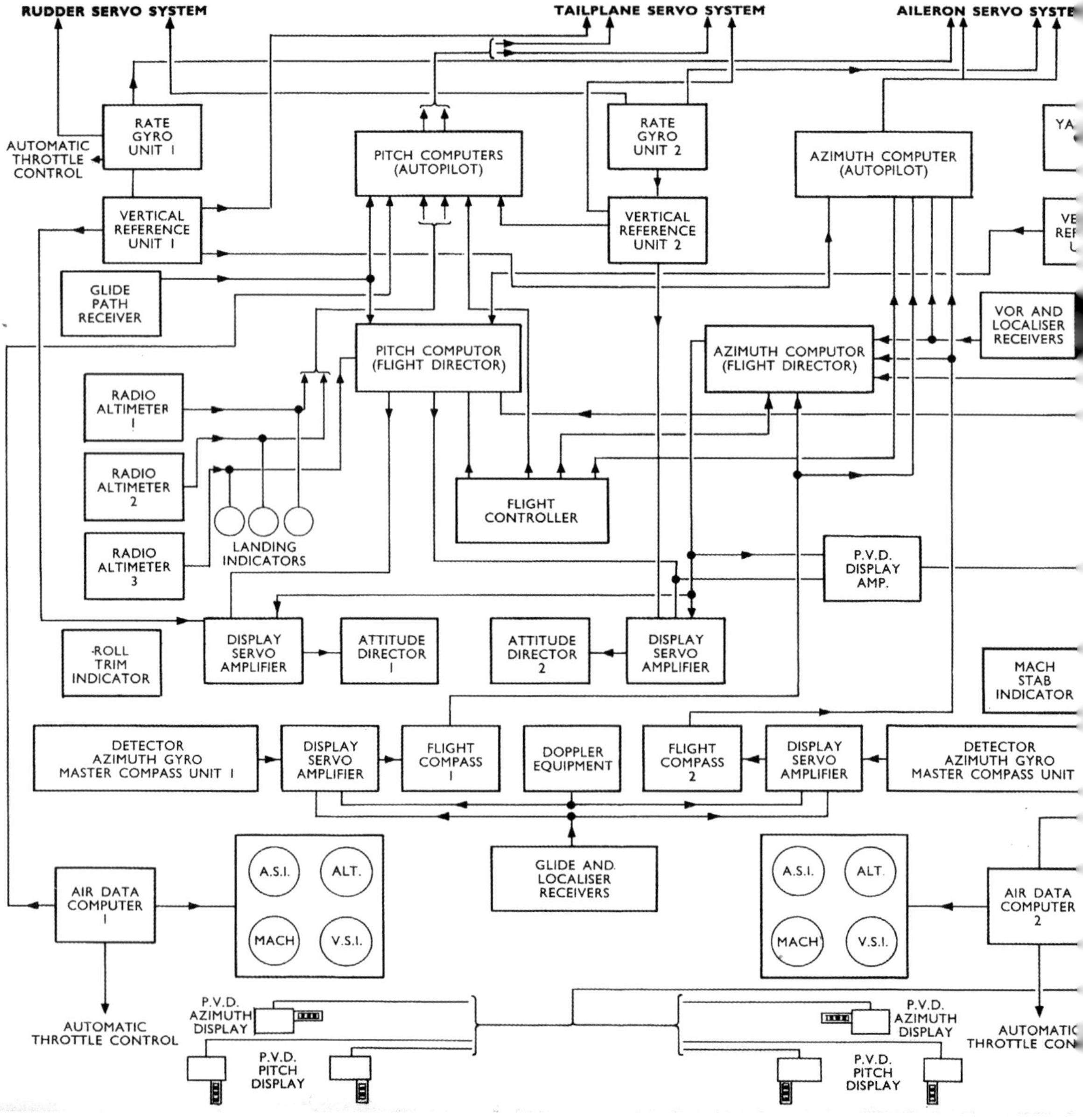

manually. Still, in the lower limits of visibility, his task will be much eased if he was provided with prominent director commands on how to fly the aircraft to complete the landing. This was the role of the Para Visual display. To ensure the availability of its commands after an autopilot failure, the pitch information for the director was provided by a separate computer independent of the two autopilot pitch computers, thus providing a form of triplex integrity in pitch control. This requirement also necessitates the installation of three radio altimeter sub-systems.

If the autopilot failed at any time, it will disconnect automatically and passively, leaving the aircraft in trim and exposing the Para Visual display. Should the auto throttle fail, it also will automatically disconnect bringing up a flashing warning light. If the monitoring pilot considered that the approach (down to about fifty feet) was not going satisfactorily he could initiate an automatic overshoot by opening the throttles to full power.

The Smiths Flight Control System, a key component of the Autoflare landing system, was responsible for managing and executing the various flight control functions necessary for a successful landing.

The operational nerve centre of the autopilot was the Flight Controller which carries the switches and controls necessary for setting up all automatic and flight director modes and facilities. The controller was mounted horizontally on the throttle pedestal and the disposition of the controls and indicators was arranged to coincide as far as possible with the basic instrument display on the instrument panel, for example the height-lock controls on the controller were in the position occupied by the altimeter on the instrument panel. In the detailed description which follows, this logical sub-division of the controls had been retained.

The three engage levers control the engagement of the autopilot pitch and azimuth axes, and the yaw damper. When these levers were latched to the rear position, disengagement of the autopilot was positively confirmed.

Engagement of an axis was effected by moving the lever forward and then allowing it to return to centre. Disengagement was normally effected by the instinctive cut-out on the control column. Emergency disengagement could also be achieved by pushing or pulling on the control column with a force greater than that normally used.

In addition the autopilot could be isolated either by switching off at the Flight System panel, or by switching olf the autopilot circuit breakers.

The A/P READY flag indicates that the autopilot power supplies were on, all gyros have run up and the autopilot could be engaged.

Pulling on the F/D switch connects the flight director signals to the Attitude Director. All pull-on switches on the controller have a white indicator on the knob to show whether they were 'in' or 'out'. When the F/D switch was off, and the flight director signals were disconnected, the flight director warning flag was made to appear and interrupt the director indices in each Attitude Director. The F/D switch dropped off automatically when the attitude reference signals to the flight director disagrees with the two attitude displays.

With no airspeed lock engaged, the IAS counter repeats the airspeed indication from the air data system. If the selector was set to IAS and the ENGAGE knob was pulled on, the aircraft pitch attitude will be controlled, either automatically or by the pilot following flight-director demands, to maintain constant IAS. The datum airspeed could be varied by turning the SPEED trim wheel until the IAS counter indicates the airspeed required.

When the selector was set to MACH, pulling on the ENGAGE switch controls pitch attitude to maintain a constant Mach number. The datum Mach number could be varied by turning the SPEED trim wheel until the required Mach number was indicated on the machmeter.

Setting the selector to THROTTLE and pulling on the ENGAGE switch engages the automatic throttle control. Thereafter, the throttles were controlled automatically to maintain constant airspeed. The datum airspeed could be varied using the SPEED trim wheel with the IAS counter.

When pulled on, the AZIMUTH switch connects radio and heading signals from the Flight Compass to the autopilot and flight director index. The switch could be turned to alternative bank-limit positions before being pulled on, and bank angle demand was limited to the selected value.

The PORT-STB'D switch selects the Flight Compass from which radio and heading information was fed into the autopilot and flight director. The unselected Flight Compass could be set as necessary, and when required, it could be coupled by changing over the PORT-STB'D switch.

The PRIME switch provided automatic glide path acquisition. The switch was set to GLIDE when the aircraft was correctly established on the localizer. The aircraft will then continue to fly along the localizer until the centre of the glide path was reached and will be coupled automatically to the glide path. The G.P. gives a visual indication of glide path coupling via the flag on the controller, while the corresponding BEAM flag appears in both the VOR and ILS modes.

When the aircraft was coupled to the glide path, the PRIME switch was set to LAND; the landing sequence was then automatically initiated at the appropriate height. An interlock between the PRIME switch and the radio altimeter in-flight check ensures that the pilot was warned of failure to set the switch to LAND.

The SELECT HEIGHT counter was set by pushing in the 'Height' knob and rotating it. Pulling out the knob and rotating it changed the set barometric pressure, which was indicated on the SET PRESSURE counter.

With the height selector set to ACQUIRE and the ENGAGE knob pulled on, the aircraft could be made to climb or dive as required using any appropriate lock, to reach the height set on the SELECT HEIGHT counter. When this height was reached, the selector automatically changed over to LOCK, and the aircraft was then maintained at the selected height.

The SELECT DESCENT control knob could be set at a desired rate of descent. When the ENGAGE knob was pulled on, the aircraft will descent at the selected rate either until a pre-selected height was reached or until the select descent facility was disengaged. Airspeed during the descent must be controlled manually by the pilot.

If the operational procedure for an approach precludes the automatic acquisition of glidepath coupling, the ENGAGE GLIDE button provided conventional manual coupling to the glidepath when required.

Flight Instruments

The flight instrument system was of new design, every effort having been made to provide the maximum in clarity of presentation so important for all—weather operation. Five-inch instruments were used for the combined horizontal and flight-director display, called the Attitude Director and for the combined compass and navigation-situation display called the Flight Compass.

Attitude Director

The Attitude Director was a remote-indicating instrument which replaces the conventional artificial horizon and in addition presents

Another Queens Building rooftop viewing area shot, this time G-AWZJ in the process of being pushed back to start another trip. *[John Stride collection]*

compensatory flight-director information by movement of an index on the display.

The horizon was displayed on a roller blind coloured light and dark grey. Changes in pitch attitude were indicated by movement of the blind over its rollers, and changed in roll by rotation of the blind. Aircraft bank angle was indicated by movement of the bank pointer over the bank scale and a fixed circular pitch scale was superimposed on the attitude display.

Demand signals were presented by movement of the flight-director index over the attitude display. To follow the director index signal, the pilot applies pitch and bank as necessary to fly the centre ring on the pitch scale on to the director index. When the centre scale ring was centred on the director index, the aircraft was in the attitude required to execute the desired manoeuvre.

When the Flight Control System was coupled to a radio navigation receiver on a VOR frequency, a BEAM flag will appear on the attitude director. If the receiver was set to an ILS frequency, the G.P. flag also will appear. Provided that the radio signals were adequate, these flags remain steady, but if the signals were weak or non-existent, the flags pulse in and out of view under approach conditions.

The director flag was in view when the flight director system was disengaged; it also appears when the attitude- reference signals for the flight director disagree with the attitude indicated by the two displays. When the flag was in view, the flight director index was withdrawn.

The attitude-failure flag appears when the attitude display on one attitude system differs significantly from that on the other and from the attitude signals to the flight director. A reset button on the front of the Attitude Director was depressed to clear the attitude failure flag when initially switching on, or when a fault had been cleared.

Flight Compass

The Flight Compass was a remote indicator of the compass system, with additional information superimposed on the display.

When the compass controller was set to

The Smiths Flight Controller as fitted to the BEA Tridents.
[Photograph courtesy of British Aerospace Hatfield]

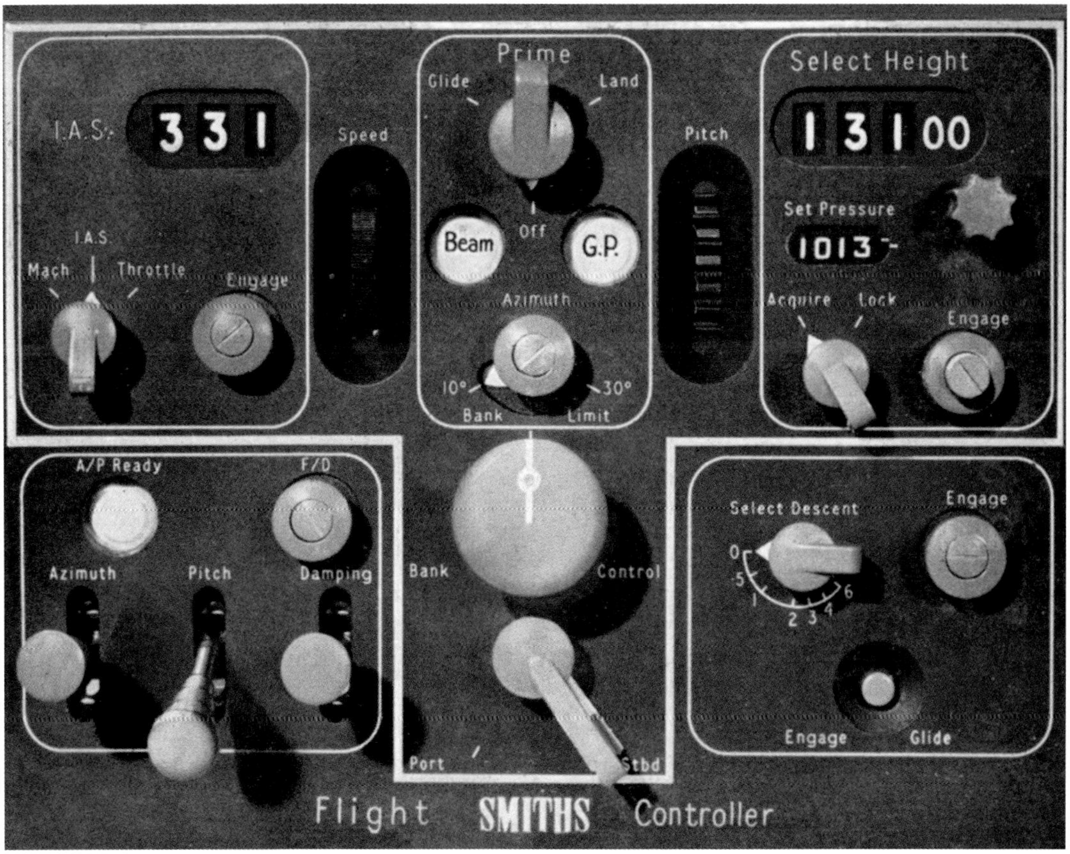

COMP., the magnetic heading of the aircraft was displayed by rotation of the compass card relative to the fixed lubber-line at the top of the dial. Fast synchronizing of the compass system was provided when the SYNC. button in the centre of the compass controller was pressed.

Setting the compass controller to DG disconnects the magnetic monitoring from the compass system, at the same time displaying the DG flag. The instrument then functioned as a directional gyro indicator, and could be aligned as fast or slow rates by turning the compass controller to F or S as required.

When the shutter covering the drift-index knob was open, rotation of the knob provided manual setting of drift on the drift index, on either side of the fixed lubber. Alternatively, with the shutter closed, the drift index was set automatically by signals from the aircraft Doppler Navigation System. The drift index provided the datum for heading error signals from the Flight Compass.

The track pointer normally rotates with the compass card, and in straight flight will normally be opposite the drift index. The Flight Compass then displays heading, track and drift in a clear, unambiguous form, with the track bearing repeated on the 360-degree counter. With the shutter set to AUTO, the drift index was automatically set by Doppler so that correct drift was constantly maintained.

When the setting knob was pushed in and turned, the track pointer and roller blind rotate relative to the compass card and drift index. This facility was used to orientate the display before coupling to various forms of track guidance. For VOR coupling, setting the track pointer also selects the radial required and displays the selected radial on the counter; thus, no separate VOR radial selector was required.

The steering index rotated typically with the

The basic Instruments of the Smiths Flight Control System as fitted to the BEA Tridents.
[Photograph courtesy of British Aerospace Hatfield]

A fish-eye view so popular by photographers in the 1960s shows a Trident fight deck...

...At the controls are Capt H J Booth (left) and First Officer J W Mahany.

compass card. Pulling and turning the setting knob rotates the steering index relative to the compass card.

When the radio coupling switch was set to the 'track pointer head' position, heading-error signals, proportional to the displacement of the track pointer head from the drift index, were fed to the autopilot and flight director. Similarly, setting the switch to the 'steering index' position feeds signals, proportional to steering-index displacement, to the autopilot and flight director.

The Flight Compass was typically used by setting the track pointer as appropriate to the stage of flight, e.g., to the airway routing or to the QDM of the runway, and setting the radio coupling switch to 'track pointer head'. With the shutter set to AUTO, Doppler drift was now coupled to the autopilot and flight director to maintain track.

When the radio coupling switch was set to 'track pointer head', suitable guidance signals (VOR, ILS, Doppler) were also fed to the autopilot and flight director, and the aircraft will then lock on to the defined track. If the aircraft was displaced from the track, automatic interception at an angle of 45 degrees was provided followed by subsidence and lock on to the track required.

If no suitable radio aids were available, the pilot sets the radio coupling switch to the 'steering index' position, and uses the steering index to command suitable headings with drift set manually. A further use for the steering index was to set headings when short-term deviations were necessary, that is, during instrument procedures based on a selected track.

Setting the radio coupling switch to the 'track pointer tail' position provided reverse coupling to a radio beam, for use when flying the reciprocal of a selected radio beam.

Heading steering was available as an alternative to track steering, by setting the drift index manually under the fixed lubber.

The background display of the Flight Compass was in the form of a roller blind, and was changed automatically to indicate the input set on the radio selector.

In the ILS mode, a glidepath-deviation pointer was displayed, with deviation from the glidepath

Not so much mystery pictures; more like mystery captions! HSA Hatfield authorised numerous brochures for Trident, often produced by Davidson, Pearce Berry and Tuck Ltd of Marylebone Road, London. One such brochure contained these two pictures, the one above having the caption *'On March 3, 1964, an Hawker Siddeley Trident landed at the Royal Aircraft Establishment, Bedford, piloted by a Smiths SEP.5 duplex autopilot. On the same day, the Trident made five more automatic landings at Bedford, followed by a further four hands-off landings at its home base, Hatfield. Subsequently, hundreds of autoland and autoflare approaches have been made by Trident'.*

The picture below claims to have been taken during an automatic approach to London (Gatwick) Airport - it was an everyday autoflare - the 485th. in fact, since the beginning of the Trident autoland flight programme. Close examination suggests that this was not Gatwick, but is almost certainly the final stages of an approach into Hatfield, coming from the south. - no doubt someone will argue!
[Photographs courtesy of British Aerospace Hatfield]

indicated on the vertical scale on the face of the instrument. In all radio—coupled modes, deviation from the selected beam was indicated by lateral movements of the roller blind relative to the beam-deviation scale. The background in the ILS mode was the blue and yellow pattern of approach charts.

Each of the two radio selectors was associated with one Flight Compass, and was used to select the radio information to be fed to that Flight Compass. The selectors could be set differently, since the signals from only one Flight Compass at a time could be used to the autopilot or flight director.

Full use was made of the two air-data computers, needed to provide inputs to the duplex autopilot, by utilising them each to drive a set of four three-and-a-quarter inch air-data instruments. As they were remote-indicating repeaters, no pitot or static connections were made to them and the long pipe runs of previous installations have given way to short and reliable connexions between pitot and static points and the air data computers. The presentations were simple and unambiguous.

Altimeter

The Altimeter was a counter-and-pointer instrument. The barometric pressure was on a separate counter, and was set by the knob on the front of the case.

A warning flag appears if the power supply to the instrument was cut off.

Airspeed Indicator

The dial of the Airspeed Indicator was helical in form, so that at speeds above 250 knots part of the pointer disappears behind the outer helix. This presentation combines the accuracy of a much larger instrument with an easily read display.

An adjustable index, which could be set to any airspeed within the low-speed range, was controlled by the knob on the instrument front. The warning flag appeared when the airspeed indications on the two airspeed indicators disagreed; the flag also appeared if the power supply to the instrument was cut off.

Landing Indicator

The Landing Indicators were repeater instruments of the radio altimeter system, scaled from five hundred feet down to ground level. Adjustable dial markings indicate the heights at which the various phases of the landing operation was automatically initiated.

A warning flag in the lower half of the dial appears when power to the instrument was cut off. In the upper half of the dial was a green 'ready' flag to indicate that automatic kick-off-drift facility was serviceable. At the correct height for kicking off drift, an IN flag appeared on the dial, and the rudder and rudder pedals moved in the appropriate manner.

PVD Display Unit

Three units were provided for each pilot, the centre unit presenting azimuth demand signals and the two outer units presenting pitch demand signals. The signals appeared as lateral movements of the black stripes in the indicators varying in speed and

G-AVFA, the first 2E is seen in what was known as the 'Red Square' colour scheme. The two black rectangles painted on the roof are flight test timing marks. *[Photograph courtesy of British Aerospace Hatfield]*

direction with the magnitude and sense of the demand signal.

When the PVD displays were not required, they were masked by internal shutters which lower automatically to cover the display. The shutters were also used to indicate malfunction.

Engage and Trim Indicators

Engagement of the autopilot pitch and roll axes was indicated by flags on the dial, while roll trim was indicated by rotation of the pointer relative to the two fixed indices opposite the ends of the pointer.

No autopilot pitch-trim indication was provided for the Trident, since automatic pitch control was injected through the trim mechanism.

Flight Systems Panel

A Flight Systems panel was provided at the systems station on the flight deck which enables the crew to check the operation of vital equipment of the Flight Control System.

Yaw Damper

Individual switches for the Yaw Damper System were provided on the panel. The yaw damper actuator positions were indicated by two dials, one for each sub-system.

Warning Indicators

Three warning indicators were provided which will appear under the following conditions:

- If the two yaw dampers' actuator positions differ.
- If the two flight compass indications disagree by more than five degrees.
- If the attitude signals to the flight-director system disagree with the attitude-system indications.

These warnings were tied into the aircraft's central warning system.

Two engagement indicators mounted in the centre of the pilot's panel indicated when the yaw dampers were switched IN.

Roll Damper

A switch for the roll damper was provided on the Flight Systems Panel, and the roll damper actuator position was indicated by a dial. An engagement indicator mounted in the centre pilots' panel shows when the system was switched IN.

Autopilot Indicators and Switches

Engagement indicators were provided for each simplex channel. Additionally, indicators (Y circuit) were fitted to provide a continuous indication that the autopilot clutch circuits were correctly isolated.

Individual switches were provided for each autopilot channel in the pitch and roll axes. Normally, setting one of these channel switches to OUT or OFF will disengage both channels in that axis. For test purposes, or for reversion to single-channel operation in an emergency, a DUPLEX OFF switch was provided in each axis. When this switch was set to OFF, setting a channel switch (1 or 2) to OFF disengages that channel only.

The TEST ADC switch operates built-in test circuits to provide a complete functional check of the air data system.

Typical Operating Instructions for Approach and Landing.

Having looked at the elements that made up the Trident Autoland System, let us now see how it was used in typical BEA service. The Trident installation had a duplex autopilot, but the pitch information for the flight director and PVD was provided by a separate computer independent of the two autopilot pitch computers, thus effectively providing triplex integrity in pitch. Automatic pitch control could therefore remain engaged right down to touchdown.

It was assumed that the aircraft was approaching the airfield and was VOR coupled under autopilot control.

The PVD System was switched on, and the VOR signal was being received on the NAV.2 radio. On the Flight Controller, the PORT-STBD switch was at STBD and the AZIMUTH switch was on, at 30 degree bank limitation.

The IAS lock was engaged and the shutters on the Flight Compass were set to AUTO.

(1) On Flight Controller, set ground pressure on SET PRESSURE counter. Set height counter to 2,000 ft. Set SELECT DESCENT control to required rate of descent.

Set height selector to ACQUIRE. Pull on height ENGAGE and select descent ENGAGE knobs. Adjust power for IAS required during descent.

When the select descent ENGAGE knob was pulled on, the IAS. ENGAGE knob will drop off,

Opposite page: Come on feel the noise! BEA's G-ARPP powers up into the skies from Zurich. *[Kirk Smeaton Collection]*

HSA test pilots Jimmy Phillips in the Captain's seat, with Pat Fillingham on the right during a 'look no hands' moment on an autoland demonstration into Hatfield that became a major selling point for the design.
[Photograph courtesy of British Aerospace Hatfield]

and the aircraft will descent on the VOR radial at the selected rate. During the descent:—

(2) Set track pointer head on port Flight Compass to QDM of runway in use. Set NAV.1 radio receiver to correct ILS frequency. Set port radio selector to NAV. 1.

The port Flight Compass will now show the ILS background with the glidepath deviation pointer in view and the BEAM and GP flags suitably displayed.

At 2,000 feet the aircraft will automatically level out, the 'height' selector will change over to LOCK, and the aircraft will fly along the VOR radial at 2,000 feet. The starboard Flight Compass was still displaying the VOR background and showing correct drift.

(3) When BEAM flag was steadily in view, set PORT-STB'D switch on Flight Controller to PORT.

The aircraft will now be manoeuvred automatically to intercept the localiser at the optimum angle. If a lower limit on maximum bank angle was required during this manoeuvre, the AZIMUTH switch could be set to '20 deg.' Throughout the manoeuvre, the port Flight Compass displays aircraft track and the position of the aircraft relative to the centre-line of the beam. When the aircraft was correctly established on the localizer:—

(4) Turn speed selector on Flight Controller to THROTTLE and pull on ENGAGE knob. Check GP flag on port Flight Compass was steadily in view. Set PRIME switch on Flight Controller to GLIDE. Check Y circuit indicators on Flight Systems panel do not indicate clutch circuit fault.

The aircraft will continue to fly along the localiser, with the glide path deviation pointer on the port Flight Compass gradually moving downwards as the aircraft approaches the centreline of the glidepath.

At any convenient time, the adjustable index on the port airspeed indicator should be set to the approach speed.

Just before the aircraft reaches the glidepath centreline the glidepath signals were automatically switched to the autopilot, the GP flag appears on the Flight Controller, and the aircraft pitches nose-down on to the glidepath. Height lock was automatically disengaged.

(5) Carry out in-flight check on radio altimeter system.

The in-flight check on the radio altimeter system cannot be completed until the PRIME switch was set to LAND. The switch cannot therefore be left at GLIDE in error. The PVD display units were hidden by the shutters, but these will open automatically if the autopilot was disengaged for any reason.

(6) *Set PRIME switch to LAND and check that Landing Indicators revert to correct indication.*

If the PVD switches have been left off in error, the central warning system will operate to indicate a PVD fault when the PRIME switch was set to LAND.

The throttles were now automatically controlled to maintain the approach airspeed on the glidepath. This speed may be trimmed if required by the SPEED trim wheel on the controller.

At any height down to the start of the flare, automatic overshoot could be initiated by opening the throttles manually. The aircraft will then be uncoupled from the glidepath, and will climb away at approach airspeed on existing track. If it was operationally desirable to overshoot on a different heading, this heading could be pre-set if required on the starboard Flight Compass steering index, and the PORT-STB'D switch set to STB'D after overshoot was initiated.

(7) *At break-off height, check roll trim and pull AZIMUTH lever on Flight Controller fully back.*

Right: On the Trident 1E's flight deck during performance measurement en route from Karachi to Kuwait.

Below: The Trident 1E co-pilot's working environment during high speed cruise. The Machmeter shows 0.86, an indicated air speed of 400 knots and a true air speed exceeding 510 knots.
[Photographs courtesy of British Aerospace Hatfield]

The aircraft was now flown manually in roll but was still under autopilot control in pitch. Flare was initiated and the throttles were automatically closed at the optimum rate.

(8) After touch-down, disengage autopilot by instinctive cut-out button.

Flight testing and publicity.

To support fully automatic landings targeted for BEA's 1970 service, the Trident required a triplex autopilot. Initial deliveries, however, featured the duplex fit, which provided 'autoflare' capability from 1964.

The second Trident to be built, registered G-ARPB, took on much of the Hawker Siddeley/Smiths Autoland flight testing from 1962 to 1967. After its first flight on 20 May 1962, Papa Bravo spent considerable time developing autopilot-coupled approaches, but when not testing, the aircraft flew around the

Obviously another publicity picture and a very good one at that, but one that contains something I had never noticed before. The markings above the central window show the letters Yankee Zulu, clearly the 'last two' of G-AWYZ, but also there is the number '3', denoting that it was a Trident 3.

Welcome on board! A special greeting for a young Trident passenger - Note the BEA Stewardess is wearing the then obligatory white gloves!
[Photographs courtesy of British Aerospace Hatfield]

northern hemisphere for demonstrations and hot-and-high trials.

Papa Bravo's autopilot development led to ARB (Air Registration Board) approval in February 1964 to operate the Smiths duplex flight system for passenger-carrying use, with the autopilot, flight director, compass, and autothrottle cleared for both en route and approach. The Trident then entered service the next month with partial automatic approach capability. By November 1964, system assessments allowed Tridents to perform coupled approaches down to 150 feet, with RVRs (Runway Visual Range: the distance a pilot can see down the runway) as low as 450 yards at certain airfields.

It was planned from the start to equip the Trident's forward instrument panels with 'howgozit' indicators, a type of display that shows whether the aircraft is above or below the desired glide path during approach. As part of the Autoland instrumentation, the Para Visual Director (PVD) was devised. This device, mounted on each pilot's glare shield, consisted of a striped visual indicator resembling a barber's pole that provided the crew with visual cues for bank angle and roll-out commands. It was mounted on each pilot's glare shield.

On 3 March 1964, Papa Bravo completed the Trident's first duplex automatic landings: ten Autolands, including six at RAE Bedford and four at Hatfield. This paved the way for Autoflare clearance approval at duplex level, followed by subsequent duplex and triplex Autoland approvals. Though formally delivered to BEA on 30 April, Papa Bravo was immediately leased back for further Autoland development.

ARB approval of the duplex Autoflare system (in Category 1 conditions) was received on 3 June 1965, and the world's first Autoflare touchdown on a commercial service was made a week later on 10 June by Trident 1C G-ARPR when it arrived at Heathrow from Paris, carrying just ten passengers. By now, Papa Bravo had completed some six hundred approaches in the proving of Autoflare and Autoland.

G-ARPB was upgraded with the automatic landing system at the triplex level. This featured three sub-channels working together simultaneously on two of the three axes of the autopilot. The likelihood of two parts of the 'triplex' system failing simultaneously was extremely remote, thereby providing the necessary reliability and safety. The triplex system provided a safety factor of ten million to one, somewhat greater than that of a 'human' pilot, and was planned to use the automatic landing capability in all weather conditions due to the increased accuracy it would provide during the approach and landing phases of flight.

In November 1965, Papa Bravo made its first Autoflares with its triplex Autopilot at Hatfield and, as work continued on the system, the aircraft carried out fifteen triplex Autolands at Heathrow on 7-8 September 1966, during two days of demonstrations to world civil aviation heads. By this time, it had conducted over 1,500 Autoflares and Autolands, including 500 at the triplex level.

The following month, on the morning of 4 November, during really foggy weather conditions, Papa Bravo made an automatic landing on Heathrow's runway 28L, the first time an airliner had done so at the airport in Category 3B conditions. During the day, three landings were made on two of Heathrow's runways, whilst all other aircraft diverted due to the weather. Papa Bravo then returned to its Hatfield base, where it again landed in fog.

Previously, as part of the test programme, Papa Bravo had been making automatic landings using the triplex system with the pilot's windscreen blanked off with opaque panels to simulate fog conditions. Of the landings in fog, Hawker Siddeley's Test Pilot Jim Phillips said, 'It was all very relaxing - even more so than practice landings under the hood. All the landings were very smooth and right on the runway centre-line.'

On 24 November, there was more fog in southern England, and again no movement was possible at Heathrow, with flights diverted to Luton, so the opportunity was taken to test the system again. This time, a team of engineers and pilots from BEA was on board the aircraft to obtain firsthand experience of the system, and five takeoffs and landings were completed in an hour.

At the same time BEA's Chief Executive, Henry Marking, was returning from Rome, but due to the fog his flight was diverted to Manchester. He was due to attend an important meeting of BEA directors in London that evening, so it was arranged that G-ARPB flew up to Manchester and bring him to Heathrow, where he was duly landed, in the fog and in the dark, so making the sixth successful automatic landing that day. At the BEA board meeting the following day, the decision was taken to equip its entire Trident fleet with triplex Autoland to enable operations in full Category 3B conditions.

All of this made for national headlines in the newspapers the next day, with Captain Arthur Johnson, BEA's Trident Flight Manager, commented, '(the system) *puts us five to 10 years ahead of any other airline in the world. By 1970, BEA will be the only airline anywhere able to keep on operating in the sort of fog we had today. I visualise that we could be the only airline operating anywhere in Europe on a really foggy day.'*

On 20 January 1967, the Category 3 automatic landing programme with Papa Bravo was completed. Beginning in May 1965, it included more than 2,000 automatic landings at 'duplex' and 'triplex' levels and ended with a demonstration of 200 landings using equipment proposed for BEA certification.

Among the advanced facilities demonstrated during the programme were automatic kick-off drift, ground roll guidance during take-off and roll-out, and the ability to overshoot automatically at any height during the approach - literally right down to ground level - and included simulated engine failure. During the series of two hundred landings required for certification, the system was shown to perform satisfactorily in crosswinds of up to twenty-five knots and in heavy turbulence associated with winds of up to thirty-five knots. These demonstrations were designed to prove to the ARB that the system would perform satisfactorily in Category 3 operations.

Although these advances were considerable, there was an ironic side to this new automation. Shortly after the Trident entered revenue service, BEA discovered that inexperienced passengers were unsettled by the frequent engine power shifts and noise on approach - something I can atest to first hand! This was a direct result of the aircraft's all-weather design.

Certification of Autoland at the duplex level was achieved on 19 April 1967, initially in Category 1 conditions. On 16 May, G-ARPP carried out the first automatic touchdown on a scheduled passenger service when it arrived at Heathrow after a service from Nice. This landing marked the commencement of 'Operation Automatic', which involved Papa Papa making

I always thought that the Channel Airways 'Continental Golden Jet' scheme looked supurb on the Trident.
[Kirk Smeaton Collection]

Iraqi Airways' YI-AEB climbs away on another service...
[Kirk Smeaton Collection]

twenty-seven duplex automatic landings during a week of scheduled operations. This programme involved Autolands at fifteen airports in nine countries, including Amsterdam, Basel, Brussels, Cologne, Frankfurt, Hanover, Madrid, Milan, Palma, Paris, Rome, Stockholm, Venice, Zurich, and, of course, London Heathrow.

Operation Automatic ended at 12.45pm on 23 May, when G-ARPP touched down automatically at Heathrow Airport after flying from Frankfurt. During the exercise, 1,400 passengers were landed automatically, and a total of 34.5 hours of flying was logged, of which, on average, only forty seconds per hour was under manual control, mainly during the take-off.

Papa Bravo was finally delivered to BEA in December 1967, and the airline's Trident 1s were cleared for duplex Category 2 auto approaches on 26 January 1968, with full Category 2 Autoland approval following on 7 February. Triplex Category 2 Autoland operations were cleared in September 1968. By this time, BEA had carried out 3,000 Autoflares and 700 Autolands in revenue service, and Papa Bravo had flown 600 development hours on Autoflare and Autoland. The intention was then to work towards Category 3 clearance through in-service proving.

The first Trident 2E, G-AVFA, which was the first machine to be equipped with a triplex fit from the start, replaced Papa Bravo as the flight development aircraft, and the programme commenced to achieve the ultimate BEA requirement: approval of passenger-carrying landings and take-offs in Category 3 conditions, initially at the Category 3A level. Foxtrot Alpha, or 'Sweet FA', as it was nicknamed by its crew, completed 170 hours of Category 3 development, flying from April 1968 to May 1969, before being handed over to BEA.

By 1969 autoland development flying had forged ahead, and as a result of it's success, Tridents were cleared to operate commercially in Category 2 conditions with a decision height of one hundred feet and an RVR of four hundred metres.

Permission was granted in late 1968, but it was not until 14 February 1969 that the ILS facilities at Cologne/ Bonn, Hamburg, Paris and Zurich were officially upgraded to Category 2 standard, becoming the first airfields so equipped in Europe. Heathrow was upgraded to Category 2 shortly afterwards.

During the remainder of 1969 and into 1970, many other airports throughout Europe were upgraded. At last BEA was able to reap some benefit from the vast sum of money they had invested in autoland.

Landings in Category 2 conditions were not the ultimate goal however. The airline was working towards Category 3 landings, with initial

... while sister ship YI-AEC heads for a smooth touchdown!
[Kirk Smeaton Collection]

development flying aimed at securing commercial operations in Category 3A conditions; a decision height of twelve feet and an RVR of three hundred metres. BEA set the winter of 1972/73 as the target date for commercial use of autoland under those conditions. Beyond lay the ultimate goal of Category 3B landings, with an RVR or only fifty metres. In recognition of the tremendous achievement of the autoland project BEA was awarded the Queens Award to Industry for Technological Achievement in April 1970, a fitting reward for twelve years hard work.

The same year, the prototype Trident 3, G-AWYZ, took over Category 3 clearance, and her equipment fit included ground roll control, ground roll guidance, and ground run monitoring. The ground roll control kept the aircraft on the centreline from touchdown until eighty knots, after which the ground roll guidance system provided steering information to the pilot using the PVD for the remainder of the ground run. The ground run monitor displayed ground speed and the remaining runway distance. The ground run monitor displayed ground speed and the remaining runway distance.

The final flight in the development of Trident Autoland occurred on 6 March 1972, when a sequence of fully automatic landings was flown at Bedford by G-AWYZ in adverse weather conditions. This cleared the way for full Category 3A operations for the BEA Trident fleet. Following these successful trials, final CAA approval for Category 3A operations was granted in May of the same year. However, the clearance of the ultimate goal, Category 3B, was not received until 1975.

So which WAS the first to Autoland??

This is a difficult question to answer definitively. As already described in this chapter, there was the first autoflare, all the BLEU flying, along with all that was done in 'Operation Automatic'. There is also the flight from Nice flown on 16 May 167 by G-ARPP. I suppose the question is the First Autoland with, or without the self-loading freight? I have a recording that sadly is undated, and done by a very BBC-type fellow with a very clipped aristocratic accent as was the broadcast style of the day that refers to the first passenger-carrying Autoland; *'Flight BE 343 today is... just in a few moments from now - an important milestone in aviation history will be reached. The BEA Trident jetliner, callsign Papa Romeo, left Paris thirty-two minutes ago, having flown at twenty thousand feet across the channel and southern England at a speed of six hundred miles an hour, is now on its final approach into Heathrow.*

Aboard are eighty passengers. We're making a very steady approach. Runway One Zero Left is right ahead. About half a mile from touchdown, the aircraft lined up with the runway, the altimeter showing three hundred feet... we're gradually descending... Captain Paul and Captain Atkins, still with no hands on the control column at all. The threshold of the runway - we're just coming over the err approach lights. Fifty feet on the altimeter...

'Captain Paul speaking. Ladies and gentlemen, the landing you have just made differs from any landing that has ever been made before. If differs because you are the very first passengers in the world to experience an automatic touchdown on a scheduled passenger service. This is a significant milestone in the history of civil aviation and is another step towards achieving our ultimate goal - all-weather operations in perfect safety.

It gives the flight number - BE 343. callsign Papa Romeo, which must be G-ARPR and as Captain Paul directly spoke to the passengers after the landing, making that claim - that's what my money is on!

Chapter Seven

To the Skies!

In January 1960, De Havilland unveiled the Trident's flightdeck mock-up, which was a three-crew design (three pilots in BEA's case) configured so that all three members would face forward for the first and last ten minutes of each flight.

Key features to the layout included a large pictorial map display on the centre panel flanked on the left by the weather radar and the right by the Central Warning System (CWS) and engine instruments; distinctive Y-shaped 'ram's horn' style control yokes; three large hydraulic levers emanating from the overhead panel; and the Smiths Autopilot controller on the pedestal between the two seats. As part of its all-weather capability, it was planned to equip the forward panel with a 'howgozit' indicator for information on the progress of the final approach.

Smiths Instruments was working on the 'Autoland' system, the development of which was progressing well and is covered elsewhere. It had been decided that a triplex autopilot fit would be required for the full automatic landings BEA aimed to introduce into revenue service from 1970. However, it was planned that the Tridents would be delivered with a duplex fit from the start to enable the aircraft to have 'auto-flare' capability from 1964.

Production and assembly of the Trident took on a very low profile during 1960 and 1961, although in January 1960 the first pictures of a DH.121 component were seen when *Flight* published a picture of the nose section undergoing pressure testing in a water tank at Hatfield. After the 11lb/sq ft test had been successfully completed, the nose section underwent some 40,000 ninety-minute 'flights'.

Production of the first Trident commenced on 29 July 1959, with the construction of components, like the design, split amongst the partners. The wings and three-quarters of the fuselage, including the nose, were to be constructed by the De Havilland division at Hatfield, with the forward fuselage - except the nose - initially manufactured at the old Airspeed works at Portsmouth airport. It was later transferred to the Hawarden, Chester, plant, a former Shadow Factory De Havilland acquired in 1948 and was a final assembly line for the Comet 4 series.

Fairey Aviation was responsible for the moving parts of the tail and the powered flying controls, whilst Hunting constructed the flaps on the first three aircraft. Production was geared to allow a rate of up to six aircraft per month to be achieved.

The first production nose structure was completed at Hatfield by March 1960. The first aircraft's final assembly commenced soon after the first forward fuselage section arrived from Portsmouth on 5 April, which was readied for mating. As the first Trident took shape at Hatfield during mid-1960, it was rather apt that the last of the Comet 4Bs for BEA was being completed under the same roof, production being transferred to Chester after several years of simultaneous assembly.

In February 1960, Sir Roy Dobson of Hawker Siddeley announced the details of a bigger DH.121 'Mk 2', aimed at the more extended range 727 market. While studies continued on the larger development, Hawker Siddeley undertook a simpler development of the basic aircraft for its current and potential customers.

A longer-range version of the Trident was revealed in January 1960, which would feature an increased 112,000 pounds gross weight, centre section fuel and a range of 1,400 miles with full payload from a 6,700 foot runway. Despite a number of false starts and projected export developments, this higher-weight model eventually evolved into the Trident 1C of late 1961, which was to become BEA's initial production Trident.

It is now known that when the Trident was designed in the late 1950s, the aircraft was tailored so tightly around BEA's need for a short-range aircraft with very low operating costs that the standard of passenger amenities assumed for the aircraft was somewhat lower than those which were required when the Trident became operational (i.e., no allowance was made for hot meals on board, or for reclining seats). As the design was refined and BEA required the incorporation of more cabin equipment, it was necessary to increase the gross weight, and by the second half of 1961, De Havilland had decided to adopt 107,000 pounds as the MTOW for the standard aircraft. The Mk 1C was a higher-weight option with an MTOW of 115,000 pounds and the centre section fuel. The 1C was, in fact, to be the first production model, and all BEA's 24 aircraft were to be 1Cs, but without the centre fuel tank, and hence the 107,000 pounds version was dropped.

Very little was seen of the Trident assembly line. Still, the new machine was proudly unveiled to the world at 5.30 pm on the warm sunny evening of Friday, 4 August 1961, when the first Trident, registered G-ARPA, manufacturer's serial number (MSN) 2101, was rolled out at Hatfield. Equipped with only two Speys, and wearing the full BEA 'Red Square' colour scheme, the roll-out of Papa Alpha was witnessed by Sir Geoffrey de Havilland along with De Havilland's Chief Pilot and director, John Cunningham, Managing Director HG. Sturgeon, Chief Designer J.P. Smith, and Technical Director Charles T Wilkins.

G-ARPA was initially fitted with non-flight-rated pre-production Speys, and the engine commenced flight testing on 12 October 1961 when Vulcan B1 XA902 took off from Rolls-Royce's flight test centre at Hucknall with Speys fitted in the two inboard Olympus positions. Two flight tests were carried out lasting four hours. Additional ground tests were undertaken to test the Trident's side pylon installation and, more importantly, the S-duct centre engine layout. By this stage, the engine was expected to exceed its guaranteed thrust level of 9,850 pounds and attain at least 10,400lb. The engine was now selected to power the BAC One-Eleven twinjet and the Blackburn Buccaneer strike aircraft. Blackburn was the source for the Trident's Auxiliary Power Unit, the Artouste, which was to be located in the lower fuselage centre section.

Papa Alpha undertook engine runs with three non-flight Speys, but by November, three flight engines were installed in readiness for its first flight the following month. Papa Alpha was cleared for flight on 21 December, but the onset of Hertfordshire's worst blizzard for fifty years was to dash any hopes of flying the Trident before the new year. The flight crew had prepared for the first flight by practising procedures on a computerised experimental control rig.

After being held up by snow on the runway and taxiways, Papa Alpha ventured out on 6 January for five high-speed ground runs, which were followed by three more on 8 January during which it lifted off and remained airborne for about ten seconds. These checks revealed that although the gearing for the tailplane and rudder was adequate, the lateral control gearing for the ailerons and linked spoilers was on the high side.

A break in the weather finally allowed G-ARPA to take to the air from the 6,000 foot Hatfield runway at precisely 12.14 on 9 January 1962. At the controls for the Trident's one hour twenty-onr minute flight was the De Havilland chief test pilot John Cunningham, accompanied by Peter Bugge (co-pilot), E. Brackstone-Brown ('Brax') (flight engineer), Anthony Fairbrother (flight test manager), John Johnston and John Marshall (flight observers).

The test flight involved a take-off at around 90,000 pounds gross weight, with the aircraft lifting off at around the 3,000 foot mark at a speed of 130 knots. Papa Alpha reached a maximum altitude of 15,000 feet and achieved a maximum speed of 330 knots (380 mph) at 12,000 feet. During the flight, a problem with the undercarriage was experienced during a routine deployment/retraction test. The starboard mainwheel jammed semi-retracted against the undercarriage door. The problem was overcome by Brax, who had the bright idea of depressurising the relevant hydraulic systems to allow the gear and door to freefall.

On its return, the Trident made a low pass along the runway with flaps and undercarriage down before making a climbing turn to port and completing one last circuit to land. The thrust reversers, which were fitted to the pod engines, were used during the landing roll, and Papa Alpha was brought to a halt at around 3,000 feet. The aircraft taxied in and was swamped by all and sundry. In all the excitement. the engines were momentarily forgotten about and were left happily whirring away quietly at the back.

Commenting on the first flight. John Cunningham said. *'I am delighted with the Trident handling qualities; she is superb to fly'.* Three Tridents were to participate in what was planned to be an eight hundred to one thousand hour flight test programme, which was due to be completed with the awarding of its Certificate of Airworthiness and first deliveries in June 1963.

Speaking at the first flight ceremony, H. G. Sturgeon, Managing Director of Hawker Siddeley's De Havilland division, said of the 727 and the Trident that they were quite different though both were cast in the same mould. *'Ours is of a size that will match airline needs more exactly than any other coming along in the next five years.'* Lord Douglas, Chairman of BEA, said *This is a great day for BEA. The Trident has a big edge on any comparable airliner in sight.* Nevertheless, only BEA had ordered the aircraft to date, and Sir Aubrey Burke remarked that ...*we didn't sell any Comets until the first one had flown. People don't believe in brochures any more.* He also revealed that there had been sales enquiries to justify a second production batch of twenty-five aircraft.

The preliminary flight test phase of forty-three hours was completed on schedule on 28 February. By the time the second Trident G-ARPB made its first flight on Sunday, 20 May, Papa Alpha had completed some one hundred and eighteen hours in one hundred and eleven trouble-free flights, putting it twelve hours ahead of schedule. Papa Bravo, which had a partly furnished forward cabin, was to be used mainly for system testing. Commenting on the trials to date, De Havilland stated that there had been *'a marked absence of engineering faults of any kind and only three occasions on which snags have even slightly delayed take-off'.*

The initial flight tests consisted of general handling assessments, with the extreme centre of gravity (CG) positions at low speeds being concentrated on. The aircraft's airfield and climb performance was checked out, as was the effect of a simulated engine failure just before take-off. High-weight take-offs with the tail bumper dragging on the runway were also carried out and successfully illustrated that there was no problem with a ground stall. lnflight reverse thrust trials proved that this was a safe and effective way to reduce speed, without a resulting change in trim or loss of lift. Reverse had also been successfully demonstrated in the flare.

Papa Alpha had achieved a maximum Mach number of 0.88 at 32,000 feet (592mph) in level cruise. Simulator tests before the first

Left: John Cunningham acknowledges the attending media from the steps of the Trident. The rest of the flight crew is behind him.

Below: V1, Rotate!
[Photographs courtesy of British Aerospace Hatfield]

Two pictures from *The Aeroplane and Astronatutics* - Left: John Cunningham brings Papa Alpha in for a low pass and preliminary check approach before landing back at Hatfield

Below: was The Trident taxies past the Control Tower at Hatfield. *[Photographs courtesy of British Aerospace Hatfield]*

flight had suggested that the outboard ailerons would not be needed, and they had been locked out from the first flight. This belief was confirmed, and later, aircraft that were built did not incorporate the outboard ailerons. Testing had established that the Trident's low-speed lift was less than expected, and it was clear that some major changes to the leading edge system would be required to improve low-speed handling and performance. Tests were carried out to establish the optimum flap and droop angles, and a form of movable leading edge flap at the wing root working in conjunction with the droop was tested. It was also found necessary to modify the wing to droop sealing plate to improve airflow.

The Trident was equipped with a novel 'Main Gear As Airbrake' switch next to the lever on the centre pedestal, along with the conventional airbrakes and spoilers. It allowed the main wheels to be lowered independently of the nose gear at speeds of up to 300 knots to allow it to serve as a second-stage airbrake. This rather over-complicated facility to slow the aircraft was deleted fairly soon after service entry, for it was rumoured someone tried to land with the nose gear retracted. Still, all the gear was permitted for operation at airspeeds of up to 230 knots.

By the time the third Trident G-ARPC had flown on 25 August, the Mk 1C offering had been joined by an export model, the longer range Mk 1E, which had been launched into production seventeen days earlier when Kuwait Airways placed orders for two plus one option. The new model featured higher weights, increased fuel and more sophisticated high lift slats replacing the 1C's droop. Papa Charlie was the first Trident not to be fitted with the outboard ailerons, saving around 1001b in weight and, like Papa Bravo, featured a partially furnished cabin. The aircraft was to be used for supplementary low-speed handling tests, performance measurement with production engines and route proving.

By August 1962, the quoted thrust rating for the Trident's Rolls-Royce Spey engines had been reduced to 9,850 pounds, somewhat less than the expected 10,400 pounds. Although Rolls-Royce had only guaranteed a rating of 9,850lb, the anticipated 'brochure thrust' was some 10,400lb, and previous experience with the company had led De Havilland to believe that this would be provided for certification.

Tests of the No 2 engine's then-novel S-duct intake had proved that there was no problem with the layout and that there were no intake problems or compressor stalls even at high angles of incidence. There had been some surge problems during ground running in crosswind conditions, which were eliminated by modifying the intake lip, and the engines.

One problem discovered early on was that the range of adjustment for the pilot's seat was inadequate for short-legged crew and could result in the wheel brakes being inadvertently applied when large rudder pedal movements were called for. During some touch-and-goes being carried out by a pilot converting to the Trident, all four tyres on the starboard undercarriage burst, and the aircraft then had to make a landing with four flat tyres. A modified undercarriage was also fitted to Papa Charlie to reduce the harshness characteristic of the original design.

On 30 August, just before Farnborough week, Papa Bravo made some demonstration flights for the press.

Papa Charlie made its public debut, being based at Farnborough for the air show week in early September. The aircraft made demonstration flights each day and was joined by the other two Tridents who synchronised their arrival, flying over from Hatfield each day.

After the final Farnborough flypast on 9 September, that was flown by Peter Bugge and Pat Fillingham, Papa Bravo made the Trident's first landing at London-Heathrow Airport, a location that

The packed tight Flight Shed at Hatfield. Closest to the camera is G-ARPD. The aircraft on the right is thought to be G-ARPA, for it has the two black vertical stripes on the upper fuselage, a known featre of Papa Alpha. Behind that is G-ARPE and 'RPF. *[Photograph courtesy of British Aerospace Hatfield]*

was destined to be the type's home for the next twenty-four years. The aircraft then made its first overseas flight to Dublin, carrying twenty delegates and their wives, including BEA Trident Flight Manager Capt Eric Poole, to an IATA meeting. A second visit to Dublin was made on 11 September.

Following its demonstrations at Farnborough, Papa Alpha was grounded for a period to allow the installation of equipment required for the flutter test programme. During the airliners first eight months, G-ARPA had completed an average of twenty-two and a half hours a month of testing, which compared favourably with the target of twenty-three hours.

The high speed flutter tests commenced with Papa Alpha in the autumn, whose new equipment fit included two electronically controlled linear hydraulic inertia exciters in the nose in place of the radar, and the other above the centre engine intake replacing the HF notch aerial. The tests involved the aircraft flying at the required height and speed over a course in East Anglia, which had been specifically selected as it gave good telemetry reception at Hatfield.

Papa Bravo departed for hot weather trials in Khartoum and Aden on 21 November 1962, with John Cunningham at the controls. Accompanying him was Capt W R Mitchell of BEA's Trident Development Flight. The first leg of the flight was

John Cunningham, executive director and chief test pilot (Hatfield) of Hawker Siddeley Aviation Ltd., was photographed while flying the Trident IE out of Nairobi during tropical trials. The superb handling qualities of the 1E are the measure of the knowledge and effort which Cunningham and his colleagues have contributed to the development programme. *[Photograph courtesy of British Aerospace Hatfield]*

Six Trident publicity photos taken on BEA BE102 and BE107 flights to Nice Cote d'Azur on 22 August 1965. *[De Havilland Aircraft Co.]*

a nine hundred and thirty mile leg from Heathrow to Ciampino airport in Rome, which was covered in 1one hour, thirty-seven minutes, giving an average cruise speed of 575 mph. The time, although not a record attempt, represented the fastest ever recorded between the two cities by an airliner and only three minutes slower than the record set by Bill Bedford in October 1956 - in a Hawker Hunter! Papa Bravo returned to the UK on 2 December after a successful eleven-day test programme.

Having returned to Hatfield for the Christmas break, the roving Papa Bravo departed for Malta via Nice on the day before the first anniversary of the type's first flight, 8 January, under the command of De Havilland test pilot Jimmy Phillips. Also on board for the tests at Luqa airport, Malta, was BEA's Capt W. R. Mitchell, along with seventeen observers and technicians. Based at Luqa, Papa Bravo flew an average of five and a half hours daily. Meanwhile, Papa Charlie carried out slush drag tests in the snow at Hatfield.

While the Trident flight testing was ongoing, Boeing quietly got on with its 727 programme and began gathering more orders. By the time the first 727 flew from Renton on 9 February 1963, total orders for the type stood at an impressive one hundred and thirty-one aircraft from eight customers. The fourth Trident, registered G-ARPD, joined the test programme on 17 January 1963 and was fitted with the leading edge slat system of the Trident 1E. Papa Delta was to fly a parallel 1E aerodynamic test programme for about ten months.

Five hundred and fifty hours of flight testing had been completed by February 1963, but there was still a long way to go before route-proving trials with BEA could begin. As a result of flight-testing, several minor modifications had been made to the basic Trident 1C wing, which included revised positioning and a reduction in the number of wing fences. As first flew, the Trident featured a large inboard fence on each wing wrapped around the leading edge and a smaller fence on the top of each wing further outboard. The final configuration involved just one small fence about three-quarters of the way outboard on the top of each wing, which extended from the leading edge aft. The droop and flap settings were revised, and the design of the wing root Krueger flap was changed. Retractable vortex generators were installed on the outboard leading edge behind the droop, but they were only extended when the droop was deployed

The Trident was also found to have a problem in that it tended not to exhibit the classic nose-down pitch at the stall, but this was eventually rectified by

Kuwait Airways Trident G-ASWU before registration as 9K-ACF starts it's take-off roll for another test flight. The airliner is seen from the flight deck of a HS 125 chase aircraft.
[Photograph courtesy of British Aerospace Hatfield]

fitting a stick pusher. This involved a hydraulic ram that physically pushed the control column forward at extreme angles of attack and speed in response to signals from duplicated incidence sensors on the forward fuselage. The Trident was the first commercial airliner to be certificated with this device.

In early March, Papa Bravo flew to Sweden to conduct a number of SAS demonstrations in Stockholm. Three demonstration flights were made from Stockholm's small domestic airport, Bromma. The return journey to Hatfield of almost 1,000 miles was completed in a record 1hr 43 min.

On 23 April, BEA Chief Executive Anthony Milward hinted that the airline was about to take up its twelve Trident options, and it was thought that the airline would plump for the longer range Mk 1E, or perhaps a higher capacity development, the 1F. Negotiations over the options, however, ended up being as protracted as the original contract, with several years passing before the deal for more Tridents was finalised.

High-speed trials were completed in April 1963, and it was revealed that high speed cruise was 0.88 Mach at 25,000 feet (530 knots), slightly faster than expected. In testing, the Trident had achieved 0.96 Mach (652 mph) in shallow dives at altitudes between 30,000 and 24,000 feet.

The fifth Trident, G-ARPE, which was the first fully furnished example, made its first flight on 3 June 1963, having been delayed slightly to allow the incorporation of the first set of low-speed modifications in production form. Papa Echo immediately departed to Paris to display at the opening day of the Le Bourget air show before returning to continue testing. The aircraft was destined to be used for BEA acceptance checks. During the summer, more hot and high trials were carried out in Cairo and at the Torrejon US Air Force base near Madrid.

By October 1963, BEA pilot training had commenced at Hatfield. BEA's first Trident 1C, G-

ARPF, was delivered on 13 December 1963, having first flown on 18 October. Papa Fox was immediately used for crew training at Stansted during which it was flown by the Duke of Edinburgh on a seventy-five minute flight, who expressed great interest in the type. The leading edge slat-equipped Papa Delta meanwhile carried out stall tests fitted with a tail parachute installation.

G-ARPE returned to Hatfield on 29 October after completing a 35,000 mile, eighty flight-hour sales demonstration and route proving tour of the Far East. Demonstration flights had been given to airlines in five countries: Japan, Hong Kong, Singapore, Pakistan and Syria. On its return, the aircraft was put into the Hawker Siddeley Group's Avro Whitworth Division plant at Bitteswell to bring it up to the latest mod standard to allow it to commence route proving with BEA. In early December, Papa Echo carried out a series of demonstration flights for Alitalia at Rome's Fiumicino airport.

A substantial amount of Papa Echo's flying time on the sales tour was put towards the mandatory two hundred hours of route proving required for the Certificate of Airworthiness (C of A). Flown jointly by De Havilland and BEA flight and cabin crews, the BEA route proving commenced on 12 December and involved flights from Heathrow to sixteen airports in eleven countries. The sixteen-day, one hundred and thirty-three hour BEA route proving programme was completed in early January and saw 61,000 miles flown. Most of the flying was carried out between Heathrow and Rome, Madrid and Athens, although other airports visited included Zurich, Lisbon, Nice, Frankfurt, Paris, Copenhagen, Stockholm, Helsinki, Prestwick and Manchester. Eight hours and twenty minutes flying per day was averaged, with a typical day involving sectors such as London - Rome - Madrid - London - Rome - London for a total of 4,320 miles in nine hours twenty minutes flying. On several occasions, fog at Heathrow saw diversions to Paris, Madrid and Prestwick. Only a handful of minor technical problems were encountered during the period.

The final flight assessment by the Air Registration Board in preparation for the C of A took place in January 1964 at Torrejon Air Force base. Final autopilot and systems testing were carried out at Hatfield soon after, and on 18 February 1964 the Trident received its C of A after sixteen hundred hours of flight testing. The Trident was also the first airliner to be approved with a duplex flight control system.

G-ARPG flew on 9 January 1964, and by February 1964, the seven Tridents had completed a total of 2,300 flying hours, of which just under 1,600 had been used in direct development, with the split as follows - low and high speed handling thirty-one per cent, systems and engineering tests twenty-nine per cent, performance twenty-two per cent, autopilot eighteen per cent.

BEA planned to have three Tridents in service by 31 March. Trident 1C G-ARPG was officially delivered on 19 February and was flown to Heathrow for its naming ceremony on 28 February, during which Lord Douglas' wife poured a bottle of champagne over Papa Golf's nose. At the presentation, Lord Douglas said, *'While others wax lyrical about supersonic airliners, I pin my faith on*

A ray of sunshine in a wet and dreary Manchester - Cyprus Airways' Trident Sun Jet 5B-DAD.
[Simon Peters Collection.]

In the Trident 1E mock-up at Hatfield, flight attendants of Pakistan International Airlines make their first acquaintance with the Trident's attractively styled passenger cabin.

Charles Butler Associates of New York, one of the world's most experienced design consultants, gave the Trident interior a clean, smooth appearance by skilled use of concealed lighting and close attention to detail.

The passenger service units, neatly recessed in the overhead racks, are an example of design detail in the Trident. Airline operators may achieve varying elfects of cabin colours and textures by individual choice of materials and have the availability of expert consultant services in the whole range of cabin decor. *[Photographs courtesy of British Aerospace Hatfield]*

the Trident. We have bought British aeroplanes not because we were instructed to do so, but because we consider them the best available tools for the job.'

BEA's planned purchase of Trident 1Fs stood at twenty-four.

On 3 March, Papa Bravo carried out the Trident's first automatic landings under the watchful eyes of Jimmy Phillips. Ten automatic landings were carried out, six at RAE Bedford and four at Hatfield, all using the Smiths duplex flight control system. Five days later on 8 March, a BEA Trident set a new speed record for Stockholm to London, completing the 900 miles in 1hr 40min, eclipsing the one hour fifty-five mnute record held by a BEA Comet 4B.

The Trident's first revenue earning flight was made on 11 March by G-ARPG, on the morning flight from Heathrow to Copenhagen substituting for a Comet 4. On board for the inaugural service were 79 rather surprised passengers. Later the same day, Papa Golf operated a London - Dusseldorf service. Until 1 April, when the Trident was to

Whether boarding or looking out the windows, HSA pushed the ease and modernity of the Trident in their publicity material. Access to the main cabin in theTrident 2 was via a pair of plug-type doors which slid 'up and over' to give unrestricted entry with more than six feet of headroom, unlike the earlier Trident 1 which had hinged doors. *[Photographs courtesy of British Aerospace Hatfield]*

officially enter service, it continued to fly ad hoc on normal scheduled services, mainly to Geneva and Nice at a frequency of about four per week.

As delivered, BEA's Trident 1Cs could seat eighty passengers in a mixed-class layout, with four-abreast first-class seating convertible to six-abreast economy. Up to ninety-three passengers could be accommodated in a single class six-abreast layout. The Tridents had two galleys, one forward and one central, and three toilets, one adjacent to the forward galley and two aft. The seating layout was novel in that the forward cabin featured a two rows of aft-facing seats, whilst the main cabin had three aft-facing rows extending as far back as the overwing exits. Sitting in these gave a very strange sensation duing a steep climb-out after take-off!

Papa Golf launched the scheduled Trident services on 1 April 1964, operating the 09.50 London-Zurich flight BE564. This route and London-Nice were operated daily from 1 April, with London-Frankfurt and Geneva added the following month. Services to Helsinki, Stockholm, Copenhagen, Milan and Rome were added throughout the summer. By the end of the year, Tridents were also flying to Valencia, Brussels, Barcelona, Munich, Prague, Venice and Vienna.

A little piece of BEA history

was made on the Thursday before Easter 1964 when BEA's outgoing Chairman, Lord Douglas, completed his farewell flight with the airline, flying on Trident G-ARPG on the type's inaugural service to Vienna. Lord Douglas was piped aboard the Trident by a Scots Piper at the ceremony. The trip to Vienna took one hour forty minutes. Lord Douglas was succeeded by the former Chief Executive Anthony Milward, who was replaced as Chief Executive by Henry Marking.

The Trident got off to a promising start, and new Chairman, Anthony Milward, praised the Trident at his first press conference. 'On the London-Frankfurt route, the hottest and most competitive on which there are 18 different jet airline flights a day, we could not hold our own with the Viscount, but with the Trident, we have increased our load factor by 10 per cent since June.' Milward had also revealed that he expected the Trident to cost around £10 million to introduce, around twice that of the Vanguard.

Meanwhile, the Trident's overseas competitor, the 727, suddenly loomed as large as life in Europe in May 1964, when Lufthansa began operating the type on its regional routes.

Shortly after its introduction into BEA service, the Trident suffered a series of centre engine surges, which had never occurred during flight-testing. De Havilland launched a test programme at Hatfield to investigate the problem, and Rolls-Royce conducted tests on the engine at Derby. The cure was found to be the installation of four vortex generators in the centre engine intake. Considering these problems, Anthony Milward stated that 'teething problems with the Trident have so far been remarkably few, which is particularly gratifying in view of the fact that the aircraft represents such a technological advance over its predecessors'.

Rumours that the Trident 1C's performance was below par on some BEA sectors began circulating in June 1964 after the aircraft had been in service for several months. BEA was forced to concede that the Trident could not operate with a full load on specific routes because of runway limitations and obstacles or hot temperatures at the destination.

Other routes, such as London - Athens, could not be operated nonstop. However, BEA explained in a rather mealy-mouthed manner that when 'the Trident specification was decided upon in 1959, such single stage operations were not envisaged'. The problem of the higher-than-anticipated weight of the Trident combined with the lower-than-expected thrust from the Speys had seemingly caught up with the aircraft. It was revealed in 1966 that all the Trident 1Cs were to be re-engined with five per cent more powerful Spey 1As.

In the summer of 1964, the three test Tridents were sent to the Bitteswell site to remove test equipment. Papa Charlie was the first of the three to leave in August and was delivered to BEA the following month. Papa Bravo had been officially delivered to BEA in June 1964 but had been immediately leased back by Hawker Siddeley to carry out Autoland tests.

By 31 March 1965, when the Trident had completed one year in service, fourteen of the type had been delivered to the airline. During these 12 months, the Tridents had carried 322,351 passengers and flown 3,660,000 miles. The aircraft was proving popular with BEA's passengers, and the only complaints came when passengers switched from a Trident to another type. The aircraft began regular operations to Paris - Le Bourget on 1 April 1965, inaugurating the new BEA Quicksilver Service which comprised thirteen flights a day, mostly every hour. The Trident completed the scheduled fifty-five-minute flight in around forty minutes.

The world's first 'Auto Flare' touchdown on a

A very wintry scene as northeast's Trident G-AVYD - part of the British Air Services Group - is seen about to roll.*[Author's Collection]*

Air Ceylon's Trident 1E 4R-ACN. *[David Lee Collection.]*

commercial service was made by Trident 1C G-ARPR when it arrived at Heathrow from Paris - Le Bourget on 10 June 1965, operating Bealine 343. At the controls were Captain Eric Poole (Flight Manager Development), Captain Tom Atkins (Trident Training Captain) and Captain M Mitchell. Each passenger was presented with a certificate to commemorate the historic achievement. Capt Poole commented on the landing, *Although I was completely confident, my pulse rate was probably a little faster than normal.*

A BEA Trident was used for the first air-bridge loading at London-Heathrow on 15 November 1965 when BEA introduced the novel system experimentally at the Europa terminal (now Terminal 2). The system was initially used for the airline's Trident services to Paris, allowing BEA to introduce trickle-loading. The 'power nose loader' was planned to be standard equipment at Heathrow's new northeast-facing terminal, which was due to open in 1968 (now Terminal 1).

As part of the ongoing product improvement programme, operational experience had led Hawker Siddeley to relocate the APU from the wing centre section to the base of the fin. It also allowed more room for additional fuel capacity on later variants. Trident 1C G-ARPR was the first aircraft to be delivered (on 12 April 1965) with the APU relocated on the line, whilst Trident 1C (G-ARPN was the first to be modified with the relocated APU).

In July 1965, BEA introduced Trident services from Manchester to Paris replacing Viscounts. By the following summer, the type was serving six European points from the airport include Copenhagen, Brussels, Amsterdam, Dusseldorf, Zurich, and Paris. The airline also modified the colour scheme on its Tridents, the polished metal undersides being painted grey and later, the name 'Trident' being added to each side of the centre air intake.

On 14 November 1967, the Queen had her first taste of the Trident when G-ARPX had the honour of flying her and Prince Philip to Malta. The following month, BEA finally took delivery of its last Trident 1C, G-ARPB, which had been retained by the manufacturer for Autoland development work.

From BEA to BA

In 1969 the Committee on British Air Transport, presided over by Sir Ronald Edwards - to be known forever as 'the Edwards Committee' - recommended

Tucked away from public view, the 'Cul de Sac'was an area of BA Engineering in the eastern side of Heathrow where many of the Tridents were serviced or repaired. It was also the site a number of years later where the 'Trident Massacre' occurred when a number were broken up by the scrappers. *[Author]*

G-AVYC in northeast colours, but with British airways titles. The dayglo Northeast yellow, and Cambrian orange roof top and fin colours did not weather well, for they rapidly faded, looking very pale. *[Author]*

that the country's two national airlines, BOAC and BEA, should be controlled by a single organisation termed the 'British Airways Board' (BAB). The then Labour government, however, decided to take this one step further and actually merge the two airlines.

Thus BAB came into effect on 7 October 1971, and acquired the assets of the two state airlines on 1 April 1972. From this point on the wheels were in motion to create what we all know now as British Airways from two very proud and single-minded airlines. However, the two airlines were

Yet another view of Charlie Pier at Heathrow Terminal One *[Author]*

Definately something of a hybrid paint scheme! When looking closely at G-ASWU there are elements of the Cyprus Airways paint livery, a modified Speedjack on the vertical fin, fuselege lettering that appears to be made up of aircraft registration letters and a union flag on the cowling that comes from goodness knows where! *[Author's Collection]*

not to officially cease to exist until 31 March 1974. It was by no means the last merger.

In September 1972, the European Division (ED) of British Airways was created and BEA began to trade as such twelve months later, with the Trident the mainstay of its fleet. In July 1973 the new British Airways colour scheme was unveiled, taking what the advertising department and graphic designers thought was the best from the existing BEA and BOAC schemes, but as an interim solution, from August 1973 the fleet had their old titles replaced by 'British Airways'.

The first Trident to be painted as such was G-ARPU, followed by Trident 2 G-AVFA and 3 G-AWZC. An interesting change was the use of a lower case rather than capital 'T' for the mark of Trident painted on the tail. Fox' Alpha was called upon for an air-to-air photo session resplendent in the new colours. It was to be some years before time was found to paint all the hard working Tridents in the new colours and as such some aircraft ended up looking scruffy while others found themselves in some very hybrid schemes.

From 1 April 1973, British Air Services, meaning northeast and Cambrian became part of British Airways and the three ex-northeast 1Es were repainted to carry British Airways titles, before being repainted to wear the full red, white and blue colour scheme.

The three 1Es continued to operate the old northeast services and carried small 'northeast' titles on the forward fuselage. Earlier, in April 1972 Trident 1E, G-AVYD, had been named 'Vicky' by Vicky Leandros, the winner of the 1972 Eurovision Song Contest.

Meanwhile 'the Channel Islands Division Trident 1E, G-AVYE, was replaced by BAC One-Elevens from November 1973 and so the aircraft joined the three others operating the old northeast routes.

It was a Trident that operated the last BEA service, BE943 from Dublin to London, on the evening of 31 March 1974. However, it was to be some time before the 'BE' flight number prefix was replaced by 'BA', and so the callsign 'Bealine' gave way to 'Speedbird'.

Trident Three G-AWZW in British airways 'Speedjack scheme on the stand. *[Author's Collection]*

Catch the Shuttle!

British Airways introduced Europe's first Shuttle service on 12 January 1975 on the London-Glasgow route with nine specially reconfigured Trident 1s. The idea was 'borrowed' from the Americans, who had pioneered the shuttle service between major East Coast cities, including Boston, New York, and Washington. In the early 1960s, Eastern Air Lines customers could march to some of America's busiest airports and rely on getting a ticket just before boarding. London had a similar status as a critical business and financial hub that connected the world, and the airline adopted the shuttle programme to its leading domestic destinations.

The BA Shuttle offered hourly service Monday through to Saturday and a two-hourly service on Sunday. No booking was required for a guaranteed seat, and the regular hourly departures were intended to give the airline a competitive advantage over other modes of transport. All passengers had to do was turn up at least ten minutes before the flight! To ensure all passengers have a seat, a permanent backup aircraft was stationed at each airport.

It was, of course, an era of restrictive practices and role demarcation, and plans to allow passengers to buy tickets on board the aircraft had to be curtailed initially due to objections from trade unions. Aimed at convenience, the service was no-frills: the aircraft was configured in one class, there was no galley, and passengers would not be provided any meals or drinks.

The nine Trident 1's standard 109-seat interiors were refurbished at a total cost of £48,000 to seat 100 passengers at a more comfortable 33in seat pitch. The plan was to add 140-seat Trident 3s to the Shuttle fleet when load factors demanded.

When the airline first launched the service, it was a big gamble, noting that British Airways lost millions of pounds; however, after just one year of service, the operating losses were halved. Two years later, the service operated in the black and carried over a million passengers.

The Shuttle operation was gradually expanded with Edinburgh being added in April 1976, Belfast in April 1977 and Manchester in April 1979. As the Shuttle established itself, the Trident 3 became the main aircraft allocated to the service, with the Trident 1s and 2s being used as Shuttle back-ups.

A promotional picture that breaks so many rules! Cannot really make out the airliner type - yes, it's a Trident 3 - certainly cannot see which airline, shooting into the sun, lens flare, but what a shot! *[Author's Collection]*

Trident 2E G-AVFL was delivered in 1967 to BEA, and is seen here in the full 'Negus' scheme. It ended it's days in Southend in 1985. *[Kirk Smeaton Collection]*

In 1977, fatigue cracks were discovered in the wings of British Airways Trident G-AWZL during routine maintenance. Cracks were then discovered in other machines as well - the problem was thought to have been at least partially caused by the extrememly short sectors the aircraft had flown since BAs introduction of their Shuttle Service. There entire fleet of Trident 2 and 3s where progressively withdrawn for the repairs to be carried out at Hatfield, Bournemouth and Chester - a process that took two weeks per aircraft. The aircraft were discretely ferried back to the manufacturer, where they had strengthening plating fitted in the areas affected, as well as the replacement of the low drag Küchemann wingtips with conventional Trident 1 style units. Later the same year BA claimed up to £5.25 million in compensation for the cost of the wing repairs and the loss of revenue that resulted in the aircraft having been temporarily withdrawn.

Colours

For several years after the merger, the component airlines' aircraft wore their old colours with British Airways titles applied. Sometimes the tail was painted into the initial BA scheme, but the fuselage kept its original colours.

The initial overall scheme was designed by the graphic design firm Negus & Negus, formed by Dick Negus. The 'Negus' livery had a white crown with a dark blue belly and blue Speedbird logo near the cockpit. The latter harked back to the BOAC days. The new tail design represented a stylised quarter Union Jack flag with red tail top and bore hallmarks of BEA 'Speedjack'. Even though British Airways itself didn't come into being until 1974, the livery was unveiled in 1973. At the beginning of the 1980s, BA dropped the Airways titles in favour of enlarged 'British' lettering. The rest of the livery was kept the same as the original Negus scheme.

The next scheme was designed by the famous design house Landor Associates. This updated scheme was unveiled in December 1984. It was quite similar to the Negus scheme, but the white roof of the aircraft was replaced with 'Pearl Grey' and the blue belly replaced with 'Midnight Blue'. The Speedbird was replaced with a 'Brilliant Red' speedwing running along the lower fuselage. The red tail top was replaced with a blue one featuring British Airways' coat of arms. The title font was also changed and capitalised. Aircraft remained individually named. All in all, it was a very elegant scheme.

Of all the colour schemes applied to the Trident I feel the Landor scheme works the best - there is something decidedly classy about it, as seen on G-AWZX here. *[Kirk Smeaton Collection]*

Among the spotters at Heathrow in the late 1960s, BEA was nicknamed 'Back Every Afternoon' due to the short-haul nature of many of their routes. Here Papa Oscar is seen on a stand undergoing overnight maintenance.

Chapter Eight

Variants

Trident 1C

Much of what has already been written applies to the Trident 1s so here for completeness, is a synopsis.

The first Trident entered service on 1 April 1964. By 1965, fifteen Tridents were in BEA's fleet, and by March 1966, the fleet had increased to twenty-one. Hawker Siddeley proposed an improved 1C, the Trident 1E. This would be powered by 11,400 pound thrust Spey 511s, have a gross weight of 135,600 pounds, an increased wing area by extending the chord, leading-edge slats for improved field performance, different take-off flap settings and the same fuselage, but with up to 140 seats in a six-abreast configuration. This specification brought the 1C closer to the original DH.121's larger concept, but with 7,000 pounds less thrust. Only a few sales of the new design were made: three each to Kuwait Airways and Iraqi Airways, four to Pakistan International Airlines (later sold to CAAC), two each to Channel Airways and Northeast Airlines, and one to Air Ceylon. Channel Airways' aircraft were equipped with cramped, twenty-one-inch seat pitch, seven-abreast seating in the forward section, seating 149 passengers.

Trident 2E

BEA decided that the Trident was too short-legged for its ever-expanding routes and that an even longer-ranged version was needed. Hawker Siddeley responded with the Trident 1F. It would have the Spey 511 engines, a nine foot two inch fuselage stretch, a gross weight of 132,000 pounds, and up to 128 seats in the original five-abreast configuration.

By January 1962, BEA expressed interest in acquiring improved developments of the Trident, and on 23 April 1963, the Corporation's intentions were made clear when the airline's Managing Director, Anthony Milward, hinted that BEA's twelve Trident 1 options were about to be confirmed as larger 1Fs, with an additional number on option. Two months later, on 6 June, Lord Douglas announced that negotiations had commenced for the acquisition of a total of twenty-four 128-seat Trident 1Fs, including firm orders for ten.

BEA's negotiations with Hawker Siddeley stalled, although it is thought that at some stage during 1963 a commitment for ten 1Fs was signed. By mid-1964, with the BEA 1F order no nearer, Hawker Siddeley dropped any immediate plans to develop a stretched Trident variant and instead

The first Trident 2E, MSN2140, comes together at Hatfield in early 1967. *[HSA/BAe Hatfield.]*

Royalty and the Trident!

Left: Prince Phillip, the Duke of Edinburgh tries out the Captain's seat of a Trident in 1964.

Below: Prince Charles, the Prince of Wales, leaves Heathrow for Malta by Trident in 1969.

concentrated on improving the longer-range 1E model. BEA was still planning to have 50 Tridents in service by 1970, and was now looking towards the 1E as a basis for its next requirement. In September 1964 the airline was rumoured to be close to finalising an order for ten 95-seat Trident 1Es, with options for at least ten more.

The arrival of the Trident 1 in BEA's fleet allowed their Comets to operate the airline's longer sectors, whilst Trident services were concentrated in Western Europe.

The need for a Trident-based replacement for the Comet initially led BEA to specify a version capable of flying the 1,400 nautical mile London-to-Athens nonstop with a full payload, something the 1E could do. However, the purchase 'off the shelf' of Hawker Siddeley's independently developed export model, the Trident 1E, was apparently far too easy, far too immediate, and BEA soon decided that it needed a London-Beirut and 2,000 nautical mile Tel Aviv capable machine. This put the BEA requirement beyond the 1E's capabilities. As work continued on the 1F, the changes became so widespread that it was renamed the Trident 2E, E for Extended Range.

In early 1965, BEA was ready to order the new Trident and was looking to introduce a ninety-four-seater on its long-range routes in 1967-68. By February 1965, the name '2E' was being applied to BEA's new long-range Trident. It was thought that the increased range and fuel capacity over the 1E would be achieved by combining higher thrust engines with either increased wingspan or the installation of wing slipper tanks similar to those on the Comet 4. The fact that the 1E could not meet BEA's needs and therefore necessitated the development of an all-new version held up negotiations, as Hawker Siddeley and Rolls-Royce discussed the costs and financing methods for the all-new aircraft. At the end of July, the Ministry of Aviation agreed to the financial terms with the parties involved, clearing the way for the contract to be signed.

BEA confirmed their order on 5 August 1965, when the two parties jointly announced a £30m order for fifteen aircraft, plus ten options, for delivery from 1968. Press reports suggested that the Ministry of Aviation would pay around £2m towards the development costs of the new aircraft, which would be shared equally with Hawker Siddeley.

Not long after, on 26 August 1965, the Trident 2E contract was formally signed at a ceremony in London. Present were Anthony Milward, BEA Chairman, Henry Marking, BEA Chief Executive, and Sir Arnold Hall. Chairman of Hawker Siddeley Group and Air Cdre FR Banks, Chief Executive (Civil), Hawker Siddeley Aviation. The first Trident 2E was scheduled to fly in the summer of 1967.

Milward proclaimed that he had bought the Trident not because it was British, but because it was best. *'We have made a profit in nine of the past eleven years, and if that does not prove that we buy the right aircraft, I don't know what does'.* He added that he was sure more Tridents would be wanted. At the time of placing the Trident 2E order, Milward announced that the Corporation would require thirty-six aircraft of the airbus type with first deliveries in 1970.

As launched, the 2E featured an increased gross weight of 142,500 pounds compared to the 134,000 pounds of the 1E, and more powerful Spey Mk 512Ws, which would develop 11,930 pounds thrust each. In an effort to meet the BEA range requirement, Rolls-Royce had examined possible higher-thrust versions of the Spey featuring a new, larger compressor. This, however, would have had substantially more mass airflow and would therefore have necessitated major changes to the centre-engine S-duct air intake and vertical fin, as well as completely new pod installations.

The launch costs for the engines alone would have been unjustifiably high, so a less radical approach was adopted. Rolls-Royce found that by redesigning the first compressor stage of the 1E's Spey 511, take-off thrust could be increased to just under 12,000 pounds, and the engine did not require any significant changes to the airframe. So

An unidentified Trident of BEA undergoes a strip-down maintenance check at Heathrow.
[The late John Stride Collection.]

it was that the Spey 25-512 was born.

To utilise the higher thrust, increased fuel capacity was needed. With the wing and centre section already full of fuel, the only area left available was the fin. This was to be sealed on the Trident 2E to allow a 350 Imp gal fuel tank to be created there.

John Thomson Stonehouse MP (*b.* 28 July 1925, *d.*14 April 1988) Stonehouse was Minister of Aviation in Harold Wilson's Labour goverment.

Although it featured the basic wing section of the 1E, the new Trident was fitted with special low-drag 'Küchemann' wingtips, which increased the wingspan to ninety-eight feet. The new tips were to be tested on a 1E prior to the completion of the first 2E.

The fuselage also received aerodynamic attention through a drag improvement programme. The areas of improvement included a slimmer tailplane bullet; the deletion of the fin and bullet de-icing system; the fitting of drag-reducing doors on the thrust reverser outlets; the suppression of the rear external fuel pipe and many of the aerials; smaller pitots; and a general tidying up of external structural joints. Additionally, the continuing weight-reduction programme aimed to achieve a saving of seven hundred pounds compared with the previous variant.

Like the 1E, the 2E's maximum seating capacity was one hundred and fifteen, although BEA planned to arrange its aircraft typically to seat ninety-four. The 2E had a range of around 2,200 miles with maximum passenger payload, increasing to 2,550 miles with ninety passengers, allowing BEA to easily operate a nonstop London-Beirut or Tel Aviv service even against headwinds.

On 22 November 1965, the Minister of Aviation, John Stonehouse, confirmed the government's support for the Trident 2E when he announced in the House of Commons that was £1,875,000 would be put towards the project.

Paradoxically, considering the effort Hawker Siddeley and Rolls-Royce had put into increasing the range of the 2E for BEA, at a press conference in April 1966 Chairman Anthony Milward flatly denied that BEA had any plans to operate nonstop services to Beirut, conceding that Athens was as far as it planned to go in one hop.

Alterations to the Trident 2E's structure were mainly confined to detailed strengthening, with slightly thicker panels on the wing and fuselage.

The undercarriage was also strengthened, and although the 1E's tyres were utilised, the tyre pressures were increased. The Trident 2E was to

G-AVFA, the first 2E is seen in what was known as the 'Red Square' colour scheme. The two black rectangles painted on the roof are flight test timing marks. *[HSA/BAe Hatfield.]*

G-AVFA at it's naming ceremony at Heathow, the day after G-AVFD became the first fully certified Trident 2E in 17 April 1968. Here Lady Milward, the wife of the BEA Chairman pours a bottle of champagne over the nose. *[HSA/BAe Hatfield.]*

be the first of the overall design equipped with an Artouste APU cleared for operation in the air.

By March 1967 the first Trident 2E, G-AVFA, was nearing completion at Hatfield, and the newaircraft was rolled out on Monday, 10 July 1967 wearing BEA's full red square colours, as the first Trident had done six years earlier. The aircraft, however, carried large additional 'Trident Two' titles on the centre engine intake to distinguish it from the short-range Trident 1s in service with BEA.

Foxtrot Alpha was the first Trident to leave the production line equipped with the full Triplex Smiths flight control system. One noticeable cosmetic change on the 2E was that a small window had been fitted on each side aft of the overwing emergency exits, whereas on the 1E it was simply a blank panel.

Foxtrot Alpha took to the air under the command of John Cunningham on 27 July, the 18th anniversary of the first flight of the Comet. By now the machine was wearing smaller 'Trident Two' titles which were painted below the centre engine intake. The first flight of 3 hour 30 minute was completed without any hitches. Deliveries to BEA were scheduled to start in spring 1968.

55.5 hours were flown in August, and until the beginning of September, Foxtrot Alpha was engaged in handling tests and preliminary performance measurements. Tests included maximum-weight ground-stall checks, flight stalls, and fully forward/fully aft C of G positions. In the first half of September, the new air-start capability of the APU was verified, and flutter tests were carried out with a full fuel tank.

By the end of September, G-AVFA had completed 46 hours of testing, and the aircraft was taken into the workshop for minor modifications, including the fitting of a production Spey Mk. 512s. The second 2E, G-AVFB, joined the flight test programme on 2 November 1967, and three days later, on 5 November, Fox Alpha departed for Nairobi to carry out high-altitude hot-weather tests, flown by John Cunningham and Captain W R Mitchell of BEA, along with thirty other personnel. After testing, Fox Alpha departed Nairobi on 17 November for Port Darwin, Australia, for more hot weather tests, this time at sea level. The airliner's route took it via Djibouti, Bombay, Colombo in Ceylon and Singapore. The results of the overseas testing proved highly satisfactory.

Foxtrot Bravo, meanwhile, completed thirty-six hours of flying in the first fourteen days, after which it was withdrawn to be fully furnished to allow air conditioning and cabin noise tests to be conducted. In December, Foxtrot Alpha donned a special nose boom pitot head and conducted several high-speed tests, including a maximum 0.97 Mach. At the end of 1967, Foxtrot Bravo was used to complete the cruise performance programme. These confirmed that the 2E's range was five per cent better than expected, payload on certain routes was up four to five thousand pounds, guaranteed speeds were twenty-five mph faster in hot conditions than expected, and the required landing distance was one thousand feet less than anticipated.

The third 2E, G-AVFC, flew on 3 January 1968 and was the first to be operated by BEA, being handed over on 15 February 1968 with a special category C of A, for crew training and route proving before the delivery of the first fully certificated aircraft. The airliner was then returned to the manufacturer to be brought up to the latest specification before being officially delivered to the airline later that year.

G-AVFD, the fourth Trident 2E, flew on 15 March, and by the time the C of A was issued on 16 April 1968, the gross weight had been increased by a further 1,000 pounds to 143,500 pounds.

Foxtrot Delta, which was the first fully certificated Trident 2E - called 'Trident Two' by BEA - was delivered on 17 April and was officially christened at Heathrow the next day by Lady Milward. Later the same day the machine entered service on an ad hoc basis on the London-Milan route, substituting for a Trident 1.

The Trident Twos were delivered with the Smiths Triplex Autoland equipment already installed and were used on an ad hoc basis to back up Trident 1s until 1 June, when regular operations began. The aircraft were operated in one of three layouts: ninety-three seaters with eighty-five tourist and eight first class; eighty-nine seaters with seventy-three tourist and sixteen first class; or ninety-seven seats all tourist. Galley and toilet layouts were similar to those of BEA's Trident 1s.

Despite the improved performance of the new Trident, the aircraft's handling characteristics were considered to be similar enough to the Trident 1 to allow both variants to be operated as a single fleet, meaning that crews would fly both the Mk 1 and the Mk 2.

The initial routes served by BEA's 2Es included London-Madrid, Stockholm, Dublin, and Milan. As more Trident Twos were introduced, Alicante and Lisbon were added to the destination list, and it also replaced Comets on the longer-haul routes such as Moscow and the eastern Mediterranean destinations - Athens, Beirut, Nicosia and Tel Aviv. As the Trident Two fleet was built up during 1968, so BEA was able to take its Comet 4Bs off these routes, and a number were transferred to the airline's Berlin-based German operation.

On 3 July 1968, an accident at Heathrow saw the loss of two Trident 1s when an Airspeed Ambassador crashed into them whilst they were

Cyprus Airways' Trident Sun Jet 5B-DAB . *[Simon Peters Collection.]*

parked. Hawker Siddeley stepped up deliveries of Trident 2Es G-AVFC and G-AVFG to fill the sudden capacity shortfall. In the *BEA Magazine,* Anthony Milward praised Hawker Siddeley for its assistance in the matter, which had enabled BEA to *'continue services with the minimum of disruption for passengers'.*

Trident 2E G-AVFI, which first flew on 6 August 1968, was the first to fly in the new BEA 'Speedjack' or 'Quarterjack' colour scheme. Officially unveiled on 20 August, the new scheme, designed by Henrion Design Associates, consisted of a 'peacock blue' cheatline and tail with a 'high speed' partial Union flag on the tail. The 'hollow' BEA logo was painted in red on the forward fuselage, and the old scheme's red wings were retained to keep repainting costs down. Foxtrot India showed off the new colours when it was displayed at the 1968 Farnborough Air Show the following month.

The capabilities of the new Trident allowed it to succeed the 1E as Hawker Siddeley's export Trident. The first foreign order for the variant was received on 26 March 1969 when the BEA associate Cyprus Airways placed an order for two aircraft, the first of which was delivered as 5B-DAA on 19 September. The early delivery was achieved as BEA had allowed one of its allocated airframes to be transferred to the order. Cyprus Airways commenced Trident services on 1 November between Nicosia and London, Frankfurt, Athens, as well as on some other regional routes. The airline's second machine, 5B-DAB, followed on 1 May 1970. The aircraft were operated in ninety-eight or one hundred and two-seat layouts on Cyprus Airways' regional services out of Nicosia to Athens, Beirut, Ankara, Istanbul, Tel Aviv, Cairo, Rhodes and Rome, as well as on longer routes to Manchester via Brussels and London. After a period in service, the airlines'

Aristotle Onassis' Olympic Airways had jointly operated a number of Comet 4s with BEA in the 1960s (see *Olympic Airways; a History* Air World 2019 by the same author). By the late 1960s OA were considering replacing them and looked at the Trident, but eventually decided upon the 727. Just how seriously HSA took the idea was this 1/12th scale model discovered in the archives removed from the Public Relations Department . *[Stuart Howe via Simon Peters Collection.]*

G-AVFI shows the 'Speedjack' scheme as applied to the BEA Tridents. *[HSA/BAe Hatfield.]*

trijets were christened 'Trident Sun Jets'.

Commenting on the introduction of the Trident, Cyprus Airways' Chairman George Eliades said. *...the Trident has come fully up to our expectations and we are happy with our selection.*

Meanwhile, the last BEA Trident 2E, G-AVFO, was delivered to the airline on 23 June 1970, bringing its fleet up to the fifteen ordered in 1965. The first Trident 2E, Foxtrot Alpha, was, in fact, the second-to-last to be delivered to BEA when it was handed over on 23 December 1969. It had been retained by Hawker Siddeley, replacing Trident 1 G-ARPB as the Autoland development aircraft. Foxtrot Alpha demonstrated Autoland skills to the press on 15 May 1969 when the airliner carried out a series of automatic landings at RAE Bedford. John Cunningham occupied the right-hand seat, and Jim Phillips the left, and opaque screens were used to obscure the pilots' view forward to simulate the effects of fog on visibility.

On 6 April 1970, the Trident 2 inaugurated BEA services from London to Bucharest, and two months later the variant launched another new BEA route, a twice-weekly service from Heathrow to Sofia via Belgrade. By the summer of 1970, the Trident 2 had completely replaced Comets on the airline's scheduled services.

In October 1971, BEA Trident 2 G-AVFE had the honour of flying the Queen, Prince Philip and Princess Anne on a Royal visit to Turkey. The five-man flight crew for the occasion included BEA Flight Operations Director Captain Charles Owens, Trident Training Captain Maurice Chick, First Officer Paul Woodburn and First Officer Pratt. Following a three-week interior refit to reconfigure the aircraft for its VIP-carrying role, Foxtrot Echo departed Heathrow at 8.40 am on 18 October, bound for Ankara. After arriving at Ankara at lunchtime, it was then positioned to

AP-ATK of Pakistan International. *[Author's Collection]*

A stunning head-on air to air of Trident 3 G-AWYZ. *[Author's Collection]*

Izmir in the afternoon, returning to Ankara in the early evening. On 20 October, Foxtrot Echo flew to Istanbul via Izmir, where the airliner remained until 25 October, when it made the return flight. Although the plan called for a stop in Venice, bad weather at the Italian airport forced a stop in Zurich instead. Foxtrot Echo arrived back in London just after 02.45 local.

Cyprus Airways' Trident operations suffered a blow on 15 March 1972 when 2E 5B-DAA was involved in an accident at Nicosia whilst being used for crew training. On the final approach to the airport, the aircraft was allowed to descend below the correct VASI glideslope, resulting in a heavy landing short of the runway threshold and ground-looping, damaging one wing and its undercarriage. 5B-DAA was exchanged for the BEA Trident 2 G-AVFB, which became 5B-DAC with Cyprus in June 1972. 5B-DAA was ferried back to Heathrow and, after repairs, entered service with the airline as G-AZXM in October of the same year.

Cyprus Airways' Trident operations came to an abrupt end on the night of 22 July 1974 when its four Tridents were caught on the ground at Nicosia when the Turks invaded the island. It is understood that UN troops may have used the Cyprus Airways fleet to help block runways, and all four Tridents sustained damage. One 1E was destroyed, and Trident 2E 5B-DAB was declared an insurance constructive total loss as it was riddled with over two hundred bullet holes.

2E 5B-DAC and the ex-Kuwait 1E 5B-DAD were both held in Nicosia until May 1977 when they were ferried back to Heathrow. The former BEA Trident 2 5B-DAC was overhauled, restored to G-AVFB, and then re-entered service with British Airways. Meanwhile 5B-DAB remains to this day substantially complete, parked at Nicosia airport.

Pakistan International Airways sold its four 1Es to CAAC in 1970, which led to a substantial series

And now for something completely different - AP-AUG of Pakistan Air Force. *[Authors Collection]*

of export orders from China for new Trident 2Es, and later 3Bs, worth an estimated £118 million. A telephone call from Peking to Hatfield on the morning of 24 August 1971 from the Hawker Siddeley marketing team led by Mr J A Johnson confirmed that CAAC had signed an initial contract for six Trident 2Es worth around £20m, for delivery 'over the next two years'. The order was the airline's first for Western-built short-haul jets. The airline's first Trident 2E was handed over at Hatfield on 13 November 1972. The aircraft was formally delivered to the airline on 2 December 1972, carrying British marks G-AZFT, as did all Chinese Trident deliveries, before taking up Chinese marks (240, later B-240) upon arrival in China.

The Chinese 2Es were delivered with the Garrett AiResearch APU in place of the Artouste unit, and the BEA Trident Twos were retrofitted with the US-built unit during the 1970s. The Chinese Tridents were unique in that they were equipped with a dedicated fourth flight crew member position adjacent to the systems station, in place of the coat closet. This navigator's position featured a working top, a second radar display, an altimeter, an ASI, and ADF radio navigation station boxes. Apparently, the Chinese planned to use their Tridents in some remote regions of the country! The pilots' 'ram's horn' yokes were also replaced with more conventional 'U'-shaped control wheels.

CAAC paid for its Tridents in cash, with a deposit paid at contract signature and the remainder upon acceptance in China. Initially, Hawker Siddeley had several technical representatives based in the country, but from November 1979, these were replaced by regular visits every four months. During 1972 and 1973, CAAC added a further twenty-seven orders for the Trident 2E, as well as two for the longer-range Super 3Bs with additional centre fuel and increased gross weight. CAAC's order placed in November 1973 for 15 2Es was to be the last order received for the Trident.

In China, CAAC's Trident 2 fleet was expanding, with the aircraft operating long-range domestic services from Beijing, Guangzhou and Shanghai, as well as some international services to Hong Kong, Rangoon and Manila. Some of the Chinese cities served by the Trident included Chongqing, Fuzhou, Guilin, Kunming, Nanjing, Nancheng, Shenyang, Xi'an, Xiamen, and Zhengzhou.

With the completion of BEA Trident 3B deliveries in April 1973, all Trident production at Hatfield was for CAAC. The last and 117th Trident to be completed, MSN 2189, was rolled out at Hatfield on 23 March 1978 as G-BBWH, bringing to an end the Trident era at the Hertfordshire site that had lasted seventeen years. The last Trident built made its first flight on 17 April of the same year and was handed over to the airline on 17 July, taking up the marks B-271. This, however, was not to be the last Trident delivered.

MSN 2185/G-BBWD had flown the previous June but suffered a fire in its forward equipment bay during its second test flight from Hatfield and had to be put back on the production line for repair. As a result, its delivery was delayed, and G-BBWD became the last Trident to be handed over, departing Hatfield on 13 September 1978 for China via Istanbul and being officially delivered to CAAC as B-263. In all, fifty Trident 2Es were built, of which fifteen were delivered to BEA, two to Cyprus Airways and thirty-three to CAAC.

Over the years, several CAAC aircraft were transferred to Chinese regional airlines and the Chinese Air Force. During the late 1970s, the Chinese Tridents underwent the same wing modifications as the British Airways aircraft, which required wing skin reinforcements to address weaknesses discovered in 1977.

In the early 1980s, as the problems of noise pollution and fuel burn became ever more important, the Chinese considered the retrofit of the Trident's three 11,970-pound-thrust Speys with two 24,000-pound-thrust CFM International CFM56-2 turbofans. A US export licence was applied for in 1981 and granted in mid-1982. The plan involved installing the two CFM56 engines in place of the two podded Speys. The centre Spey would be removed, and that area would be modified and strengthened. The engine pylons would also be modified. Although two engines were shipped to China for the project, it never got beyond the proposal stage.

With the withdrawal of the entire British Airways Trident fleet by the beginning of 1986, the only commercial Trident operations were undertaken by Chinese regional airlines. However, the Zairean airline ACS operated a couple of ex-British Airways Trident 3Bs for a time in the mid-1980s. By the end of the decade, the Chinese Tridents were operating only within China, as noise regulations banned them even from Hong Kong, and the airline was taking delivery of new generation replacements such as Boeing 737-300s and McDonnell Douglas MD-80s.

In 1990, the Tridents were operating services on behalf of Air China and China Northern, and China's last service is thought to have been a scheduled flight from Guangzhou to Tianjin. Some Tridents will remain for teaching purposes at civil aviation training schools, whilst others have survived to be exhibited in museums. Most of the aircraft were withdrawn from use at Shenyang, Shanghai, Guangzhou and Beijing.

As of 1993, some Trident 2E passenger services were still operated by the Chinese Air Force's' airline', China United, which is thought to have a ten-strong Trident fleet, including two 1Es, six 2Es, and two 3Bs. The aircraft are used for general transport and charter duties, as well as for some VIP work.

Fourteen Tridents and one 1-11 on the ground at once? It could only be London Heathrow! *[Author's Collection]*

Somewhere on a wet and windy airfield BEA Chairman Sir Anthony Milward is seen in front of a Trident with a BEA Ford Prefect alongside. *[Author's Collection]*

Trident 3B

As the trend for larger airliners gripped the western world during the 1960s and the concept of the short-range, high-capacity airbus evolved, Hawker Siddeley began exploring developments of the Trident to meet these needs. The company had already dipped its toes into the market with its Trident 1F proposal of the early 1960s, but a bolder, more radical approach to the concept was required.

BEA produced a specification for its proposed 'air bus' in June 1964. It saw a need for a short-range, 150-200-seat aircraft to operate on high-density routes such as London-Manchester. London-Paris and London-Amsterdam, from the early 1970s.

Hawker Siddeley offered two new designs in 1965: a larger 158-seat two-engine aircraft otherwise similar to the Trident known as the HS.132 'Bident'; and the 185-seat HS.134, which moved the engines under the wings, a design very similar to the Boeing 737. The HS.132 proposal utilised the Trident wing and had a gross weight of 150,000 pounds. Range with maximum payload was around 800 miles. Both were to be powered by a new high-bypass engine under development at the time, the Rolls-Royce RB.178 as replacements for the Speys. BEA opted for Boeing 727s and 737s to fill the roles of both the BAC 1-11 and Trident, but the Labour government vetoed the plan.

Two months later, when BEA placed its order for fifteen Trident 2Es, Anthony Milward, announced that the Corporation would require thirty-six aircraft of the 'airbus type' with first deliveries in 1970. It was also evident that airlines were becoming more aware of the noise problem, as it was stated that the new aircraft should have a noise level no greater than 90 dB. However, BEA's Chairman was quick to point out that he felt that the HS132 was too small, and that the aeroplane he had in mind should have 'at least 200 seats'. Significantly, BEA felt that the 'airbus' should be an Anglo-French project, possibly with German participation.

As Hawker Siddeley reached agreements with various French aerospace companies to develop a European airbus, there was talk that the HS132 could serve as the basis for the programme. BEA felt that the aircraft was too small, but it was attracted to the design because of the commonality it would offer with its existing and future Trident fleet.

The cool reception of the HS132 concept did not deter Hawker Siddeley, and while development work continued, a less radical approach to meet BEA's requirement was adopted. This was the 140-seat Trident Mk 3 of early 1966. which was effectively a simple stretch of the Trident 2E. It was considered an interim solution and would only be ordered if the government was prepared to pay for its development. The alternative was that BEA would follow its European contemporaries into ordering Boeing 727-200s - a 140-160 seat stretched development of the -100 - until the arrival of the 'definitive air bus' in 1973.

As in the mid-1950s when it ordered the Caravelle, Air France's orders again prompted a 'kneejerk' reaction from BEA. This time, the French airline intended to order 148-seat 727-200s for delivery from March 1968. In early March 1966, it became public that BEA was considering acquiring 727-200s and DC-9-40s for its Internal German Services (IGS). Air France finalised its 727 order in June 1966, placing an initial order with Boeing for four aircraft.

BEA saw a desperate need for some 'interim'

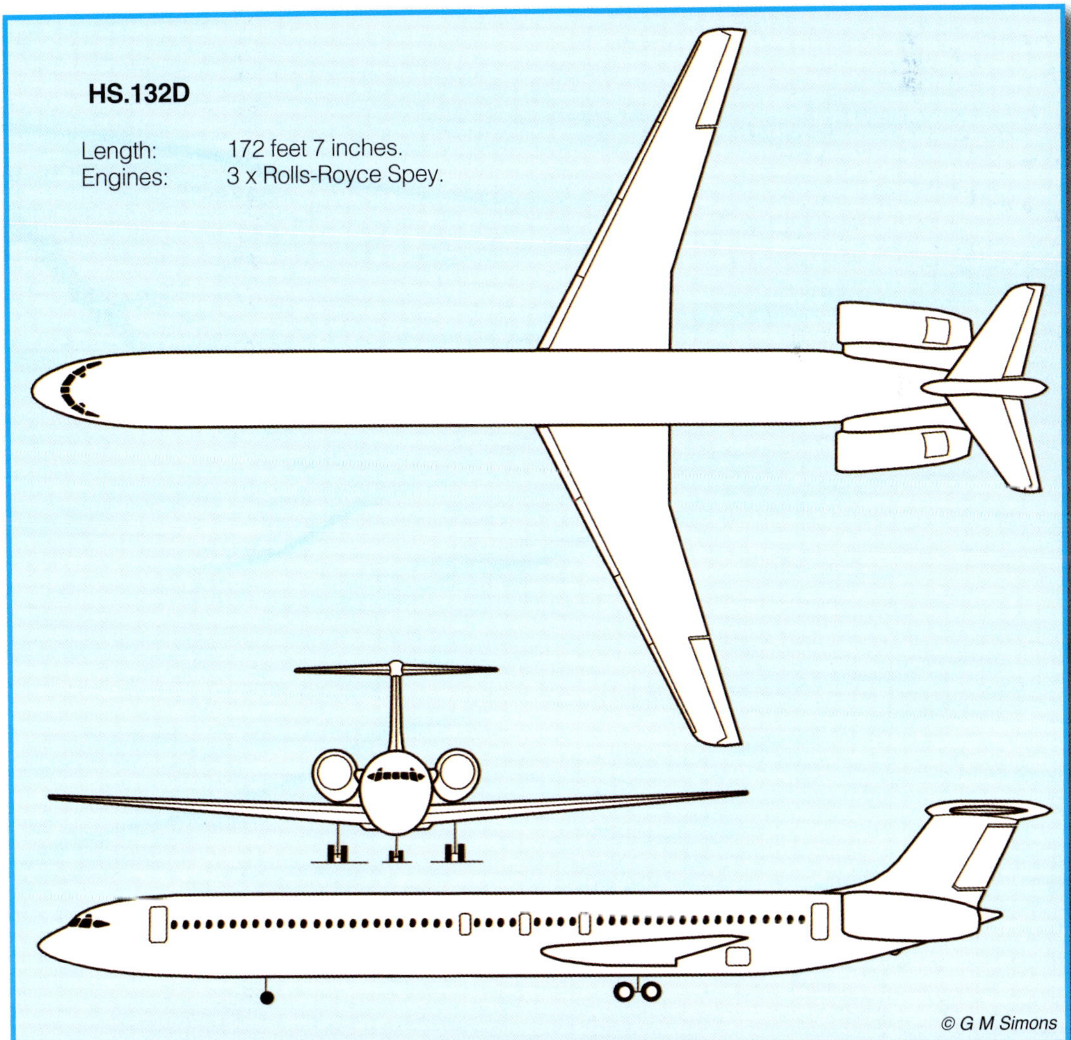

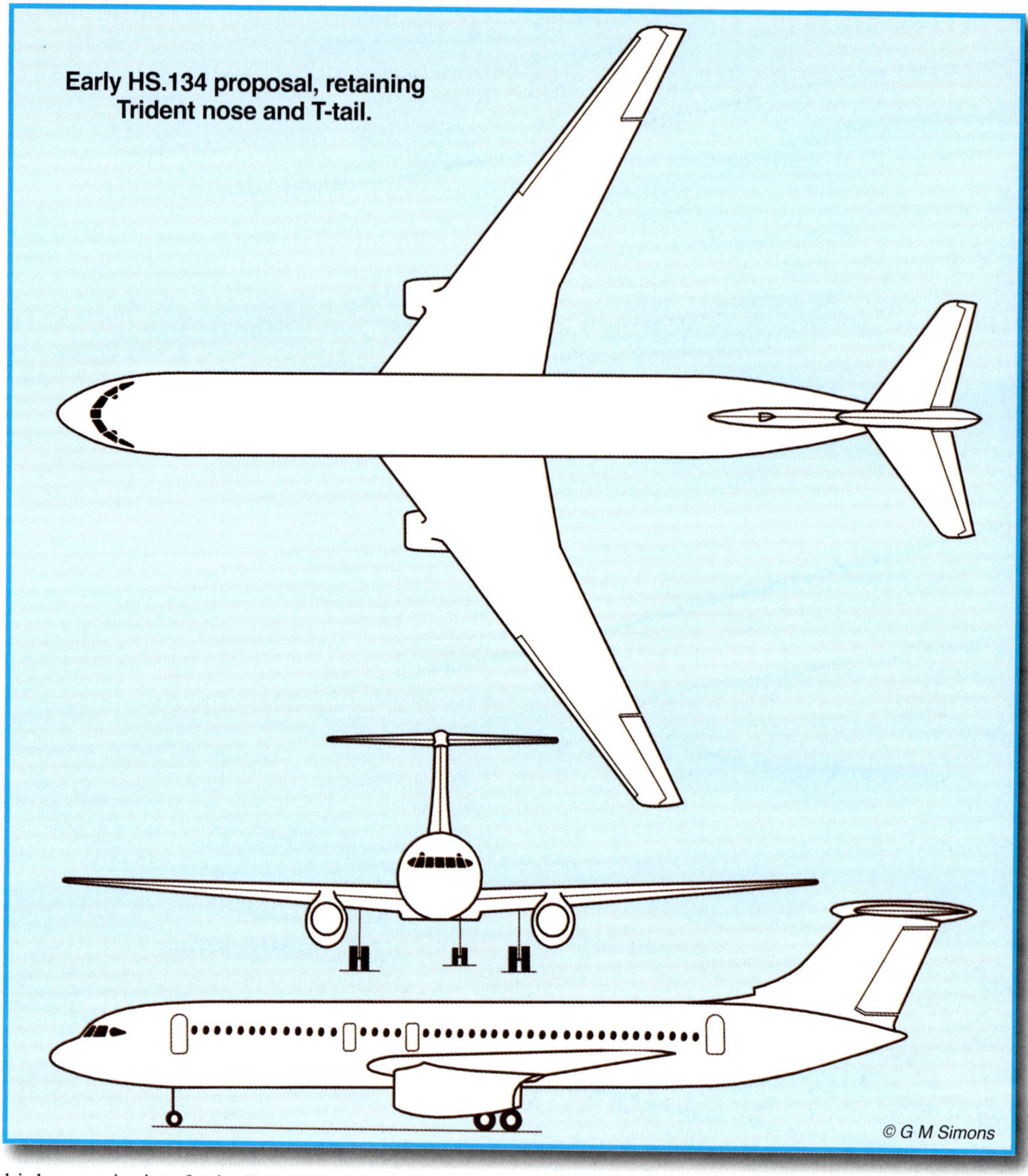

high-capacity jets for its European network before the anticipated arrival of the 300-seat European Airbus in the mid-1970s. Writing in the *BEA Magazine* in March 1966 - often used by the Board as a mouthpiece to either leak their intentions or to 'stire the pot' - Anthony Milward claimed that BEA had *'a positive lack of capacity from about 1968-69 onwards'*, and confirmed that BEA had recently received visits from both Douglas and Boeing, saying that *'this does not necessarily mean that we are looking to America for our future aircraft needs'*, but warning that although *'BEA's inclination is to buy British, it does not mean we can afford to buy British if the product is not the best on the market'*.

By May 1966, an order from BEA for either a stretched Trident, a stretched BAC One-Eleven or even a 208-seat short-haul version of the VC-10 was being alleged. The 727-200, 737-200 and DC-9-40 were being examined, and Milward dangled a carrot at the British manufacturers and the Labour government by stating that *'if a British aircraft to do this job were available at the right price, we would be delighted'*. He did warn that *'at the moment there are no signs that such a British aircraft is available'*. Pundits in the media suggested that no British airliner would likely evolve without significant government financial support.

With the increasing popularity of the stretched 727-200 amongst Europe's airlines, BEA's need for its new 'interim airbus' suddenly become more urgent, and deliveries were now required from April 1968. BEA felt that the proposed stretched 135-seat Trident 3 would be 'too small, too late and too expensive'. The HS132 was still a possible solution to BEA's anticipated capacity shortfall, but it was felt that its expected £30 million development costs would probably find little reassurance with the government.

Writing in the May 1966 edition of *BEA Magazine,* Milward confirmed that the airline's plans for re-equipment would be presented to the Minister of Aviation immediately, once the BEA board had agreed to the recommendations at a meeting at the end of May. He added that the newly ordered aircraft would *'not only fill the capacity gap, but will also eventually replace Comets, Vanguards and some Viscounts which were nearing the end of their useful life with BEA'.*

Frederick William 'Fred' Mulley, Baron Mulley, PC (*b.*3 July 1918, *d.*15 March 1995). Minister of Aviation in Harold Wilson's Labour Government.

By the end of June 1966, it was revealed that BEA had sought government approval to acquire up to thirty-five 727s and 737s for delivery from 1968. It came as a bombshell to many as the suggestion that the airline appeared to have had turned its back on the country's aviation industry, particularly as the original Trident's lack of sales success could be directly attributed to the airline's insistence that the aircraft be made smaller at a critical stage of its development!

During June, the HSA (Hatfield) shop stewards committee issued a statement urging BEA to order the enlarged Trident, saying *'the information available would indicate that the quoted figure of £10 million for developing an extended version of the Trident is an exaggeration and the final cause of strong feelings in the factory is that the original design of the Trident was for 126 seats and was tailored to its present size to accommodate BEA.*

The first Trident 3B MSN 2301 - later G-AWYZ - comes together at Hatifield. *[Authors Collection]*

This action has lost the company orders in the past and the final irony would be for the government to sanction the purchase of American aircraft because the British aircraft industry does not have the required size (of aircraft) on the shelf.' One has to wonder if this was really the committee, or the company itself who were using the unions as a mouthpiece to pressure the airline!

On 2 August the Minster of Aviation, Fred Mulley, announced that BEA should *'buy British'* despite BEA's selection *'on purely commercial grounds of American aircraft'.* The Labour government, however, informed BEA that *'it would take steps to ensure BEA is able to operate*

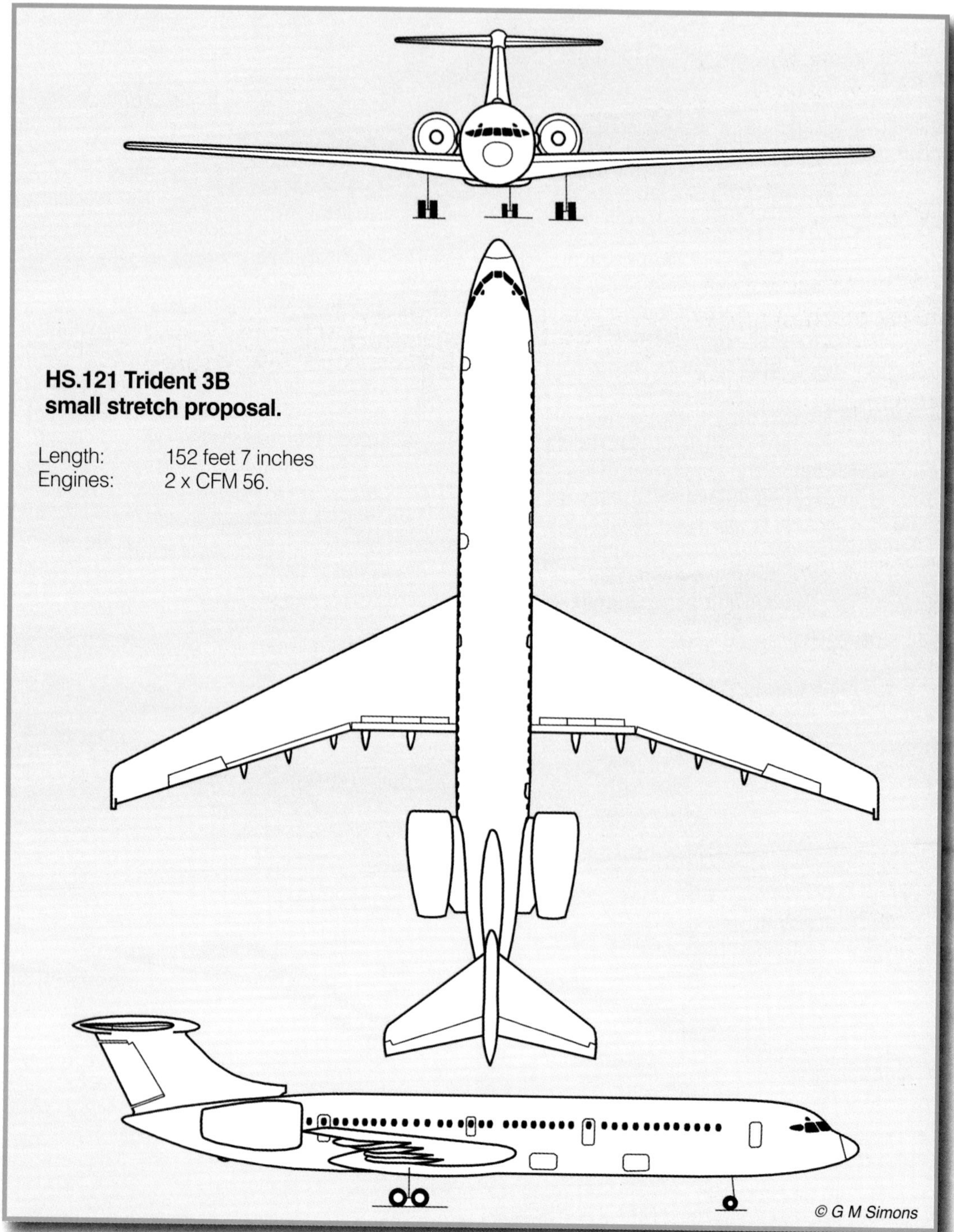

8 August 1970 - Sir Anthony Milward Chairman of British European Airways - seen speaking at BEA's Report cress conference, at the Waldorf Hotel. Seated next to him is Henry E Marking, Chief Executive.

as a fully commercial undertaking with the fleet it acquires', effectively meaning that an operating subsidy (or compensation) would be provided to the airline to cover the costs incurred of not having the aircraft which and when it wanted. It was also confirmed that the government would provide launch aid for the selected types.

As work on the HS132 progressed, a more radical Trident-based twin-engined derivative was proposed, the H8134 Airbus of December 1966. It featured a fuselage stretch of around thirty feet, increasing the overall length to one hundred and forty six feet three inches and seating for up to 210 passengers. The design used The Trident's nose, fuselage, and an extended 'supercritical' wing, it had a completely new configuration with a low-set tailplane, a new tail fin, and the RB.178s mounted under the wing. Gone was the Trident's offset nose

'I saw them out, I saw them back!' Pier Charlie at London Heathrow was a regular haunt for the spotters up on the Queens Building Terrace in the late 1960s, early 1970s. There were always Tridents coming and going and the range of different colour schemes on display was phenominal! *[author]*

wheel and swivelling double main bogeys; in their place were a conventional forward retracting nose unit and four-wheel truck main gear. The aircraft bore more than a passing resemblance to the Boeing 757, which itself evolved from the 727, admittedly some ten years after the HS134.

Both these Trident-based twinjets offered seat-mile costs some 25-30 per cent below types currently in service and, being of derivative design, have had launch costs around half of an all-new design. In the end, the RB.178 was not proceeded with, although it did provide impetus fo the RB211 turbofan, and the required European partner for these complex Trident developments was never obtained. Hawker Siddeley's offering remained the stretched Trident 3, and this would only be sanctioned if its launch costs were relatively low, no more than a third of the estimated cost of the HS132 or 134.

BEA's German requirement was fulfilled by an order for up to twenty-four 99-seat BAC One-Eleven 500s announced in January 1967. By this stage, the high-capacity BAC VC-10 project was discarded by BEA, favouring instead the HSA Rolls-Royce Spey 512-powered Trident 3 proposal.

The need to operate the new aircraft on both short high-density routes as well as on longer holiday routes to the Mediterranean resorts meant that a high standard of take-off performance was needed.To keep development costs down, HSA came up with a solution to the problem of the stretched Trident's required increased thrust, and in late 1966 was proposing a Mk 3B version of the aircraft which featured an additional 6,000 pound thrust Rolls-Royce RB.162 booster turbojet to improve take-off and climb performance. The RB.162 was a lightweight lift engine that had been under development for the experimental vertical take-off/landing Dornier 31 aircraft, and was to be fitted above the centre engine in the position occupied by the APU. As an alternative to the RB.162, the Bristol Siddeley Orpheus was being considered which, although being slightly heavier, was a production engine that could be developed for the Trident far more cheaply.

The need to operate the new aircraft on both short high-density routes as well as on longer holiday routes to the Mediterranean resorts meant that a high standard of take-off performance was needed. To keep development costs down, HSA came up with a solution to the problem of the stretched Trident's required increased thrust, and in late 1966, it was proposing a Mk 3B version of the aircraft, which featured an additional 6,000-pound thrust Rolls-Royce RB.162 booster turbojet to improve take-off and climb performance. The RB.162 was a lightweight lift engine under development for the Dornier 31 experimental vertical take-off/landing aircraft. It was to be fitted above the centre engine on the Trident, in the position occupied by the APU. As an alternative to the RB.162, the Bristol Siddeley Orpheus was being considered, which, although being slightly heavier, was a production engine that could be developed for the Trident far more cheaply.

BAC was keen to 'clean up' with the BEA order and meet the airline's larger capacity requirement as well, and, from the ashes of the dead short-haul VC-10, the 170-190 seat BAC Two-Eleven was born. Initially powered by two of the VC-10's Rolls-Royce Conways, the aircraft

Tri-jets together! British airways' Trident Three G-AWZR in front of Boeing 727 from Lufthansa. This picture allows a good comparason of of the two designs. *[author]*

evolved during early 1967, powered by two of the new 30,000 pounds thrust high-bypass ratio Rolls-Royce RB211 turbofans. BEA seriously considered the proposal, and in early 1967, Milward sought government permission to order thirty Two-Elevens plus ten options worth £110 million, for service entry in 1972. Government support would be needed to help raise the estimated £60 million in development costs for the launch of the new airliners.

By April 1967, BEA was again looking to the Boeing 727, frustrated by the government's heel-dragging over the launching the Two-Eleven, to meet their requirements. As Sir Anthony Milward said *'Every week that goes by drives us nearer and nearer to buying the Boeing 727'.*

The agreement involved transferring £25 million of the airline's current borrowings into a special account on which no interest would be paid. This could then be transferred as needed into BEA's profit and loss account. There was also a possibility of *'a further sum of £125 million for consideration later should that be needed'.* The plan was that *'in 1972 the Board of Trade would consult BEA on the basis of experience up to then and of the latest forecasts to determine whether BEA still needed this further sum to be transferred from 1 April 1972 to 31 March 1975'.*

Sir Anthony Milward described the government's settlement as *'fair - but not generous'.* The £80 million Trident 3B contract was signed in London on Friday, 16 August by Sir Anthony Milward and Mr J. T. Lidbury, Managing Director of HSA. Part of the contract stipulated the fitting of Smiths Autoland equipment at the triplex level.

As launched, the Trident 3B featured a fuselage extension of sixteen feet five inches over previous models, with an eight feet five inch stretch forward of the wing and eight feet aft, increasing the overall length to one hundred and thirty one feet two inches. The extension forward of the wing featured a twenty-inch plug between the forward and centre doors to allow an extra row of seats to be fitted in the forward cabin. The remainder of the forward extension was a six foot-nine inch plug in front of the wing. 146 passengers could be accommodated in a standard economy-class layout, although the maximum seating could be increased to 180 if denser layouts were adopted. The Trident 1E/2E's two 36-inch by 20-inch Type IV over-wing emergency exits on each side were replaced by a single 41-inch by 20-inch Type III item, whilst an additional 48-inch by 24-inch

Close up of a Trident Three 'rear end showing the fourth engine. *[Kirk Smeaton Collection]*

service door/emergency exit was added on the starboard side just forward of the engine.

Although the wingspan of the 3B was unchanged from the 2E, to help lift the higher weights of the larger aircraft, the outer wing featured an increase in chord, which in turn

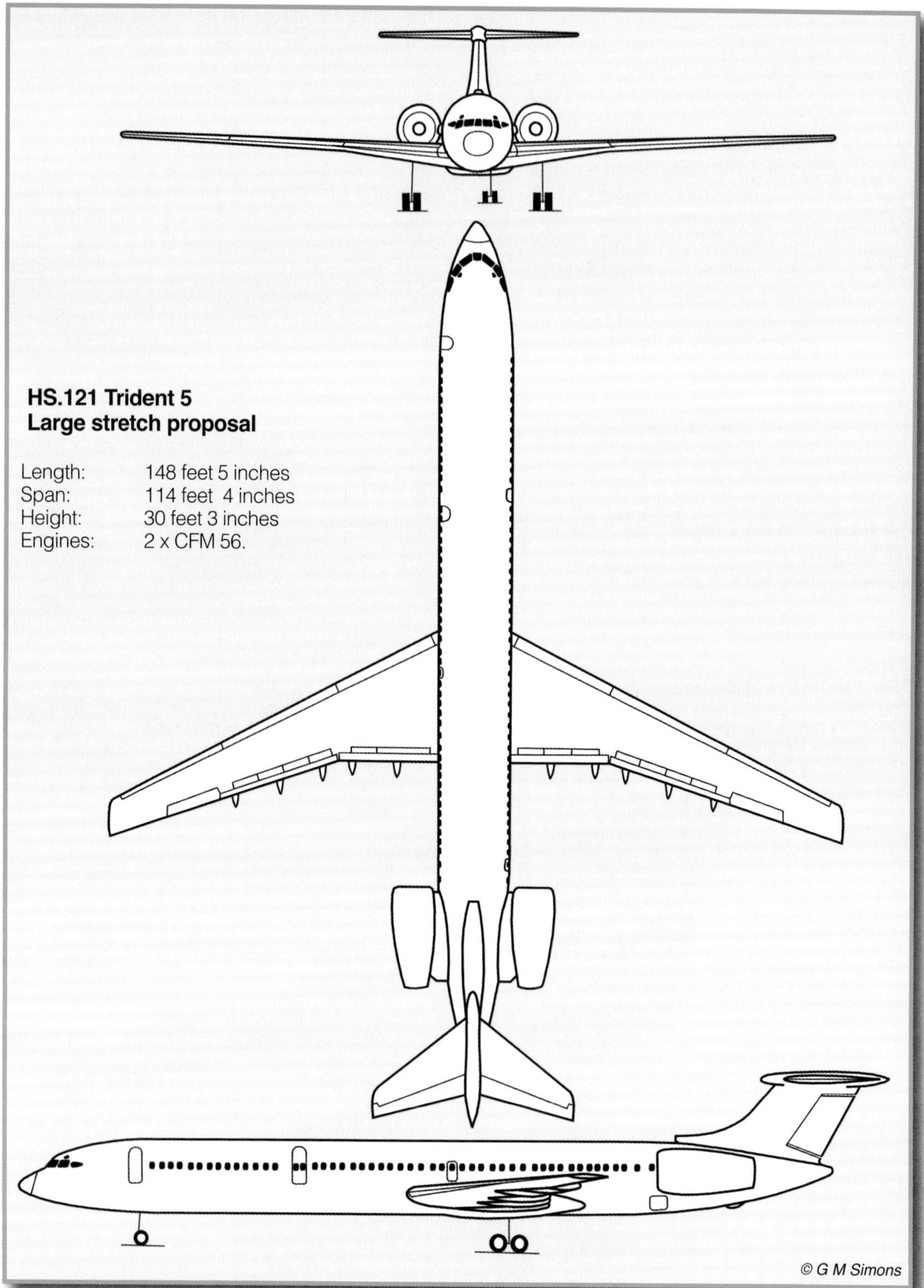

Chinese Trident G-BAJM, later to become B-270 is seen in flight over the English countryside. *[Kirk Smeaton Collection]*

increased wing area by thirty-two square feet. This also provided larger span outboard flaps, which increased the area by about twenty-six per cent, and the lift dumper area was increased by thirty-five per cent. The ailerons were reduced in size and moved outboard as reliance on spoilers for roll control increased, necessitating an increase in their maximum differential angle from ten totwenty degrees. The angle of incidence was increased by two and a half degrees to allow for the same rotation angle on take-off with the lengthened rear fuselage.

The 5,230-pound thrust Rolls-Royce RB.162-86 booster was installed at the base of the fin replacing the APU, which was relocated above the central air intake. As a result, the Trident 3B's rudder was somewhat smaller than on previous models. The booster, which would be used for take-off and initial climb when needed, allowed either a 14,500 pounds increase in payload or a 1,800 foot reduction in the take-off run. The 3B's Speys were the 11,960 pound thrust Mk 512s of the 2E, but a Garrett AiResearch GTCP85C model replaced the Trident's original Bristol Siddeley Artouste APU.

Fuel capacity was less than that of the 1E and 2E, with the deletion of the 400 Imperial gallon aft centre tank and the 350 Imperial gallon fin tank, thus reducing overall capacity to 5,620 Imperial gallons. Gross weight was increased to 155,000 pounds, and range with 146 passengers and baggage was around 1,230 miles, increasing to 1,700 miles with 92 passengers and baggage. Cruise speed would be 0.84 Mach at 25,000 feet, equivalent to 581mph.

Once the compensation details had been sorted out, Hawker Siddeley received the 'intent to proceed' letter in July 1968, and the assembly of the Trident 3B's major sub-assemblies commenced. The first centre section and stub wing were moved from their jigs at Hatfield by the middle of February 1969, and the following month, the first front fuselage section arrived after completing its 200-mile journey on the back of a lorry from the HSA site at Brough in Yorkshire. The outer wings for the new Trident were produced at the HSA factory at Hamble, whilst other sub-assemblies came from plants at Chester and Manchester. Rear fuselage assemblies were produced at Hatfield.

Trident 3B production was integrated with that of the 2E. By now, the last of the 2Es were being built for BEA, whilst aircraft were also being assembled for Cyprus Airways. The main Trident jigs could be quickly adjusted to either 2E or 3B, allowing both types to be readily interspersed on the line to suit demand.

The first Trident 3B, registered G-AWYZ, was rolled out at Hatfield on 17 November 1969, wearing the BEA 'Speed Jack' colours, with the words 'Trident Three' on the centre engine air intake. Before its first flight, Yankee Zulu was supported by special cradles to allow resonance tests. Yankee Zulu made its first flight at 12.15 on 11 December, piloted by John Cunningham. A mock-up of the RB.162 was installed, and Yankee Zulu was airborne for 2hr 50min. Five Trident 3Bs were to be used in the flight-test programme, which was planned to include at least 500 hours of flying, and the first flight-rated RB.162 was expected to become available in the early summer.

The second Trident 3B G-AWZA was rolled out on 17 February 1970 and joined the flight-test programme on 9 March, by which time the first machine had completed over eighty hours of testing. Tests undertaken included a general assessment of the performance of the new features and the clearance of C of G position, weight and design speed boundaries. Several Autolands were also carried out.

By April 1970, the final clearance testing of the boost engine installation had been completed, allowing flight tests to commence with the first operational unit. This was installed in Yankee Zulu, which then initiated performance measurements of the engine while continuing

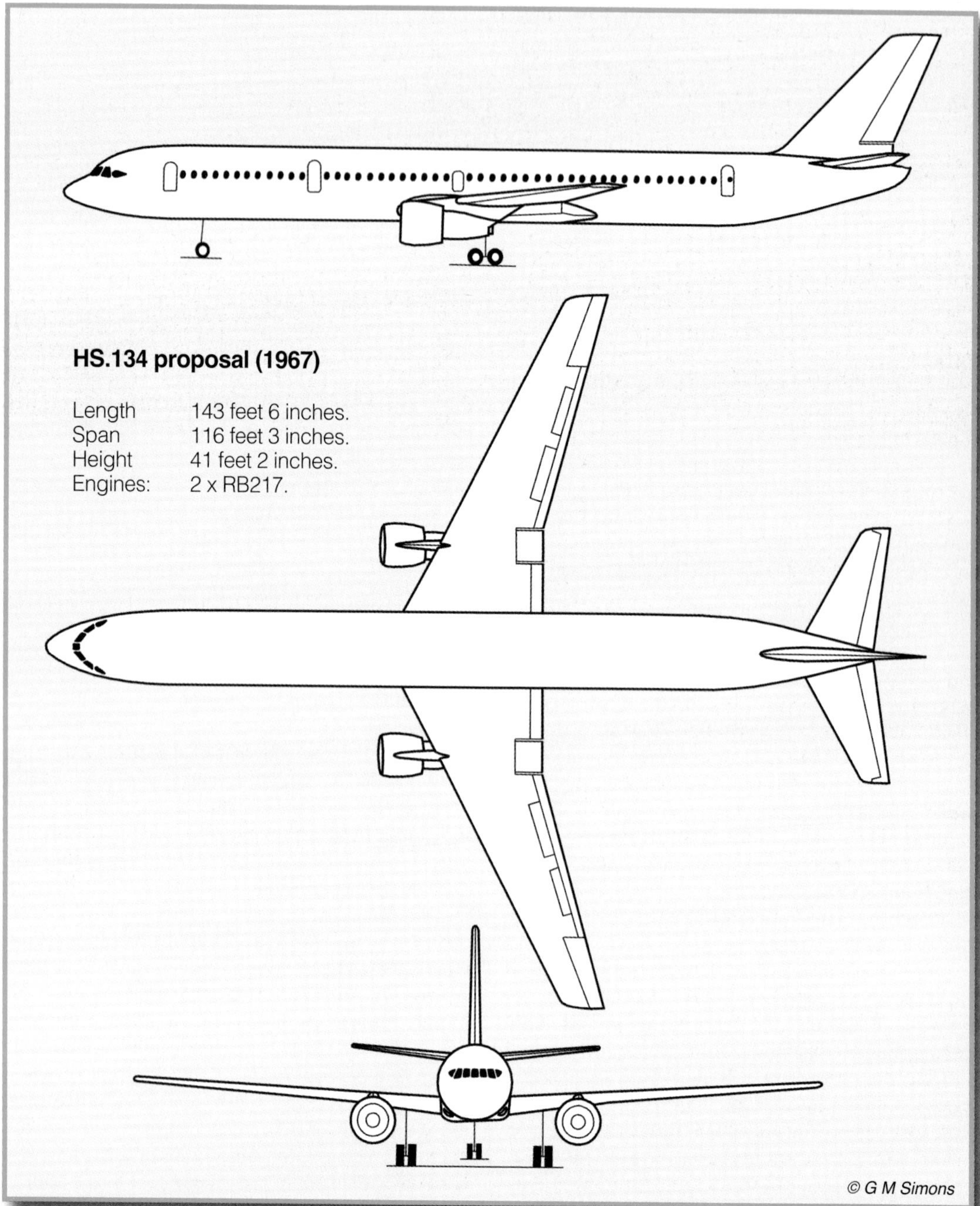

Chinese Tridents under construction at Hatfield - the hull on the left, is MSN 2185, intended as B-263, but originally registered as G-BBWD. It was transferred to the People's Liberation Army Air Force as 50055. Behind that is 2182, intended as B-294, but first flew as G-BBVZ, then registered as B-2207. In the centre is 2183, intended as B-296, but first flew as G-BBWA. before being re-registered as B-2220. Finally, to the right of that and in front is 2184 intended as B-298, but first flew as G-BBWB. At some stage it was re-registered as B-2221.

Incidentally, for anyone curious to know, the 'production line' is moving away from the camera as more and more work is completed on each hull, the aircraft eventually going out of the doors in the distance.
[Photograph courtesy of British Aerospace Hatfield]

Autoland trials. The boost engine's air intakes were sealed by pneumatically operated doors that lay flush when closed.

Zulu Alpha was being used to investigate low-speed handling and stall characteristics. The Trident 3B differed from the previous models in that it was equipped with a triplex, rather than a duplex, angle-of-attack stick pusher installation.

During June, Yankee Zulu dropped out of the test programme for a flying visit to Nicosia to carry out a publicity exercise for BEA. The aircraft was extensively photographed and filmed both in the air and on the ground, before returning to Hatfield nonstop on 23 June.

On 13 August, Yankee Zulu departed for Madrid to commence tropical trials, as its forebear Papa Bravo had done seven years earlier. Take-off performance was measured at 153,000 pounds, both with and without the boost engine, and at all four take-off flap settings.

Engine failures were also simulated. After completing the Madrid tests, Yankee Zulu flew via Athens and Baghdad to Dubai to conduct high-temperature climb performance tests. The efficiency of the cabin air conditioning system was also tested. The trials were completed in early September and Yankee Zulu positioned back to Hatfield via Baghdad and Athens. Meanwhile, the third 3B, G-AWZB, had flown on 18 August 1970 and was then demonstrated at the 1970 Farnborough Air Show the following month.

By the end of 1970, the flight test programme was progressing so well that a Trident 3B was able to be handed over to the airline for crew training and route proving. At the ceremony at Hatfield on 7 December, attended by Sir Anthony and Lady Milward, Henry Marking, and Air Chief Marshal Sir Harry Broadhurst, the Deputy MD of Hawker

An unidentifiable Trident for the Chinese is rolled out at Hatfield.
[Photograph courtesy of British Aerospace Hatfield]

Siddeley Aviation, the airline's first Trident 3, G-AWZA, was officially named when Lady Milward carried out the traditional pouring of champagne over the nose as BEA took delivery of the aircraft. At the ceremony, Sir Anthony Milward spoke of the *'great five engine Trident'* (ie, three Speys, one RB.162 and one APU), and continued *'I am particularly proud to see the introduction and arrival of this very splendid aircraft which has improved in looks as it has grown in size'.*

Zulu Alpha was used for pilot training at Stansted before being returned to the manufacturer for reconditioning to production specification and redelivered to the airline on 11 May 1971. Unfortunately, on 19 January 1971 G-AWZA was involved in an accident with a Comet 4 XP915 at Thurleigh airfield near Bedford whilst being used for crew training. The Trident 3 was on approach to the runway, with a planned go-around at 100 feet. On the runway was XP915, a RAF Comet waiting to take off. For some reason, Zulu Alpha descended below one hundred feet and, whilst overshooting, struck the fin of the Comet with the underside of its port wing and flaps. The Comet seemed to come off worse, losing most of its tail fin.

The Trident 3B received its C of A on 8 February 1971, after a 14-month, 700-hr flight-test programme. The first fully certificated Trident 3B, G-AWZC was delivered to the airline on 18 February, and the airline received its second aircraft, G-AWZB, six days later on 24 February. The final results of the flight testing revealed that the Trident 3B had exceeded its performance guarantees by a handsome margin. The aircraft's weight was around 3,000 pounds below estimates, and drag was lower than expected, resulting in 3-

Chinese Trident 2E B-254 comes in to land.
[Kirk Smeaton Collection]

4 per cent less fuel burn in the cruise. From performance-limited airfields the mission payloads were bettered by between 4,000 and 9,000 pounds.

BEA's first Trident 3 revenue service took place on Monday, 1 March 1971, when G-AWZB operated a service between Heathrow and Paris-Orly, whilst regular operations began on 1 April on routes from London to Paris and Lisbon. On this date, BEA was divided into various new divisions, with the Heathrow-based Trident fleet falling under the 'BEA Mainline' banner. Interestingly, unlike the Trident 2, BEA set up a new Flight for the operation of the Trident Three, meaning that Trident pilots converting to the 3B would no longer fly the 1 or 2. Initial Trident 3 operations were flown with the boost engine inactive.

BEA configured its new Trident 3B with a two-class cabin that included one hundred and nineteen economy-class seats six-abreast and fourteen convertible first-class seats four-abreast at thirty-six in pitch. The aircraft were operated in either a two-class one hundred and thirty-three-seat layout or a one hundred and forty-seat all-tourist layout. The Trident 3s were equipped with burgundy seats featuring beige base cushions, pigskin armrests, and cork-patterned pull-down tables.

Two galleys were installed in BEA's Trident 3B, one at the front of the aircraft and the other in the centre, whilst the toilet layout was similar to the previous Tridents, with one forward and two aft. Interestingly, BEA's Trident 3s introduced a new concept for the airline's cabin service: a trolley serving system.

Other routes operated by the type during the first few months included Dublin, Palma, Glasgow, Oslo, Milan, Amsterdam and Madrid. Brussels and Rome was added later, replacing Trident Ones and Twos. By November 1971, Pisa, Zurich, Nice, Geneva, Copenhagen, Naples, and Malta had been added to the Trident 35 destinations from London, whilst some Birmingham-Malta services were also flown with the aircraft.

A Trident Three brochure published by BEA during 1971 featuring a number of the photographs taken on Yankee Zulu's visit to Cyprus, described

No apologies for using yet another BEA publicity picture taken from an air-to-air sortie that made use of Trident Three G-AWYZ. *[Author's Collection]*

the new Trident as *'the most beautiful, most advanced jetliner flying in Europe'*. Somewhat hypocritically, the text boasted that BEA had *'once again decided to buy British'*. The airline, apparently, really had decided to lump it and like it!

The first Trident 3B, G-AWYZ, was retained by HSA to continue Autoland trials and was eventually delivered to BEA on 23 March 1972. BEA's last Trident 3, G-AWZZ, was handed over to the airline on 19 April 1973, being the sixty-fourth and last Trident to be delivered new to BEA.

On 9 November 1972, CAAC, which had placed a large number of orders for the smaller Trident 2E, became the second and last customer for the Trident 3B when it ordered two longer-range versions of the aircraft dubbed the 'Super 3B'. These featured additional centre fuel- the 400 Imperial gallon tank on the 1E/2E -and a gross weight of 158,000 pounds that was later increased to 159,900 pounds. The two Super 3Bs were completed in mid-1975, flying in July and August that year. The aircraft were delivered to CAAC on 8 September and 17 October, carrying the British marks G-BAJL and G-BAJM, before being registered B-268 and B-270. In 1981 it is thought that the two aircraft were transferred to the Chinese Air Force where they remained in operation for a number of years.

Although Trident 3B production had ceased, that of the 2E continued and, in an effort to revive interest in the Trident and extend production, I have discovered tens of studies from Hawker Siddeley on re-engined twin and trijet versions of the Trident under the project names 'Trident 4 and 5'.

Throughout the early seventies, Hawker Siddeley continued to study VSTOL, RTOL and STOL derivatives of the Trident airliner. The STOL project included adapted Trident 2 designs seating one hundred and nine passengers over a range of 800 miles, with take-off and landing distances of between 3,500 and 4000 feet with an

An image that certainly has the feel of BEA's Public Relations Department! Obviously taken in the late 1960s early 1970s, this BEA Trident 2E disembarks its passengers from the forward door. There is just something about this that promotes the holidays in the sun vibe, but I cannot help feeling it was an unused still from *'Carry On Abroad'* which did feature some Trident stock footage! *[Author's Collection]*

G-ARPH *[Kirk Smeaton Collection]*

additional six RB202s in pods, or four RB.162s in sponsons. A study was also made of a Trident 1C STOL demonstrator aircraft, with two General Electric lift-fans of 13,650 pounds thrust, Trident 2E wing tips and a low-speed aileron based on the first prototype Trident design. The RTOL Trident was to be powered by a pair of Rolls-Royce RB211 engines and would operate from 3,000-foot runways, with accommodation for up to 200 passengers.

Alongside these developments were stretched and re-engined variants. Four Trident developments were looked at in detail: the 3B with two ten-ton engines - either the CFM.56 or Pratt and Whitney JT10D - a twinjet powered by CFM.56s with a stretched Fuselage and centre section, a stretched fuselage twin with a new wing based on technology from the A.300B and a trijet powered by re-fanned Speys - the RB.163-67 which eventually led to the Tay - with a stretched fuselage and centre section.

In July 1975, a proposal was made to British Airways under the Trident 4 legend. This development featured two rear-mounted CFM56 engines, eliminating the centre-engine intake, combined with a stretched fuselage. The model 4A was lengthened by twenty inches. Other changes included a wing of reduced sweep with increased area and span, with Fowler-type flaps. The Trident 1 rudder was utilised, and there was to be improved silencing of the RB.162 booster engine. Further developments included the 4B, which was stretched by an additional thirteen feet six inches with leading-edge slats and centre-section fuel, and the double-bubble 4E seating up to one hundred and fifty-five passengers.

By the middle of 1976 the Trident 4 and 5 plans had been dropped, although the studies led to the European collaborative CAST (Civil Aircraft Study Team) and JET (Jet European Transport) proposals from which the one hundred and fifty-seat Airbus A320 evolved. By now, HSA - soon to merge with BAC and Scottish Aviation to become British Aerospace and later BAe - had decided upon the eighty-seat HS.146 feederjet for its future civil programme, production of which was undertaken at Hatfield.

The various proposals would have seated between 142 and 180 passengers in mixed class layouts, and effectively meaning that Hawker Siddeley had come full circle and returned to the concept of the HS132 'Bident' project of 1965.

The HS.132 - nicknamed the Bident - was first proposed in 1964 as a twin-engined Trident development, designed specifically for low-cost operation on high-density routes. Power would have been provided by two Rolls-Royce RB.178-14H engines of 28,100 pounds thrust with an all-up weight of 1 44,500 pounds. Major parts of the 121 Trident were retained, in fact more than sixty per cent of the HS.32 utilised the same components. The major changes were a fuselage stretched by twenty-four feet, and a redesigned rear fuselage to accommodate the twin-engine installation, and to provide the necessary tail-down ground angle with the longer fuselage. The new stretch accommodated up to 164 passengers in economy class. The Trident IE wing was utilised with a three-foot increase in span, and the replacement of double-slotted flaps by large chord—tabbed Fowler types. The horizontal tail of the Trident was retained, together with a

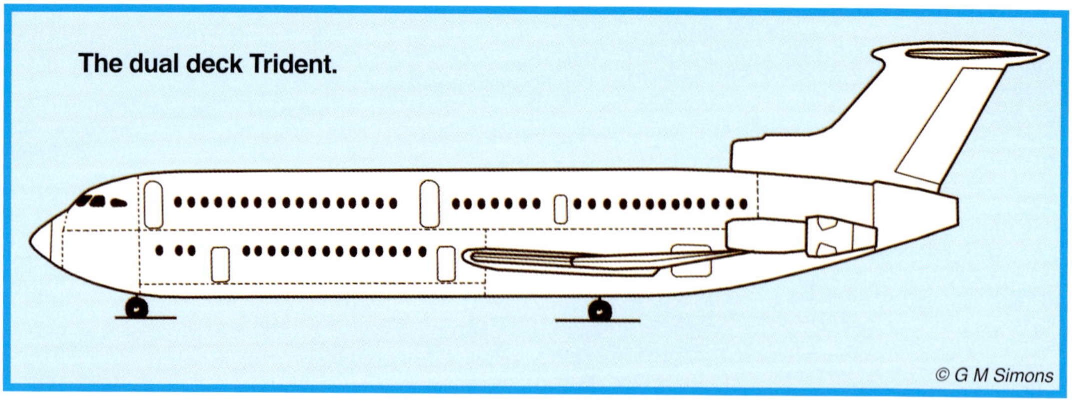

substantial part of the fin and rudder. The major difference was in the lower part of the fin, which was redesigned due to the removal of the centre engine. Final development costs of the project were put at around £30 million.

Later studies included the HS.132B/C with 180-192 seats, and the HS.132D with 219 seats. The major problem with the HS.132 was that with aft engines, the majority of any stretch had to be forward of the wing, which caused severe nodding loads. In later variants, a deeper forward fuselage was considered to provide greater rigidity. Hawker Siddeley did talk to the French aerospace industry about collaborating on the project, but BEA was of the impression that the aircraft was too small for their needs, so Hawker Siddeley turned their attention to a larger underwing-engine Trident development.

Following on from the HS132, Hatfield put forward the HS.134 Airbus. The first designs from 1966 utilised the Trident's T-tail unit, combined with a stretched fuselage to seat up to 183 passengers, and a new wing with twenty-five degrees sweepback, beneath which were mounted two Rolls-Royce RB.178 engines in pods. By the time of the final configuration in 1967, the new design featured a swept fin, a tailplane mounted on the rear empennage, and two underwing-mounted Rolls-Royce RB.207 engines of 28,000 pounds thrust. In this new design, up to 210 passengers could be accommodated. The project, now very similar in design to Boeing's later 757 model, looked like a winner, but Hawker Siddeley did not have the resources to fund it and again needed to find a European partner to share the costs and risks.

Other studies by Hawker Siddeley included double-deck designs seating 226 passengers and single-deck designs seating 183 passengers, both powered by the RB.178. Other Trident variants considered were powered by Conway engines or had a new wing and engines to seat up to 190. They also designed new studies with integrated fuselages and a raised flight deck, similar to the later 747, to accommodate 236 passengers.

There were also studies done in conjunction with Airbus Industries. Much of this came about as a result of BEA's specification for its proposed airbus, an ultra-short-haul low-cost airliner that was issued in 1964, and was for a 150- to 200-seater able to operate high-density routes such as London-Amsterdam, Paris and Manchester, and was seen as a replacement for its Vanguard fleet. With the likelihood that this would be one of the last major subsonic domestic orders for many years to come, it was natural that the major airframe companies would turn their attention to meeting such a potentially large order. With its Trident just entering service, Hawker Siddeley looked at how best to adapt its new jet to meet this new specification. Various derivatives were proposed, from simple trijet stretches to 120-seater twin designs. However, some more ambitious proposals were also put forward.

The 'double-bubble' or twin-deck Trident saw the aircraft's original upper fuselage lobe combine with a new lower fuselage. The upper fuselage provided seating at six abreast, while the new lower fuselage had five-abreast seating, with a well provided for the passenger aisle. In total, up to 200 passengers could have been accommodated. The passenger cabin in the new lower deck would have been provided forward of the wing box, with the lower deck aft of the wing box being used for freight. The total height of the new fuselage would have been fifteen feet one inch. Proposed powerplants included the Rolls-Royce Conway and aft-fan Rolls-Royce Spey.

Chapter Nine

Accidents and Incidents

Following the string of accidents that befell the early Comets, it was not surprising that the highest priority in the concept of the Trident was safety. From its triplex redundancy in powerplant, hydraulics, electrics, and autopilot, to its strenuous fatigue and systems testing, the Trident featured the ultimate in designed-in safety.

After the industry debate in the late 1950s regarding how many engines the world's new short-haul jets should have and, more importantly, their configuration, it is somewhat paradoxical that the Achilles' heel of nearly all these designs should be their 'T-tailed' layout. The manufacturers almost universally decided that the rear fuselage was the best place to put the engines, and as a result, the horizontal stabiliser was set at the top of the fin.

Early on in flight-testing, it was discovered that the Trident had a tendency not to exhibit the classic nose drop at the stall but instead pitched up steeply, thereby exacerbating its predicament. The result became known as the 'superstall' or 'deep stall', from which recovery was technically impossible.

The Trident was not alone with its deep stall problem, as this phenomenon affected all the T-tail machines - the prototype BAC One-Eleven crashed in September 1963 whilst exploring the type's stall characteristics, with the loss of all seven crew on board.

The problems that arose when stalling the T-tailed aircraft stemmed from the tailplane being positioned higher than the main plane, rather than being directly behind it and, therefore, safely outside the wings wake at the stall.

As a result, when the wing angle of attack increased to the point where the air passing over it was no longer 'clean', the tailplane was fed this turbulent, low-energy air significantly reduced its effectiveness when the pilot commanded a nose-down response to recover. To add to the problem, the fact that the tailplane was stalled contributed to the tail-down/pitch-up tendency.

Many pilots believed that there is no recovery from a genuine deep stall. However, it is reported that a Boeing 727 also entered a deep stall during its certification trials, but the pilots were able to recover the aircraft. They still had some lateral control available and used that to rock the aeroplane to increasingly higher bank angles until the nose finally fell through, and normal control response was recovered. While this recovery approach is technically possible, it relies on experienced pilots with sufficient altitude to be successful, and there is still a high chance of failure.

Development and Production Testing

Part of the intensive pre-production test programme for the Trident was devoted to examining the stalling characteristics. Ideally, there should be a clear warning of an imminent stall; at the stall, an aircraft should pitch nosed down so strongly that the pilot cannot keep the wing stalled by applying a nose-up elevator, and there should be no tendency for a wing to go down. Such characteristics were challenging to achieve with aircraft of the physical shape of the Trident. High lift devices and a powerful tailplane increased the difficulty.

Despite a programme of over three thousand stalls and much wind tunnel testing, it was not found possible to produce the ideal stalling characteristics in the Trident aerodynamically, and an electrically operated stall warning system - the stick shaker - was therefore incorporated to comply with British Civil Airworthiness Requirements. As the natural nose-down pitch of the aircraft could only be detected by meticulous handling and as the tailplane was powerful enough to permit the pilot to overcome this nose-down pitch, a stall recovery system was installed. This consisted of a pneumatic stick-pusher triggered by the same incidence detecting system as the stall warning device to push the control column forward and pitch the aircraft nose-down before the wing fully stalled. It included compensation for the rate of change of pitch attitude. This innovation has become standard on modern commercial aircraft. The Trident was the first airliner to be certificated with a stick push system.

It was agreed between the constructor and the Air Registration Board that before any newly constructed Trident was delivered to the operator, it would undergo a series of flights covered by a Production Flight Test Schedule. During these flights, checks were made to ascertain, among other things, that the stall warning and stall recovery systems worked as intended. After one or two of the first batch of aircraft had shown that a wing drop might be encountered at or near the stick-push, so a further stall check was added to ensure that the aircraft would remain reasonably level laterally through the stall.

When the stall warning and recovery systems had been found to operate satisfactorily, and at the correct speeds, the pilot was required by the test schedule to switch them off and, using as a datum the airspeed at which the stall recovery system had operated, to explore the speeds between the onset of the stall and the speed at which the greatest permissible deployment of the stall ever the wing occurred.

Many hundreds of tests on the final Trident 1 configuration, including a series flown by Peter Barlow to investigate detailed problems on production aircraft showed that the normal breakdown of flow at the stall took three to four knots of the pilot's Airspeed Indicator reading to spread from the initial small local area over the whole of the inner wing. This spread was always accompanied by a sharp increase in buffet in a lag stall. A wing drop could result from either a delay in matching the stall's spread or both inner wings or from a premature loss of lift over one tip section; in the latter case, the buffet was usually not so marked.

For performance purposes, the operation of the stick-pusher at low rates of approach to the stall had been accurately tied, in terms of incidence, to the peak of the lift curve and hence the start of the development of the stall. There was agreement between the manufacturer and the ARB that there should be a small margin beyond this point, which provided a safeguard against an uncontrollable wing drop developing as a result of a delayed stick-push.

The initial accident - G-ARPY

At 16:52 on 3 June 1966, Trident 1C G-ARPY, the twenty-third BEA Trident off the production line, took off from Hatfield on its first flight, to carry out the first of a series of production test flights under the command of Peter Barlow. The other crew members included George Errington (P2), Edgar Brackstone-Brown (P3) and Charles Patterson as navigator.

Peter Barlow, aged 39, held a valid commercial pilot's licence endorsed in Part 1 for HS 104, HS 125, Comet and Trident aircraft. He qualified as a pilot in the Royal Ravy in 1949 and, in 1953, completed a course at the Empire Test Pilot's School; he served with the Naval Test Squadron until 1958 and then joined the De Havilland Aircraft Company as a development test pilot on Sea Vixens. He joined the Trident development programme in 1962 and later assisted Iraqi Airways and Kuwait Airways with Trident 1E crew training. His total flying experience amounted to about 4,500 hours, including about 1,600 hours of test flying of the Trident. He first flew as test pilot-in-command of the Trident after eighty flights as co-pilot and two flights in command under the supervision of the chief test pilot. Since then, he made 416 test flights in command of Trident 1 aircraft and 52 in command of Trident IE aircraft. He had taken part in about 2,195 stalls on the Trident in various configurations including 750 as pilot-in-command.

George B S Errington, OBE, aged 64, had held a valid private pilot's licence since 1930. He qualified as a ground engineer in 1932. In 1935, he joined Airspeed Limited as a test pilot and became chief test pilot in 1939. In 1949, he developed and produced test flight programmes for the Airspeed Ambassador. At Hawker Siddeley he was responsible for operations liaison with airlines flying Comets and Tridents and helped as required on test work at Hatfield. At the time of the accident, his licence was endorsed for group A and B aircraft, and he had accumulated a total of 6,800 flying hours.

Edgar Brackstone-Brown, aged 47, was chief flight test engineer with Hawker Siddeley Aviation at Hatfield and had been in charge of flight engineering in the flight test department from 1949. Since that time, he had flown over 2,000 hours of development and production testing in Comets and Tridents.

Charles W. Patterson, aged 43, joined the De Havilland Flight test department as a radio navigator in 1958 after eleven years as a radio officer in BOAC. His flying experience in Trident aircraft amounted to fifty-seven hours.

Papa Yankee was a standard production machine fitted with standard equipment. When the additional check on the stall was added to the test schedule, there were no simple readily available means of incidence presentation for production Trident 1 aircraft and, as later versions of the aircraft with leading edge slats had regularly operated to much higher incidences without problems, an incidence meter was not considered necessary. Instead, a specially calibrated airspeed indicator was fitted.

Above: G-ARPY seen at Hatfield, just before it's first - and last - flight. *[De Havilland Aircraft Co.]*

Below: the wreckage of the same aircraft in a field near Felthorpe, Norfolk. *[Eastern Counties Newspapers]*

Given the extensive development experience, it was considered a safe test flying technique first to make an accurate correlation of airspeed and incidence during a stall with the stick-pusher operating and then to switch it off and to reduce this speed by the three to four-knot margin established for the deployment of flow separation. As flow separation developed, it produced a sharp increase in the buffet, and as an additional safeguard, the pilots were told to recover immediately if any buffet was felt, regardless of the ASI reading. This additional check was carried out by the manufacturers only and was not to be repeated in the aircraft's service life.

At the time of the accident, the aircraft's weight was approximately 32,800 kgs, and the centre of gravity was at 0.246 mean aerodynamic chord, the normal position for these tests.

Papa Yankee was flown out to the northeast and carried out her flight tests over Hawker Siddeley's regular testing ground, East Anglia. At 18.30, the stall tests were commenced and three approaches to the stall were made. With the aircraft in the landing configuration, Papa Yankee's stick shaker operated at 102 knots and her stick pusher at 93 knots. A fourth landing configuration stall was carried out at a height of 11,600 feet but this time, in accordance with the established test schedule, the two stall protection systems had been made inoperative. The crew disconnected the stall warning systems to ascertain the actual margin left after the warning had been given before the aircraft stalled. On this particular flight, the aircraft was being operated with its centre of gravity towards its aft limit.

Shortly after 18:30, and at an altitude of 10,000 feet with the aircraft configured for landing, the pilot reported that the aircraft was in a 'superstall'.

As it stalled, the airliner started to pitch down, and the airspeed dropped off rapidly; the nose-down motion ceased as the aircraft entered a deep stall. The nose was seen to pitch up by thirty to forty degrees before turning to port, followed by the starboard wing dropping.

The last radio call was received at 18.34 when the crew calmly reported, 'We are in a superstar at the moment'. The starboard wing then dropped suddenly, and following a short burst of engine power, Papa Yankee began to descend rapidly in a flat spin to starboard, turning once every six to eight seconds. It was not fitted with an anti-spin parachute.

Papa Yankee impacted the ground around one and a half minutes after the stall had commenced, in open farmland about a mile from the Norfolk village of Felthorpe. It hit the ground in a flat attitude with a very high rate of descent but very low airspeed, breaking apart on impact and killing all four crew. A small fire broke out in the area of the No 2 engine but this quickly burnt itself out.

The impending crash was reported by RAF personnel living in the vicinity. RAF Coltishall dispatched fire and rescue appliances and called up helicopters from RAF Manston. Norwich Fire Service also attended and removed the bodies of the crew members. The injuries to the occupants of the aircraft could not have been prevented by anything in the nature of safety equipment, stronger seats or the flight deck structure. The accident was, therefore, classified as non-survivable.

This accident represented the first fatal accident for the type in the four years it had been flying.

An on-site examination showed that the aircraft had struck the ground with a flat attitude, little forward speed, and a high rate of descent while spinning to the right. The fuselage was grossly flattened in the impact and the tail unit, which had rolled and skidded to part, had detached at the rear pressure dome. The engine installation and rear equipment bay had been demolished. A localised ground fire that had been initiated in the region of the centre engine on impact affected the No. 1 engine.

The main planes, particularly the port, had broken up in the violent impact with the ground. It was concluded that the aircraft was complete at impact. It was considered that all three Rolls Royce engines had been running, and the centre (No. 2 engine) was running at a higher speed than the other two engines, which were probably throttled to flight idle.

The wreckage was dismantled and transported to Hawker Siddeley Aircraft Ltd. premises at Hatfield, where the company further examined it in conjuction with the AAIB.

After the accident, further studies were made using the flight simulator at Hatfield. These examined in detail the relationship between the rate of approach to the stall, recovery action and the probability of the occurrence of a superstall. The studies showed that the safety margins were insignificant with the stick-pusher inoperative. In addition to these studies, the Royal Aircraft Establishment undertook a more specific investigation to compute an approximate history of tailplane deflection that occurred during the fatal test. For this investigation, the aerodynamic and other characteristics of the aircraft were taken to be the same as those used in the simulator. The history of the pitch attitude was also assumed to be known and given by the recorded data corrected for instrument error. On this basis, deducing the other flight parameters and the tailplane angle was possible. This was not, however, a simple matter of inverting the calculation procedures since the accuracy of the recorded data was not such as would permit successive differentiation of the attitude angle with respect to time. The situation was further complicated by the fact that no information was available an the level of engine thrust being used at various stages of the test. This again made it necessary to do additional exploratory calculations to assess the most plausible assumption on which to proceed.

The final report into the crash of Papa Yankee was published two years later concluded that the probable cause of the accident was that *during the stall test decisive recovery action was delayed too long to prevent the aircraft entering a superstall from which recovery was not possible.*

The loss of 9K-ACG

Flight KU32 was a was Kuwait Airways scheduled service flight from Beirut, Lebanon, to Kuwait City. It departed Beirut at 1855 hrs GMT on 30 June 1966, and apart from a tendency for the autopilot pitch lock to disconnect, the flight to the descent point was uneventful. Some reports say that on board were eleven crew and seventy-two passengers - others, including the ICAO verson say that there were eight crew and sixty-four passengers. The aircraft was cleared to commence descent at 20:28 from flight level 300 to flight level 95 by the DY NDB - the pilot-in-command decided to carry out a visual approach and advised the co-pilot accordingly.

The aircraft reached flight level 95 some three minutes before reaching the DY NDB and

9K-ACG deplanes passengers, ‘somewhere in the Gulf’. *[Simon Peters Collection]*

maintained this level until passing the beacon at about 20:39, at which time it was cleared to descend to 3,000 feet, it being agreed that the aircraft would report to base leg for Runway 33R.

At about this time, when at flight level 50, the flight reported ‘airfield in sight’. The pilot-in-command and flight engineer sighted the airport rotating beacon and the co-pilot the rotating beacon and some airport lights. The aircraft was cleared for final approach.

A left-hand turn onto the final was commenced at around 4,000 feet, and the flight reported its position as six miles from the airport at 2,300 feet. The rate of descent was 1,500 feet per minute and an airspeed of 178 knots. During all this, the aircraft was being flown on autopilot, and the co-pilot was asked to set 1,500 feet in the autopilot’s ‘acquire height’ box. The ADF was turned to the KWS locator, which was 2,224 metres from the runway threshold, and the co-pilot was occupied with the landing checks.

At this point of the flight, the aircraft was at 1,830 feet, almost above the MG NDB inbound and eighty seconds from impact with the ground. The desired approach speed was 154 knots, with a descent rate of 700 feet per minute and a threshold speed of 134 knots. According to the Flight Recorder, the flight progressed thus:

80 seconds	Altitude	1,830 ft.
	Rate of descent	1,500 ft/min.
	Airspeed	176 knots.
	Pitch attitude	0.1°
	Course	009°
74 seconds	Altitude	1,685 ft.
	Rate of descent	1,500 ft/min.
	Airspeed	177 knots.
	Pitch attitude	0.1°
	Course	001°

73 seconds — Pilot-in-Command engaged the rate of descent lock on the autopilot which had been set for 500ft/min. This rate of descent was acquired without any change of power.

66 seconds — Calculated time when the aircraft was abeam the MG NDB.

63 seconds — The rate of descent decreased to 500-600ft/min; indicated airspeed was 168 knots and decreasing pitch attitude was +6°.

59 seconds	Altitude	1,400 ft.
	Rate of descent	500-600ft/min.
	Airspeed	163 knots
	Pitch attitude	+6°
	Course	334°
50 seconds	Altitude	1,300 ft.
	Rate of descent	500-600ft/min.
	Airspeed	154 knots
	Pitch attitude	+6°
	Course	334°
47 seconds	Altitude	1,265 ft.
	Rate of descent	500-600ft/min.
	Airspeed	150 knots.
	Pitch attitude	+7°
	Course	334°

The pilot-in-command decided to abandon the autopilot appraoch and disconnected the autopilot. He called for 10,500 RPM on all three engines and this was set by the co-pilot.

46 seconds — The nose of the aircraft was lowered, the pitch attitude changing from 6.8° to 0.6° in two seconds. The rate of descent increased.

The pilot-in-command, who was now flying the aircraft manually, cancelled the flight director, asimuth master and descent locks on the FCS panel.

44 seconds	Altitude	1,200 ft.
	Rate of descent	1,800ft/min.
	Airspeed	149 knots
	Pitch attitude	-0.6°
	Course	333°
42 seconds	Altitude	1,140 ft.
	Rate of descent	2,600ft/min.
	Airspeed	151 knots
	Pitch attitude	-0.9°
	Course	333°
27 seconds	Altitude	640 ft.
	Rate of descent	1,500ft/min
	Airspeed	158 knots
	Pitch attitude	1.5°
	Course	332°

During the period 44 - 27 seconds, the pilot-in-command observed and was concerned that the airspeed was below 150 knots and that the altimeter was passing through 700 feet on QNH. He was also concerned that the ADF indicated he was to the left of the runway centreline. His attention was on the airspeed indicator, altitude director and the ADF indications. He did not monitor the vertical speed indicator, and he was unaware that the aircraft had a high descent rate.

19 seconds The pilot-in-command called for 11,500 RPM on all engines, and the co-pilot set this up. A turn to the right was initiated at about this time to align with the anticipated position of the runway. The co-pilot, still performing his pre-landing checks, glanced out the side window and observed that the aircraft was close to the ground. He glanced ahead, expecting to see the runway lights, but none were visible. He checked the instruments and observed 350 feet on his altimeter(QNH), a rate of descent of about 1,500ft/min and an indicated airspeed of 148 knots. He immediately warned the pilot-in-command and applied full engine power - the pilot-in-command now called for 12,000 RPM.

11 seconds	Altitude	250 ft.
	Rate of descent	1,350ft/min
	Airspeed	151 knots
	Pitch attitude	3.0°
	Course	334°
3 seconds	Altitude	85 ft.
	Rate of descent	1,200ft/min.
	Airspeed	157 knots
	Pitch attitude	2.6°
	Course	341°

0 seconds The aircraft struck the ground and crashed approximately 4 km short of the runway threshold, slightly to the left of the centreline at an elevation of roughly 185 feet. The accident occurred at approximately 20:46 GMT at night.

9K-ACG is seen under guard out in the desert following the landing accident. *[Simon Peters Collection]*

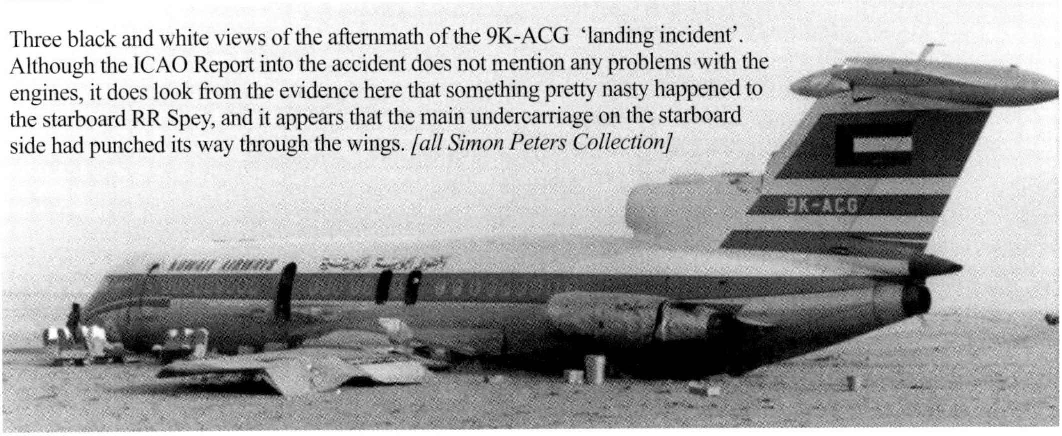

Three black and white views of the afternmath of the 9K-ACG 'landing incident'. Although the ICAO Report into the accident does not mention any problems with the engines, it does look from the evidence here that something pretty nasty happened to the starboard RR Spey, and it appears that the main undercarriage on the starboard side had punched its way through the wings. *[all Simon Peters Collection]*

The aircraft struck the ground in an area of soft and level sand, first with the starboard wheels and ten metres further along with the port wheels. Three metres further along, the starboard wheels left the ground, making contact again twenty-one metres distant. They created a deep trench six metres long at the end of which the first traces of the undercarriage collapse were found. Twelve metres after this, another trench indicated where the port undercarriage had collapsed. The aircraft then slid on its belly, leaving various components along its track, and came to a stop approximately 450 metres from the first contact point on a heading of 109°.

Later investigations revealed that a special procedure had been published three days before the incident, on 27 June 1966, instructing pilots to be at 1,300 feet on QFE when passing abeam the MG NDB and not to descend below 500 feet unless the runway was in sight. The rate of descent was not to exceed 1,000 feet/min, and special instructions for undershoot procedure were given. The QFE setting, which should have been used below the transition level, was not requested by the pilot-in-command, and his altimeter was found on the QNH setting.

The procedure specified in the operations manual for the approach and landing of Trident aircraft was not followed by the pilot-in-command, resulting in a rate of descent in excess of that desired. Although it was considered that the indicated airspeeds through the approach were completely safe, it would appear that the pilot-in-command became unduly concerned about them, and he directed his attention to the airspeed indicator at the exclusion of any other instruments.

The cockpit check should have been completed before passing the MG NDB, which was still being carried out when the aircraft struck the ground. Consequently, the co-pilot, who should have been monitoring the approach and looking for the runway, could not do so.

A subsequent Committee of Inquiry found that the pilot-in-command did not follow the procedures laid down in the operations manual for approach and landing of the aircraft type. Furthermore, the cockpit check for the approach and landing was still being carried out when the aircraft hit the ground and the pilot-in-command's altimeter was set on the QNH instead of the QFE.

The Enquiry recommended that:

1. The airline take immediate steps to introduce the following operating techniques and procedures for was Trident operations.

   a. During the approach to landing all cockpit checks (except the final check) are to be completed before the aircraft turns on to final and, in any case, at a height never less than 1,500 feet above ground level.

   b. During the final stages of the approach from 1,500 feet the rate of descent is to be maintained at 5-700 ft/min and never allowed to exceed 1000 ft/min.

   c. The co-pilot should monitor the aircraft's speed, altitude and rate of descent, calling the readings to the pilot-in-command at 1,500 ft and thereafter at 500-foot intervals at any intermediate holding altitude. Should the rate of descent at any time exceed 1,000 ft/min, he is to warn immediately the pilot-in-command.

   d. Unless the autopilot is serviceable and a coupled ILS approach is being carried out the autopilot is to be disconnected at 1,500 feet above ground level.

   e. When landing on Runway 33 R at Kuwait the final approach is to be from the KWS beacon using the approved instrument let-down pattern or is to be initiated from the Alpha Hotel beacon at a height of no more than 4,000 feet nor less than 2,500 feet.

2. The airline should make urgent and strong representations to the Airport Authorities in an effort to get more adequate radio and visual aids installed on the 33/15 runway.

Disasters at Heathrow - The Ambassador Incident

The 3 July 1968 was a dark day for BEA's Trident fleet at Heathrow. That afternoon G-AMAD, a BKS Airspeed Ambassador was on final approach to Runway 28R bring in eight racehorses from France.

The aircraft left Deauville at 15:35 as Flight No. C.6845, and made an uneventful flight to London at flight level 70. It was cleared to land on runway 28 Right, and at 16:24, it was reported that it had passed the outer marker inbound. The approach proceeded normally, and the aircraft came into the view of air traffic control personnel in the tower when it was about 200 feet, and close to the airport boundary. It was in a normal approach attitude. However, at a position near the threshold of runway 28 Right, the port wing was seen to drop, and the aircraft turned slowly to the left off the runway centreline. The bank increased, and the port wing tip, followed by the port mainwheels, touched the grass surface of the airport. Witnesses near the runway threshold heard engine power applied as if for an overshoot, and the aircraft then became airborne again, with the bank further increasing, it flew towards the partly constructed Terminal One building on the northeast side of the airport's central area. Whilst still steeply banked, it struck two British European Airways Trident aircraft parked at a terminal building pier and burst into flames.

The Ambassador then rolled onto its back, and after demolishing a twelve-foot-high metal blast barrier came to rest against the ground floor of the terminal building between two of the embarkation piers. Twenty-seven people on the ground in the

G-ARPI minus tail, surrounded by other wreckage. *[Simon Peters Collection]*

Tail damage!

Left: a close-up of the damage done to Papa India's rear end. Note the APU housing that has been twisted over ninety degrees out of position.

Below: The entire rear section of Papa Tango lies wrecked on the ground. *[both Simon Peters Collection]*

Above: G-ARPT at Heathrow.
Below:The fuselage was later disposed of to Channel Airways as a training aid. *[both Simon Peters Collection]*

area received slight injuries, and two people were seriously injured.

Three BEA aircraft, two of which were Tridents, was had been parked nose-in to the Terminal. The first aircraft to be hit by the Ambassador was Trident G-ARPI which lost it's tailfin above the S-duct after being hit by the wing of the stricken aircraft that went on to hit Trident G-ARPT that was destroyed, being severed forward of the rear toilets. The entire afterpart of that Trident, including the engines became detatched and were thrown about thirty feet away.

The accident investigation found that the accident was caused by the failure, due to metal fatigue, of the actuating rod for the port flap. This caused the flap to retract, resulting in an asymmetric condition that led to the Ambassador's loss of control.

Papa India's tail above the 'S'-duct was smashed off, but the damage was deemed repairable and the airliner returned to service the following February. Papa Tango, however, was so badly damaged that it was later broken up with the fuselage going to the Stansted and Southend-based Channel Airways as a training aid.

The loss of these two Tridents, combined with the temporary withdrawal of G-ARPR for repairs following a heavy landing during training at Shannon in June 1968, left BEA suddenly short of Trident capacity. Hawker Siddeley, however, was able to bring forward the delivery of Trident 2s G-AVFC and G-AVFG to assist.

No Smoking aboard the Aircraft was - G-ARPS

On 29 July 1969 Trident 1C of BEA was parked up at London Heathrow when a cabin fire started - the aircraft was written off.

A foretaste of what was to come - G-AVFH

Shortly after take-off from Heathrow on 8 May 1970, the crew of a BEA Trident 2 was G-AVFH bound for Naples found themselves experiencing a 'stick shaker' stall warning. There was no immediate explanation for this as airspeed and attitude were normal, but suddenly the 'stick pusher' stall recovery system operated, pushing the nose down and disconnecting the autopilot. With no immediate reason for the stall evident and height low, the Captain overrode the push, bringing the nose back up, during which time he just kept the aircraft level, and the Trident only just managed to stay flying.

A second stick push occurred, and as Foxtrot Hotel was only 1,000 feet above the ground then, the third pilot was instructed to pull the circuit breakers on the rear bulkhead to override the system. As the co-pilot turned to the rear of the centre pedestal to pull the stall recovery override lever, he noticed that the droop lever was in the 'up' position and immediately redeployed it.

Although it was established that the droop lever had been moved, no crew member remembered moving it, so the Captain decided that it had moved due to a mechanical failure. Fox Hotel's controls were comprehensively checked after the incident, and no faults were found.

Both BEA and Hawker Siddeley conducted tests to establish what, if anything, had gone wrong with the system but came up with nothing. It, therefore, became apparent that there had not been any mechanical malfunction, and it was also established that a similar incident had befallen a Trident shortly after take-off from Paris-Orly a few years before. However, it was two years before the potential air disasters that had only been avoided were fully realised.

Go Round! Go Round! - G-AWZA

XP915, a Comet operated by the Blind Landing Experimental Unit (BLEU), crewed by Flight Lt B M Barclay, Aircraft Commander, Co-pilot I L McGrath and Flight Engineer R E Anstee. Also on

G-ARPS awaits another load of passengers. *[Author's Collection]*

G-AVFH in the BEA 'Red Square' scheme. *[Author's Collection]*

board were four supernumerary crew. The Comet was about to make a training flight, and was in the take-off position on Runway 27, on the centreline, about five hundred feet in from the end of the runway at Thurleigh near Bedford, awaiting take-off clearance.

The Trident, G-AWZA, operated by BEA, was one of several civil aircraft flying in the Bedford aerodrome circuit and using the Instrument Landing System (ILS) on Runway 27 for training. Instructor Captain Anthony John Angus, Trainee Captain Leslie Wallis and Trainee First Officer James Alan Passmore crewed it. There were also two supernumerary crew on board. These aircraft were under radar surveillance and were being positioned and sequenced by the Bedford approach controller as required for the various exercises they were engaged in.

The local weather throughout the relevant period was visibility 4 to 6 nautical miles, cloud base varying from 1,500 to 21000 feet and surface wind varying from 190° (T) to 210° (T) at speeds from ten to fifteen knots. There were occasional flurries of light rain.

Trident G-AWZA was engaged in conversion training to an approved BEA syllabus. At the time of the accident, the particular manoeuvre being practised, in simulated Category III weather conditions, was designed to familiarise crew members with various failure scenarios during an automatic ILS approach to land. A screen in front of the left-hand pilot was being used to simulate Instrument Meteorological Conditions (IMC) and an aperture in this screen was being opened and closed at the relevant heights to simulate the appropriate visual reference limitations.

The operating crew consisted of a training captain who was in overall command and was occupying the P2 position, right-hand seat, a captain under training occupying the P1 position, left-hand seat, and a first officer under training in the P3 position, the centre seat. Although P1 and P3 were under training in Trident 3B G-AWZA both of them had considerable previous experience of Trident 1 and 2 operations and of auto-approach procedures. In addition to his instructional role, the training captain was fulfilling the P2 function for the various cockpit drills and procedures involved.

The two extra crew members on the flight deck were another BEA training captain and a Hawker Siddeley flight engineer. The latter was operating the shutter of the blind-flying screen as directed by the training captain in command, but, except for this, neither of the two extra crew members took part in the operation.

Before the approach on which the accident occurred four exercises had been successfully completed. These had involved automatic approaches down to about twelve feet, each followed by an automatic overshoot; the last three exercises had included a simulated engine failure during the overshoot phase.

In the fifth exercise, the overshoot was originally planned to be initiated at a height of about seventy feet, with the visibility shutter on the screen in front of P1 closed at about this height, thus triggering P1 to call for overshoot action as defined in the relevant BEA crew procedures. Almost simultaneously with overshoot initiation, there was to be an autopilot 'failure'. The training captain had briefed P1, P3 and the flight engineer on the details of this intended exercise. '

When the aircraft was inbound at the outer marker, approximately three miles out on the approach, the Trident pilot reported that he was on finals for a low approach and overshoot. The controller acknowledged this by informing the pilots that the Comet aircraft was back-tracking on the runway and that they were therefore cleared only to make an overshoot; the Trident pilot replied with the word 'understood'. At about 900 feet the training captain introduced a 'failure' by switching off one of the roll channels of the autopilot system; both P1 and P3 noted it and took account of its consequential effects. In this case, the primary consequence was to increase the decision height (DH) from the twelve feet which was permitted with a fully triplicated autopilot system to a height of one hundred feet, which is appropriate for an autopilot system operating only in duplex.

The training captain reported that it was raining, but forward slant visibility was good, and he could see the Comet lined up on the runway near the threshold. His own vision was not impaired by the screens in front of P1, and as the aircraft seemed to be correctly aligned both laterally and vertically, he was satisfied to continue the approach. Having established the Comet's position on the runway, he decided not to continue the exercise down to the originally intended seventy feet but to overshoot at one hundred feet. He did not consider it necessary to inform the crew of this change and decided that he could still get some value from the exercise by having P1 overshoot from one hundred feet.

When the radio altimeters showed five hundred feet, P3 called '500 - RADIO' thereby indicating to P1 and P2 that subsequent height calls would be given by reference to the radio altimeters. At 300 feet, P3 called 'AUTOLAND - 100 feet' to indicate that the status of the relevant equipment was satisfactory for the approach to be continued to a landing on automatics, subject to P1 making his decision by 100 feet. P1 repeated '100 feet' to acknowledge this call from P3.

At about 190 feet, P1 went 'head up' preparatory to seeking external visual reference and at 150 feet, the screen shutter was opened, giving him the appropriate 'visibility'. At 130 feet, P3 called '30 ABOVE'; almost immediately, P1 called 'LAND'. The Training Captain (P2) called 'OVERSHOOT' immediately after this and opened the throttles fully. P1 said that when P2 called 'OVERSHOOT', he went 'head down' and reverted immediately to his flight instruments, checking speed and attitude and noted that the aircraft had rotated to about a nine-degree nose-up attitude; All crew members said that they felt the aircraft continue to 'sink'.

At seventy feet, the flight engineer closed the screen shutter as he had been previously briefed to do. The aircraft continued to descend, and at a radio altimeter reading which P1 reported was about 20 feet there was an impact; P1 disengaged the autopilot by pressing his thumb button, called 'AUTO-PILOT OUT', took over manual control and climbed the aircraft back to circuit height. The pilots of another Trident aircraft in the circuit then made a visual check of the damage to G-AWZA. They established that it was confined to the port inner flap after which the aircraft made a successful landing at Bedford using a 'flaps up' technique as a precautionary measure.

The Comet crew were uncertain of the extent of the damage to their aircraft and, after shutting down the engines, left the aircraft with the assistance of the Fire Service, which arrived quickly in response to ATC instructions. The aircraft was towed away, and the runway was cleared of wreckage so the Trident could land. There was no fire in either aircraft.

Subsequent investigations revealed that the Trident sustained damage to the underside of the port wing and to the port inner flap, and the fin and part of the rudder of the Comet were torn off, and

G-AWZA, the aircraft that collided with a Comet on landing at Bedford. *[Authors Collection]*

there was some compression damage to the fuselage structure.

What did happen to PLAAF 256?

The Lin Biao incident was an aircraft accident at 03:00 on 13 September 1971 involving Lin Biao, the Vice Chairman of the Chinese Communist Party. Lin Biao was allegedly attempting to defect to the Soviet Union after a failed plot to assassinate Mao Zedong. Following Lin's death, there has been widespread scepticism in the West concerning the official Chinese explanation, while a forensic investigation conducted by the USSR that recovered the bodies has confirmed that Lin was among those who died in the crash.

According to the Chinese government, in the early morning of 13 September, Lin Biao, Ye Qun, Lin Liguo, and several personal aides attempted to flee to the Soviet Union and boarded a prearranged Trident 1E of the People's Liberation Army Air Force, registered as PLAAF 256, piloted by Pan Jiangyin, the deputy commander of the PLAAF 34th division. The aircraft did not take aboard enough fuel before taking off, ran out of fuel, and crashed near Öndörkhaan in Mongolia on 13 September 1971. Everyone on board, eight men and one woman, was killed.

The exact circumstances surrounding Lin's death remain unclear due to a lack of surviving evidence. Many of the original government records relevant to Lin's death were secretly and intentionally destroyed, with the approval of the Politburo, during the brief period of Hua Guofeng's interregnum in the late 1970s.

Western historians have contended Lin did not have either the intention or the ability to usurp Mao's place within the government or the Party. One theory attempted to explain Lin's flight and death by observing that he opposed China's rapprochement with the United States, which Zhou Enlai was organising with Mao's approval. Because the Chinese government never produced evidence to support their report that Lin was on board the aircraft, Western scholars originally doubted Lin had died in the crash.

Other scholars suggested Mao ordered the Chinese army to shoot down Lin's aircraft over Mongolia.

An investigation by Western scholars in 1994 examined evidence in Russia, Mongolia, mainland China, the United States, and Taiwan. It came to several conclusions, some contrary to the official Chinese version of events. The study confirmed Lin Biao, Ye Qun, and Lin Liguo were all killed in the crash. Lin's aircraft was travelling away from the Soviet Union at the time of its crash, making the exact sequence of events before Lin's death more confusing and casting doubt on the possibility that Lin was attempting to seek asylum in the USSR. Lin's wife and son may have forced Lin to board the aircraft against his will. Several senior leaders within the Communist Party hierarchy knew Lin and his family would flee but chose not to attempt to stop their flight.

At 22:00. The night before Lin's party fled, Ye Qun announced that the family would board an aircraft at 07:00 the following day to fly to Guangzhou. Lin's 27-year-old daughter, Lin Liheng - known by the nickname 'Doudou' - opposed the escape plan and contacted Lin's bodyguards to request that they guard her father from Ye.

Zhou received Doudou's message shortly after Doudou's phone call directly from the general office of the Central Committee responsible for guarding China's senior leaders. The message contained Doudou's warning that Ye Qun and Lin Liguo were attempting to persuade Lin Biao to flee the country using an aircraft currently being prepared at Qinhuangdao Shanhaiguan Airport. Zhou called Wu Faxian, the Air Force commander, who verified the aircraft's existence. Zhou then issued orders that the aircraft could not take off without the written

PLAAF 50051, a Trident 1E similar to 256 involved in the Lin Biao incident. *[Author's Collection]*

permission of himself and several other senior military officials, including Wu Faxian, general chief-of-staff Huang Yongsheng, and the commander of the navy and general chief-of-staff, Li Zuopeng. At 11:30, Ye Qun called Zhou and informed him Lin Biao was planning to fly to Dalian and denied they had prepared an aircraft at Shanhaiguan. Zhou then told Ye to wait for him to travel to see Lin before they left Beidaihe, where they were staying, issued orders to neutralise Wu Faxian and Huang Yongsheng, two potentially disruptive officers close to Lin, and ordered two aircraft be readied in Beijing so he could fly to Lin's residence to deal with the matter personally.

One soldier shot at Lin Biao's limousine as it left Beidaihe but missed. Most soldiers the party encountered on its way to the airport allowed the limousine to pass. According to the driver of Lin's limousine, there was no time to place mobile stairs next to the aircraft's entrance, so the party boarded via a rope ladder. Lin Biao was so weak he had to be lifted and pulled onto the aircraft.

Zhang Ning observed the aircraft after it left the airport. Lin's aircraft initially travelled southeast in the direction of Guangzhou. The Trident returned twenty minutes later and circled the airport several times as if trying to land, but the runway lights had been turned off. Soviet officials and Mongolian witnesses reported the aircraft then flew north, over Mongolia and almost to the Soviet border, but then turned around and began flying south before it crashed. A Mongolian who witnessed the crash reported the aircraft's tail was on fire when it crashed. The crash occurred at around 03:00.

None of Zhou's instructions prevented Lin's flight, and he learned Lin's aircraft had taken off before he could fly to see Lin. Zhou then ordered all aircraft nationwide grounded without the written permission of Mao, himself, and several senior military leaders. He rushed to Zhongnanhai to brief Mao on Lin's flight and asked Mao if he wanted to order Lin's aircraft shot down, but Mao replied that they should 'let him go'.

At 08:30, 13 September, the Mongolian Foreign Ministry summoned the Chinese ambassador to make a formal complaint about the unauthorised entrance of an aircraft into Mongolian airspace and reported to the ambassador that the Trident had crashed, killing all on board. The Chinese ambassador to Mongolia then phoned Zhou Enlai, who instructed the ambassador to tell the Mongolians the aircraft had entered Mongolian airspace because it had gone off course.

Mongolian investigators were the first to inspect the wreckage, arriving later that day. They found an identity card belonging to Lin Liguo, confirming Lin Liguo's presence on the flight. Markings on the aircraft and surviving miscellaneous personal items confirmed the aircraft and passengers had originated from China. Still, the Mongolians were uncertain whether any of the dead were Lin Biao or Ye Qun. After inspecting the crash, the Mongolians buried the dead onsite.

Through the Chinese ambassador, Zhou requested and received permission for Chinese embassy staff to inspect the wreckage of Lin's aircraft, which they did on 15–16 September. The staff reported to Zhou that the aircraft had caught fire while attempting to land and then exploded. Zhou then sent additional staff to interview Mongolian crash witnesses and perform a detailed technical assessment. The report concluded the aircraft had approximately thirty minutes of fuel when it crashed but attempted to land without activating its landing gear or wing flaps.

Later, in 1971, a Soviet medical team secretly travelled to the crash site and exhumed the bodies, which were by then modestly decomposed. The team removed the heads of two of the corpses suspected to be Lin Biao and Ye Qun and took them back to the Soviet Union for forensic examination. In 1972, the team concluded that the heads belonged to Lin Biao and Ye Qun, but apparently, somewhat gruesomely the heads are allegedley still stored in Russian archives. To corroborate their findings, the team returned to Mongolia a second time to inspect the body, which was believed to be Lin Biao's. The Soviet team was not able to determine the cause of the crash but hypothesised the pilot misjudged his altitude while intentionally flying low to evade radar. Judging from the fires that burned after the crash, the Soviets estimated the aircraft had enough fuel to fly to the Soviet cities of Irkutsk or Chita. The work and its results were kept secret from the public: outside of the investigative team, only KGB chairman Yuri Andropov and Soviet leader Leonid Brezhnev were informed. The report remained classified until the early 1990s, after the end of the Cold War.

Another undershoot - 5B-DAA

On 15 March 1972 Trident 5B-DAA lost its starboard undercarriage when it undershot the runway during a training flight at its Nicosia, Cyprus base.

After extensive repairs lasting seven months and repainting in BEA colours, the aircraft was ferried back to Heathrow. It is interesting to note that pilots

Three views of the undershoot of 5B-DAA, where literally the starboard undercarriage unit was ripped off. Note how the airline name and logo has been hurredly painted out! *[Yanis Caramalides Collection]*

of the former 5B-DAA reported that it flew, 'one wing, slightly down', although remarkably, legend has it that this aircraft performed better than any other Trident in the BEA/BA fleet!

The Tragedy of Papa India

Sunday, 18 June 1972 was set to go down in British aviation history as the day that the country witnessed its worst air crash. Indeed to this day, the accident that befell the BEA Trident 1 at Staines was the worst air 'accident' this country had experienced to date.

Trident I G-ARPI called, as usual by 'the last two' letters of it's registration 'Papa India', owned by British European Airways (BEA) and operated by them under a valid air operator's certificate, crashed in a field near Staines at 16:11 hours' shortly after taking off from London Heathrow en route for Brussels on a scheduled flight BE (Bealine) 548. All those on board suffered fatal injuries. They comprised three pilots, Captain Stanley Key and Second Officers Jeremy Keighley as P2 and Simon Ticehurst as the third pilot. There were also two stewards, one stewardess and 112 passengers, of whom three were a BEA Merchantman (cargo conversion of a Vickers Vanguard) positioning crew in transit. One of these was seated in the P4 position on the flight deck. The aircraft had a valid Certificate of Airworthiness and a valid Certificate of Maintenance.

The crew had been on stand-by duty and had only been called upon to undertake this assignment because the originally designated crew had been delayed.

During the flight Captain Key was in the first pilot's (Pl) position on the port side, Second Officer Jeremy Keighley in P2's on the starboard, Second Officer Simon Ticehurst in the central P3 position, slightly aft of the control pedestal and of P1 and P2, and Captain Collins in the P4 or jump seat behind the Captain. Captain Key was the handling pilot. The cabin crew consisted of Senior Steward Frederick Farey, Steward Alan Lamb and Stewardess Jennifer Mowat, the youngest crew member on the flight, at age 19.

The weather at Heathrow at the time was primarily dictated by a cold front approaching south-eastwards across England and lying some thirty nautical miles distant. The main layer of cloud was 8/8 with its base at 1,000 feet. There were small amounts of cloud below this, the lowest being at 600 feet. It was raining. The surface wind was 2100/ 17 knots. There was considerable turbulence. Clearly, at the crucial early times of the flight, the aircraft was in the cloud, and the crew had no visual reference. In other words, it was a wet and blustery afternoon.

At the start-up time, there were 8,550 kilograms of fuel onboard Papa India. The estimated fuel weight for take-off was 8,200 kilograms. Since the engines were running for some minutes before taxying the actual figure for fuel on board would be slightly lessened. After engine start last-minute load alterations were made in order to keep the figure below the permitted Maximum Zero Fuel Weight for the aircraft of 41,730 kilograms.

Start-up clearance was given at 15:39 hrs for a scheduled departure time of 15:45. Push-back was not requested until 16:00 due to load re-adjustment. Clearance to taxi was given at 16:03.

At 16:06, a Dover One Standard Instrument Departure clearance was given, and instructions were given to select the transponder to standby 6615. This was acknowledged. At 16:06:53, the crew reported ready for take-off, and Papa India was cleared for take-off on Runway 28R.

There was then a delay of forty-two seconds, after which the aircraft was finally cleared for take-off at 16:08:24. Brake-release was probably 16:08:30.

The standard BEA practice for this particular flight involved a take-off with 20° flap, leading edge droop extended and the engine thrust at settings below full power. After take-off, speed should be increased to the initial climb speed VNA (i.e., take-off safety speed, V2 plus 25 knots). The scheduled value of VNA for this flight was 177 knots, Indicated Air Speed. At 90 seconds from brakes-off, flaps are to be selected fully up, and the engine thrust is reduced to the noise-abatement settings. At 3,000 feet, climb power is to be set, and then as the aircraft accelerates and reaches 225 knots, the leading edge is retracted, and the en-route climb is established. The minimum droop retraction speed is placarded by the lever and is well-known to all pilots. Also well-known is the injunction against retracting the droop in a turn.

In the case of Papa India, the sequence of events derived from the FDR readout was very different. Times are given in seconds from brake-release.

The take-off was normal and at forty-two seconds after brakes release the aircraft rotated, leaving the runway two seconds later at 145 knots IAS. At sixty-three seconds, the autopilot was engaged 355 feet above the runway at 170 knots IAS; the IAS speed lock was selected shortly thereafter. At seventy-four seconds, the aircraft started a 20° banked turn to port towards the Epsom Non-Directional Beacon. At eighty-three seconds, Captain Key reported, 'Climbing as cleared'. He was then instructed to change the frequency and contact the London Air Traffic Control Centre on 128.4 MHz.

At 93 seconds, the noise abatement procedure was initiated. Assuming that Captain Key was the handling pilot, this would involve Second Officer Keighley selecting the flaps fully up and operating the thrust levers to reduce power to the pre-calculated figure. At 100 seconds, Captain Key called 'Passing 1500' and at 103 seconds, the aircraft was cleared to climb to Flight Level 60 and to 'squawk' 6615 on the transponder. This message was acknowledged by Captain Key at 108 seconds with the terse call 'Up to 60'. This was the last message received from Papa India. In the wreckage was found Second Officer Ticehurst's log, on which he had duly entered this clearance up to Flight Level 60.

At 114 seconds, when the airspeed was 162 knots and the altitude 1,772 feet, the droop lever was selected up, putting the aircraft into the area of the stall as the droop started to move. At was 116 seconds, the stick-pusher stall recovery device operated, causing the autopilot automatically to disengage, the nose of the aircraft to pitch down, and the stick-push to cease as the incidence

G-ARPI in the new BEA 'Speedjack' scheme pulls into a stand at London Heathrow. *[Simon Peters Collection]*

The overview of the accident site at Staines in a field adjacent to the A30 road. *[Simon Peters Collection]*

decreased. Since the elevator trim would stay at its position on autopilot disengagement, which at that speed with the droop up would be tail-heavy, the incidence then increased, causing a second stick-push at 124 seconds and a third at 127 seconds since brake release. At 128 seconds, the stall recovery system was manually inhibited by pulling the lever. The aircraft then pitched up rapidly, losing speed and height, entering the true aerodynamic stall very soon afterwards and then a deep stall from which no recovery was possible at that height. Impact was at 150 seconds.

The aircraft crashed in a field on the Staines side of the A30 Staines By-Pass opposite the King George VI Reservoir. According to eyewitnesses, the aircraft had hit the ground with a very high rate of descent but very little forward airspeed, having apparently just 'fallen out of the sky'.

Trevor Burke, aged thirteen, witnessed the crash on a nearby footpath. With great presence of mind, he ran and told Mrs Castledine, who lived about a quarter of a mile away. - Mrs Castledine was previously a nursing sister at Ashford Hospital and was familiar with accident procedures. She was one of the first on the scene, and she made heroic efforts amidst the wreckage to help any of the victims who were still alive. Her actions cannot be praised too highly. However, the decelerative forces of the impact were too great for the human frame to survive. Only one person was alive (though deeply unconscious) on arrival at Ashford Hospital and he died soon afterwards.

From 16:20 onwards, there was a rapid build-up of police and other rescue services. The field was on the boundaries of three separate police divisions, and there was no manpower shortage.

The first ambulance on the scene was a Berkshire vehicle, which happened to be passing. The crew notified their control headquarters and went to assist. Surrey ambulance vehicles began arriving at 16:26. The first fire engine arrived at 16:27, followed by several other vehicles.

The field was sufficiently inaccessible to prevent all but the most persistent sightseers from reaching it. The police successfully controlled spectators, and contemporary reports that members of the public had impeded rescue services by their presence near the scene are not borne out by the facts.

Upon examination of the wreckage, it was found that each of the four men on the flight deck had had his headset plugged in, and all four switches were set to 'intercom'.

Captain Key's seat, contrary to earlier assumptions, was in the notch where one would expect it to be had he been the handling pilot. It had not been slid back before impact.

The UK AIB removed the wreckage from the site and transported it to the Royal aircraft Establishment at Farnborough where it was minutely examined.

The AIB found in the subsequent investigation that Papa India's leading edge droop high lift device had been retracted at 162 knots which indicated air speed of around 60 knots below the safe droop retraction speed of 225 knots. As a result the aircraft entered what was known as a 'change of configuration stall', which rapidly led to a 'deep' or 'superstall', similar to G-ARPY's, from which recovery was not possible. Although the droop retraction was almost certainly executed in error, the exact circumstances and member of the crew responsible were not established.

The Trident I was fitted with high lift devices on both the leading and trailing edges of its wings, the former being referred to as 'droop', the latter flaps. Unlike other aircraft, the two systems were controlled by a separate rather than a single lever. The sequence of events after take-off called for the flaps to be fully retracted at around 190 knots and the droop at 225 knots. Interconnections between the two levers prevented the droop lever from being moved whilst any value of flap was selected, eliminating the possibility of mistaken 'up' selections. However, once the flaps were up, the droop lever was unprotected from premature retraction. After the accident, a speed lock was added to the droop lever to prevent it from being moved until a speed of 225 knots had been passed, regardless of the flap position.

We will never know the truth about what happened on that miserable afternoon. Still, regardless of whether Key or Keighley inadvertently retracted the droop, it was the system as much as the crew that was to blame for the accident.

It was inevitable that in the wake of the public inquiry and investigation that failed to identify the culprit, the press would drag all the crew through the mill. And that they did, tarring Key as an 'ogre' and claiming Keighley was 'sluggish' and 'very inexperienced'. There was even one suggestion that the Merchantman Captain, John Collins had been spraying air freshener around the cockpit just after take-off, distracting the pilots. It is true that a can of air freshener was found in the wreckage near the cockpit, but this was not unusual as the cans were standard issue to the Merchantman crews as they often carried livestock as cargo.

At the time of the accident, it was not mandatory to equip aircraft with Cockpit Voice Recorders (CVR) and as such, G-ARPI was not fitted with one. This made establishing the exact circumstances impossible. The Papa India accident has been the subject of many articles and books and still not one conjecture stands out as the most likely scenario on the flightdeck that afternoon.

This then takes us away from the world of physical, electronic, mechanical or hydraulic items to the much more ethereal realm of 'human resources.'

What is known is that Capt Key was an experienced and much respected (some might say feared) pilot, but also someone who was suffering from a very severe heart condition and should not really have

The flight deck crew of Papa India.

Above: 51 year old Captain Stanley Key, the pilot-in-command had had 15,000 flying hours experience, including 4,000 on Tridents.

Left: 24 year old Second Officer Simon Ticehurst, had over 1,400 flying hours, including 750 hours on Tridents.

Right, 22 year old Second Officer JeremyKeighley had joined line flying a month and a half earlier, with 29 hours as P2. *[all Author's Collection]*

Firemen, police and members of other emergency services attended the accident, seen here in front of the tail unit of Papa India, which came down a distance away from the main wreck site. *[Simon Peters Collection]*

been flying at all. The two co-pilots were very young and inexperienced, particularly 22-year-old Jeremy Keighley, who held less than forty hours as P2 on the Trident. The ethics of putting two inexperienced pilots together in line operations had been a point of contention for some months before the accident.

It was thought that Key's illness had reached a critical condition during and just after take-off that afternoon, impairing his judgement enough to account for his low toleration of speed, which could have resulted in him retracting or ordering to retract the droop in mistake for the flaps.

Part of the Human Resources aspect involved investigating the crew's physical condition. The fact that there was no fire on impact enabled detailed autopsies to be carried out on the bodies of those who had been on the flight deck. There was no trace of alcohol or other drug. The autopsies demonstrated nothing abnormal in the case of Second Officer Keighley, Second Officer Ticehurst or Captain Collins.

It was otherwise with Captain Key. The condition of his heart was abnormal. Although there was no sign of any damage to the myocardium (that is to say no scarring of the heart muscle due to earlier coronary incidents), the three coronary arteries each showed throughout their length severe atherosclerosis.

This is a narrowing of the lumen (or bore) due to the deposit of fibrous or fatty tissues on the walls. It was a long-standing condition that must have been developing for thirty years or more. By the time of death it had reached a point where, in places at least, the effective diameter of the lumen had been reduced by fifty to seventy per cent. In addition to this abnormal condition, there were two points of more specific damage discovered near each other in the left coronary artery. The first was an area of localised calcification, fibrin deposition and aggregation of foamy phagocytes. This indicated a cardiac incident in the past, which the process of nature had resolved. It may have been symptomless.

In the same area of this artery, there was also a tear of the intima (the: is the lining of the arterial wall). In effect, a section of the pathologically thickened wall of the artery had become partially detached so that it was lying in the already diminished lumen but still leaving the lumen adequate for the flow of blood.

For reasons explained by Group Captain Mason, which convinced all the medical experts and the Accident Investigations Branch, it was as sure as anything can be that the intimal tear preceded and was not caused by the impact. The cause of the tear was probably this. As the thickening of the arterial lining takes place, so small blood vessels form in the new tissue. In the nature of things, since this is an unhealthy development, these blood vessels are not robust. Should there be any sharp rise in the

Three pictures of some of the wreckage of Papa India at Farnborough. *[Author's Collection]*

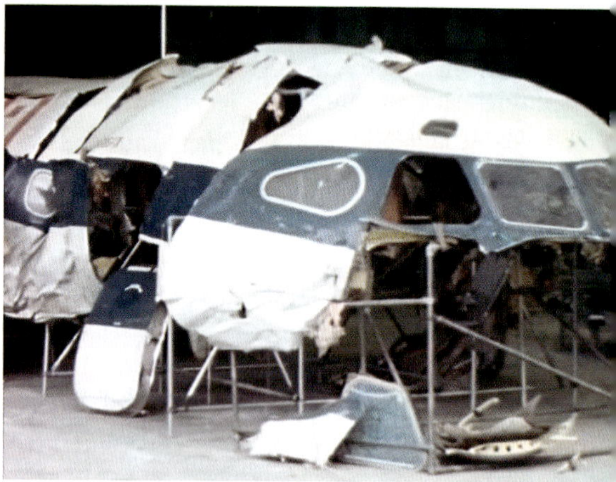

blood pressure passing through the vessels, they would be set to rupture, and the resulting haemorrhage could, by creating its own pressure, force part of the intima to separate. The pathologists could tell from the colour and composition of that blood that bleeding had started not more than two hours before death and not less than about a minute. Precise timing must be tricky because it is rare for a person to suffer from a cardiac incident such as this and then die shortly afterwards from extraneous causes. Experience is, therefore, limited.

The next question was, what was the likely cause of the rise in blood pressure and consequent haemorrhage? It is common knowledge that any form of stress, whether physical or emotional, is expected to produce such an effect. On 18 June, unfortunately, there was no shortage of events which might have had such an effect upon Captain Key.

On the more trivial level was the rostering as a stand-by crew on a Sunday. Days of the week are all much the same to an airline pilot, but it appears from a letter that he wrote that Captain Key set some store on spending Sundays at home. There were other possible irritations of a minor nature, namely the graffiti in the aircraft if he saw them - which I shall come to shortly - and the unexpected and no doubt irritating delay before push-back caused by the necessity to alter the load. However, the one incident that stands out as the most likely cause is the altercation in the crew room. Captain Key was very angry indeed, though his anger was short-lived.

Since this event took place about an hour and a half before take-off, it is not unreasonable to suppose that it may have been the cause of the initial rise in blood pressure, which resulted in the rupture of the small blood vessels.

The crew room incident came about because in June 1972, there was a long-standing dispute between BEA and the British Airline Pilots' Association about pay rates and work conditions. Some pilots, opposed by others, favoured strike action. The effects of this dispute emerged at many stages. The dispute affected relations between management and pilots and between pilots and pilots. It evinced itself in the following ways:

The graffiti: On P3's table in Papa India after the crash, there was found a series of offensive scribbles or graffiti, some of them directed at Captain Key, some of them at members of the BEA management staff. Those in charge of mustering the evidence realised early on that these graffiti might be evidence that a dispute had actually occurred between members of the crew of Papa India whilst they were on board the aircraft before or during flight.

Accordingly, the handwriting was subjected to expert examination to determine whether it was Second Officer Ticehurst or Second Officer Keighley. The handwriting expert concluded that, in all probability, neither of the co-pilots was the author of any of the writings. Still, that Second Officer Ticehurst might have been responsible for one of them. All the evidence showed that Second Officer Ticehurst's views about the threatened strike coincided with Captain Key's.

Other matters strengthened this conclusion: the graffito most closely resembling the handwriting of Second Officer Ticehurst was, by its position, almost certainly not the last to be written. Also, on 6 June 1972, First Officer Spain flew as a co-pilot on Papa India with Captain Key in command. Many of the graffiti were then already present on the table. Whilst on the ground preparing for flight, Mr Spain said to P2, *Look at this lot!* At that moment, Captain Key appeared and asked, *What's that?* First Officer Spain put his flight log over the writing and passed the matter over with some non-committal remark. He did not think that Captain Key saw the writing. Nor did he believe that it would have provoked more than an acid comment if he had.

After the crash, an inspection of other Trident aircraft revealed further offensive inscriptions on the P3 tables. Thus, what at first sight appeared to be a sinister fact, namely that on P3's table in an aircraft with Captain Key in command were found offensive remarks directed at Captain Key, turns out to be no more than an exercise in puerility which could have been found repeated in several other places and aircraft. The graffiti was no basis for even suspecting any dissension on the flight deck of Papa India on this occasion. It is just possible that had he seen them on this occasion, Captain Key might have felt some twinge of annoyance, but if he did see them, it must have been before Mr Coleman came on board to discuss the load, and he observed nothing untoward about the Captain or crew.

Then there was the matter of the much-reported crew-room incident. About an hour and a half before Papa India's departure, Captain Key was in the crew room. Also, there were many other pilots, including First Officer Flavell. It seems that Captain Key, who was opposed to pilots taking strike action in support of their claim for higher salaries, had been enlisting the support of some of his fellow Senior Captains. First Officer Flavell asked Captain Key how these efforts were progressing.

Some of the graffiti on the P3 tables of BEA's Trident fleet. *[Authors Collection]*

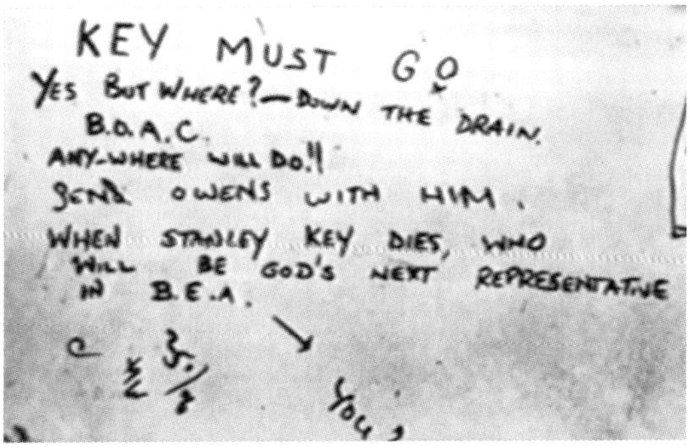

This question provoked an outburst from Captain Key, who told was Flavell that the matter was just as confidential as the BALPA ballot. This outburst was described by at least one eyewitness as the most violent argument he had ever heard, although it was less of an argument than a one-sided expression of views. Whichever it was, although Captain Key was very angry indeed, it subsided as quickly as it had erupted and the Captain took First Officer Flavell by the arm and apologised for what he had said. Thereafter, he seemed to have outward appearances as if he were his normal self.

Among the AIB's recommendations following its investigation into the accident were to fit a baulk to prevent droop being retracted prematurely; to improve pilot training in the area of stall recognition and recovery, to install CVRs; to increase the amount of experience required by young pilots before operating as co-pilots in line service; to improve the ability to detect significant heart disease in flight crews; and to involve the AIB in the investigation of potentially disastrous incidents.

The AIB eventually issued a huge report on the accident and a summary. They concluded:

- Captain Key failed to achieve and maintain adequate speed after noise-abatement procedures.
- Retraction of the droops at some sixty knots below the proper speed caused the aircraft to enter the stall regime and the stick shaker and pusher to operate.
- Failure by the crew to monitor the speed errors and to observe the movement of the droop lever.
- The dumping by the crew of the stall recovery system.

The underlying causes were these:

- The abnormal heart condition of Captain Key led to a lack of concentration and impaired judgment sufficient to account for his toleration of the speed errors and his retraction of, or order to retract, the droops in mistake for the flaps.
- Some distraction, the nature of 'which is uncertain, possibly due to the presence of Captain Collins as a passenger on the flight deck, which caused Second Officer Ticehurst's attention to wander from his monitoring duties.
- Lack of training directed at the possibility of 'subtle' pilot incapacitation.

- Lack of experience in Second Officer Keighley.
- Lack of knowledge in the crew of the possibility or implications of a change of configuration stall.
- Lack of knowledge on the part of the crew that a stick-shake and push might be experienced almost simultaneously and of the probable cause of such an event.
- Lack of a mechanism to prevent the droops' retraction at too low a speed after flap-retraction.

Trouble in Cyprus

1964 to 1974 was a turbulent era for Cyprus, with the apparent breakdown of relations between the Greek Cypriot and Turkish Cypriot sides across the social and political ties. In 1963, the Turkish Cypriots had abandoned their constitutional presence in the Cyprus Government, both voluntarily and by external pressure. Violence in Nicosia followed soon after. In 1964, the Cyprus National Guard intervened militarily against a Turkish Cypriot militant threat in the northwest of the island, in and near the Kokkina enclave, leading to a confrontation with Turkey, who responded militarily but stopped short of invasion. During the unrest, the island began to incubate fanaticism on both Greek and Turkish Cypriot sides of Enosis and Taksim, respectively, polar opposite ideologies. Enosis was an effort to unify the island with Greece, while Taksim simultaneously called for the island's partition between Greeks and Turks.

On 15 July 1974, the Cyprus National Guard, under the command of the Greek junta in Athens, launched a coup against the democratically elected President, Archbishop Makarios III. A large force of troops and tanks descended on the Archbishopric in Nicosia and laid siege to it, though Archbishop Makarios himself was able to escape. Troops defending the Presidential Palace resisted, and fighting between pro-Makarios and junta supporters continued for much of that day. A former EOKA member, Nikos Sampson, was promptly placed in power as de facto President of the Republic, though he later resigned on 23 July after support for his regime collapsed. The coup represented both a provocation against Turkey and an opportunity for Turkey to invade, citing concerns for the safety of the Turkish Cypriot community as its primary goal.

Out at Nicosia Airport, on 22 June 1974 the Turkish Air Force straffed a number of Cyprus Airways aircraft on the ground there. Trident 2E 5B-DAB was damaged, and 5B-DAC was also damaged but was later repaired and returned to British Airways.

Flight CY317, Trident 1E, 5B-DAE, was being prepared for its scheduled flight to Nicosia via Rome. Due to the dramatic events on the island, only six passengers were booked.

Concerned that an invasion was very likely, Captain Adamos Marneros contacted Cyprus Airways management in Nicosia to request the cancellation of the flight. The idea behind this was that it would be better to have at least one aircraft that could be used from a base outside Cyprus to continue some form of service should Nicosia become unusable. However he was directed to operate the flight.

Upon arrival in Rome, he again requested to cancel the flight, still concerned for his aircraft's safety. When it was refused once more, he decided

The tail unit of 5B-DAE is cleared away from Nicosia Airport following the straffing by the Turkish Air Force. *[Yanis Caramalides Collection]*

to take on extra fuel so that if he could not land in Nicosia, he had sufficient reserves to return to Rome.

Passing Rhodos, the crew noticed a flotilla of ships heading for Cyprus on their radar. Once over Cyprus, despite the possible threat of Turkish fighters, Captain sMarneros decided to fly around the island to look at the current situation.

The majority of the ships were around the northern coast of the island. While overflying the bay of Famagusta, he noted another large ship and four smaller ones, which later turned out to be the British aircraft carrier *Hermes* and other British ships which had arrived there to evacuate British citizens in case of a conflict.

Captain Marneros then asked the Nicosia control tower to contact the military commander of Kyrenia and advise him of what they had seen on their radar. The reply from the commander was: *'All is quiet in Kyrenia…'* Not satisfied with that response, he then asked the controller to request that the general manager of Cyprus Airways divert back to Rome. But, he was ordered to land at Nicosia which he did at 03:55am local time.

Less than an hour after the arrival of flight CY317 the airport was subjected to a fierce bombardment. This resulted in the total destruction of Cpt. Marneros's aircraft 5B-DAE.

Spanish Splashabout - G-AVYD

15 September 1975 was rainy in Bilbao, Spain. Yankee Delta operated British Airways flight NS552, a scheduled service from Bilbao to London Heathrow Airport. Earlier in the day, the aircraft and crew had operated scheduled service NS55I from London to Bilbao, and after an uneventful flight had landed at Bilbao on Runway 10 at 12:31. At the time of landing, light rain was falling, and the runway was wet. The Commander nor the First Officer saw no standing water on the runway during the landing run.

While the aircraft was being prepared for the return, flight rain fell intermittently, varying in intensity from moderate to heavy but abating to light as the aircraft taxied out for take-off. Before starting up the crew requested the airfield information on RTF from Bilbao Tower and were passed the following at 13:21:30:

Surface Wind - calm:
Runway in use - 28;
QNH - 1014 mbs.

The Commander had given a full take-off briefing before the aircraft left London that morning. As permitted by normal company procedures, he curtailed his briefing at Bilbao andsimply called for:

Standard emergencies;
510 (normal) take-off power
engine relight switches on wet V1".

Start-up was normal, and at 13:37, the aircraft was cleared to taxi and to hold short of the runway because of landing traffic - a Caravelle. The crew watched the Caravelle land on Runway 10 and the Flight Engineer commented to his two colleagues on the considerable amount of water spray being thrown up at the rear of this aircraft during its landing run. The Commander remarked that he would assess the runway conditions while back-tracking to the take-off position from the taxiway entrance to the runway.

He noted a number of pools of standing water on the runway surface as the Trident back-tracked along the runway. Although he could not estimate their area or depth, the pools appeared to be well within the limits imposed for take-off using 510 (normal) power. As the greater part of the runway surface he had looked at was damp he did not change his take-off briefing.

The taxi drills were actioned by the First Officer and the Flight Engineer during this time, and 'runway items' were completed after the Commander turned the aircraft through 180° close to the threshold of Runway 28, aligned it on the

G-AVYD in full British Airways scheme. *[Author's Collection]*

Not strictly an accident, but Cyprus Airways' 5H-DAB was abandoned following the Turkish invasion of the northern part of the island. At the time of writing, there are plans to save the hulk and restore it for display. *[Simon Peters Collection]*

runway centre line, and selected the wheel brakes to park. A one hundred per cent thrust power setting was made, all engine indications were checked as correct, and the engine relight switches were selected 'ON' before the wheel brakes were released. The take-off run commenced at about 13:46, and the Captain piloted the aircraft.

According to crew statements taken after the accident, the aircraft accelerated normally; the First Officer called out the indicated airspeeds at eighty and one hundred knots knots and called 'Wet V' at 117 knots, then removed his hand from the throttles. At the time, or just after 'Wet V,' the Flight Engineer and the First Officer heard a noise, which the latter crew member attributed to the aircraft's entry into standing water. According to the flight engineer, the aircraft appeared to decelerate when he heard the noise.

The Commander has stated that as 'Wet V' was called, he felt a marked deceleration consistent with a loss of engine power, whereupon he immediately closed the throttles, called 'Abandon', deployed the airbrakes and lift dumpers and applied the wheel brakes fully. However, the flight engineer said all engine indications were normal before the throttles closed. On seeing a hand close the throttles, the First Officer selected emergency reverse thrust on the pod engines, checked the engine indications were correct and maintained the application of emergency reverse thrust until the aircraft eventually came to rest. The First Officer and the Commander checked the indicated pressures on the wheel brake gauges, which showed that the wheel brakes were fully applied. The initial deceleration felt satisfactory to the crew, then quickly deteriorated, and the First Officer formed the impression that the aircraft was aquaplaning.

According to the First Officer and Flight Engineer, the Commander commented on the poor deceleration rate. The Flight Engineer then noticed that the aircraft had begun to drift gradually to the left of the runway centreline, apparently due to a deliberate action by the Commander. Subsequently, it became evident to the Commander that he could not bring the aircraft to a halt within the runway confines. Some 200 to 300 metres before the end of the runway, he turned the aircraft to the left using nosewheel steering and applied a full left rudder. As the nosewheels ran off the runway onto the grass, the aircraft slewed to the left, then skidded broadside to the right for a short distance before it came to an abrupt stop at the side of the runway in a right wing-down attitude with the right wing tip close to the threshold lights of Runway 10.

As soon as the aircraft had come to rest, the First Officer shut down the engines and, on instructions from the Commander, operated the engine fire extinguishers. At the same time, the Flight Engineer carried out the emergency electrical shutdown drills. Evacuation drills were initiated, and the passengers left the aircraft reasonably orderly, the majority by sliding from the main exit doors and, foremost, the right overwing emergency exit. Catering equipment in the galleys came out of stowage during the accident, obstructing access to the forward emergency exit door and preventing using this exit and its slide during the evacuation. The Airport Fire Services were quickly on the scene and discharged extinguishers into the engines as a precautionary measure. They were followed by an ambulance and airport personnel who arrived in time to assist passengers from the aircraft. There was no fire, and the passengers and crew sustained no injuries.

In their efforts to recover the aircraft to get the runway operational as soon as possible, the Spanish authorities managed to inflict even more damage on

G-AVYD in the weeds adjacent to the runway at Bilbao.
[Simon Peters Collection]

the aircraft. By the time they were finished the state of the Trident was such that British Airways decided not to repair it. It remained at Bilbao for some time and was later broken up.

No Smoking Aboard the Aircraft - G-ARPC

On 28 December 1975 while parked on Stand A3 at London Heathrow Trident 1C of British Airways experienced a cabin fire thought to have been started by an electrical fault - the aircraft was written off.

Collision over Zagreb - G-AWZT.

As I have said earlier, British Airways operated twenty-six Trident 3s, which accrued 560,000 hours of trouble-free service with the airline. Twenty-five of the aircraft was retired after serving the airline well for eleven to fourteen years, but sadly, one example was to see a premature and horrific end to its days.

On the morning of Friday, 10 September 1976, British Airways' Trident 3B G-AWZT took off from Heathrow at 08.:32 (GMT). The flight, BE476, proceeded via West Europe and was cruising at 33,000 feet along airway Upper Blue 1 (UB1) whilst en route from Heathrow to Istanbul. On board were fifty-four passengers and nine crew. The commander that day was Captain Dennis Tann, with First Officers Brian Helm (P2) and Martin Flint (P3) alongside him.

In the mid-1970s, the Zagreb air traffic control region was one of the busiest in Europe despite being seriously understaffed and poorly equipped. The Zagreb VOR was a reporting point for a number of congested airways between northern Europe and southeastern Europe, the Middle East, and beyond. The airspace was divided into three sectors by altitude: the lower sector below 25,000 feet, the middle sector from 25,000–31,000 feet, and the upper sector above 31,000 feet.

On entering Yugoslav airspace from Austria, BA476 established radio contact with the Area Control Centre 'Upper Sector' in Zagreb on the frequency 134.45 MHz.

10:04:12:	Bealine 476:	Zagreb, Beeline 476, good afternoon'.
	Zagreb:	Bealine 476, good afternoon, go ahead".
10:04:19	Bealine 476:	476 Klagenfurt at 02, 330 estimating Zageb at 14.
	Zagreb:	Beeline 476, roger, call me passing Zagreb, flight level 330, Squalk Alpha 23121.
10:04:40:	Bealine 476:	2312 is coming.

No further calls were received from the Bealine 476, which was obliged to keep active listening on 134.45 MHz.

Immediately after the report to Zagreb Control, the crew heard a Turkish Airlines reporting to Zagreb Control its position over point 'Charlie', just ahead of was Zulu Tango at flight level 350. The cockpit voice recorder on the Trident recorded the comments of the crew that shortly afterwards, they saw the aircraft passing overhead in the opposite direction.

About twenty-five minutes before Zulu Tango was expected overhead Zagreb, an Inex Adria McDonnell Douglas DC-9 Series 32, YU-AJR, had taken off from Split in Yugoslavia with five crew and 108 passengers on board operating a German charter flight JP550 to Cologne. At 10:12, amid some confusion because of overloading in the Zagreb Air Traffic Control Centre that morning, Adria 550 was handed to the upper sector controller, Gradimir Tasic. As a result of the overloading, the fact that the aircraft was climbing through the Trident's cruising height was not clarified to the controller.

At around the same time, JP550 contacted middle-sector controller Bojan Erjavec asking for a higher flight level; the aircraft was at flight level 260, but FL280 and FL310 were unavailable, so Erjavec informed JP550 of the situation and offered flight level 350, which the pilots accepted. To get clearance for a higher level, obtaining permission from the upper-sector controller was necessary. Erjavec waved his hand to get Tasić's attention. Still, Tasić - who was working the upper sector on his own, as his colleague Mladen Hochberger had gone to search for Nenad Tepeš, Tasić's replacement who was running late, and was far too busy to be interrupted. Middle sector controller Gradimir Pelin was then instructed to coordinate the climb out for the DC-9 with Tasić.

According to Pelin, he walked to the upper sector console holding JP550's flight progress strip. He asked Tasić if the DC-9 could climb to FL350. Tasić took the strip from Pelin, looked at it, and then asked where the aircraft was. Pelin then pointed to a blip on the screen approaching Kostajnica. Tasić's response was, 'Yes, it could climb'. Pelin then noticed an aircraft on the screen coming from the direction of Metlika and asked Tasić about it, who said, 'Wait until they cross.' Pelin referred to the middle-sector screen to ensure he had identified the DC-9 positively on the upper-sector screen. He then returned to Tasić, and they both watched the targets pass each other. At this point, Tasić authorised JP550 to climb. Pelin then called out to Erjavec and said, 'Yes, climb it.' Upon Erjavec receiving the OK from Pelin, he instructed the DC-9 to climb to FL350. That was at 10:07:40.

At 10:12:03 JP550 called the Zagreb middle-sector controller to inform them that the aircraft was out of flight level 310. The last instructions given by Erjavec to JP550 were to call the upper-sector controller on 134.45 MHz and to stop squawking the assigned squawk code. By instructing JP550 to squawk Standby, Erjavec simply released a code allocated for the middle sector. The data tag for the DC-9 would now disappear from his screen, and the aircraft would become a point among many others. If everything about this handover had been normal, the DC-9 would have been given a new code on initial contact with the upper sector controller and positively identified on the upper sector screen with its flight number and altitude readout. But this was not a normal handover because of the ill-handled coordination for the climb. Also, Tasić was busy with other traffic, and JP550 did not immediately contact the upper-sector controller. This could have been because the frequency was busy, but the pilots

G-AWZT approaches its stand at London Heathrow. *[Authors Collection]*

might have delayed the call for unknown reasons.

When JP550 contacted the upper-sector controller at 10:14:04, it had reached the Zagreb VOR and was already climbing through flight level 325. The controller immediately asked for confirmation of the aircraft's level.

Tasic suddenly realised that a conflict existed with the Trident. Still, in his excitement to avert potential disaster, he broke into Serbo-Croat, informing the DC-9's crew that an aircraft was in front of them and to level off immediately. This unfortunate slip prevented the Trident's crew from having any warning of the ensuing danger. By the time the DC-9 had levelled off, it was cruising at exactly FL330.

Zulu Tango maintained a heading of 120-122° until two minutes fifty seconds before ZAG VOR at flight level 330, with a ground speed of 489 knots. It was flying along the airway centreline with a 1-2 km side deviation to the right due to a wind of 220°/45 knots.

At two minutes fifty seconds before the collision, the aircraft changed heading to 115°. Five seconds before the collision, the heading was 116°, maintained until the collision. From plotted data, it could be concluded that at the moment of impact, the aircraft was one and a half to two kilometres northeast of the high cone of ZAG VOR at flight level 330 and at a speed of 295 knots IAS.

As fate would have it, the DC-9 was now travelling from right to left across the Trident's bows at exactly the same height, with the two aircraft closing on each other at around 1,100 mph. At 10.14:41, the outer fifteen feet of the DC-9's left wing smashed through the forward fuselage and cockpit of the Trident at about window level, killing all three pilots instantly. The Trident then plummeted earthward out of control, spilling some of its contents as it fell. It impacted the ground near the village of Gaj, and all sixty-three people on board were killed.

The DC-9, meanwhile, also went out of control and partially broke up as the remains of its left wing erupted in a fireball and the wreckage impacted the ground in an area some four miles from the Trident. All 113 people on board the DC-9 perished.

Tasić attempted to call BA476 and instruct it to report passing the next waypoint at Našice but was answered by a different flight. Tasić continued to call BA476 and JP550, ignoring calls from other aircraft, but to no avail.

Meanwhile, a Lufthansa Boeing 737 was travelling eastbound on UB5 at flight level 290 (approximately 29,000 feet towards Zagreb, only fifteen miles behind the Trident The co-pilot saw the collision as a flash of lightning and afterwards, two aircraft fell towards the ground out of a ball of smoke. The Lufthansa captain, Josef Kröse, reported the sighting to Erjavec, the middle-sector controller.

A total of 176 people had died that morning, apparently as a result of the momentary lapse of the Zagreb ATC.

The official report of the accident determined that improper air traffic control operation was the probable cause. Immediately after the accident, a number of Zagreb's air traffic controllers were arrested and charged with criminal misconduct, with the possibility of twenty-year jail sentences if found guilty.

Eventually, all but one - Tasic - was was released and found not guilty. Tasic was left to shoulder all the blame, and in May 1977, he was sentenced to seven years imprisonment. Fortunately, appeals were made to have Tasic released, as it was felt that the whole system, as much as any individuals, was to blame for the disaster. After initially halving his jail sentence, Tasic was eventually released in November 1978, having served some two years and three months.

Chinese Whispers - B-274

Reports vary as to what was behind this incident on 14 March 1979. An unqualified pilot allegedly took the aircraft from was Beijing - although some state it was Guangzhou - and subsequently crashed after takeoff into a local factory, causing a large number of fatalities. Indications are there were twelve crew on board, and thirty were killed on the ground.

Beware of stuffed clouds - B-266

On 26 April 1982, CAAC flight 3303 crashed into a mountain, about sixty kilometres km SE of Guilin, on a flight from Guangzhou-Baiyun Airport. All 112 on board were killed. The aircraft, a 2E, was attached to the Chinese Air Force's 34th Air Division and operated for CAAC.

Brake! Brake! Brake!- B-260

On 22 February 1983 CAAC Airlines Trident 2E overshot the runway on landing at Fuzhou Airport, China, causing the landing gear to collapse. The aircraft was written off.

Unlawful Interference - B-296

Trident B-296, a 2E, was en route from Shenyang Airport to Shanghai-Hongqiao Airport on 5 May

1983 when six hijackers demanded to be taken to South Korea. In the process, a CAAC crew member was injured after being shot in the leg. The Trident landed on the US Army Camp Page runway at Chunchon. It overran the runway by about one hundred metres but did not sustain damage. The airliner, crew and passengers were later returned to China.

Two aircraft, One Space! - B-264

An Ilyushin Il-28 collided with the aircraft whilst taxiing at Guilin Airport, China, on 14 September 1983, resulting in 11 fatalities aboard the Trident.

Going for a Swim? - B-2218

Scheduled passenger flight CCA301 departed Guangzhou in the People's Republic of China at 00:33 (all times are UTC) on 31 August 1988 for Hong Kong International Airport using the callsign 'China 301'. The flight deck crew of the Trident 2E comprised two Captains, a Flight Engineer, a Navigator, a qualified Radio Operator and a Radio Operator under training. The Captain designated as the aircraft commander occupied the right-hand control seat and acted as a non-handling pilot, whilst the other Captain acted as the handling pilot from the left control seat. The crew consisted of three female cabin attendants and two male security officers in the passenger cabin. There were seventy-eight passengers on board. The planned flight time to Hong Kong International Airport was 30 minutes, and the cruising altitude was 10,000 feet.

At 00:43 China 301, whilst still in the Guangzhou FIR, contacted Hong Kong Approach Control on 119.1 MHz gave its position as SHILONG NDB at 10,000 feet and confirmed receipt of an ATIS Information Delta.

This was acknowledged by the approach controller, who instructed them to call twenty miles before RUHBT. The reporting point on A461 marked the Guangzhou/Hong Kong FIR boundary. At 00:45, China 301 contacted Hong Hong Approach again and advised of its intention to deviate twelve miles left of track to avoid cumulonimbus. The deviation was approved, and shortly afterwards, China 301 was told of weather returns showing on the approach radar in the letdown area associated with the runway 13 Instrument Guidance System (IGS). In ILS approach to runway 31, monitored by Precision Approach Radar (PAR) was offered and the following weather passed: *...the surface wind is between 090 to 140 degrees at 10 knots... heavy shower over the airfield...the visibility on runway 31 is 5,000 metres and on the IGS is 3,000 metres...advise.*

China 301 elected to make an ILS approach. The time was 00:48. At 01:07, China 301 was

The remains of B-2218, at the base of the sea wall at Hong Kong bordering Kowloon Bay...

heading 270 degrees at 5,000 feet, approaching the runway 31 centreline from the east. To facilitate a departure from runway 13, the controller intended to take the aircraft through the centreline before initiating a right turn onto the localiser. At 01:09, the aircraft was told to turn right onto a heading of 360 degrees to intercept the localiser; however, a left turn was requested to avoid cumulonimbus. This was approved, and at 01:12, China 301 was at 4500 feet, heading 360 degrees to intercept the localiser and cleared for an ILS approach. The latest weather was then broadcast: .....*wind 120 to 150 degrees..5 to 10 knots..runway surface wet.. visibility 4500 metres in rain...* China 301 acknowledged the weather broadcast and confirmed its intention to use runway 31.

At 01:14, when the aircraft was established on the localiser, it was again cleared for an ILS approach and informed that PAR would monitor the approach. This was acknowledged, and after a frequency change to 119.5 Mhz, two-way contact with Hong Kong PAR was confirmed at 01:15, at which time the aircraft was approximately ten to twelve nautical miles from touchdown. Although the precision radar controller could see from his adjacent approach radar that China 301 was maintaining the localiser centreline, he could not gain radar contact on the PAR due to rain clutter. He immediately advised China 301 that there was no precision radar contact - advised the surface wind was 090/07 knots - and cleared the flight to land.

The last recorded transmission from China 301 was the acknowledgement of this clearance at 01:16:59.

The aircraft's right outboard trailing edge wing flap struck the innermost approach light, twenty-one feet above MSL and twelve before the runway promontory. Almost simultaneously, the right main landing gear tyres struck the runway promontory just below the sloping lip of the sea wall, and three of the four tyres on the axle burst. The complete right main landing gear with its support structure, upper and lower wing sections, and the inboard wing flap and flap tracks were then torn from the wing.

The left main gear touched the paved surface approximately two metres from the sea wall. The aircraft then bounced and continued to track just to the right of the runway centreline until it contacted the ground again, approximately six hundred metres down the runway. From this point, it started to yaw to the right, departed from the runway and slid sideways across the grass toward the parallel taxiway. The yaw continued past the travel direction until the aircraft slid almost completely sideways. As it traversed the grassed runway strip, the left main and nose landing gears collapsed. The aircraft continued until it crossed the parallel taxiway, slid

...the nose broke off and the tail ended up resting on the rocks. *[Both the late John Stride collection]*

over the sea wall and fell off the runway promontory into Kowloon Bay.

When it came to a halt, it was resting in a slightly nose-high attitude, heading East North-East, with the rear extremity of the fuselage supported on a ledge of stone blocks at the base of the sea wall. It had travelled 1485 metres from the point of first impact with the runway promontory.

The main part of the fuselage remained above the water but the rear of the passenger cabin was partially submerged. The flight compartment and the front portion of the forward passenger cabin remained attached to the fuselage only by control cables and secondary structure and drooped steeply down into the water with the nose resting on the sea bed. At the rear of the aircraft the centre engine detached from the airframe and a fire started in the centre engine intake duct. A thin layer of fuel spread over the surrounding water.

At 01:19 was the duty officer at the Airport Fire Services substation, on the northern edge of the runway promontory, saw a landing aircraft pass by in an unusual attitude on the runway and pressed the crash alarm. As a result, it took less than a minute for the rescue services to arrive on the scene.

The fire in the centre engine intake duct was soon extinguished by a fireman climbing onto the fuselage with a handline and spraying water into the intake. Meanwhile foam was sprayed over the fuel floating on the surrounding water and the wreck secured by lines to the shore.

The passengers escaped from the aircraft through the forward right overwing emergency exit and the midships passenger door. Some stood on the wing in the heavy rain and waited to be rescued, others jumped into the water and a few were able to scramble ashore. Two remained trapped in the wreckage and were extricated by the rescue personnel. Forty-one of those rescued were taken on board the fire services rescue launch and five on to junks that happened to be in the vicinity. The land rescue crews rescued the remainder to the runway promontory.

The two security officers and one cabin attendant were seated in the first two rows of the front passenger cabin and were cut off from the rest of the passenger compartment by the break in the fuselage. They could not help in the evacuation and left the wreck through a break in the side of the fuselage. The remaining two cabin attendants were seated at the amidships passenger door.

One was rendered unconscious and later rescued from the water by emergency services personnel. The other opened the midships passenger door and directed the evacuation of the passengers. After checking that the passenger cabin was clear she left the aircraft.

The rescued passengers were taken to a First Aid Point, and the uninjured were transported to the airport terminal building. Those suffering from injuries were removed directly to the Queen Elizabeth Hospital for treatment. One passenger later died in hospital from his injuries.

Divers attempted to enter the submerged flight deck, but the abysmal visibility hampered them in the polluted water, the substantial current and wreckage blocking the entrance to the flight deck. When entry was finally gained approximately seventy-five minutes after the accident occurred, all flight deck crew members were found drowned.

Despite intensive investigations by the Hong Kong Civil Aviation Department. it was thought there was insufficient evidence to determine the cause of the accident.

Having converted to visual references at some point before Decision Height, the commander elected to continue the approach even though heavy rain had caused a sudden marked deterioration in the visual references in the final stages.

There was no conclusive evidence that the aircraft encountered significant windshear on the approach but given the meteorological conditions that existed at the time it cannot be ruled out, and therefore windshear may have been a contributory factor in destabilising the approach.

Runway Excursion - B-2208.

On 22 March 1990 Trident B-2208 was flying from Shanghai-Hongqiao Airport to Guilin-Qifengling Airport in China. On board were one hundred and seven people. The Trident approached high and touched down far down the runway at Guilin Airport. The aircraft overran the runway onto soft ground. The runway was very wet following heavy rainfall. There were no fatalities, but the aircraft was written off.

Chapter Ten

The Twilight Years

The beginning of the Trident's end came in the late 1970s, when ICAO began drafting new noise regulations that would require first- and second-generation jet airliners to fit hush kits to the engines. ICAO Annex 16, Chapter 2 required all Stage 1 aircraft to be phased out by the mid-1980s. These regulations would go into effect on 1 January 1986. British Airways, the type's main operator, saw the refits as not viable and instead chose to phase the Trident out of their fleet in 1985, the final flights were made on 31 December 1985.

By 1975, British Airways had introduced its first 'air buses' into service on its European network in the form of the Lockheed TriStar. This, combined with the merger and an economic downturn, led the airline to experience significant overcapacity. In 1974, BA made efforts to sell up to 13 of its Trident 1s, particularly in the Far East, but these came to nothing, and so it was decided to retire some Trident 1Cs. Seven aircraft were ferried to Prestwick for storage, where later they were broken up. Amongst these, Trident 1Cs was the prototype G-ARPA, which was scrapped in early 1976. Additionally, one Trident 1C, G-ARPU, was scrapped at Heathrow.

BA began taking delivery of its first Boeing 737s in early 1980, and the gradual decline of its Trident fleet began. The used 1Es it had acquired were withdrawn in 1980 and broken up at Heathrow in 1981, including the prototype G-ASWU. Trident 1E G-AVYE operated British Airways' last 1E service on 30 September 1980, and was flown to Wroughton in April 1981 at the request of John Bagley, the Collections Manager to be preserved as part of the Science Museum collection.

More Trident 1s and the first Trident 2s were withdrawn in late 1981; the first four 2s were broken up at Heathrow in 1982. The same year, G-AVFB was ferried to Duxford for preservation with

Murder Row - the infamous cul-de-sac at BEAs Heathrow maintenance base at Heathrow where a number of Tridents were no-so-discreetly scrapped. *[Author's Collection]*

the Duxford Aviation Society, whilst Trident 1 G-ARPH joined the British Airways collection at Cosford Aerospace Museum. Fox Bravo has since been restored to her former BEA glory, repainted in the airline's classic 'Red Square' colours of the early 1960s.

During the early 1980s, the Trident found favour with a new employer, assorted airport fire services, and aircraft were delivered to various UK regional airfields to be used as non-destructive trainers. Far more sinister was the interest that the CAA's Fire Service Training School at Teesside showed in the Trident, for they had every intention of setting fire to its charges. The first Trident, G-ARPD, was flown to Teesside in August 1981 and, in all, the school destroyed eight Tridents, including four 1s, one 2, and two 3s.

When British Airways' Boeing 757 operations began in January 1983, its Trident fleet was down to thirty-six aircraft, including three 1s, nine 2s, and twenty-four 3s. The 757 was so much slower - by around twenty knots - than the Trident on final approach, so ATC found that separation had to be increased to 3.5 miles to prevent the Trident from being too close inside the outer marker. The arrival of the 757s further enhanced the airline's 'new generation' fleet and paved the way for Trident 3 withdrawals to begin, as well as the withdrawal of more 1s and 2s.

Retirement brought forth incidents, some amusing. When one crew found itself operating an end-of-the-day Shuttle flight into Manchester, they noted that it would be the aircraft's last, as it was slated for retirement to the Manchester Museum of Science and Industry for preservation. The next morning, the Shuttle service was to be taken over by company 757s. The local weather had other thoughts. The morning dawned foggy, and visibility was outside the 757's operating limits, so the Trident crew were rapidly called upon to resurrect the Trident and to fly four Category 3 landings at Heathrow and Manchester that day!

BAs' last Trident 1C revenue flight took place on 4 April 1983 when G-ARPZ operated the Shuttle service from Glasgow to Heathrow. The last Trident 1 flight occurred on 12 December 1983 when G-ARPO was ferried to the CAA Fire School at Teesside as 'Speedbird 9614M'. Papa Oscar was then left to the destructive devices of the firemen and was eventually burned.

The first Trident 3, G-AWZA, was withdrawn in late 1983, and six of the variant were broken up at Heathrow during 1984, whilst two others were delivered to fire services.

By early 1985, BA's operational Trident fleet consisted of just three 2s and 15 3s. During the early part of 1985, six 2s were ferried to Southend for immediate scrapping by contractors. The last two Trident 2 positioning flights occurred on 13 February, when G-AVFE and' FO respectively positioned to Belfast for the airport's fire department and Southend for scrapping , leaving just G- AVFG to soldier on for two more months.

Oh Dearie Me!

At least one Trident achieved immortality of a kind when it prominently appeared in the opening title sequence of a British Comedy TV series *The High Life* that was written by and starred Forbes Masson and Alan Cumming as Steve McCracken and Sebastian Flight respectively.

The series followed the cabin crew at the fictional airline, Air Scotia, flying out of Prestwick Airport. The crew consisted of the camp, alcohol-loving, narcissistic and vindictive steward, Sebastian Flight ; his sex-obsessed colleague, Steve McCracken; their uptight, antagonistic chief stewardess, Shona Spurtle; and the eccentric pilot, Captain Hilary Duff. Sebastian and Steve longed to be promoted to long-haul flights to see exotic locations, instead of the current short-haul trips with their superior Shona, played by Siobhan Redmond,

This unidentified, but very smart-looking enginelessTrident represents quite a number that were used by assorted fire services. *[Authors Collection]*

The pair of Tridents retired into the care of John Bagley and the Science Museum's outstation at Wroughton. Furthest from the camera is 1E-140 G-AVYE that was scrapped in June 1989, after the Museum acquired what it saw as a better representative in the form of 3B-101 G-AWZM on 28 February 1986. *[Author's Collection]*

whom they described as 'Hitler in tights', 'Mussolini in Micromesh' and 'Goebbels in a Gossard'. The deranged pilot, Captain Duff, played by Patrick Ryecart, would need to be frequently reminded who he was, where the cockpit was and where he was flying to by a single word 'Heathrow'. All very surreal, but great fun, and a lot closer to the truth than many thought!

Despite its short run, it is remembered for Steve and Sebastian's joint catchphrase: 'Oh dearie me!' and for the opening sequence, which featured the cast performing a dance routine to the title song. At the time it was broadcast, I was working for Dan-Air and there were very strong rumours going around that Masson and Cumming did their research on our Heathrow-Inverness service!

There were also rumours circulating over the years that Dan-Air considered obtaining the surviving Iraqi Airways fleet to supplement their Comet operations. Tales have surfaced that at least one Trident Sales Brochure was spotted at their mainenance base of Lasham, but nothing has been discovered to conclusively prove this rumour.

The third and last Trident 3B operator was the Zairean airline Air Charter Service (ACS), which acquired five Trident 3Bs from British Airways during 1984, 1985 and 1986, as the airline retired the last of its trijets. The five aircraft were operated on passenger and cargo charter flights on behalf of Zairean oil companies, operating mainly in Africa and the Middle East. It is understood that the aircraft did operate with cargo on the main deck, loaded through the narrow passenger doors. By 1988, all the ACS machines were thought to have been

9Q-CTM - the former G-AWZC - of ACS. *[Authors Collection]*

BEA

Appendix One

Production List

MSN	Variant	Reg.	F/F	Del.	Oper.	WFU	Remarks
2101	1C	G-ARPA	09/01/62	18/08/65	BEA	07/02/75	Orig reg with UK CAA 13/04/61. To British A/W 01/04/74. Std Preswick. B/U recorded as 01/04/76. Recorded as some parts preserved since 2008 at The Heathrow Trident collection.
2102	1C	G-ARPB	20/05/62	30/04/64	BEA	1975	Orig reg with UK CAA 13/04/61. Lsd HSA. Ret. to BEA12/67. To British A/W. 01/04/74. Std Preswick 01/04/76. To British Airports Authority 1/78. B/U 01/85.
2103	1C	G-ARPC	25/08/62	09/09/64	BEA	28/12/75	Orig reg with UK CAA 13/04/61. To British A/W 01/04/74. W/O 28/12/75.
2104	1C	G-ARPD	17/01/63	08/01/66	BEA	30/04/81	Orig reg with UK CAA 13/04/61. To British A/W 01/04/74. To Teeside 27/8/81. To Fire School. Burnt.
2105	1C	G-ARPE	30/06/63	10/07/64	BEA	1975	Orig reg with UK CAA 13/04/61. To British A/W 01/04/74. Std Preswick. B/U 05/76.
2106	1C	G-ARPF	18/10/63	19/12/63	BEA	1975	Orig reg with UK CAA 13/04/61. To British Orig reg with UK CAA 13/04/61. To British A/W 01/04/74. Std Preswick. B/U 05/76.
2107	1C	G-ARPG	09/01/64	19/02/64	BEA	31/03/75	Orig reg with UK CAA 13/04/61. To British Orig reg with UK CAA 13/04/61. To British A/W 01/04/74. Std Preswick. B/U 05/76.
2108	1C	G-ARPH	08/03/64	25/03/64	BEA	26/03/82	Orig reg with UK CAA 13/04/61. To British A/W 01/04/74. To RAF Museum, Cosford 02/04/82. Scrapped 01/05/2006. Nose Section preserved at Museum of Flight East Fortune Scotland.
2109	1C	G-ARPI	14/04/64	02/05/64	BEA	18/0672	Orig reg with UK CAA 13/04/61. To British A/W 01/04/74. W/O 18/06/72.
2110	1C	G-ARPJ	01/05/64	26/05/64	BEA	03/75	Orig reg with UK CAA 13/04/61. To British A/W 01/04/74. Std Preswick. B/U 05/76.
2111	1C	G-ARPK	13/06/64	26/06/64	BEA	27/03/82	Orig reg with UK CAA 13/04/61. To British A/W 01/04/74. Bought 3/82 by Manchester Airport Authority used as fire trainer, b/u 14/03/06.
2112	1C	G-ARPL	27/07/64	06/08/64	BEA	26/03/82	Orig reg with UK CAA 13/04/61. To British A/W 01/04/74.To Edinburgh Airport Fire Service. Scrapped.
2113	1C	G-ARPM	28/09/64	09/10/64	BEA	03/75	Orig reg with UK CAA 13/04/61. To British A/W 01/04/74. Std Preswick. B/U 05/76.
2114	1E-101	9K-ACF	02/11/64	19/03/66	Kuwait A/W	01/08/80	Orig reg with UK CAA 01/10/64 as G-

							ASWU for HSA. To Kuwait A/W 23/11/65. To BEA 04/02/72. To Cyprus A/W 5B-DAD 12/03/73. To British A/W 12/05/77 as G-ASWU B/U LHR 05/81.
2115	1C	G-ARPN	21/11/64	04/12/64	BEA	26/03/82	Orig reg with UK CAA 13/04/61. To British A/W 01/04/74. To Aberdeen 27/03/82 for Airport Fire Servce..
2116	1C	G-ARPO	13/01/65	31/01/65	BEA	16/03/83	Orig reg with UK CAA 13/04/61. To British A/W 01/04/74. To Teeside 12/12/83 for Fire School. Preserved at North East Land, Sea and Air Museums Sunderland, UK in Northeast Airlines (UK) livery.
2117	1C	G-ARPP	12/02/65	25/02/65	BEA	23/02/83	Orig reg with UK CAA 13/04/61. To British A/W 01/04/74. Previously preserved as a fire training airframe at Glasgow Airport from Feb 1983 until May 2005 Broken Up. The cockpit section on display at the Dumfries and Galloway Aviation Museum, Scotland, Preserved Aug 2009, at the Solway Aviation Museum, cockpit section only.
2118	1E-101	9K-ACG	09/06/65	27/05/66	Kuwait A/W	30/06/66	Orig reg with UK CAA 01/10/64 as G-ASWV for HSA. To Kuwait A/W 23/11/65 W/O near Kuwait City 30/06/66, with 72 pax and 11 crew on board.
2119	1C	G-ARPR	01/04/65	12/04/65	BEA	31/03/81	Orig reg with UK CAA 13/04/61.To British A/W 01/04/74. To Teeside 16/09/81. Burnt.
2120	1C	G-ARPS	23/05/65	01/06/65	BEA	07/69	Orig reg with UK CAA 13/04/61. dbr at LHR after an electrical fire broke out in the cabin whilst parked W/O 29/07/69.
2121	1C	G-ARPT	30/06/65	09/07/65	BEA	03/07/68	Orig reg with UK CAA 13/04/61.DBR 3 Jul 1968 at LHR after being struck by a BKS Air Airspeed Ambassador that had lost control and crashed on the apron of terminal 1. The Ambassadors wing ripped through the rear fuselage of the Trident, tearing the aircraft in half.
2122	1C	G-ARPU	13/08/65	27/08/65	BEA	11/74	Orig reg with UK CAA 13/04/61. To British A/W 01/04/74. Std LHR. B/U 11/75.
2123	1C	G-ARPW	07/10/65	15/10/65	BEA	26/03/82	Orig reg with UK CAA 13/04/61. To British A/W 01/04/74. To Teeside 26/03/82 for Fire School. Burnt.
2124	1C	G-ARPX	13/05/66	25//05/66	BEA	23/10/82	Orig reg with UK CAA 13/04/61. To British A/W 01/04/74. To Perth 29/11/82 for Air Service Training. Broken up Sep 1996.
2125	1E	YI-AEA	07/09/65	01/10/66	Iraqi A/W	01/06/77	Std Baghdad and poss W/O 1991.
2126	1C	G-ARPY	03/06/66	-	BEA	-	Orig reg with UK CAA 13/04/61. Not delivered. W/O near Felthorpe Norfolk 06/03/66 while on test fight. 4 crew killed.
2127	1E	YI-AEB	17/02/66	05/03/66	Iraqi A/W	19/04/77	Std Baghdad. Possibly W/O 1991.
2128	1C	G-ARPZ	22/06/66	01/07/66	BEA	04/83	Orig reg with UK CAA 13/04/61. To British A/W 01/04/74.To Dunsfold for RFD Aviation. WFU 20/04/83. B/U 09/2000.

2129	1E	YI-AEC	27/04/66	13/05/66	i A/W	08/06/77	Std Baghdad. Possiby W/O 1991.
2130	1E-103	AP-ATK	31/11/65	01/03/66	PIA	-	Orig reg with UK CAA 14/01/66 for HSA. F/F as G-ATNA. To Pakistan 21/02/66. To CAAC as 232. To People's Liberation Army Air Force as 50056.
2131	1E-103	AP-ATL	16/03/66	11/04/66	PIA	12/09/71	To CAAC as 256. W/O 12/09/71.
2132	1E-103	AP-ATM	26/05/66	17/06/66	PIA	1990?	To CAAC as 236. To People's Liberation Army Air Force as 50050. To Datam Shan Museum.
2133	1E-103	AP-AUG	24/08/66	14/02/67	PIA	-	To People's Liberation Army Air Force as 50152.
2134	1E-101	9K-ACH	19/10/66	21/12/66	A/W	22/07/74	To Cyprus A/W as 5B-DAE. W/O 22/07/74.
2135	1E-140	4R-ACN	28/05/69	19/07/69	Air Ceylon	09/07/78	Orig registered G-AVYA to Channel A/W 13/11/67. Reg ntu. . To Ceylon 11/11/68. Stored Columbo.
2136	1E-140	G-AVYB	13/02/68	13/05/68	Channel A/W	31/08/80	Orig registered to Channel A/W 13/11/67. To Northeast A/W. To British A/W. B/U LHR 08/81. Fusleage to MoD.
2137	1E-110	G-AVYC	15/10/69	3/01/69	BKS A/T	31/07/80	Orig registered to Channel A/W 13/11/67. To HSA 13/11/68. To Northeast A/W. 08/12/71. To British A/W 01/04/74. B/U LHR 04/81
2138	1E-110	G-AVYD	17/02/69	05/03/69	BKS A/T	5/09/75	Orig registered to Channel A/W 13/11/67. To HSA 13/11/68. To Northeast A/W. 03/12/71. W/O Bilbao Airport, Spain 15/09/75, with 110 pax and 7 crew aboard.
2139	1E-140	G-AVYE	23/04/68	14/06/68	Channel A/W	30/09/80	Orig registered to Channel A/W 13/11/67. To BEA 01/02/72. To British A/W. To Science Museum, Wroughton 24//04/81. B/U 06/89.
2140	2E-101	G-AVFA	27/07/67	23/12/69	BEA	29/03/83	Orig registered 0102/67. To British A/W. 01/04/74. B/U. LHR 01/84.
2141	2E-101	G-AVFB	02/11/67	06/06/68	BEA	27/03/82	Orig registered 0102/67. To Cyprus Airways as 5B-DAC 19/06/72. Ret British A/W 12/05/77/ To Duxford Aviation Society 13/06/82.
2142	2E-101	G-AVFC	03/01/68	0608/68	BEA	23/10/81	Orig registered 01/02/67. To British A/W. 01/04/74. B/U LHR 1982.
2143	2E-101	G-AVFD	15/0368	16/04/68	BEA	22/03/82	Orig registered 01/02/67. To British A/W. 01/04/74. B/U LHR 04/82.
2144	2E-101	G-AVFE	19/04/68	08/05/68	BEA	08/02/85	Orig registered 01/02/67. To British A/W. 01/04/74. To Belfast 13/02/85 for Fire Service.Broken up Apr 2019 leaving only the cockpit & forward fuselage.
2145	2E-101	G-AVFF	14/05/68	30/05/68	BEA	30/11/84	Orig registered 01/02/67. To British A/W. 01/04/74. To Southend10/01/85. B/U 01/85.
2146	2E-101	G-AVFG	19/06/68	04/07/68	BEA	25/04/85	Orig registered 01/02/67. To British A/W. 01/04/74. To British A/W Ops training. Preserved at London Heathrow as an instructional airframe for British Airways engineers from 1985 until September 1990, painted into 'British Airways Landor' livery. To LHR Fire Service 09/90 until 03/2000.Used as a TV prop to replicate a plane crash for the British TV drama 'Always and Everyone' in March 2000. To Manchester as a fire training

							airframe from April 2000 until May 2013 with fake registration 'G-SMOKE'. Broken up May 2013
2147	2E-101	G-AVFH	17/07/68	01/08/68	BEA	24/10/81	Orig registered 01/02/67. To British A/W. 01/04/74. B/U LHR 05/82. Forward Fuselage to Mosquito Aircraft Museum.
2148	2E-101	G-AVFI	06/0868	27/11/68	BEA	11/09/81	Orig registered 01/02/67. To British A/W. 01/04/74. B/U LHR 05/82.
2149	2E-101	G-AVGJ	02/10/68	21/12/68	BEA	26/03/82	Orig registered 01/02/67. To British A/W. 01/04/74. To British A/W. To Teeside 24/06/82 for Fire School. Burnt.
2150	2E-101	G-AVFK	01/11/68	17/01/69	BEA	28/12/81	Orig registered 01/02/67. To British A/W. 01/04/74. WFU Heathrow Dec 1981. B/U 5/82. Fuselage, minus vertical fin and partial wings to Metropolitan Police Vickers Row, Hounslow Heath May 1982 for use as an anti-terrorist trainer. Moved to Shawbury, then Valley by 1997 and Lyneham in 1998. Supposedly scrapped at Lyneham 2011 but has been reported as early as 2001. Was painted blue and red when with Met Police.
2151	2E-101	G-AVFL	31/01/69	18/02/69	BEA	05/12/84	Orig registered 01/02/67. To British A/W. 01/04/74. To Southend 31/01/85. B/U 02/85.
2152	2E-101	G-AVFM	25/03/69	26/04/69	BEA	28/11/83	Orig registered 01/02/67. To British A/W. 01/04/74. To Bristol for Brunel College13/01/84. Broken up May 2004. Preserved at DGX 16 Apr 2019, at the South Wales Aviation Museum (SWAM), cockpit section only
2153	2E-101	G-AVFN	07/05/69	25/05/69	BEA	08/12/84	Orig registered 01/02/67. To British A/W. 01/04/74. To Southend 10/01/85. B/U 01/85.
2154	2E-101	5B-DAA	28/08/69	17/09/69	Cyprus A/W	01/85	To British Airways as G-AZXM 28/06/72. To British Airways 01/04/74. To Southend 04/02/85. B/U 02/85.
2155	2E-101	5B-DAB	23/04/70	01/05/70	Cyprus A/W	22/07/74	W/O 22/07/74.
2156	2E-101	G-AVFO	22/06/70	23/06/70	BEA	31/01/85	Orig registered 01/02/67. To British A/W. 01/04/74. To Southend 13/02/85. B/U 02/85.
2157	2E-107	240	21/10/72	02/12/70	CAAC	1990?	Orig reg with UK CAA 29/09/71 To HSA. F/F as G-AZFT. Transferred to China 15/1272 and re reg as B-2201. Std Bejing. B/U 1991
2158	2E-107	242	30/12/72	08/02/73	CAAC	early 1991	Orig reg with UK CAA 29/09/71. To HSA. F/F as G-AZFU.Transferred to China 16/03/73 and re reg as B-2202. Std Tianjn.Preserved at the 21st Century Hotel in Beijing, China as a nightclub venue. Preserved Changping, Beijing, China 2003, at the Beijing Air and Space Museum, forward fuselage & wing stubs only.
2159	2E-107	244	19/05/73	03/07/73	CAAC	31/08/88	Orig reg with UK CAA 29/09/71. To HSA. F/F as G-AZFV. Transferred to China 23/07/73 and re reg B-2218. W/O 31/08/88.
2160	2E-107	246	04/07/73	19/08/73	CAAC	1990?	Orig reg with UK CAA 29/09/71. To HSA. F/F as G-AZFW. Re reg B-2219.

							Std Guangzhou. Known preserved Mar 2024, as an instructional airframe at the Guangzhou Civil Aviation College Shijiazhuang, China Mar 2024.
2161	2E-107	248	05/09/73	26/10/73	CAAC	1990?	Orig reg with UK CAA 29/09/71. To HSA. F/F as G-AZFX. Re reg B-2223. Std Shenyang. B/U 1991
2162	2E-107	250	09/11/73	06/01/74	CAAC	1987?	Orig reg with UK CAA 29/09/71. To HSA. F/F as G-AZFY Re reg B-2212. Std Shanghai. B/U 1991
2163	2E-107	B-252	21/06/74	06/06/74	CAAC	1990?	Orig reg with UK CAA 29/09/71. To HSA. F/F as G-BABP. Re reg B-2214. Std Bejing. B/U 1991.
2164	2E-107	B-254	24/08/74	16/10/74	CAAC	1990?	Orig reg with UK CAA 29/09/71. To HSA. F/F as G-BABR. Re reg B-2209. Std Bejing. B/U 1992.
2165	2E-107	B-256	25/10/74	21/12/74	CAAC	22/03/90	Orig reg with UK CAA 29/09/71. To HSA. F/F as G-BABS Re reg B-2208. W/O 22/03/90.
2166	2E-107	B-258	31/12/74	03/03/75	CAAC	1990?	Orig reg with UK CAA 28/02/72. To HSA. F/F as G-BABT. To China 07/03/75 and re reg as B-2215. Std Bejing. B/U 1990.
2167	2E-107	B-260	08/02/75	01/04/75	CAAC	27/02/83	Orig reg with UK CAA 21/08/72 To HSA. F/F as G-BABU. To China 11/04/75. W/O 27/02/83
2168	2E-107	B-262	31/03/75	22/05/75	CAAC	1990?	Orig reg with UK CAA 21/08/72. To HSA. F/F as G-BABV. To China 03/06/75 and re reg as B-2203. Std Bejing. B/u 1991.
2169	2E-108	B-264	24/10/75	07/12/75	CAAC	14/0983	Orig reg with UK CAA 28/11/72. To HSA. F/F as G-BAJF. To China 22/12/75. W/O 14/09/83.
2170	2E-108	B-266	02/12/75	24/01/76	CAAC	26/04/82	Orig reg with UK CAA 28/11/72. To HSA. F/F as G-BAJG. To China 06/02/76. W/O 26/04/82 near Guilin. All 104 pax and 8 crew killed.
2171	2E-108	B-272	12/01/76	06/03/76	CAAC	-	Orig reg with UK CAA 28/11/72. To HSA. F/F as G-BAJH. To China 18/03/76. To People's Liberation Army Air Force and re reg 50052. Known Ppeserved Haidian District, Beijing, China 1994,
2172	2E-108	B-274	20/02/76	15/04/76	CAAC	14/03/79	Orig reg with UK CAA 28/11/72. To HSA. F/F as G-BAJI. To China 03/05/76. W/O 14/06/79.
2172	2E-108	B-276	31/03/76	25/05/76	CAAC	1990?	Orig reg with UK CAA 28/11/72. To HSA. F/F as G-BAJJ. Re reg as B-2213. Preserved Changping, Beijing, China, at the Beijing Air and Space Museum until being scrapped in March 1997.
2174	2E-108	B-278	13/05/76	03/07/76	CAAC	-	Orig reg with UK CAA 28/11/72. To HSA. F/F as G-BAJK. To CAF. Re reg 50158. B.U 1998.
2175	2E-108	B-280	30/06/76	08/09/76	CAAC	early 1991	Orig reg with UK CAA 03/01/74. To HSA.F/F as G-BBVS. Re reg as B-2204. Std Tainjin. Preserved as an instructional airframe for the Civil Aviation University of China
2176	2E-108	B-282	24/08/76	30/10/76	CAAC	1990?	Orig reg with UK CAA 03/01/74. F/F as

							G-BBVT. Re reg as B-2205. Std Shenyang. B/U 1992.
2177	2E-108	B-284	28/09/76	24/01/77	CAAC	1990?	Orig reg with UK CAA 03/01/74. F/F as G-BBVU. Re reg as B-2216. Std Tainjin.Preserved as an instructional airframe for the Guangzhou Civil Aviation College
2178	2E-108	B-286	03/11/76	18/01/77	CAAC	1990?	Orig reg with UK CAA 03/01/74. F/F as G-BBVV. Re reg as B-2210. Std Nanjin.
2179	2E-108	B-288	31/12/76	01/04/77	CAAC	1990?	Orig reg with UK CAA 03/01/74. F/F as G-BBVW. Re reg as B-2217. Std Guangzhou. B/U 1991
2180	2E-108	B-290	04/02/77	30/04/77	CAAC	1990?	Orig reg with UK CAA 03/01/74. F/F as G-BBVX. Re reg as B-2211. Std Shanghai. BU 1992
2181	2E-108	B-292	23/03/77	13/06/77	CAAC	early 1991	Orig reg with UK CAA 03/01/74. F/F as G-BBVY. Re reg as B-2206. Std Tainjin. Preserved Haidian District, Beijing, China 1994,
2182	2E-108	B-294	13/06/77	15/08/77	CAAC	1990?	Orig reg with UK CAA 03/01/74. F/F as G-BBVZ. Re reg as B-2207. Std Tainjin. Preserved at Civil Aviation Museum, Beijing, China. Preserved Enping, Jiangmen, Guangdong Province, China, on a lakeside plinth.
2183	2E-108	B-296	13/07/77	25/0977	CAAC	1990?	Orig reg with UK CAA 03/01/74. F/F as G-BBWA. Re reg as B-2220. Std Dalian.
2184	2E-108	B-298	24/08/77	29/10/77	CAAC	1990?	Orig reg with UK CAA 03/01/74. F/F as G-BBWB. Re reg as B-2221. Std Shenyang. B/U 1991
2185	2E-108	B-263	07/10/77	11/10/77	CAAC	-	Orig reg with UK CAA 03/01/74. F/F as G-BBWD. To People's Liberation Army BU 1991.
2186	2E-108	B-265	07/11/77	20/01/78	CAAC	-	Orig reg with UK CAA 03/01/74. F/F as G-BBWE To People's Liberation Army Air Force. Re reg 50054. Preserved

50055 of the People's Liberation Army Air Force. *[Authors Collection]*

							Chengdu, Sichuan, China, at the Moon Bay Park until being scrapped in 2004.
2187	2E-108	B-267	13/01/78	02/04/78	CAAC	-	Orig reg with UK CAA 03/01/74. F/F as G-BBWF. To People's Liberation Army Air Force. Re reg 50057. Preserved Changsha, Hunan, China 2021, as a memorial, previously preserved elsewhere in Changsha as an advertisement billboard at a shopping complex since 1999.
2188	2E-108	B-269	16/02/78	28/04/78	CAAC	-	Orig reg with UK CAA 03/01/74. F/F as G-BBWG. To People's Liberation Army Air Force. Re reg 50055. WFU 10/92
2189	2E-108	B-271	17/04/78	17/07/78	CAAC	-	Orig reg with UK CAA 03/01/74. F/F as G-BBWH To People's Liberation Army Air Force. Re reg 50053.
2301	3B-101	G-AWYZ	11/12/69	23/03/72	BEA	16/10/83	Orig reg with UK CAA 14/01/69 To British A/W 01/04/74. B/U LHR 06/84.
2302	3B-101	G-AWZA	09/03/70	11/05/71	BEA	23/10/83	Orig reg with UK CAA 14/01/69. To British A/W 01/04/74. B/U LHR 01/84.
2303	3B-101	G-AWZB	18/08/70	24/02/71	BEA	05/11/83	Orig reg with UK CAA 14/01/69. To British A/W 01/04/74. B/U LHR 06/84
2304	3B-101	G-AWZC	24/12/70	18/02/71	BEA	1987?	Orig reg with UK CAA 14/01/69. To British A/W 01/04/74. Last British A/W service 31/10/84. To ACS (Zaire) as 9Q-CTM. B/U 1989?
2305	3B-101	G-AWZD	05/03/71	08/04/71	BEA	1988?	Orig reg with UK CAA 14/01/69. To British A/W 01/04/74. Last British A/W service 02/03/85. To ACS (Zaire) as 9Q-CTI. B/U. 1990?
2306	3B-101	G-AWZE	28/03/71	08/04/71	BEA	22/05/83	Orig reg with UK CAA 14/01/69. To British A/W 01/04/74. B/U LHR 06/84.
2307	3B-101	G-AWZF	30/04/71	11/05/71	BEA	04/86?	Orig reg with UK CAA 14/01/69. To British A/W 01/04/74. Last British A/W service 08/01/85. To ACS (Zaire) as 9Q-CTZ. damaged and B/U 04/86.
2308	3B-101	G-AWZG	03/06/71	12/06/71	BEA	1989?	Orig reg with UK CAA 14/01/69. To British A/W 01/04/74. Last British A/W service 01/05/85. To ACS (Zaire) as 9Q-CTD. B/U 1989?
2309	3B-101	G-AWZH	07/07/71	15/07/71	BEA	06/09/85	Orig reg with UK CAA 14/01/69.To British A/W 01/04/74. B/U.06/86.
2310	3B-101	G-AWZI	04/08/71	09/08/71	BEA	01/05/81	Orig reg with UK CAA 14/01/69. To British A/W 01/04/74. B/U LHR 06/87. Fuselage reserved as a training airframe at the Surrey Fire and Rescue Service Headquarters from June 1987 until November 2002. Broken up Nov 2002, leaving only the cockpit section. Jan 2004, to the Farnborough Air Sciences Trust Museum.
2311	3B-101	G-AWZJ	09/09/71	16/09/71	BEA	09/12/85	Orig reg with UK CAA 14/01/69. To British A/W 01/04/74. To Prestwick for Fire Service.
2312	3B-101	G-AWZK	08/10/71	16/10/71	BEA	01/11/85	Orig reg with UK CAA 14/01/69. To British A/W 01/04/74. To BA Ops Training. 1985 - 2001, as a ground trainer for aircraft towing and de-icing, during this time it wore 'British Airways Landor' livery. Preserved at Runway Visitor Park

Examples of the graphic designers art from the Trident years, featuring the aircraft's iconic tail on the BEA Timetables.

[Author's Collection]

							Manchester 11 Sep 2005, in 'BEA' colours
2313	3B-101	G-AWZL	08/11/71	23/11/71	BEA	21/11/83	Orig reg with UK CAA c To British A/W 01/04/74. B/U LHR 06/86.
2314	3B-101	G-AWZM	08/12/71	16/12/71	BEA	13/12/85	Orig reg with UK CAA 14/01/69.To British A/W 01/04/74. To Science Museum, Wroughton 28/02/86
2315	3B-101	G-AWZN	12/01/72	20/01/72	BEA	22/12/85	Orig reg with UK CAA 14/01/69. To British A/W 01/04/74. To Cranfield 07/03/86.
2316	3B-101	G-AWZO	09/02/72	16/02/72	BEA	31/12/85	Orig reg with UK CAA 14/01/69. To British A/W 01/04/74. To Hatfield for BAe 18/04/86 as an instructional airframe for British Aerospace. Broken up Aug 2002.
2317	3B-101	G-AWZP	08/03/72	21/03/72	BEA	31/10/85	Orig reg with UK CAA 14/01/69. To British A/W 01/04/74. B/U LHR 06/86. Nose to Manchester Museum of Science and Industry.
2318	3B-101	G-AWZR	05904/72	13/04/72	BEA	27/09/85	Orig reg with UK CAA 14/01/69. To British A/W 01/04/74. To Teeside 19/03/86 for Fire School. Burnt.
2319	3B-101	G-AWZS	29/04/72	05/05/72	BEA	05/12/85	Orig reg with UK CAA 14/01/69. To British A/W 01/04/74. To Teeside 12/03/86 for Fire School. Burnt.
2320	3B-101	G-AWZT	26/05/72	07/0672	BEA	10/07/76	Orig reg with UK CAA 14/01/69. To British A/W 01/04/74.W/O. 10/09/76
2321	3B-101	G-AWZU	28/06/72	10/07/72	BEA	31/12/85	Orig reg with UK CAA 14/01/69. To British A/W 01/04/74. To Stansted 05/03/86 for Fire Service. Subsequently G-AWZU went to GJD AeroTech, at Bruntingthorpe Aerodrome, for disposal, and from where Jet Age Museum acquired the 'cockpit' from Gary Spoors including the forward cabin section of the fuselage. This acquisition was made because of the significant link which Gloucestershire has with this aircraft, being the 1st passenger aircraft to adopt the Smiths Autoland system.
2322	3B-101	G-AWZV	02/08/72	09/08/72	BEA	1988?	Orig reg with UK CAA 14/01/69. To British A/W 01/04/74. Last British A/W service22/12/85. To ACS (Zaire) as 9Q-CTZ. B/U 1990?
2323	3B-101	G-AWZW	15/11/72	29/11/72	BEA	19/10/83	Orig reg with UK CAA 14/01/69.To British A/W 01/04/74. B/U LHR 06/84
2324	3B-101	G-AWZX	24/01/73	29/01/73	BEA	01/10/84	Orig reg with UK CAA 14/01/69.To British A/W 01/04/74. To Gatwick 01/10/84 for Fire Service. Broken up Jul 2004.
2325	3B-101	G-AYVF	01/03/73	14/03/73	BEA	04/11/84	Orig reg with UK CAA 14/01/69.To British A/W 01/04/74. B/U LHR 06/84
2326	3B-101	G-AWZZ	03/04/73	19/04/73	BEA	01/02/84	Orig reg with UK CAA 14/01/69.To British A/W 01/04/74. To Birminham 04/11/84 for Fire Service.
2327	3B-104	B-268	09/07/75	08/0975	CAAC	-	F/F as G-BAJL. To People's Liberation Army Air Force and Re reg 50059.
2328	3B-104	B-270	26/08/75	17/10/75	CAAC	-	F/F as G-BAJM. To People's Liberation Army Air Force and re reg 50058.

Production List Decode

G-ARPA	2101
G-ARPB	2102
G-ARPC	2103
G-ARPD	2104
G-ARPE	2105
G-ARPF	2106
G-ARPG	2017
G-ARPH	2108
G-ARPI	2109
G-ARPJ	2110
G-ARPK	2111
G-ARPL	2112
G-ARPM	2113
G-ARPN	2115
G-ARPO	2116
G-ARPP	2117
G-ARPR	2119
G-ARPS	2120
G-ARPT	2121
G-ARPU	2122
G-ARPW	2123
G-ARPX	2124
G-ARPY	2126
G-ARPZ	2128
G-ASWU	2114
G-ASWV	2118
G-ATNA	2130
G-AVFA	2140
G-AVFB	2141
G-AVFC	2142
G-AVFD	2143
G-AVFE	2144
G-AVFF	2145
G-AVFG	2146
G-AVFH	2147
G-AVFI	2148
G-AVFJ	2149
G-AVFK	2150
G-AVFL	2151
G-AVFM	2152
G-AVFN	2153
G-AVFO	2156
G-AVYA	2135
G-AVYB	2136
G-AVYC	2137
G-AVYD	2138
G-AVYE	2139
G-AWYZ	2301
G-AWZA	2302
G-AWZB	2303
G-AWZC	2304
G-AWZD	2305
G-AWZE	2306
G-AWZF	2307
G-AWZG	2308
G-AWZH	2309
G-AWZI	2310
G-AWZJ	2311
G-AWZK	2312
G-AWZL	2313
G-AWZM	2314
G-AWZN	2315
G-AWZO	2316
G-AWZP	2317
G-AWZR	2318
G-AWZS	2319
G-AWZT	2320
G-AWZU	2321
G-AWZV	2322
G-AWZW	2323
G-AWZX	2324
G-AWZZ	2326
G-AYVF	2325
G-AZXM	2154
G-AZFT	2157
G-AZFU	2158
G-AZFV	2159
G-AZFW	2160
G-AZFX	2161
G-AZFY	2162
G-BABP	2163
G-BABR	2164
G-BABS	2165
G-BABT	2166
G-BABU	2167
G-BABV	2168
G-BAJF	2169
G-BAJG	2170
G-BAJH	2171
G-BAJI	2172
G-BAJJ	2173
G-BAJL	2327
G-BAJM	2328
G-BAJK	2174
G-BBVS	2175
G-BBVT	2176
G-BBVU	2177
G-BBVV	2178
G-BBVW	2179
G-BBVX	2180
G-BBVY	2181
G-BBVZ	2182
G-BBWA	2183
G-BBWB	2184
G-BBWD	2185
G-BBWE	2186
G-BBWF	2187
G-BBWG	2188
G-BBWH	2189
240	2157
242	2158
244	2160
246	2160
248	2161
250	2162
232	2130
256	2131
236	2132
50052	2171
50053	2189
50054	2186
50055	2185
50055	2188
50056	2130
50058	2328
50059	2327
50050	2132
50152	2133
50057	2187
50158	2174
B-252	2163
B-254	2164
B-256	2165
B-258	2166
B-260	2167
B-262	2168
B-263	2185
B-264	2169
B-265	2186
B-266	2170
B-267	2187
B-268	2327
B-269	2188
B-270	2328
B-271	2189
B-272	2171
B-274	2172
B-276	2173
B-278	2174
B-280	2175
B-282	2176
B-284	2177
B-286	2178
B-288	2179
B-290	2180
B-292	2181
B-294	2182
B-296	2183
B-298	2184
B-2201	2157
B-2202	2158
B-2203	2168
B-2204	2175
B-2205	2176
B-2206	2181
B-2207	2182
B-2208	2165
B-2209	2164
B-2210	2178
B-2211	2180
B-2212	2162
B-2213	2173
B-2214	2163
B-2215	2166
B-2216	2177
B-2217	2179
B-2218	2159
B-2219	2160
B-2220	2183
B-2221	2184
B-2223	2161
AP-ATK	2130
AP-ATL	2131
AP-ATM	2132
AP-AUG	2133
YI-AEA	2125
YI-AEB	2127
YI-AEC	2129
5B-DAA	2154
5B-DAB	2155
5B-DAD	2114
5B-DAE	2134
9K-ACF	2114
9K-ACG	2118
9K-ACH	2134
9Q-CTD	2308
9Q-CTI	2305
9Q-CTM	2304
9Q-CTZ	2307
9Q-CTZ	2322
4R-ACN	2135

Bibliography

4/73. Report into the Crash of Trident G-ARPI, 18 June 1972. AAIB.

AIB Report: British Airways Trident 1E G-AVYD on the accident at Bilbao Airport 15 September 1975. Translated from Spanish investigation released July 1978.

AIB Report: British Airways Trident G-AWZT/Inex Adria DC9 YU-AJR 10 September 1976. From re-investigation, Belgrade, February 1982.

Aircraft Accident report No.1/90. report on accident to Hawker Siddeley Trident 2E B-2219 at Hong Kong International Airport 31 August 1988. Issued June 1990.

An Illustrated History of British European Airways: Phil Lo Bao Browcom Group Plc Middlesex 1989.

BEA Magazine Edition 129 to 140covering the year 1960.

BEA Magazine Edition 141 to 151 covering the year 1961.

BEA Magazine Edition 152 to 163 covering the year 1962.

BEA Magazine Edition 164 to 175 covering the year 1963.

BEA Magazine Edition 176 to 187 covering the year 1964.

BEA Magazine Edition 188 to 199 covering the year 1965.

BEA Magazine Edition 200 to 211 covering the year 1966.

BEA Magazine Edition 212 to 223 covering the year 1967.

BEA Magazine Edition 224 to 234 covering the year 1968.

BEA Magazine Edition 235 to 246 covering the year 1969.

BEA Magazine Edition 247 to 258 covering the year 1970.

BEA Magazine Edition 259 to 270 covering the year 1971.

BEA Magazine Edition 271 to 282 covering the year 1972.

BEA Magazine Edition 283 to 294covering the year 1973.

De Havilland Gazette Edition No.113. October 1959.

De Havilland Gazette Edition No.114. December 1959.

De Havilland Gazette Edition No.115. February 1960.

De Havilland Gazette Edition No.116. April 1960.

De Havilland Gazette Edition No.117. June 1960.

De Havilland Gazette Edition No.118 Supplement. August 1960.

De Havilland Gazette Edition No.118. August 1960

De Havilland Gazette Edition No.119. October 1960.

De Havilland Gazette Edition No.120. December 1960.

De Havilland Gazette Edition No.121. February 1961.

De Havilland Gazette Edition No.122. April 1961.

De Havilland Gazette Edition No.123. June 1961.

De Havilland Gazette Edition No.124. August 1961.

EW/C0130. Civil Aircraft Accident Report: Trident Series 1, 3 June 1966. AIB, June 1968.

EW/C0214. Civil Aircraft Accident Report : Ambassador AS.57 Series 2 G-AMAD 3 July 1968. AIB March 1969.

ICAO Circular 96-AN/79. Civil Aircraft Accident Report: Trident Series 1E 9K-ACG 30 June 1966. Report undated.

The Challenge of BEA: Garry May, Oxley Press, London 1971.

Trident: Aircraft Engineering: Bunhill Publications, London 1964.

Wings Across The World. Harold Penrose. Cassels Ltd, London 1980.

Kuwait Airways' 9K-ACH. *[Author's Collection]*

Index

BEA

YI-AEC looking very smart in the sunshine during a turnaround at Athens' Ellinikon Airport. *[Author's Collection]*